Land of 10,000 Aches

Land of 10,000 Aches

A History of Minnesota Meltdowns

Zeke Fuhrman

Copyright © 2020 by Zeke Fuhrman.

Library of Congress Control Number: 2019919372
ISBN: Hardcover   978-1-7960-7265-5
              Softcover   978-1-7960-7264-8
              eBook   978-1-7960-7263-1

All rights reserved. No part of this book may be reproduced or transmitted in any form or by any means, electronic or mechanical, including photocopying, recording, or by any information storage and retrieval system, without permission in writing from the copyright owner.

Any people depicted in stock imagery provided by Getty Images are models, and such images are being used for illustrative purposes only.
Certain stock imagery © Getty Images.

Author photo courtesy of Forever Yours Portraits by Abby Schlauderaff

Print information available on the last page.

Rev. date: 12/06/2019

To order additional copies of this book, contact:
Xlibris
1-888-795-4274
www.Xlibris.com
Orders@Xlibris.com
804280

For my friends, teachers, faculty and staff at Staples-Motley High School and the University of Northwestern–St. Paul who encouraged, inspired, and excited me about writing.

For my fantasy football league . . . except Peter. You suck.

For Dan "the Common Man" Cole, who unknowingly led me into a career that I love.

Most of all, to my darling wife, Mandy, and our children, Esme and Judah. Daddy can finally put the computer down. I love you all.

Introduction

Have you ever tied a rope around the back of a car, tied the other end around your testicles, and had your heart ripped out through your groin?

Willingly?

That is what it is like to be a fan of Minnesota sports. The good news is that after you do that literally hundreds and hundreds of times, you eventually become numb to the pain. Numb enough to continue to root for a team that has lost four Super Bowls and six NFC Championship games, a team that has lost an MLB-record sixteen straight postseason games, a team that was eliminated from the first round of the NBA playoffs for seven consecutive years despite having one of the best players in the league, and a team that doesn't have any professional championships despite the moniker "the State of Hockey."

Don't get me wrong. There have definitely been some feel-good moments. But that's how they keep their hooks in you. For every Minneapolis Miracle, there is a Josh McCown-to-Nate Poole and Roger Staubach-to-Drew Pearson. For every Andrew Brunette overtime winner, there is a Ron Schock and Magnus Paajarvi series ender. For every Andy McPhail, there is a Bill Smith and David Kahn. For every Kevin Garnett, there is a Derrick Williams and Jonny Flynn. For every Joe Nathan robbery, there is a Herschel Walker and Brandon Roy. And the list goes on and on and on and on.

Minnesota fans have endured everything: last-second losses, historically bad teams, draft busts, missed calls, terrible trades, disappointing playoff runs, underqualified front office staff and coaches, and untimely injuries. Yet this fan base stays loyal. Even when their team sets the NFL record for points scored and fails to make the Super Bowl. Even when their team sets a major league record for most home runs hit in a season but gets swept out of the playoffs. Even when their collegiate sports programs go through scandal after scandal after scandal after scandal. People may say I was born under a lucky star: Spring Training 1987. And while I have technically lived through two Minnesota championships, I have always longed to know what it is like to see my team's confetti fall from the rafters.

"The greatest things to happen to me are my marriage, my kids, and winning the World Series . . . and not in that order," said my Chicago Cubs fan after they won their World Series.

"It feels like a weight has been lifted from my shoulders," said my St. Louis Blues fan after their Stanley Cup Finals win in 2019.

"Nick Foles is the greatest quarterback of all time!" screamed my former Philadelphia Eagles friend as I threw him out of my house during Super Bowl XLII.

While this book doesn't have all 10,000 heartbreaks in it, it does chronicle some of the worst Minnesota sports moments of all time. If you're having a good day, I wouldn't read this book.

April 20, 1948

The John Wooden Snowstorm

If fate had not intervened, I would never have gone to UCLA.
—John Wooden

In 1948, the University of Minnesota was looking for a new men's basketball coach. Dave MacMillan had just retired for a second time due to his health, and the university was looking for a long-term answer for the program.

The Gophers reached out to an up-and-coming coach from Indiana State Teacher's College (now Indiana State University) named John Wooden. Wooden had led ISTC to the Indiana Intercollegiate Conference title and had received an invitation to the NAIB Tournament (which he declined, citing the tournament's ban on African American players).

There was, however, another program looking for a new basketball coach, as well: UCLA. Wooden wanted to go to Minnesota because he and his wife, Nellie, preferred to stay in the Midwest.

In April 1948, John lined up a phone call with each institution; first with Minnesota athletic director Frank G. McCormick, then UCLA AD Wilbur Johns an hour later. He waited by the phone when McCormick was supposed to call. He waited . . . and waited . . . and waited. Eventually, about an hour later, the phone did ring.

It was Johns and UCLA. Thinking that the Gophers had lost interested in him, he accepted the UCLA job on the spot.

Minutes after accepting the Bruins job, the phone rang again. It was McCormick. There had been an April snowstorm in Minneapolis, and he had gotten stuck in the middle of it and was unable to make the phone call. He offered Wooden the job on the spot; Wooden declined the offer because he had already given his word to UCLA.

Wooden faced a challenge at UCLA. The Bruins didn't have an on-campus arena. They played their games at the practice facility until fire codes closed it down. From 1948 to 1962, Wooden's Bruins played their home games at Santa Monica City College and Venice High School.

Despite that hurdle, Wooden had immediate success at UCLA and instantly turned around a faltering program. UCLA was 22–7 in 1948. A year later, they were 24–7 and in Wooden's first NCAA tournament.

Prior to Wooden's arrival at UCLA, the Bruins had won only two conference championships in the previous eighteen years. By 1965, UCLA was a national powerhouse recruiting the likes of Bill Walton, Gail Goodrich, Jamaal Wilkes, Marques Johnson, Sidney Wicks, Lucius Allen, and arguably the best high school prospect of all time, Lou Alcindor.

Wooden led UCLA to ten national championships (including seven consecutive ones from 1967 to 1973) and transformed UCLA as one of the most successful college basketball programs in history.

The Gophers, on the other hand, hired away Michigan head coach Ozzie Cowles. Cowles was named the Big Ten Coach of the year with the Wolverines in 1947. Cowles saw immediate success with the Gophers too, finishing with 18–3 record and finished ranked number 6 in the AP Poll. He would coach the Gophers until 1959, compiling a 146–93 record.

Although he didn't have the same national success as he did at previous coaching jobs like Dartmouth (eight Ivy League titles, three NCAA tournament appearances, and NCAA runner-up in 1943) and Michigan, the O. Cowles era of Gopher basketball is often referred to as the golden era of the program.

The two big differences in the coaches (other than the ten championship banners hanging in Pauley Pavilion right now) are the coaching philosophies. Cowles was an old-style coach. In February 1949, the *Long Beach Press-Telegram* ran a lengthy story on Cowles negatively impacting an evolving game:

> Ozzie Cowles has put the brakes on basketball in the Western Conference, and speculation is rife over whether the hardwood sport has seen the limit, for the time being at least, of the "fire department" style which sent scores soaring and left fans, players and coaches breathless. Coach Cowles finds himself in a storm center.

Cowles was also opposed to the shot clock, saying that "it forces players to take shots they wouldn't normally take" and was an outspoken opponent of a rule added in 1950 limiting a player to one free throw if fouled in the act of shooting (in a game against Michigan State, he elected for a jump ball instead of shooting free throws).

Cowles had losing seasons in his final two seasons at Minnesota while the league adapted to the rule changes, and he resigned in 1959 amid anti-Cowles talks among Gophers fans and officials.

Wooden, however, revolutionized the game on his journey to becoming the Wizard of Westwood. Wooden developed a unique offensive system that included run-and-jump, 1–3–1 trapping, box-and-one, and switching man-to-man defense—a lot of strategy that the modern-day coaches are still using.

However, if it's any consolation to Gopher fans, despite all his early success, Wooden didn't initially enjoy his position. He saw the early success of the Gophers under Cowles, plus his wife didn't enjoy Los Angeles after growing up in the Midwest. Two years into his coaching career at UCLA, the coaching job at Purdue University opened. Wooden really wanted to return to Indiana with his wife and take the coaching job there, but UCLA officials dissuaded him when they reminded him that he had verbally committed to them for three years.

And after all, Gopher fans, John Wooden IS a man of his word.

November 22, 1950

Minneapolis Lakers versus Fort Wayne Pistons

Play like that will kill professional basketball.
—Lakers coach John Kundla

The Lakers had won twenty-nine straight home games when the Fort Wayne Pistons, coached by Murray Mendenhall, came to the Minneapolis Auditorium. The Lakers, led by George Mikan, were the two-time defending NBA champions but were off to a slow start by their standards. After back-to-back wins over the Rochester Royals (who would dethrone the Lakers in the playoffs that year), they were 5–4 before the matchup against the Pistons. Mendenhall knew the Lakers were almost unbeatable, especially on their home floor. So he devised a tactic that had never been used before. He stalled.

The Pistons had an 8–7 lead after the first quarter but trailed 13–11 at halftime. Whenever they had possession of the ball, they would throw it around for extended chunks of time, killing the clock. Lakers fans booed, but Mendenhall kept to his strategy.

But the Lakers kept fighting through it, feeding the ball to Mikan on offense. With six seconds left and trailing 18–17, Pistons rookie Larry Foust took an inbounds pass, drove the baseline, and laid it in over Mikan for a 19–18 win.

George Mikan scored 15 of the Lakers' 18 points on 4-of-11 shooting and 7-of-11 on his free throws. He is the only Laker with a field goal in the game. Bob Harrison made two free throws, and Jim Pollard had one. The Lakers were outscored 8–5 in the second half, had one point in the fourth quarter, and only had three shots in the second half. The game is, and always will be, the lowest scoring game in NBA history.

The Lakers' next game was in Fort Wayne, where they lost 73–63. It wasn't until the 1954 season…four years after the 19–18 game… that the NBA instituted a 30-second shot clock.

MARCH 13, 1954

NCAA Men's Hockey Championship versus Rensselaer

We were made to win that night. We didn't have any fear of losing that game.
—RPI coach Ned Harkness

The 22–5–1 Minnesota Golden Gopher men's hockey team returned to the NCAA tournament in 1954, a year after losing in the championship game to Michigan 7–3. The Gophers were led by reigning Coach of the Year John Mariucci and four All-Americans: Dick Dougherty, James Mattson, Ken Yackel, and John Mayasich. The Gophers hadn't won a championship since beating Brock Hall 9–1 in the 1940 AAU championship game while Mariucci was still a player.

The four teams in the 1954 tournament were Minnesota, three-time defending champion Michigan, and at-large teams Boston College and Rensselaer Polytechnic Institute.

The Gophers opened the tournament against 17–2–0 Boston College at the Broadmoor Ice Palace in Colorado Springs on March 11, 1954. Eighty-five seconds into the game, they were up 2–0 after goals by Mayasich and Bob Meredith. A goal by George Jetty, two goals by Gophers captain Gene Campbell, and another by Mayasich made it 6–0 after the first period. The Gophers led 9–1 after 2 and won the game 14–1 in a game that set the NCAA tournament record for goals in a game (later matched by Michigan in 1955) and the largest margin of defeat. Mayasich set the record for most points in an NCAA tournament game with 7 (3 goals, 4 assists). Dougherty had 4 goals, and Campbell added a hat trick and 2 assists.

But Mariucci wasn't impressed.

"If we play the whole game like we did tonight, Michigan will run us right off the rink," he said after the game, already assuming that top-seeded Michigan would beat RPI the following night.

They didn't. Michigan fought back from a 3–0 deficit to tie RPI at 3–3, but Frank Chiarelli scored the go-ahead goal in the second to take a 4–3 lead. Each team scored a goal in the third before RPI hit an empty-netter in the last ninety seconds of the game to knock off Michigan 6–4. The Engineers had scored four power play goals and got a hat trick from Gordy Perkins. It was Michigan's first loss since Minnesota had beaten them on January 15, 1950. There would be a new NCAA Champion in 1954.

The puck dropped on the NCAA championship game in front of a standing-room crowd of 2,800 fans, which was more than the enrollment at RPI (2,700 students). The Engineers jumped out to an early 3–0 against the Gophers, just like they had done with Michigan. All-American Abbie Moore and Chiarelli scored in the first period, with Moore adding another goal at the 2:45 mark in the second. The Gophers offense finally responded as Yackel and Dougherty scored goals less than two minutes apart. Minnesota had a two-man advantage in the third period as they tried to tie the game. RPI kept the puck out of their net until one man got back on the ice, but Mayasich scored a backhand goal on the power play to tie the game at 3–3.

Four minutes later, Dougherty scored his second goal of the game to give the Gophers their first lead of the game. Eight minutes separated the Gophers from their first ever NCAA hockey championship.

But Abbie Moore beat Gopher goalie Jim Mattson with 3:50 left to tie the game at 4–4. The Gophers had a couple chances to score on goalie Bob Fox but couldn't get the puck in the net. Fox, who was named to the All-Tournament First Team, stopped 40 of 44 shots in regulation against a team that had scored 14 goals two days prior.

The overtime period would last less than two minutes. Gordie Peterkin scored the game winner at 1:54. Minnesota wouldn't get a shot on goal in the overtime period.

The 1954 NCAA championship game was the final game of a dominant Gopher first line featuring Campbell, Dougherty, and Mayasich. Minnesota would miss the tournament in 1955 (won by Michigan). Mayasich, arguably the best hockey player ever to play at any level in Minnesota, won WCHA scoring titles in 1954 and 1955, was a four-time All-American, scored 144 goals and 154 assists (both program records) in 111 games but never won a championship with the Gophers.

The Gophers wouldn't return to the NCAA hockey tournament until 1961.

April 28, 1960

The Lakers Relocate to Los Angeles

The team might still be here if they'd had their own place to play.
—Former Lakers GM Sid Hartman

The Los Angeles Lakers are one of the world's most valuable and successful franchises, valued around $3.7 billion in 2019. They've employed NBA stars like Kobe Bryant, Wilt Chamberlain, Magic Johnson, LeBron James, Kareem Abdul-Jabbar, and Jerry West. The Lakers, as a franchise, have won sixteen NBA championships.

However: don't forget that five of those were won in Minneapolis.

In 1947, Ben Berger and Morris Chalfen bought the Detroit Gems of the fading National Basketball League (NBL) for $15,000 and moved the team to Minneapolis. The Gems were 4–40 the previous season and, since the NBL already assigned the former Gems players to other teams in the NBL, the franchise didn't come with any players. Berger and Chalfen would be building the team from scratch.

The first moves they made were hiring Max Winter as the team's general manager and John Kundla as the team's first head coach.

Winter's first job was to come up with a new team name for the franchise. He decided to have a naming contest. Winter reportedly like the name 'Vikings' for the franchise, but the radio station running the contest heard his preference and were advised not use it so the contest didn't seem fraudulent. Minnesotan Ben Frank won a $100 savings bond for coming up with the name Lakers.

With a new team identity in place, Winter and Kundla began searching for players to fill the roster. Kundla used his U of M connections to sign several former Gophers to form the 1948–49 Lakers squad: Don Carlson, Warren Ajax, Ken Exel, Tony Jaros, and Don Smith. They also added forward Jim Pollard and playmaker Herm Schaefer. All they needed was a big man to dominate the paint.

And it took the death of another basketball league to get him.

Since the Gems had the worst record in the NBL the previous year, they were awarded the top pick in the upcoming draft. Winter had one player at the top of his wish list: George Mikan. The problem? Mikan was currently playing for the Chicago American Gears. The American Gears had won the 1946–47 NBL championship, then they moved to the Pro Basketball League of America. The league folded two weeks into the league's season, making Mikan eligible for the NBL draft. Winter took him first overall. Mikan would average 28 points per game, establish himself as the NBA's first superstar, and lead the Lakers to a forty-seven-win season and the league championship.

The following year, the Lakers moved to the Basketball Association of America (BAA). Mikan and the Lakers won the title that year as well. Following the 1949–50 season, the BAA renamed themselves the National Basketball Association.

The Lakers won the 1949–50 NBA Championship as well for their third straight title. They didn't make the finals in 1950–51 but won three more consecutive championships beginning in 1951–52 after adding more Hall of Famers Vern Mikkelsen and Jim Pollard.

But while the Lakers were winning on the court, there was trouble behind the scenes. Financial issues were growing. The Lakers didn't have a true home arena. They were shuffled around among the Minneapolis Auditorium, the Minneapolis Armory, and the St. Paul Auditorium.

"It was more important in those days for the Minneapolis Auditorium to schedule events such as the Sportsmen's Show, the Builders Show and other types of entertainment to take over the building and bump aside the Lakers," Sid Hartman wrote in his *Star Tribune* column in 2015.

The Lakers wins dropped off following their NBA title in 1953–54, largely due to the retirement of Mikan. But the Lakers still made the playoffs with a forty-win season. The bottom fell out when Pollard retired following year. It got so bad that Mikan, who was working in the front office, unretired and returned to the team midseason. Even after sitting out for nearly two seasons, he was still able to average double figures in scoring, but the team went 33–39 for its first losing record since moving from Detroit.

With the decline in wins, fan attendance waned, and the team's financial issues piled up. Not interested in a rebuild or in losing more money, Berger was ready to sell the team. He had a reported offer from a group of Missouri businessmen that planned to move the Lakers to Kansas City. But before signing the deal, he decided to give people in the Twin Cities the chance to purchase the team and keep the team in Minnesota. The team was sold to a group led by Bob Short, who was elected new team president, for $150,000. Short said he was committed to keeping the Lakers in Minneapolis.

With the departure of Berger, Chalfen, and Winter, Kundla was promoted to general manager and Mikan was named head coach. Mikan's Lakers only won nine of their first thirty-nine games before Kundla retook the reigns as the Lakers finished a league-worst 19–53 and missed the playoffs for the first time in franchise history.

The Lakers were in the same position they were in a decade earlier, heading into the draft with the number 1 overall pick. They selected forward Elgin Baylor of Seattle University as their new building block.

Baylor would win Rookie of the Year and finish third in Player of the Year voting and helped take the league's worst team from the previous year to the NBA finals for the first time in five years before running into Bill Russell's Celtics dynasty. The 1958–59 season was also the last year of the John Kundla era, leaving the team to fill the University of Minnesota basketball coaching vacancy.

Looking to build of Baylor's great rookie campaign, Short brought in his college coach at Seattle University, John Castellani, to coach the team. But with expectations high, Castellani's Lakers started slow, and he was fired after an 11–25 start. Jim Pollard finished out the season as head coach as the Lakers finished the season 25–50.

Back to their losing ways, the franchise was hemorrhaging money, was losing fans, and still had no arena to call home.

In the late 1950s and early '60s, pro sports teams were starting to move west. In 1958, Major League Baseball's Brooklyn Dodgers moved to Los Angeles, the New York Giants relocated to San Francisco, and the plans were in motion to create the expansion California Angels. With rumors that the Philadelphia Warriors had plans to move west (they would move to San Francisco in 1962), Short wanted to be the first one to sow the seeds of the West Coast.

During an owner's meeting on April 26, 1960, Short announced his intention to relocate the Lakers. Not wanting to increase travel costs to get their team to West Coast games, Short's request was voted down 7–1. But after the vote, the owners learned of the formation of the American Basketball League with a play beginning in 1960 with teams in Cleveland, Washington, Kansas City, Los Angeles, and San Francisco. Not wanting to lose the West Coast to the rival league, they revoted. The motion passed 8–0.

On April 28, 1960, after contemplating moves to Chicago and San Francisco, Short announced that the Lakers would be relocating to Los Angeles. He decided not to rename the franchise.

The Lakers flourished in LA. They had a solidified home venue in the Los Angeles Memorial Sports Arena and had amazing fan attendance. Baylor had a Hall of Fame career and averaged 27 points and 13 rebounds per game the rest of his career. The team drafted Hall of Famer Jerry West in 1961 and players like Frank Selvy and Rudy LaRusso reached All-Star status. The Lakers were a mainstay in the NBA finals during the 1960s and early '70s.

Minnesota fans watched as Hall of Famer Wilt Chamberlain brought Los Angeles its first championship in 1972 after losing in the finals seven times since the move.

In the 1980s, they watched Magic Johnson and Kareem Abdul-Jabbar win five more.

In the early 2000s, Kobe Bryant and Shaquille O'Neal won back-to-back-to-back titles, with Bryant and Pau Gasol winning two more almost ten years later.

Today, LA is the hot destination for basketball. They've employed six of the top eight scorers in NBA history don the purple and yellow (Abdul-Jabbar, Karl Malone, Bryant, Chamberlain, LeBron James, and O'Neal). LA has added eleven more NBA titles to the Lakers franchise since relocating and is now the most valuable franchise in the league.

Meanwhile, Minnesota was granted an expansion franchise in 1989: the Timberwolves. In nine postseason appearances, they have advanced past the opening round only once. They made it to the Western Conference Finals behind league MVP Kevin Garnett in 2004 only to be eliminated by the Lakers.

<<BONUS ACHE>>

The Lakers Plan for Bill Russell Falls Through

The Minneapolis Lakers finished the 1955 season with a 34–38 record—their first losing season since relocating from Detroit. The early Lakers stars had retired and general manager Sid Hartman was looking for the next George Mikan to take his team to the next level.

"I had a deal in place with Red Auerbach of the Boston Celtics," Hartman recalls. "I would send Vern Mikkelsen to the Celtics for Frank Ramsey, Cliff Hagan, and Lou Tsioropoulos, who were all in the service at Andrew Air Force Base at the time."

By trading Mikkelsen to the Celtics, the Lakers likely would have finished with the worst record in the NBA and the top overall pick in the draft. The deal fell through, and Mikkelsen stayed with the Lakers. At the end of the season, the Rochester Royals had the top pick after finishing 31–41. The St. Louis Hawks would pick second, and the Lakers third.

The Royals, who had the league's top rebounder in Maurice Stokes, selected guard Si Green with the first overall pick. The St. Louis Hawks selected center Bill Russell out of San Francisco, who was traded to Boston for St. Louis native and six-time All-Star Ed Macauley and Cliff Hagan.

"My agent on the West Coast had Russell all set to come here, something Russell wrote in his books," Hartman said. "Russell himself called Lakers big man George Mikan, who Russell had met in high school, his childhood hero after his father."

The Wolves drafted Jim Paxton third overall. Paxton had a two-year NBA career. Russell played thirteen seasons, scored 14,552 points, pulled down 21,620 rebounds, and won five MVP awards and eleven NBA championships.

November 8, 1964

Jim Marshall Runs the Wrong Way

Many times, people ask coaches who their greatest player was. It's normally very hard to choose, but I don't hesitate to say Jim Marshall.

—Bud Grant

Jim Marshall's two-decade career began in 1960. He played in a record 282 consecutive regular season games (270 consecutive starts), recovered a record 30 fumbles, 127 sacks, played in four Super Bowls, and was a part of one of the most daunting defenses of all time.

Although he is not in the Pro Football Hall of Fame (yet), his number 70 has been retired by the Vikings (Hall of Famers John Randle, Paul Krause, Ron Yary, Randall McDaniel, Chris Doleman, and Randy Moss haven't had their numbers retired). It's easy to say that Marshall is one of the most beloved Vikings of all time.

But unfortunately, he is remembered for one play that occurred the afternoon of October 25, 1964. In a game against the San Francisco 49ers, Marshall recovered a Billy Kilmer fumble. He picked it up and ran sixty-six yards into the wrong end zone. He threw the ball out of bounds, celebrating what he thought was a touchdown, only to realize he had scored a safety against his own team.

"My first inkling that something was wrong was when a 49er player (Bruce Bosley) gave me a hug in the end zone," Marshall later recalled.

The safety cut the Vikings lead to 27–19. What a lot of people don't remember is that the Vikings scored what would be the deciding touchdown on a Carl Eller scoop-and-score forced by Marshall into the end zone for a forty-five-yard score.

The Vikings would beat the 49ers 27–22, but people will always remember Marshall for a ten-second, two-point mistake and not the twenty years and arguably Hall of Fame–worthy career that he had.

October 6, 1965

The 1965 World Series

It took the best pitcher in baseball to finally kill us off.
—Twins manager Sam Mele

Professional baseball had come to Minnesota in 1961 with the relocation of the Washington Senators. And with the Senators, a legacy of losing. While the Senators had won three American League Pennants (1924, 1925, 1933), including the 1924 World Series, losing and Washington were synonymous. Prior to moving to Bloomington for the beginning of the 1961 season, the Senators had only had three winning seasons since the end of the Great Depression in 1939. The moniker surrounding the Senators was "First in War, First in Peace, and Last in the American League."

The Twins had inherited a solid core of players with the move: players like Harmon Killebrew, Earl Battey, Zoilo Versalles, Camilo Pascual, Jim Kaat, and Bob Allison. The Twins finished seventh in the American League in their inaugural season in Minnesota with a 70–90 record but put together back-to-back ninety-win seasons in 1962 and 1963 (they finished five games behind the New York Yankees in 1962 and thirteen games behind them in 1963). The Twins fell back to sixth place in 1964 with a 79–83 record. Then came 1965.

In addition to the core they had groomed since 1961, the Twins had also brought in players like Jim Perry, Mudcat Grant, Cesar Tovar, and 1964 Rookie of the Year Tony Oliva. The Twins started the season 43–28 and were locked in a dead heat for the pennant with an up-and-coming Baltimore Orioles squad led by 1964 AL MVP Brooks Robinson. But the Twins scorched through July with a 22–9 record (they had six All-Stars at the Mid-Summer Classic played at Metropolitan Stadium: Grant, Killebrew, Battey, Versalles, Oliva, and Jimmie Hall in an All-Star Game that featured nineteen future Hall of Famers). They surpassed their win total from 1964 on August 23 with a walk-off win against the

Detroit Tigers and won a total of nineteen games in August. On September 26, they clinched the AL Pennant with their ninety-ninth win. It was the first time in five years that the Yankees didn't win the pennant (they had won fourteen of the previous sixteen American League pennants.) The Twins won their 102nd game on the final day of the season, beating the California Angels 3–2. The team's 102 was a new franchise, besting the previous mark set by the 1933 Senators team that lost the World Series to the New York Giants in five games. No Twins team has matched or bested 102 wins in a season since.

The National League pennant had been captured by the Los Angeles Dodgers, who finished 97–65 and two games ahead of the San Francisco Giants. The Giants had a four-game lead on September sixth after winning fourteen straight games, but the Dodgers came back with thirteen consecutive wins of their own over the final two weeks of the season to overtake the Giants and win their seventh pennant since 1952.

Like the Twins, Los Angeles had also finished in sixth place the previous season. The 1965 World Series also was the first World Series to feature two relocated teams (the Dodgers from Brooklyn in 1958 and the Twins from Washington in 1961). The Dodgers were led by a strong pitching: Sandy Koufax won twenty-six games with a 2.04 ERA and 382 strikeouts in 335 innings, and Don Drysdale won twenty-three games with a 2.77 ERA. The Dodgers added Claude Osteen in a trade with the new Washington Senators in exchange for slugger Frank Howard. Osteen chipped in fifteen wins with a 2.79 ERA in 40 starts.

The Dodgers were expecting a huge offensive season from left fielder Tommy Davis, who had won back-to-back NL Batting Titles in 1962 and 1963, but Davis broke his ankle sliding into second base seventeen games into the season and was done for the year. The Dodgers only averaged 3.8 runs per game, which was third worst in the National League. The Twins had five players with 75+ RBI that season. Right fielder Ron Fairly led the Dodgers with 70. Dodgers captain Maury Wills paced the offense with 94 stolen bases and 92 runs scored.

"We've been reading about the Dodgers' great pitching and running, but we think we can more than match them in hitting," said Twins manager Sam Mele.

While the Dodgers' weakness was their offense, the Twins' weakness was their defense having committed 173 errors that season, including 39 by eventual 1965 AL MVP shortstop Zoilo Versalles.

Game 1 of the 1965 World Series was played at Metropolitan Stadium on October 6 and featured Don Drysdale versus twenty-one-game winner Mudcat Grant. Koufax was originally scheduled to start the opener, but it fell on Yom Kippur. Koufax, who was Jewish, told management that he wouldn't pitch that day.

The game was tied 1–1 in the heading to the bottom of the third (Ron Fairly and Don Mincher had each hit solo home runs to right field), until the Twins broke it open. Frank Quillici doubled off Drysdale to lead off the inning. Grant reached on a Jim Lefebvre error at second base that allowed Mudcat to reach. Versalles hit a home run to left field to put the Twins up 4–1. Left fielder Sandy Valdespino became the fourth-consecutive batter to reach in the inning with a double to right field. Drysdale got Oliva to ground out to third for the first out of the inning. Killebrew singled, advancing Valdespino to third. Drysdale struck out Jimmie Hall for out number 2. Drysdale then walked Mincher before allowing RBI singles to Battey and Quillici. Quillici, who only played in fifty-six games for the Twins that season, became the tenth player in World Series history to record 2 hits in the same inning. Dodgers manager Walter Alston pulled Drysdale in favor of righty Howie Reed (7–5, 3.12 ERA), who got out of the inning by getting Grant to ground out.

His team now leading 7–1, Grant would cruise the rest of the way and wouldn't allow another run until the top of the ninth, when Maury Wills bunted in Lefebvre for an RBI single. Grant pitched the complete game, allowing 2 runs on 10 hits as the Twins won 8–2. The 6 runs scored by the Twins in the third innings was the most the Dodgers had given up in an inning all season. Drysdale only lasted 2.2 innings and gave up 7 runs (only 3 earned) and 2 home runs.

"You can't afford to make mistakes against a good-hitting club like the Twins and hope to survive," Drysdale said after the game.

Game 2 featured Sandy Koufax versus Jim Kaat. Sam Mele made a couple of adjustments to his lineup against Koufax, starting Bob Allison in left field and Joe Nossek in center.

Bloomington had been soaked by a rainstorm the previous night, which made for less than ideal field conditions. A helicopter was called into Metropolitan Stadium and hovered over the outfield before the game in attempt to fan dry the grass after an all-night and all-morning rain.

For Kaat, it brought back memories of the start of the season, when he had to be picked up from his home and flown to the ballpark because his neighborhood had flooded in the spring.

Kaat (18–11, 2.83 ERA in a league-leading 42 starts) matched Koufax pitch for pitch through the first five innings. Fairly singled to lead off the top of the fifth inning, Lefebvre sent a line drive down the left field line. Allison made a spectacular sliding catch across the foul line and through the mud to retire a stunned Lefebvre back to the dugout.

"That was one of the greatest catches I could remember," recalled Mele after the game.

"I was on first base, and I could have scored if Allison hadn't caught the ball," Fairly said. "Instead, he makes the grab, and we don't score."

The Twins finally broke through against Koufax in the sixth inning. After Versalles reached on an error by third baseman Jim Gilliam (who committed his third error in two games after only one in his previous thirty-one), he scored on an Oliva double. Killebrew then knocked in Oliva for a 2-0 lead. Alston pulled Koufax after six innings of work, allowing 2 runs and striking out nine Twins.

"Look, when my control is lousy and I don't have good stuff, I throw a little harder than I should and I lose my rhythm," Koufax said. "The weather didn't bother me. My arm felt fine. I tried to get the ball up and in on those guys who got hits, and I got it down and in. I only missed by four feet."

The Dodgers got one back in the top of the seventh when Fairly, who had singled off Kaat, scored on a John Roseboro (the same John Roseboro that would represent the Twins at the 1969 All-Star Game) single to cut the deficit in half.

Ron Perranoski, who would be part of a trade package to the Twins for Mudcat Grant and Zoilo Versalles after the 1967 season, relieved Koufax. He got Quillici and Kaat for the first two outs in the bottom of the seventh before giving up a triple to Versalles, who would then score on a wild pitch to make it 3-1 Twins. The Twins would add 2 more runs in the bottom of the eighth off Perranoski and win Game 2 5-1.

It was only the second time all season that Drysdale and Koufax had been beat in consecutive starts.

The Dodgers headed back to LA down two games to none in the series. A reporter for the *New York Herald Tribune*, Rod Smith, reminded his readers that the 1955 Brooklyn Dodgers came back from a 2-0 deficit in the World Series against the Yankees that year.

"Those however," he wrote, "were the Brooklyn Dodgers with hard-baked boys like Duke Snider, Jackie Robinson, Pee Wee Reese and Carl Furillo, who hit with Louisville Sluggers and not banana stalks."

Sam Mele had options for his starter in Game 3: Camilo Pascual or Jim Merritt. Pascual had won three straight strikeout crowns from 1961 to 63 and struck out 213 more in 1964 with his devastating curveball—a curveball that Ted Williams was quoted as saying was the nastiest he ever faced. But the seven-time All-Star, who started the season 8-2, would deal with arm issues in 1965 and had midseason surgery in early August to repair a torn muscle. He missed thirty-nine games before returning to action on September 6, going 1-0 in six starts with 23 strikeouts and a 3.82 ERA in thirty-three innings the final month of the season. The Twins were 3-3 in his starts, but there were reports that he wasn't in the strongest condition or in perfect control of the curve.

But Pascual's arm strength wasn't Mele's main concern. It was his slow throwing motion and the curveball.

"Pascual's motion is such that the Dodgers might run on him. We're thinking about using left-hander Jim Merritt to hold Maury Willis and company on the bases."

"If Mele doesn't think I can do the job, let him use somebody else," Pascual said after he heard Mele's comments, "I'm okay. If I didn't think I was ready to pitch, I'd say so. I want to help the club, not hurt it."

Rookie Jim Merritt was 5–4 with a 3.17 ERA in sixteen appearances for the Twins, including nine starts after moving out of the bullpen. Ultimately, Mele went with the veteran Pascual.

For the Dodgers, the Game 3 starter was a no-brainer: Claude Osteen. While with the new Washington Senators from 1961 to 64, he was 5–0 against the Twins. In fact, his first major league win was against the Twins at Metropolitan Stadium in September 1961. Although he had an even record of 15–15 in 1965, he didn't get much run support, which was the Dodgers' modus operandi. His ERA was only 2.79.

"I honestly feel I pitched as well as Drysdale this season," he said. "Not Koufax, though. He's something special. Out of this world. It's always Koufax, Drysdale, and Osteen. They never say Osteen, Drysdale, and Koufax. If I have my control, I shouldn't have any trouble against the Twins. They swing the bat the same way they did when I faced them in '63 and '64. We can't afford to make any mistakes like we did in the first two games, or they'll kill us."

The Dodgers were happy to return home for games 3, 4, and 5. A deeper fence and four hundred-foot power alley would benefit their pitching, they thought. Lou Johnson, the Dodgers outfield who had played for fifteen teams in only thirteen seasons, blasted Metropolitan Stadium and the condition of the outfield. They were 50–31 at Dodger Stadium that season and relied heavily on their pitching there. They had scored 72 fewer runs at home than they did on the road, but they only surrendered two runs per game.

Dodger Stadium was also renowned for its rock-hard infield. Before Game 3, bench coach Billy Martin asked one of the groundskeepers how they kept the infield so hard. "They use a 1,500-pound roller to keep it that way," Martin reported. "Then the groundskeeper realized he may have said something wrong and added they only use it once a year."

The stars came out to Dodger Stadium to watch Pascual and Osteen duel. The Dodgers had a special section called Millionaire's Row, which were dugout box seats behind home plate and allowed the viewers to chat with Dodgers players and gave an unobstructed view of the dugout.

"We're going to win the Series yet," said Doris Day, who attended every Dodgers game that her schedule allowed. Other stars in attendance for Game 3 included Milton Berle, Joey Bishop, Frank Sinatra, Mia Farrow, Gregory Peck, and Jerry Lewis.

Pascual and Osteen held each other's offenses scoreless through the first three innings of the game. The Twins squandered a chance for a run in the top of the first. With Earl Battey at the plate and Killebrew on first and Versalles on third base, Battey missed a hit-and-run sign. As a result, Versalles got caught in a rundown between third and home and was tagged out to end the inning.

"This has been a bread-and-butter play for us all year," Mele said after the game. "Killebrew should have run to second and let them try to throw him out rather than hold up. This might have given Versalles a chance to score from third, or the Dodgers might have made the play for Harmon at second. I wanted to get the jump on the Dodgers, because they don't score a lot of runs."

Pascual scattered 3 hits (two doubles) over the first three innings and only allowed one stolen base (to Wills).

"We had Wills out by three feet," recalled Versalles. "But Earl's throw hit the top of my glove, and I couldn't hold it."

He ran into problems in the bottom of the fourth inning. Fairly hit the Dodgers' third double of the game to lead off the inning. Lou Johnson laid down a sacrifice bunt to advance Fairly to third. Lefebvre hit an infield single to short, but great awareness by Versalles kept the runner at third. A walk to outfielder Wes Parker loaded the bases John Roseboro with only one out. Roseboro laced a single to Oliva in right field, scoring both Fairly and Lefebvre to take a 2–0 lead.

"I got a good curve ball on Roseboro in the fourth," Pascual said after the game. "But when I tried again, the ball didn't break, and he got the single that scored the first two runs."

Pascual got Osteen to pop up to third. With Maury Wills at the plate, Alston called the double steal for Parker and Roseboro, moving them both into scoring position; but Wills popped up harmlessly to Versalles to end the inning.

The Dodgers added another run in the bottom of the fifth, with Lou Johnson knocking in outfielder Willie Davis with an RBI double.

Mele lifted Pascual after the sixth inning for Merritt. The rookie gave up a leadoff single to Parker, who was bunted over to second by Osteen. Wills lifted a fly ball toward Nossek in center field, who tried to make a diving catch but missed.

"I felt I could catch the ball up to the time I dove and missed it," Nossek said. "I might have been playing Wills wrong, but the plan was to play him a shade toward right field."

Wills ended up with an RBI double as the Dodgers opened a 4–0 lead.

The Twins offense couldn't figure out Osteen as he pitched a complete game shutout, 4–0. He got sixteen ground ball outs and didn't allow a ball to get hit to the outfield until Killebrew flew out to right in the top of the seventh inning.

The game wasn't the only thing the Twins lost. In the bottom of the seventh inning, Earl Battey bruised his neck after running into the backstop chasing a Willie Davis pop-up that forced him out of the game. It was so severely bruised that Battey could barely swallow after the game. Backup catcher Jerry Zimmerman came into the game to replace Battey, but he wasn't 100 percent after spraining his ankle late in the season.

"We need Battey, and I hope he will be ready to play tomorrow," Mele said.

Another Twins star that was struggling in the playoffs was two-time defending AL Batting Champion Tony Oliva, who had hit a combined .322 in his first two full seasons.

"What's really hurting us is the fact that Oliva is only batting .167 in the series," Mele wrote in his *Star Tribune* column after the game. "He missed the last part of the season with a pulled leg muscle, and it may be hurting his timing. But I have confidence that he'll start hitting."

The Twins were only shut out four times all season that year, and now twice at Dodger Stadium. The Los Angeles Angels, who played their final season at Dodger Stadium before moving to Anaheim Stadium for the 1966 season, beat the Twins 5–0 in June.

Game 4 at Dodger Stadium was a rematch of Game 1: Drysdale versus Grant. The Dodgers used their rock-hard infield to their advantage against Grant and implemented their bunt-and-run style that had won them so many games that season. The Twins defense didn't help Grant out either. They committed two errors behind him and failed to make basic plays: hitting cut-off men, covering bases, and throwing to the wrong base.

The Twins wanted to be aggressive and take the small-ball strategy away from the Dodgers right away, but it backfired. Sandy Valdespino, who was hitting second for the Twins, was thrown out trying to stretch a single into a double.

Earl Battey was behind the plate for Game 4, and that both helped and hurt the Twins. It helped to have their All-Star catcher in the lineup but led to a lot of miscommunication in the infield. Grant gave up a run in the first inning due to sloppy play. Maury Wills led off the game with a soft grounder to Don Mincher at first base. Grant was slow covering the bag and had his head down when Mincher tossed him the ball and never saw the ball tossed his way. Normally, Battey, who was a very vocal catcher, would yell at players and directed them where they should be; but he couldn't because of his throat injury.

Wills beat the play to get on first. After colliding with Quillici, he got up and advanced to second. After Jim Gilliam flew out to left, he advanced to third on another ground ball to first base by Willie Davis. Grant was late covering first base again, and Davis was safe at first. Wills scored on a groundout by Ron Fairly. The Twins were able to get the force at second with Davis, but Versalles's spikes got caught in the infield clay and couldn't make a good relay throw to Mincher at first base. And Fairly beat out what should have been an inning-ending double play. Instead, Wills scored to take a 1–0 lead.

The Dodgers added another run in the bottom of the second after Wes Parker reached on a bunt single. Parker stole second then advanced to third on a wild pitch. John Roseboro's ground ball went through the legs of Quillici at second base, and he scored on the error for a 2–0 lead. Dick Tracewski popped out on a bunt attempt, then the Twins graciously got out of the inning on a strike out–throw out play.

The Dodgers scored 3 more runs after both Tony Oliva and Jimmie Hall missed cut-off men in the sixth inning. Mele had pulled Grant after giving up a leadoff walk to Gilliam and a single to Davis to start the bottom of the sixth inning. Gilliam and Davis ended at third and second, respectively, after a bad throw from Tony Oliva in right field. Grant was replaced by Al Worthington, who was 10–7, 2.13 ERA in 62 relief appearances that season. Ron Fairly knocked in both runners with a single to center, then he advanced to second base on a bad throw from Hall. Lou Johnson laid down a bunt to Worthington to advance Fairly, but Worthington threw the ball away down the right field line, which allowed Fairly to score the third run of the inning.

Not only did the Dodgers score with their small-ball style of play, but Wes Parker and Lou Johnson also each hit solo home runs in the game.

Drysdale was a lot better than he was in Game 1. Other than home runs given up to Killebrew in the fourth and Oliva in the sixth, he was untouchable. He struck out Mincher and Hall three times each, finished with 11 total strikeouts and scattered 5 hits over nine innings.

"Drysdale had real good stuff," Mele said. "But my guys were taking too many good pitches."

The Dodgers won 7–2 to even the series at 2–2.

"It's as simple as a three-game series now," Alston said after the win. "I'm not making any predictions, but I like our position with Koufax ready to pitch the fifth game."

The Dodgers utilized their speed once again, forcing Twins mishaps. Wills led the attack on Twins starter Jim Kaat, going 4-for-5 with two doubles and a stolen base. Wills' 4 hits tied a World Series record for hits in a game (since surpassed by Paul Molitor in 1982 and Albert Pujols in 2011 with five). Willie Davis also stole three bases, which tied Honus Wagner's World Series record set in 1909 (later matched by Lou Brock in 1967 and 1968).

Wills led off the game with a ground rule double over the head of Oliva in right field. Jim Gilliam laced an RBI single to the right field for the game's first run. Willie Davis laid down a sacrifice bunt to Killebrew at third, who threw to second to get the lead runner. The ball went through the glove of Quillici and into the right field. Gilliam scored on the error, and Davis took third.

In the third, Davis singled, stole second, then scored on Lou Johnson's RBI single. Fairly hit a double to left center that scored Johnson all the way from first base.

After pitching a complete game win in Game 2, Kaat was chased from the game without completing three innings: 2.1 innings pitched, 6 hits, 4 runs, 14 batters. Mele brought in Dave Boswell for his first World Series action, trying to keep the game within striking distance. Boswell got the last two outs of the inning to retire the side.

Wills led off the fourth inning with an infield hit to Versalles at short. Knowing Wills was a threat to steal, Boswell threw to Mincher at first six times, trying to keep him close before making his first pitch to Gilliam. When Boswell did deliver to the plate, Wills stole second base. Gilliam ripped an RBI single to center to extend the lead to 5–0 Dodgers.

With Jim Perry pitching in the eighth inning, Fairly beat out an infield single to short then was bunted to second by Parker. Roseboro was intentionally walked to set up the double play before Koufax and Wills both knocked in runs with RBI singles to make it 7–0.

The Twins couldn't buy a hit off Koufax, who finished with 10 strikeouts and 4 hits allowed in the complete game shutout. After outscoring the Dodgers 13–3 at Metropolitan Stadium, the Twins only managed to push two runs across the plate in three games at Chavez Ravine and struck out twenty-three times.

The Dodgers, criticized for their hitting all season long, were outhitting the Twins 51–33 in the five games and had raised their Series team average to .302. The Dodgers recorded 34 hits in games 3, 4, and 5 alone.

Now leading the series 3–2, the Dodgers had a chance to win their second World Series in three seasons.

"We've been faced with must-win situations before this season, and the Twins have always won the game they had to win," a confident Calvin Griffith said. "I said we could win it when the series started, and I still think so. It's sure nice to get back to our ballpark."

It would be up to Mudcat Grant, on two days' rest, to push the series to Game 7. He would be opposed by Osteen, who shut out the Twins in Game 3.

"I don't aim to pitch any differently at the Met," he said. "I've got to keep the ball down to win, and if I have my control, I feel confident."

Osteen didn't allow any runs through the first three innings, although the Twins' bats came alive, but couldn't take advantage of runners on base over the first couple innings. Versalles led the game off with a single, but Nossek hit into a double play. Then Oliva singled, but Killebrew grounded out.

In the second inning, Battey lined a single to center field but an aggressive Willie Davis attempted to make a diving catch and missed. The ball also got passed Lou Johnson in left field. When the ball finally got back into the infield, he was standing at third base with a triple. The Twins couldn't knock him in though. Bob Allison struck out for the seventh time in four games. Quilici also struck out, then Grant popped up to third base to end the inning.

In the fourth inning, Battey caught another break and reached on an error by Gold Glove-caliber second baseman Dick Tracewski. The next batter was Bob Allison, who was batting a measly .111 in the World Series. Osteen got ahead of Allison 0–2, but Allison took the next pitch 373 feet into the left field seats for a 2–0 Twins lead.

"I haven't been counting the strikeouts. I haven't been making contact with the ball. That's my main concern," said Allison. "I've been working with Coach Jim Lemon, and I felt comfortable at the plate for the first time in days."

"One bad pitch beat me today," Osteen said. "I had two strikes on him. The second strike was in a perfect spot, low and away. I wanted the 0–2 pitch to be high and tight. Instead, it was right down the middle, and Allison hit it out. My spike got caught in the dirt, and I knew it was a terrible pitch as soon as I released it."

Meanwhile, Grant had pitched four no-hit innings. Ron Fairly broke up the no-no in the fifth inning, but the Twins defense got out of the inning with a pair of groundouts. In the sixth, Dick Tracewski singled to lead off the top of the inning.

Trailing 2–0 and looking for some offense, Alston pulled Osteen for pinch hitter Willie Crawford. Osteen only allowed 1 earned run and 4 hits over five innings. Grant struck out Crawford for his third punch-out of the game. Maury Wills singled to center for his eleventh hit of the series (one short of the six-game World Series record), but Grant got Gilliam and Davis to each fly out to end the threat.

Howie Reed replaced Osteen. H got Battey to ground out for the first out of the inning, then he walked Allison. Allison stole second on a Mincher strikeout. Alston signaled for Reed and intentionally walked Quillici (a .200 hitter) to get to Grant.

"I'm really a pretty good hitter," Grant said during his postgame interview.

Grant took the first pitch he saw from Reed 392 feet into left-center field for a three-run home run.

"He hit a slider right down the pipe. And I'll have to say he hit it pretty good," said Reed. The Met Stadium–record crowd of 49,578 gave Grant a standing ovation as he rounded the bases and emphatically jumped on home plate.

"That meant more to me than the home run," he said after the game. "Imagine, looking up and seeing all those people cheering for you. I'll never forget it."

Grant's home run was just the seventh pitcher to hit a home run in the World Series and the first since Lew Burdette did it for the Milwaukee Braves in 1958. As of 2018, Grant is one of thirteen pitchers to hit a World Series home run.

While the Twins were only held to six hits by Osteen, Reed, and Bob Miller, they got all five of their runs on 2 home runs—1 unearned and two men put on base by walks.

Fairly hit a home run to lead off the top of the seventh, but that was the only run the Dodgers could muster against Grant.

"His curve ball was great today," said Fairly, who was 2-for-4. "We couldn't touch it. I hit a fast ball for the homer. He was getting his curve ball over for strikes today."

"Grant's curve saved him today," Wills said bluntly.

With the 5–1 win, the Twins forced a decisive Game 7 at Metropolitan Stadium. Mele knew he would use Jim Kaat. Alston had options with a rested Don Drysdale or Sandy Koufax on two-day rest. Drysdale had bruised a bone in his hand while batting in Game 4 and had three days' rest, but the injury was still bothering him enough that Alston didn't want to take the risk. He elected to go with Koufax, who was beaten at Met Stadium in Game 2 despite only allowing two runs and striking out nine Twins.

"It was the toughest decision I've ever had to make, choosing between Drysdale and Koufax for the final game," said Alston. Drysdale would be available out of the bullpen, if needed, as would All-Star reliever Ron Perranoski.

A new record of 50,596 fans crammed into Metropolitan Stadium for Game 7. Koufax wasn't at his best in the opening innings. He had trouble getting his curveball over the plate. He walked both Oliva and Killebrew with two outs in the first before striking out Battey to end the threat.

Koufax and the Dodgers caught a break in the third. Versalles hit a one-out single to center, then he stole second with Nossek swinging through strike 2. But home plate umpire Ed Hurley said that Nossek stepped over home plate while swinging and interfered with catcher John Roseboro's throw. Hurley sent Versalles back to first. Nossek popped up to Roseboro, then Oliva struck out.

"Hurley said I got in the way of the catcher," Nossek argued. "If anything, he got in my way. It was an outside pitch. My momentum was such that I was still going for the pitch when Roseboro made his throw. He came into me as he threw. I felt he could have thrown over me just as easily."

The game was still 0-0 in the fourth inning. Kaat was on a short leash with an arsenal of Worthington, Merritt, Pascual, Boswell, Johnny Klippstein, Bill Plies, and Jim Perry ready in the bullpen. Kaat only allowed one hit over the first two innings, then he got out of a jam with two on and nobody out in the third.

In the fourth inning, Lou Johnson sent a 1-1 pitch down the left field line, staying clear of the left field foul pole by a couple inches for the game's first run. Johnson paused momentarily at first base because he wasn't sure if the ball was fair or not. Ron Fairly (a career .266 hitter who hit .379 in the World Series) laced his eleventh hit of the series down the right field for a double. Wes Parker hit him home with a single to right field, then he advanced to second on a bad throw by Oliva. Johnson's, Fairly's, and Parker's hits were all on consecutive pitches.

Al Worthington relieved Kaat, who left the games after completing three innings and giving up 2 runs on 5 hits. Worthington pitched the Twins out of the inning and left the field trailing by only 2 runs.

Seeing his team score those 2 runs was all the motivation Koufax needed. He abandoned his curveball and threw mostly fastballs the rest of the game.

"When I got into the late innings, I could feel I had a lot of strength left," he said. "I was concerned about pitching on short rest and conserving myself a bit, but at the end of the game, I never felt better."

The Twins biggest threat to score came in the fifth inning. Quillici hit a one-out double to left, then Rich Rollins (pinch-hitting for Worthington) drew a walk. With two on and one out, Versalles pulled a fastball just inside the third base line for what looked like a double that could tie the game. John Gilliam backhanded the ball and fell but scrambled to his feet quick enough to beat Quillici to the third base bag for the second out.

"I saw Sandy didn't have his real good curve, so I cheated to the line a few feet." Said Gilliam. "If I didn't, I never would have come up with the ball. It was my best play of this Series. I've been in six World Series, and I find it hard to classify thrills or great plays."

Koufax got Nossek to ground out for the final out of the inning. He would retire the next twelve Twins in order and wouldn't give up another hit until Killebrew's single in the ninth. The Twins bullpen matched him the rest of the way. Worthington, Klippstein, Merritt, and Perry combined for five innings of no-run ball; but Koufax's fastball got better and better as the game went on. After Killebrew's one-out single in the ninth, he struck out Battey and Allison to win the game and the Series.

The Dodgers became the first team in World Series history to win the title after losing the first two games. The 1965 World Series is also the last World Series that saw complete games from the winning pitcher in all seven games.

Game 7 in 1965 is the only World Series game the Twins have lost at home (11-1 all-time).

Versalles led the Twins with a .286 average in the series, but as a team, the Twins only hit .195 as a club—way below their .254 during the regular season. The Dodgers hit .274 as a team with Wes Parker (.304), Maury Wills (.367), and Ron Fairly (.379) all batting about .300.

The Twins would finish above .500 in 1966 at 89–73 but finished in second place in the American League—nine games behind a blossoming powerhouse in the American League: the Baltimore Orioles. Baltimore swept the Dodgers out of the World Series in 1966.

November 27, 1965

The Vikings Draft Jerry Shay

We've been looking at Shay for quite a while. We think he's a good one.
—Vikings head coach Norm Van Brocklin

Although he didn't know it at the time, Vikings head coach Norm Van Brocklin was building an all-time great defense. The Dutchman was entering his sixth season as the head coach. With Bert Rose as general manager in 1961, he acquired Jim Marshall from the Cleveland Browns. After Jim Finks was named general manager in 1964, he got Carl Eller with the sixth pick in the draft and added Gary Larsen as a free agent.

But they were still a long way to what they would become. And prior to the 1965, things were still questionable on the defensive side of the ball. The Vikings finished .500 or better for the second time in their young history (8–5 in 1964) but ranked dead last in the NFL in scoring defense, giving up nearly 29 points per game.

The defense had let them down in some big games. In week 2, the Vikings led Detroit 29–24 with twenty-two seconds left in the game until Milt Plum hit Amos Marsh with a game-winning forty-eight-yard touchdown pass. In week 5, they led the Chicago Bears 37–31 with two minutes left before Gayle Sayers returned a kickoff ninety-six yards for a touchdown (the Bears scored 14 points in the final two minutes for a 45–37 win).

To make things more difficult, linebacker Rip Hawkins, who had started all but one game since the Vikings drafted him in the second round of the 1961 NFL Draft, retired from the NFL at age twenty-six. The Vikings lost another linebacker when veteran Bill Jobko was taken by the Atlanta Falcons in the expansion draft. With Fran Tarkenton, Tommy Mason, and the Vikings offense rolling (28 points per game, fourth in the NFL), the Vikings needed to continue building the defense.

Van Brocklin had four players on his wish list during the draft: Texas linebacker Tommy Nobis, Illinois fullback Jim Grabowski, Oklahoma linebacker Carl McAdams, and Purdue defensive lineman Jerry Shay.

The Vikings had the seventh pick in the draft. The expansion Atlanta Falcons had the first pick and took Nobis, who would win the 1966 NFL Rookie of the Year award and be selected to five Pro Bowls over a ten-year career. Van Brocklin and Finks selected defensive lineman Jerry Shay out of Purdue (McAdams was taken by St. Louis with the eighth pick and Grabowski was drafted by Green Bay with the ninth pick.)

Shay was also selected fifth overall by the Denver Broncos in the AFL draft. He was offered a hefty bonus to sign with the Broncos but ultimately chose the Vikings. He was signed by the team less than half an hour after being drafted.

"I didn't expect to be picked in the first round," Shay told the *Star Tribune* on draft day. "I signed with the Vikings not only because they took me in the first round but because I want to play in the NFL (instead of the AFL)."

At Purdue, Shay had played both sides of the line but preferred defense. Shay played in all fourteen games for the Vikings in 1966, starting two at defensive tackle. While the Vikings defense did improve (21 points per game, eighth in the league), their win total did not. After finishing 4–9–1, Jim Finks fired Van Brocklin (29–51–4 record with the Vikings from 1961 to 66) and hired CFL coach Bud Grant to replace him.

The Vikings decided to undergo a massive rebuild in 1967, trading their best player in Fran Tarkenton to the New York Giants for a haul of draft picks, including the second overall selection in 1967. In addition to their own pick (the eighth overall pick), they also traded tight end Hal Bledsoe, RB Tommy Mason, and a second-round pick to the LA Rams for TE Marlin McKeever and the fifteenth overall pick during the draft.

With their first two first-round picks, the Vikings took a pair of Michigan State offensive stars in RB Clint Jones (second overall) and WR Gene Washington (eighth overall). With the fifteenth pick, the Vikings took Notre Dame standout defensive end Alan Page.

While Grant was coaching with the CFL's Winnipeg Blue Bombers, he never let a rookie start. He felt that the new players should watch and learn from the veterans. But after watching the rookie Page dominate in training camp and preseason games, he decided to start Page at defensive tackle next to Carl Eller.

Shay saw his playing time decrease exponentially, only appearing in one game that season. The former two-time All-American was traded to the Atlanta Falcons after the season. The first defensive tackle taken in the 1966 Draft played in fifteen games in two seasons with the Vikings. He retired in 1972 at the age of twenty-seven and became a scout for the New York Giants.

March 14, 1967

The Vikings Draft Clint Jones over Floyd Little

I hope to play as soon as I can prove I can play. I know I've got a lot to learn, but I think I'll get a chance.
—Vikings runningback Clint Jones

The 1967 Draft was the first common draft after the NFL-AFL merger, meaning teams wouldn't have to compete for their draft picks as they had since 1960. For example, in 1961 the Vikings of the NFL and the Boston Patriots of the AFL both drafted Tulane runningback Tommy Mason, North Carolina LB Rip Hawkins, and Georgia QB Fran Tarkenton. After drafting the players, each team had to recruit the players to play for them. The Patriots offered Tarkenton, whom they drafted in the fifth round, a $17,500 contract and a $5,000 signing bonus. The Vikings drafted him in the third round and offered a $12,500 contract and a $3,500 signing bonus.

"Any reasonable person would have taken the Boston offer," Tarkenton said in an interview with KDLM radio in Detroit Lakes in 2016. "I didn't. I came to Minnesota. I gave up $5,000, but I'm glad I did." The Vikings signed all three players.

The common draft merger couldn't have come at a better time for the Vikings, who had three of the first fifteen picks in 1967. They acquired the second overall pick from the New York Giants in a deal for Tarkenton (they also got a 1967 second-round pick and New York's first two picks in the 1968 Draft), their own pick at number 8, and got the fifteenth overall pick from the Los Angeles Rams in a deal that included franchise-rushing-leader Tommy Mason and tight end Hal Bedsole during the draft.

Bud Grant had been the head coach of the Vikings for four days leading up to the 1967 Draft.

"We need speed," Grant told the *Star Tribune*.

After Michigan State DE Bubba Smith went first overall to the Baltimore Colts, another Spartan went to the Vikings: runningback Clint Jones. Jones was a two-time All-American that ran the hundred-meter dash in under ten seconds. The 205-pound running back averaged 4.8 yards per carry on 396 attempts while at Michigan State.

"He is the type of player who can turn a six- or seven-yard gain into a sixty- or seventy-yard touchdown run." Grant said after selecting Jones. "He'll be running next to a defender, then bam, he pulls away."

The Vikings selected another Michigan State player, Gene Washington, with the eighth pick then Notre Dame defensive lineman Alan Page with the fifteenth pick.

With Mason traded to Los Angeles, the starting running back job was up for grabs. The Vikings had brought in CFL veteran Joe Kapp to replace Tarkenton, but he needed somebody to hand the ball off too. Jones competed with Dave Osborn for the starting spot. Osborn won the job out of training camp (finished 1967 with 215 carries, 972 yards, and two touchdowns) with Jones handling kick returns (25 returns, 23.9 yards per return, 1 touchdown). Jones also had carries on offense for twenty-three yards his rookie year as the Vikings finished the year 3–8–3.

In 1968, he won the starting running back job over Osborn, but veteran fullback Bill Brown led the team in carries (222), yards (805), and touchdowns (11). Brown also caught 31 passes for 329 yards and 3 touchdowns. Jones finished his sophomore season with 128 carries for 536 yards and 1 touchdown.

He was shifted back to special teams in 1969 for a Vikings team that won the NFL Championship. He saw his carries drop from 128 to 54 as he fell to the fourth option out of the backfield behind Osborn, Brown, and Oscar Reed.

His best season as a Viking was 1970. He ran for 9 touchdowns but only averaged 26.4 yards per game. The next season, he had a career high 675 rushing yards and scored four touchdowns.

Over the course of six seasons, Jones ran for 2,008 yards with 19 touchdowns, averaging 3.7 yards per carry and 26 yards per game. He was signed with the San Diego Chargers for the 1973 season before retiring at age twenty-eight.

Taken four picks after Jones was Syracuse runningback Floyd Little. Little had a nine-year career with the Denver Broncos, racking up 12,173 all-purpose yards (6,323 on the ground) and 54 total touchdowns. He was elected to the Pro Football Hall of Fame in 2010.

OCTOBER 1, 1967

The Impossible Dream

It's been a wonderful year, but it's not over yet.
—Boston Red Sox manager Dick Williams

The 1967 American League pennant race was one of the most exciting finishes in the history of baseball. For Boston Red Sox fans.

Two years removed from their Game 7 loss to the Dodgers in 1965, Harmon Killebrew and the Twins were looking to return to the World Series. They finished nine games behind the eventual World Series champion Baltimore Orioles in 1966.

There were no divisions in the 1960s; just two leagues with the winner of each league facing off in the World Series. There were a couple new faces poised to make an impact for the Twins in 1967. The Twins traded Pete Cimino, Jimmie Hall, and Don Mincher to the Angels for twenty-game winner Dean Chance. They also added reliever Ron Kline in exchange for Camilo Pascual and Bernie Allen. But most notable addition to the big-league roster was the unveiling of a lanky second baseman from Panama named Rod Carew.

The 1967 season got off to a rough start for the Twins. They were 5–10 at the end of April and 20–22 at the end of May. The rough start cost manager Sam Mele his job as owner Calvin Griffith sought a fresh look to the team. He promoted longtime minor league manager Carl Ermer to the skipper of the big-league club. Under Ermer's direction, the Twins won 66 of the last 112 games of the season to jump back into a four-team pennant race.

Surprisingly, one of teams was not the ninety-seven-win Orioles from 1966. The defending champs only won seventy-six games in '67, opening the door for the AL pennant to fly in a new stadium.

On September 6, four teams were tied atop the American League standings. While Bob Gibson and the St. Louis Cardinals were running away with the NL pennant, the Chicago White Sox, Boston Red Sox, Detroit Tigers, and the Twins were fighting for the chance to head Busch Stadium for a World Series matchup with the Cards.

The White Sox hadn't won a World Series since 1917. Boston hadn't won since 1918. Detroit hadn't been champions since 1945. And though they had appeared in the World Series in 1965, the Twins hadn't won one since they were the Washington Senators in 1924. (Between 1919 and 1966, the New York Yankees won twenty-nine AL pennants and twenty World Series championships.)

The race stayed tight the entire month. After being swept in a three-game series by the White Sox in the middle of September, the Twins won six of their next seven games to take a half-game lead into the final five games of the year.

But the team to shake up the standings during the last week of the season wasn't even in the race. It was the California Angels.

The Angels, who would finish fifth in the American League, took two of three games from the Twins in the second-to-last series of the year. The Twins couldn't take advantage of Boston losing back-to-back games in Cleveland. Despite that, the Twins were still held a one-game lead in the standings over both Boston and Detroit with two games left.

Detroit played back-to-back doubleheaders with the California Angels. The Twins headed to Boston with the pennant on the line.

Only needing one win to take the AL pennant and return to the World Series, the Twins took a 1–0 lead in the top of the first inning on a Tony Oliva RBI single that scored Zoilo Versalles. Twins starter Jim Kaat was unhittable the first two innings of the game. Kaat was 7–0 with a 1.51 ERA in September and looked set to send Minnesota back to the Fall Classic. But after striking out José Santiago to start the third inning, Kaat felt a searing pain in his pitching elbow. He had to be taken out of the game and was replaced by Jim Perry. Perry would retire the side then continue in Kaat's place.

Still 1–0 in the bottom of the fifth inning, Perry allowed a leadoff double to Reggie Smith. He then fanned Santiago and Mike Andrews before giving up back-to-back run-scoring singles to Jerry Adair and Triple Crown winner Carl Yastrzemski, giving Boston a 2–1 lead.

The Twins tied the game at two in the top of the sixth on a Rich Reese single, then they had runners on second and third with two outs. But Santiago got Zoilo Versalles to pop out and end the Twins threat.

In the sixth, the Twins turned to Ron Kline, who was 7–0 in fifty-four relief appearances on the season. Kline made one bad pitch during his relief appearance. On a 2–2 pitch to the first batter he faced, George Scott hit a home run for a 3–2 Boston lead. Kline would settle down and retire five of the next batters he faced.

In the seventh, Kline gave up a one-out single to Andrews. After Adair reached on an error by Versalles, Ermer lifted Kline in favor of starter Jim Merritt. Merritt was 13–7 with a 2.53 ERA for the Twins that season.

The first batter he faced, Yastrzemski, hit a three-run home run on a full count to give the Red Sox a 6–2 lead.

The Twins mounted a small comeback in the ninth with a two-run Harmon Killebrew home run, but the Twins lost 6–4 to move into a tie for first place with Boston and a potential winner-take-all game the next night.

Meanwhile, Detroit split the first doubleheader with California to move half a game back.

Detroit would have to sweep the second doubleheader to force a one-game playoff for the World Series berth. California took care of those dreams with a win in the first game. That left the Twins and Red Sox for a virtual playoff game for the pennant.

The Twins sent twenty-game winner Dean Chance to the mound, while Boston countered with eventual Cy Young Award winner Jim Lonborg.

Again, the Twins scored in the top of the first. They added an insurance run in the third to take a 2–0 lead. But everything fell apart in the sixth when 5 Boston runs crossed the plate. The Twins added another run in the eighth, but the Twins fell short of returning to the World Series by a final score of 5–3. The Cardinals would win the World Series in seven games.

The Twins were never more than one game out of first the last month of the season and had at least a share of first place for twenty-six days in September.

January 15, 1968

Bill Masterton Passes Away

*I was sick when I heard about it. But I was always
wondering when this was going to happen.*
—Chicago Blackhawks star Bobby Hull

Bill Masterton's dream was to play pro hockey. A native of Winnipeg, he played for the University of Denver from 1958 to 1961, where he scored 66 goals and 196 points. He was a two-time All-American, was a two-time WCHA All-Star, and won the 1960 NCAA championship with the Pioneers with a record of 30–1–1.

Masterton graduated from Denver with an engineering degree but decided to turn pro. He signed a contract with the Montreal Canadiens in 1961. He was assigned to the Hull-Ottawa Canadiens of the Eastern Professional Hockey League. In 1962, he was promoted to the Cleveland Barons of the AHL, where he led the team with 82 points.

After he failed to make the Canadiens roster in 1962, he decided to complete his master's degree at the University of Denver. He accepted a job at Honeywell in Minneapolis. After taking a year off from hockey, he regained his amateur status and played two seasons for the St. Paul Steers of the United States Hockey League. After becoming an American citizen, he joined the US National Team in 1966, where he served as the team's captain.

When the NHL expanded from six teams to twelve in 1967, Masterton had another chance to play pro hockey. One of the six new teams introduced to the league set up in Bloomington: the Minnesota North Stars. Masterton was the first player signed by coach and GM Wren Blair. As a twenty-nine-year-old NHL rookie, Masterton debuted against another new NHL team: the St. Louis Blues. It was in that game, October 11, 1967, that Masterton scored the first goal in Minnesota North Star history in a 2–2 tie with the Blues.

Masterton was playing in his thirty-eighth career NHL game against the Oakland Seals at the Met Center on January 13, 1968, when tragedy struck. While carrying the puck across the blue line, he was checked by Seals defensemen Larry Cahan and Ron Harris. One of their sticks got tangled in Masterton's skate, and the other defender hit him with a clean check that knocked him backward. The impact of the hit caused Masterton to lose consciousness before hitting the back of his head on the ice.

"It sounded like a baseball bat hitting a ball," said teammate Andre Boudrias.

He was rushed to Fairview Southdale Hospital, where doctors determined the swelling in his brain was so severe that they couldn't operate. Thirty hours after the hit, his family decided to remove him from life support, and he passed away on January 15, 1968. He is the only NHL player to die from an injury suffered during a game.

"Making this team was the greatest achievement of his life," Coach Wren Blair said after the news broke that Masterton had died. "It was the thing he always wanted to do."

"I suppose we have been fortunate never to have had a fatality in fifty years," said NHL president Clarence Campbell. "But that doesn't ease the burden of this young man's family."

At the time, helmets were required in NCAA hockey, but not in the NHL. Masterton was not wearing a helmet when he fell. Only a handful of NHL players were wearing helmets at the time. It would take eleven years for the NHL to make helmets mandatory to incoming NHL players. Players who had signed pro contracts prior to June 1, 1979, were given the option not to wear a helmet. It wasn't until Craig MacTavish retired following the 1996–97 NHL season that every player in the league was wearing a helmet.

The North Stars retired Masterton's number 19 in 1987. Following his death, the NHL introduced the Bill Masterton Trophy, which is awarded to a player who "best exemplifies the qualities of perseverance, sportsmanship and dedication to hockey."

April 21, 1968

The 1968 NHL Stanley Cup Semifinals

If they're the two best in the league, then they should be playing for the Cup.
—Clarence Campbell

In 1967, the National Hockey League expanded from their Original Six teams to make a twelve-team league, adding franchises in Philadelphia, Los Angeles, St. Louis, Pittsburgh, Oakland, and Minnesota. They put the new franchises in the West Division and the Original Six (Toronto, Montreal, Boston, New York, Chicago, and Detroit) in the East Division. The playoff format also expanded from four qualifiers to eight—four from each division. That meant one of the brand-new teams would make an appearance in the Stanley Cup Finals.

The North Stars had a couple shining moments during their inaugural season: upsetting Boston in the Bruins' first ever trip to Metropolitan Stadium, RW Wayne Connelly led the team and the division with 35 goals and had the first hat trick in North Stars history against Philadelphia.

At the end of the season, the North Stars had 69 points, which was good for the fourth and final playoff spot in the West Division with Philadelphia (73), Los Angeles (72), and St. Louis (70). The East Division was understandably better. The Toronto Maple Leafs missed the playoffs in the East with 76 points, which would have led the West Division.

Minnesota was matched up against the LA Kings in their first ever playoff series. The series went to seven games with the home team winning each of the first six games. The North Stars won Game 7 in Los Angeles 9–4 to advance to the semifinals.

St. Louis, behind eventual Playoffs MVP goalie Glenn Hall, also won their series against Philadelphia in seven games to advance to the showdown with the North Stars with each franchise's first Stanley Cup Final berth on the line.

The playoff series opened in St. Louis on April 21, 1968. The North Stars led Game 1 2–1 midway through the second period before three Blues goals in just under three minutes (Frank St. Marseille, Dickie Moore, Bill McCreary Sr.). The Blues took Game 1 by a 5–3 final. The series shifted back to Bloomington the next night with Minnesota taking Game 2 in overtime thanks to a Parker MacDonald goal at 3:41. The North Stars also took Game 3 5–1 to take a 2–1 series lead.

Minnesota led Game 4 3–0 (Walt McKechnie, J. P. Parise, Wayne Connelly) heading into the third period. The Blues would score three unanswered goals in the third (Jimmy Roberts, Dickie Moore, Roberts again) to tie the game before Gary Sabourin scored his first career postseason goal to win the game for the Blues. Game 5 in St. Louis also went to overtime, tied at 2–2. This time, Bill McCreary Sr. was the hero for the Blues, putting the game winner past Cesare Maniago at the 17:27 mark to take a 3–2 series lead.

Minnesota returned to the Met Center with their backs against the wall in a must-win Game 6. Wayne Connelly scored his eighth goal of the postseason at 5:28 in the first period and never looked back, winning 5–1 to force a decisive Game 7—the second for both teams in the playoffs.

Game 7 was a defensive dual between Maniago (thirty-six saves) and Hall (forty-four saves). The game stayed scoreless deep into the third period before Walt McKechnie scored at 16:49 to put the North Stars up 1–0. They were less than three minutes away from a Stanley Cup Finals appearance. But St. Louis' Dickie Moore scored thirty-one seconds later to tie the game and send it to overtime. The first overtime was scoreless as neither team were able to get it past Maniago or Hall, who had over eighty-two minutes of ice time in the game. Minnesota outshot St. Louis 14–10 in the first overtime period.

In double overtime, Ron Schock finally sent St. Louis into the Finals with a goal 2:50 into the second overtime period.

The Blues were swept in the finals by Montreal, losing all four games by only one goal.

For the North Stars, it would be as close to the finals as they would get for another thirteen years. Three of their losses in the series came in overtime, and their Game 7 loss is one of only four Game 7s in the history of the NHL to go to double overtime.

July 9, 1968

Harmon Killebrew Tears His Hamstring in the All-Star Game

Longer throw by Fregosi. Right there, Killebrew with the big split. Is he all right?
—Curt Gowdy on NBC

When you think of All-Star Game injuries, you immediately think about Pete Rose colliding with Ray Fosse in 1970. Or Dwayne Wade breaking Kobe Bryant's nose in 2012. But there was an injury in 1968 that changed the course of Twins history.

Harmon Killebrew was making his tenth career All-Star Game appearance despite putting up uncharacteristic numbers during the first half of the season: 13 home runs, 34 RBI, and a .204 batting average. The Twins were in fifth place at the break, fifteen games behind the first-place Detroit Tigers.

The game was played at the Astrodome in Houston on July 9. Killebrew was joined in Houston by teammates Rod Carew and Tony Oliva (the second of five consecutive trips for the trio of Twins). It was the first All-Star Game played indoors and on artificial turf. With the revolutionary field turf relatively new, grounds crews were still finding to find the recipe for the perfect infield. The dirt at the Astrodome wasn't hard-packed like a sunbaked outdoor stadium. Instead, it was like fine sand.

Harmon made his third start in four years at first base, largely due to his reputation as one of the most feared sluggers of the 1960s instead of his 1968 offensive numbers. Cleveland's Luis Tiant was the starting pitcher for the American League, with Killebrew, Carew, shortstop Jim Fregosi, third baseman Brooks Robinson rounding out the rest of the infield. Tiant gave up a leadoff single to San Francisco's Willie Mays in the bottom of the first. A bad pickoff throw to Killebrew got past him, which moved Mays to second. Then Tiant threw a wild pitch to St. Louis Cardinal Curt Flood, in which Mays advanced to third.

36

Flood eventually walked. Tiant got Willie McCovey of the San Francisco Giants to ground into a run-scoring double play. He issued another walk, this time to Atlanta's Hank Aaron, before getting Chicago Cub Ron Santo to ground out to Fregosi.

LA Dodger Don Drysdale was on the hill for the National League. After giving up a leadoff double to Fregosi to start the game, he retired the next nine batters he faced, including a Killebrew pop out to second base.

Oakland's Blue Moon Odom relieved Tiant in the third inning with the AL trailing 1–0 on Tiant's unearned run. Odom got Mays on a routine ground ball to Fregosi at short. The next at bat would halt Killebrew's season.

Flood hit a deep ground ball to Fregosi, who threw low to Killebrew. He stretched to dig the ball out, but as he did, his left foot slid on the infield dirt, causing him to do the splits.

"It wasn't a bad throw," Harmon recalled in a 2002 interview. "Just a low one. I'd never done the splits before, but I did it that day. That injury was really a freak injury."

Killebrew held on to the ball for the putout but went down in immediate pain as soon as the out was made. He laid flat on his back on the infield dirt and was immediately looked at by NL first-base coach Herman Franks, and seconds later, he had teammate Rod Carew by his side.

While NBC analysts Curt Gowdy and Pee Wee Reese speculated that the injury was a pulled muscle, it was much more severe than that.

It turns out that Killebrew tore muscles in his left knee, the covering of his hamstring muscle, and pulled a small piece of bone away from his pelvis where the hamstring was attached.

Harmon was loaded up onto a stretch and carried off the field. The first person to meet him in the locker room was an inconsolable Calvin Griffith. Several doctors questioned whether Killebrew would ever play again.

"Had it torn completely away from the pelvis, I probably wouldn't have." Harmon said.

He would miss all but the last five games of the regular season. "I played those last five games because I didn't want to spend the whole off-season wondering if I'd ever play again. I really wasn't in any condition to play those last few days, but I couldn't just not play. Even after playing those last few games of the season, I sure wasn't sure if I'd play at a high level again."

The National League beat the American League 1–0 for their sixth straight win in the Midsummer Classic, but it was Minnesota that lost the most in the exhibition game.

Harmon's final stat line in 1968: 17 home runs, 40 RBI, and a .210/.361/.420 slash line, all easily career lows for the Hall of Famer. Even with his slow first-half, it would be fun to think about where Harmon's career numbers would have been with another half season in his prime.

October 4, 1969

The Inaugural American League Championship Series

We battled them all the way, but still it's a bitter pill to swallow.
—Twins manager Billy Martin

Prior to 1969, only two teams made the playoffs in Major League Baseball. The winner of the American League pennant and the winner of the National League pennant squared off in the World Series. No divisions. No wild cards. Just the two best teams in baseball.

That all changed for the 1969 season with the introduction of baseball's Eastern and Western Divisions in each league. The Minnesota Twins were placed in the American League West with the Oakland Athletics, California Angels, Chicago White Sox, and the expansion Seattle Pilots and Kansas City Royals.

The Twins finished 79–83 in 1968, good for seventh place in the American League. With the divisional split, six of the seven teams that finished ahead of them (Detroit, Baltimore, Cleveland, Boston, and New York) moved to the AL East.

Rod Carew won his first American League Batting Title in 1969, leading the league with a .332 average. Tony Oliva hit .309 with 24 home runs and 101 RBI, and Harmon Killebrew, who missed the second half of the 1968 season with a leg injury sustained in the All-Star Game, won the AL MVP award with 49 home runs and 140 RBI. Jim Perry and Dave Boswell each won twenty games (the only time the Twins have had two twenty-game winners on the staff).

At the helm was first-year manager Billy Martin, who had played for the Twins in 1961 before becoming a scout in 1962, a third-base coach in 1965, and a manager in 1969.

The Twins won ninety-seven games under Martin and the inaugural AL West Division Championship and faced the 109–53 Baltimore Orioles in the American League Championship Series.

Baltimore's roster featured future Hall of Famers Brooks Robinson, Jim Palmer, and Frank Robinson; AL MVP runner-up Boog Powell; All-Stars Davey Johnson and Paul Blair; and twenty-game winners Dave McNally and Mike Cuellar.

Game 1 at Memorial Stadium in Baltimore featured Jim Perry (20–6, 2.82 ERA) and Mike Cuellar (23–11, 2.38 ERA). Cuellar was nearly untouchable through the first four innings, with Perry matching him pitch for pitch. The series' first run was scored on a Frank Robinson home run in the fourth that put Baltimore up 1–0. The Twins answered back in the top of the fifth after Tony Oliva scored on a Bob Allison sac fly. Mark Bellanger hit a solo home run off Perry in fifth inning to take a 2–1 lead. Tony Oliva hit a two-run home run in the seventh to give the Twins their first lead of the game, 3–2.

The Twins had a great chance to add an insurance run in the top of the ninth. After drawing a walk, Cesar Tovar stole second. The next three batters were three of the best hitters in Twins history: Rod Carew, Harmon Killebrew, and Tony Oliva.

Reliever Pete Richert, pitching his first inning of relief for Cuellar, was tasked with getting them out. He struck out Carew, intentionally walked Killebrew, and then struck out Oliva. Bob Allison popped up to Boog Powell at first base to end the threat.

Jim Perry, who had only allowed the 2 home runs through eight innings, remained in the game to pitch the bottom of the ninth. Powell, who was 0–3 in the game, was the first man to bat. Powell hit a deep shot that cleared the right field wall and tied the game at 3–3. Following Powell, Brooks Robinson singled to Ted Uhlaender in left field, then he advanced to second on an Allison throwing error. With the winning run on second base, Twins manager Billy Martin called on American League Saves leader Ron Perranoski to try and send the game to extra innings.

Curt Motton pinch-hit for catcher Elrod Hendricks and reached on a Carew error at second. With runners first and second, Davey Johnson popped up to catcher George Mitterwald. Mark Belanger grounded out to second base, moving Robinson to third. With two outs and Merv Rettenmund at the place, Robinson got a little too far off third base and was thrown out by Mitterwald to end the inning.

The Twins had another chance to take a lead in the top of the twelfth inning. Orioles reliever Marcelino Lopez loaded the bases with one out before Orioles manager Earl Weaver pulled him for Dick Hall. Hall struck out Leo Cardenas. All-Star catcher John Roseboro came off the bench to pinch-hit for Mitterwald, and he grounded out to second base.

Perranoski returned to work the bottom of the twelfth—his third inning in relief of Perry. He gave up a leadoff infield single to Belanger, and the Orioles took advantage. Andy Etchebarren bunted Belanger to second, a Don Buford ground ball advanced him to third, and then Paul Blair bunted him home. The Orioles won 4–3 and led the ALCS 1–0.

Game 2 was also played at Memorial Stadium and pitted Dave McNally (20–7, 3.22 ERA) and Dave Boswell (20–12, 3.32 ERA) against each other. McNally had won his first fifteen decisions that year and didn't lose a game until August 3 in a 5–2 loss against the Twins. He nearly no-hit the Twins that season too, had it not been for a Cesar Tovar single with one out in the ninth on May 15. There were six starts during that streak in which he lasted fewer than four innings, but Baltimore had come back to tie to remove him as the pitcher of record.

After a Tony Oliva single in the fourth inning, McNally held the Twins hitless for the rest of the game. Boswell, like Perry was in Game 1, matched McNally on the scoreboard through the first nine innings. The game went to extra innings, still tied at 0–0.

George Mitterwald almost gave the Twins the lead in the tenth inning, missing a home run down the left field line by about two feet. McNally struck him out to start the inning, then he struck out Leo Cardenas and Boswell.

The Twins had another good chance to take the lead in extra. With two outs in the eleventh, McNally walked Killebrew on a 3–2 count, then he walked Oliva on four pitches. Bob Allison got ahead in the count 3–0, then took two strikes before lining out to left field.

It was déjà vu for the Twins in the bottom of the eleventh. Boswell, who had pitched ten shutout innings, walked Boog Powell to lead off the innings. Brooks Robinson bunted him to second. Boswell walked Davey Johnson to set up the double play, then he got Mark Belanger to pop out third in foul territory. Weaver and Martin played a managerial chess match, with Martin sending in Perranoski, and Weaver sending Curt Motton to the plate to pinch-hit for Elrod Hendricks.

Motton lined a ball to right field, just over the outstretched glove of Carew at second base. Powell rounded second and beat Oliva's throw from right field as Baltimore walked off on the Twins for the second day in a row, taking a 2–0 series lead. The final stat line on McNally: eleven shutout innings with 11 strikeouts.

Minnesota, who led the league in hitting with a .268 average, had only managed 7 hits in twenty-three innings in the first two games. Batting Champion Rod Carew was 1–9 with 4 strikeouts. Killebrew, Allison, Rich Reese, and Leo Cardenas went a combined 0–30. Heading back to Minneapolis, Minnesota would need to win the next three games to capture their second American League pennant in four years.

To make matters worse, Oliva threw out his arm on the final play of the game and needed three shots to calm down the swelling. His status for Game 3 was uncertain up until the first pitch.

Game 3 of the ALCS was the first postseason game at Metropolitan Stadium since Sandy Koufax shut down the Twins in Game 7 of the 1965 World Series.

Koufax was at the Met that Monday afternoon as part of the NBC broadcast team.

Martin had two options to start Game 3: Jim Kaat and Bob Miller. The veteran Kaat was a gritty competitor that baseball writers thought would have a better chance to stave off elimination. But Martin wanted to save him for a potential Game 4 matchup. The Twins' playoff hopes rested on the shoulders of Bob Miller (5–5, 3.02 ERA). Miller, an eleven-year major league veteran, was in danger of missing the roster before the season started. 1968 was the worst statistical season of his career, and he was relegated to mop-up duty. He figured either Kansas City or Seattle would draft him in the expansion draft. His name was consistently brought up in trade talks and he figured if he wasn't traded that the Twins would flat out cut him. But here he was, pitching a win-or-go-home game for the Twins.

Billy Martin thought Miller would be the best matchup against young Jim Palmer of the Orioles. The twenty-three-year-old Palmer was 16–4 with a 2.34 ERA in 1969. He had one previous playoff start for the O's: he outdueled Sandy Koufax in Game 2 of the 1966 World Series, throwing a complete game 6–0 shutout for the World Series champion Orioles. When Martin was a Twins scout in 1962, he urged Twins president Calvin Griffith to sign Palmer, but Griffith didn't want to shell out a $50,000 signing bonus for the eventual three-time Cy Young–winning Hall of Fame pitcher.

The Twins took the lead in the bottom of the first inning, stringing together a couple two-out hits against Palmer to push Tony Oliva across the plate for a 1–0 lead. Olivia, who had hurt his arm on the final play of Game 2, didn't take pregame warm-ups to try and hide the fact that he couldn't lift his arm. Earl Weaver and Baltimore already knew. "I told my players if they hit a ball to right field not to hesitate about taking any extra bases," Weaver said after the game.

Brooks Robinson led the second inning off with a double to the left field. Davey Johnson lifted a fly ball to Olivia in the right field. Oliva slipped while making the catch and dropped the ball.

Fans, who weren't informed of Oliva's arm injury, began to boo. Elrod Hendricks knocked both in with a double to center field, and just like that, Baltimore was up 2–1. Miller got Belanger and Palmer to fly out, then gave up an RBI single to Don Buford to make it 3–1.

"I'm mad." Oliva told the *Star Tribune*'s Sid Hartman after the game. "They boo me and not even know what is wrong with me. I couldn't throw the ball. I couldn't lift my arm high enough to swing the bat. But I insisted that Billy play me because this was such an important game."

Martin pulled Miller for Dick Woodson, who struck out Paul Blair to end the inning. It would be the only time the Twins got Blair out all afternoon. Miller's stat line in his final appearance as a Twin: 1.2 innings, 5 hits, 3 runs (1 earned).

Palmer retired the side in the bottom of the second, but manager Earl Weaver noticed something funny with the scoreboard. He came out to home plate umpire Frank Umont and pointed to a hole to the right of the error sign. He and Curt Motton had noticed that there was a white cloth waving over the hole. Motton had a pair of binoculars, and when he looked at the scoreboard, he noticed a man seemingly signaling pitches to the Twins batters. When Palmer was going to throw a curveball, his arms were in the air. When it was a fastball, his arms were at his sides.

Umont told Weaver that the person was working out there and told him to have Motton put the binoculars away. After the protest, the mysterious man in the scoreboard disappeared.

If the Twins were stealing signs, it didn't help. Baltimore dominated Game 3. They outhit, outpitched, and frankly outmanaged the Twins en route to an 11–2 victory. After striking out in the first inning, Paul Blair finished the game 5-for-6 with 5 RBI. Don Buford was 4-for-5 with 3 runs. Jim Palmer pitched a complete game, scattering 10 hits, striking out 4, and giving up 2 earned runs.

The Twins used seven different pitchers to get through the game: Miller, Woodson, Tom Hall, Al Worthington, Joe Grzenda, Dean Chance, and Ron Perranoski (who pitched in all three games of the series). Combined, they gave up 11 runs (9 earned) on 18 hits. The only Twins pitcher not to appear in the three-game series was Jim Kaat.

Twins batters didn't fare much better during the series. The only starter to hit over .167 for the series was Oliva (.385). Batting champ Rod Carew was 1–14 (.071/.133) and reigning MVP Harmon Killebrew was 2–8 (.125) with six walks, no home runs, and no RBI.

After the game, a reporter asked Billy Martin what the Twins needed for the 1970 season.

"A new manager," he answered.

President Calvin Griffith, upset that Martin had gone with Miller over Kaat to start Game 3, informed him that his contract wouldn't be renewed via a telephone call from New York while attending the World Series between the Orioles and the New York Mets (the Miracle Mets won the series 4–1).

"It was the hardest decision I ever had to make about a manager," Griffith said after making the move. He hired veteran manager Bill Rigney to replace Martin for the 1970 season.

To make matters worse, for Griffith anyways, the Twins missed out on an estimated $2 million in playoff revenue.

January 4, 1970

The Vikings "Lose" the Ed Thorp Memorial Trophy

Ed Thorpe was an early football referee, a rules expert, and a friend to some of the early NFL owners. When he died in 1934, the owners decided to create a trophy to honor him. The Ed Thorp Memorial trophy was awarded to the NFL champion from 1934 until 1969, and was passed on from champion to champion much like the NHL's Stanley Cup. Today's championship trophy, the Lombardi Trophy, stays with the team that wins it. A new one is created and awarded every year.

In 1966, the NFL merged with the AFL to create one National Football League. However, the league decided to continue to award the Ed Throp trophy to the winner of the NFL Conference. The last team that won the award was the Minnesota Vikings.

The Vikings only won one Ed Thorp trophy...the last one, awarded in 1969. After all, Minnesota had entered the league in 1961, but now had the building blocks in place to be one of the great franchises of the 1970s. Hall of Fame head coach Bud Grant was now in his third season as head coach and had taken the Vikings from a 3–8 team to 12–2 and to the top of the NFL. With Pro Bowl quarterback Joe Kapp at the helm, future Hall of Famers Ron Yary and Mick Tingelhoff protecting him, and Alan Page, Carl Eller, Gary Larson and Jim Marshall on the defensive line, Minnesota was poised to win multiple championships.

After losing the first game of the 1969 season to the New York Giants, the Vikings beat the Baltimore Colts (who had knocked them out of the playoffs in 1968) by 38 points en route to a twelve-game winning streak. In fact, they led the league in both points per game (27.1) and points against (9.1). The Vikings literally dominated every aspect of the game. On January 4, 1970, they shellacked the Cleveland Browns in the NFL Championship game at a freezing Metropolitan

Stadium 27–7 to advance to their first Super Bowl. The team was awarded the final Ed Thorp Memorial Trophy as the 1969 NFL champions.

And they lost it. Straight up lost it. The trophy just disappeared. But it's hard to lose something that you never had.

For years, fans attributed the Vikings' playoff struggles to the Curse of the Ed Thorp Trophy, and losing the only trophy the franchise had won. The curious thing was there was no visual evidence that the trophy ever made it to Minnesota. No photos of Joe Kapp or Bud Grant celebrating a trip to the Super Bowl with the NFL Championship trophy.

Nobody knew where the trophy had disappeared to . . . until 2015.

The trophy was discovered in a closet in Green Bay. After the Packers won the trophy for the eighth time in 1967, they never gave it back. The Baltimore Colts won it in 1968 and the Vikings in 1969, but the last name engraved into the trophy is Green Bay, suggesting that it was never given to Baltimore either.

The trophy is on display in the Packers Hall of Fame, despite being the rightful property of the Minnesota Vikings.

"Maybe they'll loan it to us," joked Grant upon hearing where the trophy ended up. "We can finally have something on display in our trophy case in the new Vikings Museum."

Jokes aside, it doesn't change the fact that the Vikings have the most playoff losses (twenty-nine) in league history. Fans will just have to find something other than the ghost of Ed Thorp to blame it on.

<<BONUS ACHE>>

The Slab of Bacon Trophy

It wouldn't be so bad if it was the first time that the state of Wisconsin had pulled this. Beginning in 1930, the Minnesota Golden Gophers and Wisconsin Badgers football teams would play for the Slab of Bacon Trophy so that the winning team could "bring home the bacon." But after the Gophers beat the Badgers 25-13 in 1943, Wisconsin didn't hand the trophy over to Minnesota and claimed that they had lost it. A new trophy was introduced in 1948: Paul Bunyan's Axe.

But, in 1994, a Wisconsin intern found the trophy in a storage closet at Camp Randall and had been maintained for some time, with the scores updated through 1970. Even though the trophy rightfully belongs to Minnesota, the Slab of Bacon is displayed at the football offices at Camp Randall.

January 11, 1970

Super Bowl IV versus Kansas City

There wasn't an upset. We really believed we were going to win.
—Chiefs quarterback Len Dawson

Super Bowl IV, held on January 11, 1970, was the final NFL versus AFL Super Bowl. The two leagues were merging to into the National Football League in 1971, and it was the AFL's last chance to prove that they were not an inferior league.

Joe Namath and the AFL New York Jets stunned Johnny Unitas and the Baltimore Colts in Super Bowl III, and now Len Dawson and his Kansas City Chiefs were trying to do the same thing to the Minnesota Vikings in Super Bowl IV.

The Vikings dominated the NFL in 1969. They led the league in both points scored (379, 27.1 per game) and points allowed (133, 9.5 per game) and finished the season 12–1, losing the first and last game of the regular season while running a twelve-game winning streak in the middle. The Vikings were led by "the indestructible" Joe Kapp. He completed 50 percent of his passes that year for 1,726 yards and 19 touchdowns. Today, most quarterbacks slide after a run. Not Kapp. He'd lower his shoulder and fight for as many yards as his five-foot-two, 215-pound frame could get. The Vikings team also featured five Hall of Fame players: Carl Eller, Paul Krause, Alan Page, Mick Tingelhoff, and Ron Yary, as well as GM Jim Finks and Coach Bud Grant.

The Kansas City Chiefs, however, had a different road to Super Bowl IV. Hall of Fame quarterback Len Dawson missed more than a month of the season with a knee injury, but the Chiefs won all six games that backup Mike Livingston was under center. The Chiefs finished 11–3, one game behind the 12–1–1 Oakland Raiders in the AFL West. Wanting to be structured like the NFL, the AFL expanded their playoffs before the 1969 season from two division winners playing for the AFL Championship and added two wild card teams to compete for the title.

The Chiefs, like the Vikings, had a smothering defense. Led by Hall of Famers Buck Buchanan, Curley Culp, and Emmitt Thomas, the Chiefs only allowed 177 points (12.6 PPG) and were second in the AFL in points scored (359, 25.6 per game). On offense, Coach Hank Stram's moving pocket offense, also dubbed Hank Stram's Wild West Variety Show, revolutionized the game. The 1965 Heisman Trophy winner Mike Garrett, Robert Holmes, and Warren McVea combined for 1,844 rushing yards and 15 touchdowns. Garrett and Holmes added 698 receiving yards and 5 touchdowns, while McVea contributed 318 kick return yards.

The Vikings were the top seed in the NFL in the playoffs that season. Their opening game against the LA Rams was a nail biter. The Vikings trailed 17–7 at halftime but held the Rams to a Bruce Gossett field goal in the second half. Kapp and Dave Osborn each scored a rushing touchdown and the Vikings defense put the icing on the cake with Carl Eller sacking Roman Gabriel in the end zone for a safety and Alan Page hauling in an interception to seal the win.

The NFL Championship game went a little smoother at Metropolitan Stadium. In frigid negative six-degree temps, the Vikings led the 11–4–1 Cleveland Browns 27–0 before a garbage-time touchdown late in the game gave the Vikings the win, their first NFL Championship, and a trip to Super Bowl IV.

The Kansas City Chiefs' road to the Super Bowl began with a matchup against the defending-champion New York Jets. Chiefs Hall of Fame kicker Jan Stenerud and Jets kicker Jim Turner each kicked two field goals for a 6–6 tie in the fourth quarter. A sixty-one-yard completion from Dawson to Otis Taylor set up a nineteen-yard touchdown pass to Gloster Richardson and a 13–6 Chiefs win. The defense held Joe Namath and the Jets to only 234 yards and had four takeaways, including three Namath interceptions.

The AFL Championship game pitted the Chiefs against the AFL West Division champion Oakland Raiders—a team that had beaten them twice in the regular season. Oakland was coming off a 56–7 drubbing of the Houston Oilers in their opening round game, and many fans and media members expected a similar result against the Chiefs.

After giving up a rushing touchdown to Charlie Smith in the opening quarter, the Chiefs Defense shut out Oakland for the rest of the game, winning 17–7.

Nobody had more to prove in Super Bowl IV than Len Dawson. The fifth overall pick out of Purdue in 1958, he spent five years as a backup with the NFL's Pittsburgh Steelers and Cleveland Browns before signing with the AFL's Dallas Texas in 1962, who would relocate to Kansas City in 1963. Dawson was the AFL MVP in 1962, was a six-time AFL All-Star, led the league in passing touchdowns four times, and won three AFL titles. But the AFL was viewed as a lesser league to the AFL. Dawson couldn't crack an NFL lineup from 1957 to 61, and the one time he had played an NFL team in Super Bowl I, the Green Bay Packers beat the Cheifs 35–10.

The Vikings entered the game as thirteen-point favorites against the Kansas City Chiefs. Writers claimed that since the Vikings dominated the superior NFL and since the Chiefs didn't even win their division in the AFL, the Vikings should run away with it.

The Vikings received the ball to start the game and had to punt after their first drive stalled. Jan Stenerud kicked a then–Super Bowl record forty-eight-yard field goal to take a 3–0 lead.

In the second quarter, an Ed Sharockman pass interference call on a third down incompletion kept a Kansas City drive alive, resulting in a thirty-two-yard Stenerud field goal to give Kansas City a 6–0 lead. On the Vikings next drive, receiver John Henderson fumbled after catching a sixteen-yard pass from Kapp, and the Chiefs recovered the football at the Vikings' forty-six-yard line. But the Vikings' defense stepped up big with an Alan Page tackle-for-loss and a Paul Krause interception at their own seven-yard line.

The Vikings couldn't capitalize on the turnover. A three-and-out forced them to punt the ball back to the Chiefs, and after a 39 punt by Bob Lee, Stenerud was able to kick another field goal, this time from twenty-five yards, to extend the Kansas City lead to 9–0.

Vikings returner Charlie West fumbled on the ensuing kickoff, and Kansas City recovered it at the Vikings nineteen-yard line. Seven plays later, the Chiefs were in the end zone with the first touchdown of the game on a five-yard trap draw play by Mike Garrett. Stram had guard Mo Moorman pull and aid in blocking Page, opening a huge hole. The play is forever known in Kansas City lore as 65 Toss Power Trap.

Stram's game plan on offense focused on double-teaming Carl Eller and Jim Marshall on the line of scrimmage. He knew that the Minnesota defensive backs played off wideouts on the line of scrimmage because pressure applied by Eller and Marshall disrupted the passing game. But taking Eller and Marshall out of the game, Dawson was able to complete quick passes to his wideouts with the defensive backs playing deep. That and a wide array of new-look offensive formations kept the Vikings' defense confused on the field.

Now trailing 16–0, Kaap and the Vikings offense needed to show some life. Kapp connected on a twenty-seven-yard pass play to John Henderson on the first play of their next drive. Kapp then threw back-to-back incompletions and was sacked by Buchannan to make it fourth and long. Bud Grant sent Fred Cox out for a fifty-six-yard field goal that fell way short, and the Vikings went to the locker room trailing by 16 points.

The Chiefs' defensive line was dominant in the first half, overpowering Tingelhoff, Yary, and Pro Bowler Grady Alderman. KC's defensive tackles Buchanan and Culp outweighed Tingelhoff by fifty pounds and clogged up the line of scrimmage, inhibiting the Vikings' rushing attack. The Vikings only had twenty-four rushing yards in the opening half and were 0 for 5 on third down conversions.

In the third quarter, the Vikings defense forced Kansas City to punt the ball on their opening drive. Kapp and the offense finally found a rhythm and the end zone, going sixty-nine yards in ten plays and scoring on a four-yard Dave Osborn touchdown run.

Three minutes later, Len Dawson hit Otis Taylor on a short pass play near the sideline. He broke an Earsell Mackbee tackle and made Karl Kassulke miss and took it forty-six yards for the touchdown.

The Vikings were shell-shocked. Kapp threw two fourth-quarter interceptions trying to get the Vikings back in the game. Kapp's final play of the game (and as a Viking) was an eight-yard sack by Aaron Brown that forced him from the game. He was replaced by Gary Cuozzo, who threw a pick to Emmitt Thomas to end the game. The final score was 23–7.

The combination of Garrett, Hayes, and McVea ran the ball thirty-one times for ninety-six yards. Kansas City had 42 carries for 151 yards as a team. Otis Taylor finished with six receptions for eighty-one yards and the backbreaking touchdown. Len Dawson, named Super Bowl MVP, finished 12 of 17 passing for 142 yards and a touchdown.

The Kansas City defense held All-Pro wide receiver Gene Washington to one catch for 9 yards and Dave Osborn (who ran for 108 against Cleveland the game prior) to only 15 yards (his longest run of the game was his four-yard touchdown). As a team, the Vikings had 19 carries for only 67 yards. The lone bright spot of the Vikings offense with John Henderson's seven catches for 111 yards.

The Vikings turned the ball over six times and committed six penalties. Safety Karl Kassulke said after the game, "We made more mental mistakes in one game than we did all season."

October 3, 1970

The 1970 American League Championship Series

Sure, we won 11 straight games coming into the playoff, but I don't believe in momentum.
—Baltimore Orioles manager Earl Weaver

A season after Cal Griffith decided not to retain manager Billy Martin despite leading the team to the playoffs, new manager Bill Rigney and the Twins improved to one more win than they did in 1969. The Twins were 98–64 (the second-best record in team history behind the 102-win 1965 squad) and finished nine games ahead of the Oakland Athletics to win back-to-back American League West titles.

Harmon Killebrew followed his 1969 MVP season with another 40-home run/100-RBI season. Tony Oliva had the arguably the best year of his career with a .325/.364.514 stat line with 107 RBI and 200 hits. Cesar Tovar hit .300 and scored 120 times; Jim Perry won the AL Cy Young; rookie Bert Blyleven was a ten-game winner; and Stan Williams (10–1, 1.99 ERA in 68 appearances), Ron Perranoski (2.43 ERA, thirty-four saves in sixty-seven games), Bill Zepp (9–4, 1.87 ERA, in twenty-three relief appearances), and Tom Hall (11–6, 2.55 ERA, 184 strikeouts in fifty-two appearances) made up one up one of the best bullpens in baseball. Rod Carew led the American League with a .376 average before hurting his knee in Milwaukee mid-June and missed all but the final four games of the season.

Just like in 1969, the Baltimore Orioles waited for them in the American League Championship Series. The Os had swept the Twins out of the playoffs in '69 before losing to the New York Mets in the World Series.

Baltimore was just as strong in 1970. With a starting rotation featuring three twenty-game winners (Jim Palmer, Mike Cuellar, Dave McNally) and a lineup with future Hall of Famers Brooks Robinson and Frank Robinson and reigning

AL MVP Boog Powell, the Orioles won 108 games and had compiled a winning record against everybody in the American League that season.

Everybody except Rigney's Twins, who beat them seven out of twelve times in the regular season.

The bad taste of the sweep still lingered in the mouths of the Twins. Questions remained from the Game 3 11–2 loss. Should the injured Tony Oliva have been in the game? Should Billy Martin have started Jim Kaat instead of Bob Miller? Would Rod Carew, who batted .071 in the 1969 playoffs, hit the ball like the Twins were used to?

Game 1 of the best-of-five series was played at very windy Metropolitan Stadium on October 3. In a game that pitted twenty-four-game winners Mike Cuellar and Jim Perry against each other, fans and analysts were expecting a low-scoring Game 1.

But Mother Nature had other plans. The wind swirling above the Met was strong enough to take a fly ball and put it over the fence. Orioles' starting pitcher Mike Cuellar, oddly enough, was the beneficiary of the thirty-miles-per-hour wind, carrying a long fly ball over the right field wall for a grand slam in a seven-run fourth inning for Baltimore.

"I don't think Mike's ball would have gone out if it hadn't been for the wind," Perry said after the game. He didn't even watch it because he thought it was going to be foul down the right field line, but the wind pushed it back into play.

"I didn't bother to run when I hit it," Cuellar said after hitting his first career grand slam. "It was three feet foul before the wind got it."

"I ran to the foul pole," recalled right fielder Tony Oliva. "The wind kept bringing the ball back in, but it was fair all the way. The ball landed three or four rows into the stands, so I didn't have a chance to catch it,"

Perry gave up 8 total runs (7 earned) on 8 hits over three-and-a-third innings pitched. Cuellar didn't fare much better, giving up 6 runs on ten hits over four-and-a-third innings of work.

Trailing 9–2 in the third innings, the Twins climbed back into the game after a George Mitterwald two-run single and, with the wind at his back, a mammoth Killebrew home run.

"I've never seen a ball hit as far or as high as Harmon's home run in all my life," said Orioles center fielder Paul Blair after the game.

Forty-year-old Dick Hall replaced Cuellar in the fifth inning and only allowed one baserunner the rest of the way as Baltimore won Game 1, 10–6.

As they did in 1969, the press second-guessed big decisions by the Twins coaching staff, namely the decision to start rookie Danny Thompson over veteran Frank Quilici at second base for the injured Rod Carew, who was still nursing his knee injury.

Thompson committed an error in the second inning after failing to complete a routine double play that led to 2 Baltimore runs. Thompson, a natural shortstop, had played eighty-one games at second after Carew was hurt but was still having issues turning the double play. Add the fact that Thompson had a .143 average against Baltimore that season compared to Quilici's .321.

"Thompson will be at second base again for Game 2," Bill Rigney said after the game. Carew pinch-hit in the bottom of the eighth but flew out. He did not play the field.

The Twins turned to spot-starter Tom Hall for Game 2. Hall, who started four only of his first forty-five appearances that season, was moved to the rotation in September. In seven starts that month, he was 5–0 with a 1.84 ERA with 61 strikeouts; and opposing hitters were batting only .160 off him.

With Rigney opting to go with the hot twenty-three-year-old to keep the Baltimore offense in check, Orioles manager Earl Weaver went with the veteran Dave McNally. McNally was tied for the league lead with twenty-four wins (with Game 1 pitchers Jim Perry and Mike Cuellar).

Hall walked the first two batters he saw in that game: Mark Belanger and Paul Blair. After a Frank Robinson fly ball advanced Belanger to third base, Boog Powell doubled to right field to score Belanger before Hall retired the side. In the third inning, Hall gave up a two-run home run to Frank Robinson; and in the fourth, McNally helped his own cause with an RBI single to left and a 4–0 Baltimore lead.

McNally had no trouble with the Twins the first time through the lineup, sitting down eight of the first nine batters he faced (he walked Killebrew in the top of the first). The Twins' bats finally broke through seeing McNally a second time. After Leo Cardenas walked to lead off the bottom of the fourth, Killebrew and Oliva hit back-to-back home runs to bring the score to 4–3.

Rigney went to his bullpen in the fifth, starting with Bill Zepp then bringing the unhittable righty Stan Williams into the game after Zepp loaded the bases with nobody out. Williams got Brooks Robinson to pop up to catcher George Mitterwald. Davey Johnson was to fly out to Tony Oliva in right field before striking out Andy Etchenbarren to end the threat.

McNally was still dealing in the fifth when Rigby lifted Williams for pinch-hitter Bob Allison in the bottom of the seventh. Williams had faced nine batters and had retired all nine. Allison walked but was stranded on the base paths.

Williams was replaced on the mound by AL Saves leader Ron Perranoski. But as Perranoski came out of the bullpen, Earl Weaver came out of the Orioles dugout. Weaver went over to home plate umpire Bill Haller and complained that Perranoski had something black on his hands. Orioles bullpen coach Jim Frey said he saw Perranoski run pine tar on his hands, which is illegal and cause for an automatic ejection from the game. Perranoski said it was resin, which is legal. Haller sent Perranoski back to the clubhouse to wash his hands, then he let him return to the game.

"I don't blame Perranoski for trying to cheat," Weaver quipped after the game. "It means money to win games and the pennant, cheating or not. But when you're caught, you're caught. Admit it."

"The very sight of Weaver upsets me," Perranoski told reporters after the game, still upset over his 1970 All-Star Game snub by Weaver, who managed the AL squad. "If I was going to rub pine tar on my hands, I wouldn't do it in front of the Baltimore bullpen coach. The only thing that blackened my pitching hand was the resin buildup with spit and rubbing down the ball. Weaver's little tirade had nothing to do with upsetting me."

The reason Perranoski was upset after the game was what happened in the ninth inning. After setting down Baltimore one-two-three in the eighth, he returned to the mound to give the Twins a chance in the ninth.

Baltimore's bats erupted, and Perranoski only got one of the six men he faced out. McNally led off the inning with a double to left, then Mark Belanger singled to advance McNally to third. Perranoski struck out Paul Blair before walking Frank Robinson to load the bases. Boog Powell knocked in 2 runs with a double to left field to extend the Baltimore lead to 6–3. Merv Rettenmund singled in Frank Robinson to make it 7–3, and Perranoski was lifted for Luis Tiant.

Brooks Robinson reached on a Rick Renick throwing error at third base, which scored Powell. Then Tiant gave up a three-run home run to Davey Johnson to make it 11–3. It was the second straight game that Baltimore had put up 7 runs in a game against the Twins.

McNally retired the Twins in order in the bottom of the ninth to take a 2–0 series lead back to Baltimore. Rod Carew did not play in Game 2.

One of the main reasons that Billy Martin lost his job as Twins manager after the 1969 ALCS was deciding to sit Jim Kaat in the decisive Game 3. Bill Rigney had two options to start Game 3: Kaat or rookie Bert Blyleven. Originally, it was Blyleven who was scheduled to face Jim Palmer in Game 3.

"I've had five days' rest," a confident Blyleven said after Game 2. "I beat them at the Met earlier this year. If we would have won Sunday to tie the series it, it would have put more pressure on me."

Rigney originally said he wasn't going to go with Kaat was because he threw in the bullpen during Game 2, but he ultimately decided to send the veteran to the mound to keep their season alive.

Kaat, who was 14–10 with a 3.56 ERA in 1970, took the mound at Memorial Stadium in front of 27,608 Baltimore fans who were looking for their second straight American League pennant.

After Jim Palmer (20–10, 2.71 ERA, 305 innings pitched) retired the Twins in order in the top of the first inning, Kaat and the defense behind him struggled.

The Twins were down 5–0 after three innings after Kaat gave up 4 runs (only 2 earned) and was chased with nobody out in the third. Blyleven replaced him and surrendered another unearned run.

The Twins were finally able to push a run across the plate. Cesar Tovar hit a towering fly ball that Frank Robinson lost in the sun. When Robinson recovered and got the ball back into the infield, Tovar was at third with a triple.

Leo Cardenas singled Tovar in to make it 5–1, and that's the only offense the Twins got against Palmer, who would pitch a complete game, scattering 7 hits and striking out twelve Twins.

Baltimore won Game 3 6–1 to sweep the Twins in the ALCS for the second straight year.

Again, the injured Rod Carew was a nonfactor, striking out while pinch-hitting in the top of the seventh. Davey Johnson knew that the absence of Carew's bat made the difference in the series. "[Last year] when the Twins had Cesar Tovar, Rod Carew, and Tony Oliva batting in succession they presented not only a strong front at the bat, but three outstanding base runners. It's important to have a god-man like Carew batting second, not only because of his ability to get on base and drive in runs but also his strength at stealing bases. Carew always hurt us. The Twins didn't scare us as much without Rod in the lineup."

Carew hit a combined .342 in the AL West Championship seasons in 1969 and 1970 but hit .062 (1–16) in the playoffs.

Earl Weaver only had to use four pitchers in the entire series: Mike Cuellar and Dick Hall in Game 1, then got complete games from Dave McNally and Jim Palmer in games 2 and 3.

Baltimore would beat the Cincinnati Reds 4–1 in the World Series.

<<BONUS ACHE>>

Harmon Killebrew Signs with the Kansas City Royals

Four years after the 1970 ALCS, the Twins championship window was closing. That included the career of the seemingly immortal Harmon Killebrew, who spent the first twenty-first years of his career with the Washington Senators/Minnesota Twins. Harmon's contract expired after the 1974 season—a season in which he hit .222 with 13 home runs and 54 RBI in 122 games. He was given three options by the Twins: stay with the major league club as a coach and batting instructor, manage the AAA affiliate Tacoma Twins, or be released. Harmon chose to be released. Eight days later, he signed a one-year contract with the Kansas City Royals. He hit .199 with 14 home runs (one of which came against the Twins at Metropolitan Stadium) and 44 RBI in 106 games. He retired following the 1975 season and became an announcer for Twins games.

March 31, 1971
The Twins Release Luis Tiant

Luis Tiant, the son of a former Negro League pitcher, was discovered in 1957 by former Cleveland Indians All-Star Bobby Avila, who was scouting talent in Cuba. With Avila's help, he signed with Mexico City Tigers of the Mexican League for $150 a month.

In 1961, the Indians purchased Tiant's contract from Mexico City for $35,000. He spent three seasons with the Indians' minor league system, and after throwing a no-hitter and a one-hitter in consecutive starts for AAA Portland in 1964, he got called up to the big leagues.

In his major league debut, he shut out the reigning AL champion New York Yankees, beating Whitey Ford 3–0. Tiant was 10–4 with a 2.83 ERA and 105 strikeouts in nineteen games his rookie year.

And he kept getting better.

In his first full season in 1965, he pitched in forty-one games (started thirty), won eleven of them with a 3.53 ERA. Over the next two seasons, his win and strikeout totals climbed, and his ERA dropped. By 1968, he was a twenty-game winner and led the American League with a 1.60 ERA—the lowest AL ERA since Walter Johnson's 1.49 in 1919. He pitched nine shutouts, including a stretch of four straight. Opponents only hit .168 off him (a major league record), and on July 3, he struck out an AL record nineteen Twins in a ten-inning shutout.

Tiant dealt with injuries in 1969 in a year that saw a career-high ERA (up to that point in his career) of 3.71, as well as career highs in losses (20), home runs allowed (37) and walks (129).

In December 1969, Tiant, only two seasons removed from a 21–9 season with a 1.60 ERA, was traded with pitcher Stan Williams to Minnesota for pitchers Dean Chance and Bob Miller, outfielder Ted Uhlaender, and third baseman Graig Nettles (who would turn into a six-time All-Star and two-time Gold Glove winner).

The Twins gave up a lot to acquire the twenty-nine-year-old Tiant, and they were hoping for the twenty-win version rather than the twenty-loss Tiant. The Twins had won ninety-seven games the previous year but were swept by the Baltimore Orioles in the first ever American League Championship Series.

Williams had a great season for the Twins coming out of the bullpen in 1970 (10-1, 1.99 ERA). And it looked like Tiant was poised for a bounce-back year with the reigning AL West champion Twins as well. He began the season 6-0 with a 3.12 ERA in his first ten starts (the Twins were 10-0 in those games) before landing on the disabled list in June with arm troubles. Tiant dealt with the injury, which turned out to be a fractured shoulder blade, all season long and tried to come back down the stretch as the Twins chased back-to-back division titles, but went 3-5 with a 3.94 ERA in thirty-two innings. In three of his last four starts, Tiant lasted four innings or less. He finished Game 2 of the 1970 ALCS against Baltimore Orioles, who also repeated at AL East champions. After Ron Perranoski gave up 5 runs in the top of the ninth, Tiant came in and gave up a two-run home run to Davey Johnson in an eventual 11-3 Twins loss.

Tiant was released by the Twins during spring training in 1971. He was signed and released by the Atlanta Braves before being signed by the Boston Red Sox.

Still coming back from the broken shoulder blade, he was 1-7 with a 4.85 ERA with the 1971 Boston Red Sox, but from 1972 to 1978, he returned to form 121-74 with a 3.30 ERA, including a league-leading 1.91 in 1972, and would be a twenty-game winner three times for the Red Sox during that span. He would pitch for the New York Yankees, Pittsburgh Pirates, and California Angels before calling it a major league career in 1982.

Tiant would finish his career with 229 wins, a 3.30 ERA, 2,416 strikeouts, and three All-Star appearances.

January 28, 1971
The Vikings Draft Leo Hayden

If you're a die-hard Vikings fan and have never heard of Leo Hayden, there's a good reason for it. The Minnesota Vikings won the 1970 NFC Central championship with a 12-2 record. However, they couldn't make it back to the Super Bowl after being upset in the first round of the playoffs by the San Francisco 49ers, 17-14. The Purple People Eater Defense was thriving. The offense wasn't.

Quarterback Gary Cuozzo had taken over as signal called after Pro Bowler Joe Kapp signed with the Boston Patriots. In 1970, Cuozzo completed less than 50 percent of his passes for 1,720 yards, 7 touchdowns, and 10 interceptions. Backup Bob Lee was 2-0 as a starter with 610 yards and 5 touchdowns and 5 interceptions.

The running game wasn't much better. Dave Osborn led the attack out of the backfield with 681 yards and 5 touchdowns on 207 carries (3.2 yards per carry). Clint Jones added 9 touchdowns out of the backfield while splitting time with the great Bill "Boom Boom" Brown.

The offensive line was there with future Hall of Famers Mick Tingelhoff and Ron Yary. The defense was loaded with talent and only gave up 200 yards per game. The offense was inconsistent, averaging about 272 yards per game.

The Vikings needed a dynamic playmaker. And they thought they found him in the 1971 NFL Draft.

Leo Hayden was a backup running while playing at Ohio State, but when he was on the field, he flashed brilliance. Taking carries behind Big John Brockington (who was selected ninth overall by Green Bay in 1971), Hayden ranked seventh in the Big Ten in yards from scrimmage (787) and first in rushing yards per attempt (5.8). He scored 3 touchdowns on the ground that season as well.

With the first pick in the 1971 NFL Draft, the Boston Patriots selected quarterback Jim Plunkett (they were 2-12 with Joe Kapp that year). Pro Bowlers Archie Manning, Dan Pastorini, J. D. Hill, Frank Lewis, Isiah Robertson, and

John Brockington and Hall of Famer John Riggins all went in the top 10. The offense-needy Vikings watched the top quarterbacks go one-two-three and saw five running backs go off the board before they selected at 24. So maybe Hayden was a panic pick and felt the need to grab somebody. The fact of the matter was that the Vikings needed to improve on their 3.2 YPC from 1970.

It's also worth noting that Hall of Famers Jack Ham and Dan Dierdorf were still on the board, both selected in the second round. Pro Bowl caliber quarterbacks like Ken Anderson, Joe Theismann, and Lynn Dickey still available as well.

To say Hayden's Vikings career was underwhelming would be a dramatic understatement.

Hayden appeared in seven games for the Vikings in 1971, finishing the season with exactly zero touches. In 1972, he was with the St. Louis Cardinals. His stats from 1972 were 8 carries for eleven yards and a touchdown, good for 1.4 yards per carry. He also added one catch for seventeen yards. In 1973, he was on kick return duty for the Cards, returning five kicks for ninety-eight yards.

In 1974, he was out of the league.

June 29, 1971

Tony Oliva Hurts His Knee

Oh, my. One vote.
—Twins bullpen coach Eddie Guardado

Tony Oliva is arguably the best right fielder from the 1960s. His career began with eight consecutive All-Star selections (breaking Joe DiMaggio's record of six) and the 1962 Rookie of the Year award. He won three batting titles (two in his first two major league seasons), led the league in hits five times and doubles four times, and was runner-up behind teammate Zoilo Versalles for MVP in 1965 and Baltimore's Boog Powell in 1971. In addition to his great bat, he had a power arm in right field, winning a Gold Glove in 1966 and lead American League outfielders in putouts six times, double plays three times, and outfield assists twice.

In an age dominated by the pitching, Oliva hit .313 with 1,455 hits, 177 home runs, 719 RBI, and a .507 slugging percentage from 1964 to 1971.

"I was 31 [in 1971], in my prime," Oliva said. "I was hitting the ball so nice. I was killing it."

But on June 29 at the Oakland Coliseum, Oliva hurt his knee playing the outfield and missed three weeks. He was batting .375 at the time of the injury, then hobbled his way to a third batting title with a .337 average. He would only play ten games in 1972 while recovering from knee surgery. When the American League implemented the designated hitter in 1973, Tony Oliva filled the position in the Twins lineup.

But the knee continued to deteriorate, and he had eight surgeries in five years. He tried everything to alleviate the pain: magnets, brake fluid, salves, and dry ice.

"Today, they would scope it during the off-season, you would have three months to heal, and it would be no problem," said Oliva.

Tony spent his final four seasons as the DH for the Twins, hitting .277 with 43 home runs, 223 RBI in 471 games—a far cry from his .313/.361/.507 stat line before the injury. In his final season in 1976, his knee hurt so bad that he could no longer slide.

He first appeared on the Hall of Fame ballot in 1982 with 63 total votes, which steadily climbed to 202 by 1988 (321 votes were needed to get in), but that's as close as he got before falling off the ballot in his fifteenth and final year in 1996.

In 2000, he was added to the Baseball Hall of Fame's Veterans Committee ballot but wasn't elected. In 2011 he was four votes shy of induction on the Golden Era Committee, and in 2014, he fell a single vote shy of induction.

"Ted Williams said I was one of the best hitters he ever saw. Catfish Hunter and Jim Palmer said the same thing. When I was killing the ball, managers would tell left-handed pitchers to walk me to get to Killebrew."

Oliva tallied 1,917 hits in his career with a .304 average, 329 doubles, 220 home runs, and 947 RBI; and he received MVP votes in each of his first eight seasons. A fully healthy career for Oliva projects to around 3,000 hits, 350 home runs, 1,450 RBI, and no Hall of Fame debate.

<<BONUS ACHE>>

Kevin Love's Knuckle Push Ups

A far-cry from Oliva's knees, Timberwolves All-Star Kevin Love had two weird injuries early in the 2012 season. The first was a sore right elbow suffered when he slept with his arm extended off his bed that forced him to miss a preseason game against Chicago. The other happened less than a week later. While working out with trainer Rob McClanaghan, he broke his right hand doing knuckle pushups. He missed the first five weeks of the NBA season. After eighteen games, he refractured the hand again, which forced him to miss the rest of the season. He was shooting just 35 percent from the field in those eighteen games, likely because he returned from his broken hand too soon. The Wolves finished 31–51.

January 25, 1972
The Ohio State Brawl

I went blank after I was hit with the knee. The next thing I knew, I was in the emergency room at the hospital.
—Ohio State center Luke Witte

In his first year as the head coach of the Minnesota men's basketball team, Bill Musselman wasn't interested in a rebuild. When he took over a Gopher program that went 11–13 (5–9 in the Big Ten) in 1971, he was taking over a team that hadn't won an outright Big Ten title since 1919 (they split one with Illinois in 1937). The Gophers hadn't been nationally ranked since they ranked ninth on December 28, 1965.

Musselman, who came to Minnesota following a 109–20 record at Division III Ashland University, had a very tough coaching style. He liked strong, disciplined players that would push around and intimidate opponents. And he hated losing. There was a sign in the Gophers locker room that read "Defeat is worse than death because you have to live with defeat."

With Jim Brewer, Dave Winfield, Corky Taylor, and Keith Young already on the roster, he added three junior college transfers: Ron Behagen, Bob Nix, and Clyde Turner. Turner would average nearly 19 points for the Gophers that season, with Ron Behagen (16 points, 10 rebounds) and Jim Brewer (10 points and 11) averaging double-doubles. All three would get drafted into the NBA (Turner decided to play professionally in Europe instead of the NBA).

The Gophers started the season 3–3 before rattling off six wins in a row, including an upset against fifth-ranked Indiana 52–51 at the Barn. Now 9–3, the Gophers were ranked sixteenth in the AP Polls and welcomed the defending Big Ten Champion #6 Ohio State Buckeyes to Williams Arena.

Ohio State was 10–2 and had put together a four-game winning streak of their own. The Buckeyes had four players averaging double figures in scoring that season: Allan Hornyak (22 PPG), Luke Witte (17 PPG), Dan Gerhard (11 PPG) and Wardell Jackson (11 PPG).

Both teams entered the contest undefeated in conference play. Minnesota's three loses came at the hands of Bradley, Marquette, and Temple, while OSU had been beaten by in-state rival Ohio and number 1 UCLA.

A sellout crowd of 17,800 fans packed into Williams Arena on January 25, 1972, to see one of the biggest games in Gophers history. Tension built early, with Ohio State viciously booed as they came onto the court for their pregame warm-ups. Gopher fans loved the change of pace that Musselman brought and were tired of a new coach every season (four head coaches in five seasons: Jerry Kundla, Bill Fitch, George Hanson, and now Musselman). The fans especially loved the Gophers new pregame routine, which featured Harlem Globetrotter-esk ball handling and passing tricks while rock music blasted through the PA system. With the crowd whipped into a frenzy, the Gophers players were ready for the game.

Things got chippy just before halftime, when Luke Witte inadvertently elbowed Bob Nix in the head as he tried to create space in the lane. The Gophers led 32–30 with twelve minutes left in the game before OSU went on a 10–0 run and took a 40–32 lead. As Ohio State continued to pull away from the Gophers, the crowd became more and more restless. The refs had to stop the game because fans were throwing food, garbage, and coins on the floor. The PA announcer told the fans that if anything else was thrown onto the court, Minnesota would be accessed a technical foul (an announcement that was met with boos and more debris).

The Buckeyes led 50–44 with thirty-six seconds left in the game. Luke Witte had the ball for OSU and drove for what looked like an easy layup. He was fouled hard by Clyde Turner on the put back. Turner was given a flagrant foul and was thrown out of the game. Corky Taylor went to help Witte to his feet, and that's when all hell broke loose.

While helping Witte to his feet, Taylor kneed him in the groin. Witte went back down, and the benches cleared. Jim Brewer began fighting with Dave Merchant. Ron Behagen, who had fouled out of the game earlier, ran up to the helpless Witte and stomped on his face and neck. Dave Winfield tackled Mark Wagar and punched him in the face five times. Fans began flooding onto the court. Wagar was able to escape Winfield but caught a punch from a fan and went down hard. When he lost Wagar, Winfield turned his attention to forward Mark Minor. When order was restored, Witte and Wagar were both lying on the court, concussed. Even with thirty-six seconds left in the game, Ohio State was declared the winner by Big Ten commissioner Wayne Duke, who happened to be in the crowd for the big game. Witte, Wagar, and Minor were all taken to the hospital. Gopher fans booed Witte as he was carried off the court.

Duke investigated the brawl over the next couple days, watching and reviewing film and ended up suspending Taylor and Behagen for the rest of the season for their part in the brawl. Winfield was not suspended for his role because his actions were not caught on tape.

Wagar and Minor were treated for concussions. Witte spent time in intensive care after the fight, needed twenty-nine stitches, and suffered a concussion and a scratched cornea. He returned to the court for the Buckeyes a week after the incident.

Minnesota did go on to win their first Big Ten title in fifty-three years, but the brawl with Ohio State will always overshadow it. They were bounced by Florida State in the first round of the NCAA tournament.

April 16, 1972

The 1972 NHL Stanley Cup Quarterfinals versus St. Louis

We had a lot of chances. But what can you do when you don't put them in?
—North Stars winger J. P. Parise

The 1971–72 Minnesota North Stars were the best team in the young history of the franchise, led by captain Ted Harris, Bill Goldsworthy (31 goals, 31 assists, 62 points), Murray Oliver (27 goals, 29 assists, 56 points), Lou Nanne (21 goals, 28 assists, 49 points), Dean Prentice (20 goals, 27 assists, 47 points) and the goalie combo of Cesare Maniago (20–17–4, 2.65 GAA) and forty-two-year-old Gump Worsley (16–10–7, 2.12 GAA).

The Stars finished above .500 for the first time (37–29–12, 86 points) and drew the number 2 seed in the playoffs.

They matched up against a familiar foe in the postseason in the St. Louis Blues. The Stars had faced the Blues in the playoffs each of their four postseason berths in their short five-year history. The Blues beat them in overtime in Game 7 of the 1968 Conference Finals, and again in six games in the 1970 quarterfinals. The Stars got a little revenge in the 1971 quarterfinals, upsetting the Blues in six games before bowing out to the Montreal Canadiens.

The Blues had lost three consecutive Stanley Cup Finals to start their franchise history, getting swept by Montreal in 1968 and 1969 and Boston in 1970.

In 1972, the Blues featured star defenseman Barclay Plager; Garry Unger (36 goals, 34 assists, 70 points); Frank St. Marseille (16 goals, 36 assists, 52 points); Jack Egers (21 goals, 25 assists, 46 points); Gary Sabourin (28 goals, 17 assists, 45 points); and goalie Jacques Caron (14–8–5, 2.56 GAA).

The Chicago Black Hawks won the West Division with 107 points in 1972. The North Stars were second with 86, the Blues finished third with 68, and the

Pittsburgh Penguins won a tiebreaker with the Philadelphia Flyers for the fourth and final playoff spot out of the West with 66 points.

The Stars were 4–1–1 against St. Louis, but Bill Goldsworthy knew that they were going to see a different Blues team than they saw in their six previous matchups.

"They were hurt early in the season by injuries," he told Sid Hartman of the *Star Tribune*. "They're healthy now, and they strengthened their roster with good trades."

"We had gone to the finals of three Staley Cups until we lost to Minnesota last year," said Blues executive vice president Sid Salomon III. "We had an old team, and we decided to shake things up."

Through trades, they lowered their average age from thirty-two to twenty-six, which made them the second-youngest team in the league (Minnesota's average age was thirty). They sent their first-round pick (fourth overall) from the 1971 Draft Gene Carr to the New York Rangers for Andrew Dupont, Jack Eggers, and Mike Murphy. They also traded Jimmy Roberts (who they had taken from Montreal in the 1967 Expansion Draft) back to the Canadiens for Phil Roberto. They claimed Kevin O'Shea off waivers from the Buffalo Sabres. Each of the new Blues acquisitions were twenty-five years old or younger. They also purchased the contract of thirty-year-old goalie Jacques Carton, who had played in three career NHL games for the LA Kings, from the WHA's Denver Spurs. The Blues had started four different goalies before adding Caron to the roster on December 29.

At the same time, the Blues were on their third head coach that season. After firing Scotty Bowman after the 1971 season, the Blues hired Hall of Famer Sid Abel, who had coached the Detroit Red Wings to four Stanley Cup finals in the 1960s. Abel was fired after a 3–6–1 start, and the team hired Bill McCreary as interim coach. McCreary had retired as a player with the Blues following the 1971 season. He was 6–14–4 before being replaced by Al Arbor, who returned as head coach after coaching the Blues for the first fifty-five games of the 1971 season (Bowman was 13–10–5 after replacing Arbor that season). Arbor was named the permanent head coach on Christmas Day 1971, won 44 points in forty-four games, and put the Blues in the playoffs by one point. The Blues had four head coaches in one calendar year, and thirty-nine different players suited up for the team.

Game 1 between the North Stars and Blues was played at Metropolitan Sports Center in front of a record 15,482 fans. The Stars tried to set the tone physically in the first period, with Ted Harris and Doug Mohns both hitting the penalty box in the first ninety seconds of the game. Stars goalie Gump Worsley (who had won seven straight games against the Blues) with Charlie Burns, Barry Gibbs, and Tom Reid kept the puck out of the net during the two-man advantage.

The Stars got on the board at the 14:25 mark, getting the puck past Caron. Caron had blocked a Murray Oliver shot in front of the net, and Dean Prentice cleaned up the mess.

The physical play continued into the second period, with Minnesota's Dennis O'Brien and the Blue's Jack Egers picking up major penalties for fighting. The two tried climbing into the public address announcer's box to continue their fight. Phil Roberto found his way back into the penalty box and, after being harassed by Stars fans, stood up on the bench and started yelling back. Police had to get involved before he sat back down.

Prentice scored again in the third period, sending a sixty-foot slap shot past Caron. Worsley continued his domination of the Blues, stopping all twenty-seven shots he saw in the game. The closest St. Louis came to scoring was a Roberto shot that glanced off the right post late in the third period. Bob Nevin scored at 12:01 in the third as the Stars went on to win Game 1 3–0.

There was a lot more offense in Game 2. The previous record-crowd from Game 1 was even larger in Game 2, upping the total number of fans in attendance to 15,674 (after the game, the North Stars announced plans to increase seating capacity from 15,067 to over 18,000 for the upcoming season).

After beating St. Louis for the eighth consecutive time, Gump Worsley got a rest in Game 2. Cesare Maniago got the start in lieu of Worsley, who was five weeks shy of his forty-third birthday. Maniago, who hurt his leg in a March 8 loss to the Boston Bruins, was 0–2–2 since returning to the ice. St. Louis gave Caron a rest in Game 2 and started backup Ernie Wakely (8–18, 3.40 GAA). Without Caron, Blues goalies (Wakely, Jim McLeod, Wayne Stephenson, and Peter McDuffe) were a combined 14–31 and allowed 3.39 goals per game.

The Blues' Frank St. Marseille scored three times before the 5:38 mark in the second period, but Minnesota kept pace with goals by Doug Mohns, J. P. Parise, and Danny Grant. The Stars took a 4–3 lead in at the 1:45 mark when Jude Drouin scooped up a Parise miss at the crease and put it past Wakely.

Gary Unger tied the game at 8:05, then he got an assist after hooking the puck from the right corner face-off to Phil Roberto at 10:59 to give St. Louis a 5–4 lead.

But less than a minute later, Prentice, who had two goals in Game 1, scored the equalizer, bombing a forty-five-foot slap shot past Wakely at 11:32 to tie the game at 5–5.

St. Louis had outshot the Stars 38–28 in regulation, but the North Stars needed only one shot in overtime. Drouin, who finished the game with one goal and three assists, fired the puck to the right of the crease, where Bill Goldsworthy picked it up. He did his famous Goldy Shuffle, got Wakely to commit, then scored the overtime winner. Nobody was happier than Maniago.

"I gave up five goals tonight, and we still won." he said. "I don't have any excuses. My timing wasn't as sharp as it should have been. I tried to bear down, but it wasn't one of my better games."

"You can't blame either goaltender for the scoring," said Minnesota coach Jack Gordon. "It was just one of those games."

Game 3 shifted to St. Louis Arena with the Stars leading the series 2–0. Worsley and Caron were back in net for Game 3. The Blues struck first when Phil Roberto scored on a Mike Murphy rebound at 9:18 in the first period. Worsley made a fantastic save on Murphy on the right side of the net but couldn't cover the puck or move to the other side to stop Roberto's shot in time.

Roberto scored again in the second period, again on a Murphy rebound. The winger hit the left pipe and careened right to Roberto, who fired a twenty footer past Worsley for a 2–0 lead.

Minnesota tried to intimidate the Blues with their size in the second period, with Ted Harris and Bob Plager dropping gloves at center ice in the second period. Harris landed a dozen good punches on Plager before Plager headbutted Harris after the two were separated.

The fight seemed to ignite Minnesota. Drouin scored the Stars' first goal of the game forty seconds into the third period. Momentum had shifted toward Minnesota, but Caron stood on his head to keep the puck out of the net. Worsley was pulled for the extra attacker with a minute left, but the Stars didn't put a shot on net as the final seconds ticked away in a 2–1 St. Louis win.

Jacques Caron was the hero for St. Louis in Game 4. Caron started only thirteen hours after stopping twenty-nine shots in Game 3. Worsley, after losing to the Blues for the first time in eight starts, was back on the bench in favor of Maniago.

Just like in Game 2, Maniago got an early boost from his offense, with Jude Drouin scoring at midway through the first and Danny Grant early in the second. Phil Roberto got the Blues on the board with his fourth goal of the series at 12:12 on a bouncing that found the back of the net in the second period. Kevin O'Shea scored his first goal of the postseason one minute and thirty-three seconds later to tie the game at 2–2 on a shot that hit off the back leg of Stars defenseman Tom Reid.

The Blues took the lead on a power play goal at 11:50 in the third period. Roberto found Barclay Plager at the left point, who fired the puck between the legs of Reid and past Maniago, who was screened by Roberto.

"I never saw the puck," Maniago said after the game.

The North Stars had three excellent chances to score in the game. Two were great saves by Caron, and the third was a play Caron may or may not have made. After Roberto's goal, a fresh Ted Hampson had just come into the game after a shift change and had a breakaway opportunity against Caron. Caron lowered his shoulder pad and blocked his shot from close range. The next came in the closing moments of the game with Minnesota trailing 3–2. Drouin took a pass and had a good look from forty feet out. He blasted a slap shot that was deflected by Caron to end the game.

The controversial play in Game 4 came midway through the second period. At the 6:56 mark, Reid sent a gorgeous breakaway pass to a streaking J. P. Parise.

Parise shot the puck and snagged his own rebound after it slid into the crease. Caron lunged to stop the puck. He landed on it, but his momentum carried him and the puck into the net. The officials did not turn on the scoring light. They said they saw Caron land on the puck but couldn't tell if it crossed the goal or not. Referee John Ashley was trailing the play and saw both the puck and Caron cross the goal line but didn't overrule the judge. After the game, Ashley claimed to have blown his whistle to signal the play had stopped.

"I heard the whistle," said Al Arbour. "Jacques had control of the puck before it crossed the line. Then the official blew it dead."

"There was no whistle," argued Parise. "My first shot hit the goalie on the inside of the leg, and when the puck dropped, I shot it again. Everything went across the line, and there never was a whistle."

"After seeing the television replays, I'm surer than ever now that it was in," said Jack Gordon. "But you can't get it back, so there's no sense worrying about it. We just need to find more scoring."

The Stars lost 3–2 and headed back to Minnesota with the series tied at 2–2.

The injury report was full of North Stars before Game 5. Doug Mohns was in the hospital was a back injury. Barry Gibbs missed the last two periods of Game 4 with a leg injury. Tom Reid and Lou Nanne were dealing with hip injuries, and Dean Prentice needed to have a hand injury x-rayed.

"We don't want to risk too much with our defensemen hurting," Jack Gordon said before Game 5. "There's too much at stake." The defense had been shaky since Game 2. After outshooting the Blues in every period of Game 1, the Blues had outshot the Stars in all nine regulation periods since.

The attendance continued to climb at the Met. For a third consecutive home playoff game, Stars fans set another attendance record with 15,706 fans in attendance for Game 5.

Barry Gibbs scored the first goal of the game early in the first quarter to electrify the fans. St. Louis answered at the 16:34 mark with Gary Sabourin getting the puck past Worsley in net. Tom Reid put the Stars back ahead less than ninety seconds later, and Minnesota looked poised to take a 2–1 lead into the first intermission.

But with one second left in the first period, Roberto scored a power play goal to tie the game at 2–2. Worsley and Caron were each brilliant in the net in the second period, the highlight coming from Worsley. Jack Eggers forced a turnover as Tom Reid and Dennis O'Brien fell on the ice and had a breakaway toward Worsley, who came up with a huge save at 16:52. Reid was able to scramble to his feet and check Gary Sabourin before Sabourin could collect the rebound for another shot on goal.

But St. Louis benefited from another last-second goal, this time from Garry Unger with twenty-six seconds left in the period.

St. Louis led 3–2 in the third period, but the Stars had the home crowd behind them. After the game, Coach Gordon said that the third period was "best offensive period in quite a long time." The Stars outshot the Blues 13–9 (the first time since Game 1 that they outshot St. Louis in a period).

J. P. Parise, still upset about the noncall in Game 4, scored the equalizer at 2:55 after intercepting the puck from Bob Plager; and he fired it past Caron.

"I tried to deke Caron, but he wouldn't move," Parise said. "So I just fired it and hoped for the best."

Bill Goldsworthy made a great play behind the net to notch an assist on the go-ahead goal four minutes later. Caron left the circle to collect the puck from behind the net. He didn't know Goldsworthy was closing in from behind. Goldy stole the puck and slid it to Drouin, who scored the go-ahead goal at 5:45.

"I think he must have thought one of his defensemen was coming in behind him," Goldsworthy said. "But it wasn't."

The Stars won 4–3 and were one victory away from a second-round matchup with the Boston Bruins, who had won their series with the Toronto Maple Leafs in five games.

Game 6 shifted back to St. Louis with the home team winning each of the previous five games. Despite being down 3–2, Blues coach Al Arbor was still confident. "There's no way the North Stars are going to win it," he said. "Our players have had their ups and downs all year, but they've always bounced back. We're not only going to win the game tonight, but we're going to win the last one too."

The North Stars were shorthanded with injuries before the game. They were down two defensemen right out of the gate: Doug Mohns reinjured his back during warm-ups and missed the game, and Dennis O'Brien aggravated a severe bruise on his foot. Winger Lou Nanne split time between right wing and defense but played with a helmet after being hit in the head with the puck in Game 5. Bill Goldsworthy played with the stomach flu, but the real blow happened midway through the first period.

Phil Roberto scored his sixth goal of the series on a power play at 3:04. Bill Goldsworthy answered with a goal one minute later to tie the game at 1–1. The Blues scored again at 6:41 on a goal from the right point by Bob Plager.

After a Bill Pager penalty at 13:28, the North Stars were on a power play. The Blues cleared the puck. Blues penalty-killer Gerry Odrowski hustled down the ice and had drawn a holding penalty on center Murray Oliver. Bob Plager was also there and saw an opportunity to force a turnover and take a shot before play was stopped. Instead, he dove wildly into the net and crashed into Gump Worsley. Worsley, who was 2–1 with a 2.17 GAA and .935 save percentage in the series, needed to be carried off the ice on a stretcher. So on the power play, the Stars lost Oliver to the penalty box and Worsley for the rest of the game.

Maniago replaced Worsley and stopped thirteen of fourteen shots in the second period (Garry Unger snuck a puck past him at 11:07) as St. Louis took a 3–1 lead into the third period. J. P. Parise scored his third goal of the series with five minutes left in the third period to cut the Stars deficit to one goal. The Stars had plenty of other chances to score that period: Parise was stoned by Caron at 11:05, then Buster Harvey (who was called up from Cleveland before the game to add another player to the bench) whiffed on a rebound at 14:53 before Parise scored his goal at 15:01.

Frank St. Marseille fed a beautiful pass to Jack Egers, who scored his first goal of the playoffs, to clinch the game for the Blues with just under four minutes left. The Blues won 4–2 and forced Game 7 back in Bloomington.

Game 6 was played on a Thursday night, and Game 7 was originally scheduled for Saturday, April 15. But a scheduling issue forced the NHL to move Game 7 from Saturday to Sunday, much to the pleasure of Jack Gordon.

"We're better off playing Sunday," he told the *Star Tribune*. "It will give us an extra day of rest. I hope to see Doug Mohns back for the game."

Thirty-eight-year-old Doug Mohns was cleared to play on Friday after skating for an hour without any back issues. But a huge loss for Game 7 was goalie Gump Worsley. After spending Thursday night in the hospital, he was ruled out.

"I don't remember anything after [Plager] hit me," he recalled.

Cesar Maniago was back in net for the Stars and played very well, stopping twenty-one of twenty-two shots he faced in the game (Sabourin, 12:04 in the first); but Caron matched him the entire way. Caron didn't allow a goal until fifteen seconds into the third period (Charlie Burns). Maniago and Caron would go toe-to-toe for the rest of the third period as the decisive Game 7 went to overtime.

Five years earlier, a Blues versus North Stars playoff series had gone overtime in Game 7 with a trip to the Stanley Cup Finals on the line. Only ten players remained from the inaugural teams from that Game 7: Noel Picard, Frank St. Marseille, Gary Sabourin, Barclay, Bill (who played for Minnesota that season) and Bob Plager, and Terry Crisp for the Blues and Bill Goldsworthy, J. P. Parise, Lou Nanne, and Cesare Maniago.

Ron Schock, who scored the double-overtime game winner in the 1968 Game 7 winner, was traded to Pittsburgh in 1969. But the player still haunted by the loss was Cesare Maniago, who gave up the winning goal to Schock.

And back in the net in another Game 7 overtime against the Blues, Maniago didn't want to go through that again.

Minnesota peppered Caron with five shots in the first ten minutes of overtime, but Caron stood strong, stopping all five. St. Louis, who was held to twenty-two shots in regulation, also fired five shots at Maniago.

With 10:07, Kevin O'Shea sent a slap shot at Maniago from forty-five feet out that hit the post.

"I was just trying to throw the puck somewhere near the net," he said. "I thought the shot was too high at first, then I heard it hit the pipe. I was sure it had bounced out because there was no reaction from anybody."

O'Shea, who had been claimed off waivers from Buffalo five weeks earlier, did hear his shot hit the pipe. What he didn't see right away was the puck bounce off the pipe, hit Maniago in the back, and slide into the net for the game winner.

"I heard the puck clank against the post," a tearful Maniago said after the game. "I turned to look over my right shoulder to see where it would carom out. Then it glanced against the knob at the top of my stick and fell down in. It was a sorry way for a game like that to end. Why does it always have to be me? Am I a jinx or something?"

The Blues won Game 7 2–1 in overtime and eliminated the Stars. The home team won every game of the series, except the Stars in Game 7.

The Blues were swept by the eventual-champion Boston Bruins in the second round.

September 27, 1972

Sal Bando Beats the Twins Twice in One Day

Wins are the most overrated stat in baseball. For example, let's say a pitcher gives up 10 runs in a game. But if his team scores 11, he would get the win. Or if a pitcher gives up 2 runs but his team only scores 1, he would get the loss. Wins aren't unimportant, but they don't tell the whole story.

That is largely the case with Hall of Fame pitcher Bert Blyleven. Blyleven waited fourteen years to get in the Hall largely due to his win total: "only" 287 wins over a twenty-two-year career. He won twenty games one time in his career. However, he ranks ninth all-time in shutouts (60); and when he retired, his 3,701 strikeouts ranked third all-time (he is currently fifth). He also ranks near the top of the list in no-decisions. He had an MLB record twenty of them in 1979 alone.

A prime example of this came in the first game of a doubleheader in 1972 against the eventual World Series champion Oakland Athletics. Blyleven was 15–16 entering the game with 202 strikeouts and a 2.83 ERA. In all 16 of his losses, he had gotten three or fewer runs from his offense.

Bert had scattered five hits and struck out nine Athletics over nine innings and had shut out the powerful Oakland offense. The problem? A's starter Ken Holtzman had matched him pitch for pitch, also shutting out the Twins through eight innings before giving way to the bullpen.

In the top of the ninth, Harmon Killebrew singled off Rollie Fingers. Fingers came back and struck out Bobby Darwin before walking George Mitterwald to put two Twins on with one out. A's manager Dick Williams went back to the pen, sending lefty Darold Knowles in to save the shutout.

He got Eric Soderholm to fly out to leftfielder Joe Rudi and Danny Thompson to ground out to end the threat.

Blyleven also struggled to get through the ninth. He surrendered a leadoff single to Bert Campaneris, who then stole second. With Campaneris in scoring position and nobody out, he struck out Sal Bando and Reggie Jackson and got Joe Rudi to fly out to Rich Reese at first base.

The two teams went to extras, tied at 0–0.

The Twins had a great opportunity to push a run across in the top of the tenth. Rick Renick reached on a single. Blyleven, hitting in the nine hole, grounded out to the catcher Dave Duncan, who threw to second to force Renick out. With Bert safe at first, Cesar Tovar drew a walk. Up to the plate came Rod Carew, who advanced the runners with a ground out to first. With two runners in scoring position, Rich Reese, who had entered the game as a pinch runner for Harmon Killebrew after he singled in the top of the ninth, struck out.

The game remained tied until the bottom of the eleventh, with Blyleven still on the mound. Matty Alou hit a double to the left field wall. Blyleven struck out Campaneris before Sal Bando delivered the game-winning single, scoring Alou from second base.

Blyleven pitched 10.1 innings of shutout baseball, but he still picked up his seventeenth loss of the season.

To make things even sour for Twins fans, Game 2 of the doubleheader also went to extra innings in a low-scoring affair. Tied 1–1 in the tenth, the Twins offense was kept in check by Catfish Hunter and his 11 strikeouts but had managed to push Rich Reese across the plate in the fifth. Twins starter Ray Corbin had also only allowed one run and was still on the mound in the tenth inning. Both starters were still in the game in the tenth.

In the bottom of the frame, it was déjà vu for the Twins. Matty Alou singled off Corbin. Campaneris, instead of striking out, reached on an error by Corbin after laying down a sacrifice bunt. The result was still the same with Sal Bando lacing a single into left field and scoring Alou from second base for the winning run.

The Twins have been walked off in both games of a doubleheader five times in the team's history, but Sal Bando is the only player to have two walk-off hits against the Twins on the same day.

July 24, 1973

Karl Kassulke's Motorcycle Accident

Bud broke down and started to cry.

—Bob Lurtsema

Karl Kassulke was an eleventh-round draft pick by the Detroit Lions in 1963. The safety had started his college career as a running back at Marquette before transferring to Drake University and converting to safety. He was waived by the Lions and signed by the Minnesota Vikings.

A year later, he was known as one of the hardest-hitting safeties and one of the best open-field tacklers in the league. He started Super Bowl IV in the loss against Kansas City and was named to the Pro Bowl in 1970.

In July 1973, he was riding on the back of a motorcycle on his way to Vikings training camp in Mankato when it crashed into the rear of a car near Minnetonka. He was thrown from the motorcycle and sustained a broken right leg and spinal injuries. The accident left him paralyzed from his waist down, effectively ending his NFL career.

A crying Bud Grant delivered the news to the team in Mankato later that evening, when they were still unsure if Kassulke would survive the accident. Defensive lineman Bob Lurtsema later told the *Star Tribune* that it was the only time in the six years he played for the Vikings that he saw Bud Grant openly weep.

Karl Kassulke returned to Metropolitan Stadium as a spectator for Karl Kassulke Day on November 25, 1973, in a game against the Chicago Bears. With Kassulke on the sideline for the first time since the accident, the Vikings defense sacked Bears quarterbacks Bobby Douglas and Gary Huff eight times. The Vikings beat the Bears 31–13.

During his ten-year career, Kassulke started 117 games at safety for the Vikings, intercepted 19 passes, and recovered 9 fumbles.

There was a happy ending for Karl, however. While he was rehabbing from the injury at the University of Minnesota, he fell in love with his rehab nurse, Sue, and married her. The two were married for thirty-three years before Kassulke passed away from a heart attack in 2008 at the age of sixty-seven.

January 13, 1974

Super Bowl VIII versus Miami

They just ran the ball down our throats, especially with that big fullback they had, Larry Csonka.

—Paul Krause

The Vikings returned to the Super Bowl after a four-year absence in January 1974. After finishing 7–7 the previous year, Bud Grant's squad improved to 12–2. The Vikings were 9–0 at one point and were poised to match the Miami Dolphins' perfect regular season record from a year earlier. But a loss to Atlanta in Week 10 nullified the perfect season.

One key addition to the Vikings that year was rookie Chuck Foreman out of Miami. Foreman, selected twelfth overall in the 1973 Draft, would have 1,163 yards from scrimmage (801 rushing, 362 receiving) and 6 total touchdowns. Foreman would be named the Offensive Rookie of the Year that season.

The Vikings were one of two 12–2 teams that season; the other being the Los Angeles Rams (the Vikings beat the Rams 10–9 in Week 7 in a battle of unbeaten teams). The Dallas Cowboys won the NFC East with a 10–4 record, and the Washington Redskins got into the playoffs as the wild card at 10–4 after losing the tiebreaker with Dallas.

The Vikings were the top seed in the NFC Playoffs that season and matched up against Washington in the first round of the playoffs. The Vikings trailed 13–10 in the fourth quarter but rattled off 17 points (thanks to two Fran Tarkenton-to–John Gilliam touchdowns) in the fourth quarter to win 27–20.

In 1973, the top seed didn't always have home field advantage. Instead, it was determined by a rotating system (the undefeated 1972 Miami Dolphins played the AFC Championship Game in Pittsburgh). The 1973 NFC Championship Game, despite the Vikings having two more wins than the Dallas Cowboys, was played at Texas Stadium. The Vikings never trailed in the game as the defense intercepted

Roger Staubach four times in the game, one of them returned sixty-four yards by Bobby Bryant for a touchdown to seal the game. The only touchdown the Vikings allowed was on a sixty-three-yard Golden Richards punt return. The Vikings won 24–10 to advance to Super Bowl VIII.

They entered the game as eight-point underdogs against the reigning Super Bowl champion Miami Dolphins, who were looking to become only the second team in Super Bowl history to win back-to-back titles (Green Bay won Super Bowls I and II). It was the Dolphins' third straight Super Bowl appearance—a feat that wouldn't be matched until the Buffalo Bills run in the early 1990s. The Dolphins were 12–2 in 1973 and had beaten the Cincinnati Bengals (34–16) and Oakland Raiders (27–10) in the playoffs.

Super Bowl VIII was a historic Super Bowl away from the game. It was the first Super Bowl that was held in a venue that wasn't home to an NFL franchise (Rice Stadium in Houston, Texas) and was the first Super Bowl that wasn't held in either Los Angeles, Miami, or New Orleans. It was also the last NFL game to feature the goal posts in front of the end zone. They were moved to the back at the start of the 1974 season.

The first Miami drive of the afternoon was a preview of what would happen the rest of the game: future Hall of Famer Larry Csonka had five carries for thirty-six yards and a touchdown on the opening 10 play, fifty-six-yard drive. Miami outscored their opponents in the first half 69–21 that season and jumped out to a 14–0 lead after scoring touchdowns on their first two possessions (five-yard Csonka run, one-yard Jim Kiick run). The Dolphins would score 24 unanswered points in the first three quarters of the game, including touchdowns on their first two drives of the game. They led the Vikings 17–0 at the half, only allowing 31 rushing yards and four first downs. The Vikings wouldn't get their first first down by rushing the ball until forty-four minutes and seventeen seconds into the game. Bill Stanfill, Vern Den Herder, and the No-Name Defense shut down the Vikings offensive attack, not allowing Tarkenton time to throw downfield and not giving any room to Foreman or Oscar Reed.

The Vikings were hampered by uncharacteristic turnovers and costly penalties. With a chance to put points on the board before halftime, Reed fumbled at the Miami six-yard line with under a minute left in the first half. A huge kickoff return by John Gilliam to start the second half was nullified by a Stu Voight clipping penalty. Miami would score another touchdown on a two-yard Csonka run to open the lead up to 24–0. Minnesota's only touchdowns came on a four-yard Tarkenton run to start the fourth quarter. The Vikings' only other drive in the fourth quarter ended with a Tarkenton interception.

The Vikings did recover an onside kick in the fourth quarter but were flagged for an offside penalty.

The Dolphins won their second consecutive Super Bowl 24–7. Csonka ran for a Super Bowl record of 145 yards on 33 carries. He was the first nonquarterback to be named Super Bowl MVP.

In the loss, the Vikings had now scored only two touchdowns in both Super Bowls combined.

June 12, 1973
The Twins Draft Eddie Bane

The Rangers ruined David Clyde by bringing a high school kid right to the big leagues. That wasn't the case with me. I was what I was.

—Eddie Bane

Arizona State Sun Devil pitcher Eddie Bane was a can't-miss prospect. The lefty was 40–4 with a 1.64 ERA in his three years at ASU. He led the nation in strikeouts in 1972 and 1973 and still holds the program's all-time strikeout record.

The Twins drafted Bane eleventh overall in the 1973 Draft. Five days later, Bane and ASU would beat Dave Winfield and the Gophers 3–0 in the College World Series. Twins president Calvin Griffith, known for his excessive frugalness, gave Bane a team-record $55,000 signing bonus—equivalent to $300,000 in 2018.

Griffith saw dollar signs when looking at his new super prospect. That same season, Texas Rangers owner Bob Short (Minnesota fans remember him as the man that moved the Minneapolis Lakers to Los Angeles in 1960) had manager Whitey Ford start the number 1 overall pick from the 1973 Draft Dave Clyde. Clyde was a Texas native and had pitched in his final high school game only twenty days before making his major league debut. The Rangers were in last place and needed a draw to sell tickets. The Twins were in Arlington to face the Rangers for Clyde's major league debut in front of the first ever sellout crowd in Arlington Stadium history. He struck out eight Twins over five innings for a 4–3 Texas win.

Cal wanted to do the same thing with Bane. On July 4, 1973, Bane made his highly publicized debut at Met Stadium in front of a regular-season record of 45,890 fans. A sold-out Met Stadium in 1973 was worth $128,487 in tickets sales. That doesn't include standing-room-only tickets or concessions like popcorn, peanuts, and beer. The start of the game had to be delayed for fifteen minutes because people were still coming through the gates.

Griffith's gamble paid off. Not only did the Twins attract 10,000 more fans than Clyde did in Texas but Bane also pitched better: one run on three hits over seven innings. The Twins took a 3–1 lead in the bottom of the ninth, but Ray Corbin came out of the bullpen and gave up four runs as the Twins lost 5–4.

Bane was, at the time, one of only eleven players since 1965 to bypass the minor leagues to start his career. He made five more starts his rookie seasons and appeared in twenty-three total games for an 0–5 record, an ERA of 4.90, and 42 strikeouts in 60.1 innings.

Bane spent all of 1974 and most of 1975 at AAA-Tacoma, going 25–19 with a 4.09 ERA and 210 strikeouts. He was a September call-up for the Twins in 1975, starting four games for the Twins, going 3–1 with a 2.86 ERA. But he walked more batters (fifteen) than he struck out (fourteen).

He made his final appearance in the majors on September 26, 1976, at the age of twenty-four. For his major league career, Bane was 7–13 with a 4.66 ERA and 80 strikeouts for what seemed like a can't-miss career only three years earlier.

After becoming a free agent in 1976, he spent time in the minor league systems of the Chicago White Sox, Kansas City Royals, and Chicago Cubs. He pitched in Mexico in 1981 and Alaska in 1982 before retiring as a player and joining the LA Dodgers' minor league system as a pitching coach. He became a scout in 1984 and, to his credit, found some big players for the LA Angels after becoming their scouting director in 2004... most notably Mike Trout with the twenty-fifth pick in the 2009 MLB Draft.

January 12, 1975

Super Bowl IX versus Pittsburgh

*It's fitting in a championship game that our defense shut out
the National Football Conference champions.*
—Steelers head coach Chuck Noll

The main concern for the 1974 Minnesota Vikings was age. How long was the Super Bowl window going to be open? They had lost in 1969 and 1973, but now Fran Tarkenton was thirty-four years old. Jim Marshall was thirty-seven. Gary Larsen became a rotation guy off the bench, losing his starting spot to Doug Southerland. Bobby Bryant only played in one regular season game due to injury.

But the defense still had Alan Page and Carl Eller up front and Paul Krause in the secondary. The Vikings slipped from 12-2 in 1973 to 10-4 a year later, but they still had a top 3 defense in the NFL. The surprise was the offense. Despite dips in production from two of the offensive stars from running back Chuck Foreman and receiver John Gilliam, Tarkenton threw for nearly 2,600 yards (third in the NFL) as the Vikings scored 22.1 points per game—good for fifth in the NFL.

The Vikings won their sixth NFC Central division title in the last seven years with a 10-4 record, three games ahead of 7-7 Detroit. All four NFC Playoff teams were 10-4 that year: St. Louis Cardinals, Washington Redskins, Los Angeles Rams, and Minnesota. The Vikings drew the NFC East champion Cardinals in the first round of the playoffs.

The Cardinals, led by second-year head coach Don Coryell, were in the playoffs for the first time since losing the 1948 NFL Championship as the Chicago Cardinals. The Vikings and Cardinals played on *Monday Night Football* the previous November with the Vikings overcoming a 17-14 halftime deficit and 353 passing yards from Jim Hart to win 28-24 in St. Louis.

The playoff matchup six weeks later was played at a nineteen-degree Metropolitan Stadium. The defense contained Hart this time, only allowing 200 passing yards. The Vikings would beat the Cardinals 30–14, with the game broken open in the third quarter on a Nate Wright fumble return for a twenty-yard touchdown.

The NFC Championship Game returned to the Met the following week against the NFC West champion LA Rams, who beat Washington the previous week 19–10. The Rams defense—led by Hacksaw Reynolds, Jack Youngblood, Isiah Robertson, and Dave Elmendorf—gave up a league-best 12.9 points per game. The Vikings and Rams had also met in the regular season with the Rams beating the Vikings 20-17 at LA Memorial Coliseum in November.

The Vikings led 7–3 at halftime of the NFC Championship after a twenty-nine-yard touchdown pass from Tarkenton to Jim Lash. Rams kicker David Ray connected on a twenty-seven-yard field goal in the second quarter. Neither team scored in the third quarter, but the Rams came close. After Harris found Harold Jackson on a seventy-three-yard pass play, the Rams were called for a false start on the two-yard line. Harris then threw an interception to linebacker Wally Hilgenberg in the end zone.

There were eight combined turnovers in the game, with the Vikings grabbing five of them. Dave Osborn scored a fourth quarter touchdown from the one-yard line to make the game 14–3, but the Rams offense again showed their ability to score points quick with a forty-four-yard touchdown pass from Harris to Harold Jackson with 5:37 left in the game. Tarkenton and the Vikings ate the rest of the clock and won their second straight NFC championship 14–10.

Awaiting them in Super Bowl IX was the Pittsburgh Steelers, coached by Chuck Noll. The Steelers finished atop the AFC Central at 10–3–1. They had knocked O. J. Simpson and the 9–5 Buffalo Bills out of the playoffs in the first round (Simpson was held to forty-nine yards in his only playoff appearance), then held the Oakland Raiders and the league's best offense to 13 points and 29 rushing yards in the AFC Championship (they had lost to Oakland 17–0 in Week 3).

Pittsburgh's defense was solid. Glen Edwards, Joe Greene, Dwight White, L. C. Greenwood, Jack Lambert, Mike Wagner, Mel Blount, Jack Ham, and the rest of the Steel Curtain Defense only allowed 13.5 points per game. The big question was the quarterback. Chuck Noll had benched Joe Gilliam after seven games in favor of Terry Bradshaw, who was benched three weeks later for Terry Hanratty. Noll went back to Bradshaw the following week, and had it not been for the Steel Curtain defense, the Steelers would have had a much more difficult road to the playoffs.

Super Bowl IX was played at Tulane Stadium in Louisiana on January 12, 1975. The Steelers were three-point favorites in the game, and the Vikings were looking to avoid losing their third Super Bowl in six years.

Fred Cox kicked off to Pittsburgh to start the game, and the Vikings defense set the tone early. Rocky Bleier got the first handoff of the game and was tacked by Doug Sutherland after a three-yard gain. Franco Harris was tacked by Roy Winston for a one-yard loss, then Bob Lurtsema sacked Terry Bradshaw to force Pittsburgh to go three-and-out.

The Vikings managed a first down on their first play on offense with Tarkenton finding John Gilliam for a sixteen-yard gain. After a pair of incompletions and a one-yard gain by Dave Osborn, the Vikings punted back to Bradshaw and the Steelers.

The Steelers locked down on defense in the first half. The one-yard run by Osborn would be Minnesota's longest run from scrimmage in the first quarter. But Minnesota's defense bent but didn't break, allowing sixty-one yards on the ground to Harris. Pittsburgh missed a thirty-seven-yard field goal late in the first quarter. The only points of the first half were scored on a safety when Fran Tarkenton and Dave Osborn botched a handoff deep in their own territory, and Tarkenton was forced to fall on the ball in the end zone and was touched down for a safety by Dwight White. With 7:11 left in the first half, it was 2–0 Steelers.

After forcing a three-and-out on the next Pittsburgh drive, Tarkenton and the Vikings took over at their own twenty-yard line and put together their best drive of the opening half after getting a free fifteen yards on a pass interference call on Mel Blount. The Steel Curtain got a steady dose of Chuck Foreman out of the backfield and in the passing game, gaining thirty-five yards on four plays from scrimmage. A three-yard pass to Dave Osborn set up first and ten from the Pittsburgh twenty-five-yard line. With 1:17 left before halftime, and looking to take the lead, Tarkenton fired a strike to John Gilliam at the five-yard line. Gilliam had the ball in his hands, then he was lit up by Glen Edwards, who came across the field to make the tackle. The ball popped up straight in the air and was intercepted by Blount at the one-yard line and returned to the ten. Pittsburgh ran out the clock and took a 2–0 lead to the locker room.

The Vikings received the ball to start the second half. Roy Gerela's kickoff was fielded by veteran Bill Brown, who muffed the kick. It was recovered by Marv Kellum, and Pittsburgh's offense trotted out to take over at the Minnesota thirty-yard gain. The Steelers handed the ball to Harris three straight times, who took it in for the game's first touchdown. After Gerela's extra point, Pittsburgh led 9–0.

After exchanging punts with the Steelers, the Vikings offense got back into Pittsburgh territory. The Steelers kept pressure on Tarkenton though. On the second play of the drive from their own nineteen-yard line, a Tarkenton pass was batted at the line of scrimmage. He caught it then fired it for a forty-one-yard gain to Gilliam, but the play was nullified for an illegal forward pass. After a twelve-yard run by Foreman and a twenty-eight-yard reception from Stu Voigt, Minnesota was set up first and ten from the Pittsburgh 45. Foreman was wrapped up in the backfield for a two-yard loss, then Tarkenton had another pass tipped at the line of scrimmage, this time by Dwight White. And it was picked off by Joe Greene.

Three plays later, Jeff Siemon intercepted Terry Bradshaw, but Minnesota was flagged for offsides. Pittsburgh punted back to Minnesota four plays later.

Things looked to be going Minnesota's way again in the fourth quarter. Paul Krause recovered a Franco Harris fumble at midfield with the Vikings still trailing 9–0. On the next play, Pittsburgh defensive back Mike Wagner was flagged forty-two yards for pass interference on John Gilliam that put the ball at the Pittsburgh five. The five-yard line was the closest the Vikings had been to the end zone all day. On first and goal, Foreman fumbled the ball, and it was recovered by Joe Greene for his second takeaway of the afternoon.

Pinned deep in their own territory, Pittsburgh ran the ball three consecutive times then lined up to punt. Vikings linebacker Matt Blair blocked the punt, and Terry Brown recovered it for a Vikings touchdown. Fred Cox missed the extra point, and the Steelers lead was cut to three points, 9–6.

With 10:28 left in the game, the Vikings needed a stop and a score. Bradshaw would orchestrate one of the best drives of his young career, putting together a twelve-play sixty-six-yard drive that ate up nearly seven minutes. He was 3-for-3 passing on third down, picking up a thirty-yard completion to Larry Brown on third and two, a six-yard completion to Rocky Bleier on third and five, then found Brown again on third and four for a four-yard touchdown. After the extra point, Pittsburgh led by 10 points with just over three minutes left.

The first play on the next Vikings drive was intercepted by Mike Wagner—Tarkenton's third interception on the afternoon and the fifth turnover by the Vikings.

The Steelers limited the Vikings to only nine first downs, 119 total yards (17 rushing yards), and no offensive scores. Pittsburgh, on the other hand, had 333 yards of total offense, including 158 rushing yards on 34 carries by Franco Harris—more than the entire Vikings offense. For the second straight year, the single game Super Bowl rushing record was broken against the Purple People Eaters defense (they gave up 145 yards to Larry Csonka in Super Bowl VIII), and Harris was named the Super Bowl MVP as Pittsburgh won their first Super Bowl in the forty-two-year history of the franchise. The Steelers would win the Super Bowl the following year, then back-to-back Super Bowls again in 1979 and 1980.

In three Super Bowls, Minnesota had only scored two offensive touchdowns.

December 28, 1975

The Hail Mary

I just threw it and prayed.
—Cowboys quarterback Roger Staubach

Until 1998, the 1975 Minnesota Vikings was the greatest Vikings team of all time. At age thirty-five, Fran Tarkenton had the best year of his career, throwing for nearly 3,000 yards and a league-leading 25 touchdowns on his way to the 1975 NFL MVP award. Chuck Foreman ran for 1,070 yards. Ed White developed into a Pro Bowl guard while playing on the right side next to Hall of Famer Ron Yary. The Vikings led the NFC in scoring, averaging 27 points per game (377 total points). The defense was equally as dominant with anchors Alan Page, Carl Eller, and Paul Krause in addition to young breakout stars like linebacker Jeff Siemon and cornerback Bobby Bryant. The Vikings won the first ten games of the season, but none of the teams they faced would finish over .500. They lost their first game of the season to playoff-staple Washington. Trailing 21–0, Fran Tarkenton led the Vikings back to take a 30–24 lead before Redskins quarterback Billy Kilmer orchestrated a game-winning drive and a 31–30 win.

They'd bounce back and beat a terrible Green Bay team 24–3 before traveling to Detroit to play their first ever game at the brand-new Silverdome. The Vikings offense completely disappeared in Detroit, with their lone touchdown coming on a Paul Krause fumble return. Detroit won 17–10 to drop the Vikings to 11–2.

Prior to 1975, the NFL used a rotation system rather than record to determine home field advantage in the playoffs. The NFL changed the rule so that a team's record would determine home field advantage. At 11–2, they needed to beat Buffalo on the road in order to hold of the Los Angeles Rams and clinch home field advantage throughout the playoffs.

A week after not scoring an offensive touchdown, Chuck Foreman took over. He had 29 offensive touches for 172 yards (85 rushing, 87 receiving) and

4 touchdowns. The Vikings defense held O. J. Simpson to 57 rushing yards (Simpson would score both of Buffalo's touchdowns in the game) and picked off quarterback Joe Ferguson three times. Although the Vikings put the ball on the ground five times (they recovered four of them, one for a touchdown in the end zone by Jim Lash) they blew out the Bills 35–13. The Vikings finished the season 12–2, won the NFC Central champion title, secured home field advantage, and were poised to reach their third straight Super Bowl.

Their opponent in the first round of the playoffs was the Dallas Cowboys in a game in which the Vikings were eight-point favorites. Dallas, led by veteran coach Tom Landry and Super Bowl MVP quarterback Roger Staubach, snuck into the playoffs as the NFC wild card team (back when there were three division winners and one wild card team). Dallas had missed the playoffs in 1974 and featured twelve rookie starters, including Ed "Too Tall" Jones and Thomas "Hollywood" Henderson, Harvey Martin, Drew Pearson and Golden Richards.

Neither team scored in the first quarter. The closest either team came to the end zone was Dallas on Minnesota's thirty-eight-yard line.

Dallas made their first mistake of the game on a punt return in the second quarter. After a Vikings punt by Neil Clabo bounced at the four-yard line, it hit Dallas's Cliff Harris in the leg and was recovered by Fred McNeill. Foreman drew first blood in the game with a one-yard touchdown to give the Vikings a 7–0 lead.

The Vikings took the 7–0 lead into the locker room at halftime and couldn't figure out Dallas defense. The NFC's top offense had only scored fewer than seven points in the opening half twice that season. Minnesota, who averaged 354 yards of offense during the regular season, would finish the day with 250. The rushing attack was virtually nonexistent. Foreman was the leading rusher with 56 yards; Tarkenton was second with 32.

Vikings kicker Fred Cox missed a forty-five-yard field goal early in the third quarter, and Dallas drove down and tied the game at 7–7 on a Doug Dennison four-yard touchdown run to the right side. In the fourth quarter, Dallas took their first lead of the game on a twenty-four-yard Toni Fritsch field goal.

Trailing 10–7, Minnesota put together their best drive of the game: an eleven-play, seventy-yard drive that ended with Brent McClanahan fighting his way into the end zone on another Vikings one-yard touchdown run. Cox's extra point was good, and the Vikings took a 14–10 lead.

After forcing Dallas to punt after a three-and-out, Minnesota got the ball back with 3:18 left and could win the game by running out the clock. All that stood in their way was a third and two play after Dallas burned their last time-out. Offensive Coordinator Jerry Burns wanted to run the ball, but Dallas had eaten up the run all afternoon. Tarkenton called a rollout and short pass. As he rolled out to the right, he was sacked by Dallas safety Charlie Waters.

"That play cost us the game," Tarkenton said afterward. "It wasn't the Hail Mary pass. We had the game in control but couldn't make the play." Minnesota punted the ball back to Dallas and pinned Dallas at their own fifteen-yard line with 1:51 left in the game. Cowboys coach Tom Landry was "very, very depressed" because he felt that the Cowboys had outplayed the Vikings the entire game.

From the shotgun formation, Staubach targeted wide receiver Drew Pearson, who hadn't made a catch all game. Pearson made back-to-back receptions that advanced Dallas to the twenty-five-yard line.

On third and ten, Staubach had to fall on a low snap from center John Fitzgerald for a loss of six yards. Dallas faced a fourth and sixteen on their own twenty-five-yard line. One more defensive play, and the Vikings would win and head to their third straight NFC Championship Game. Dallas needed a miracle to win the game.

Staubach went back to Pearson on fourth down. He made a leaping catch out of bounds at the fifty-yard line, guarded closely by defensive back Nate Wright, who hit him midair and pushed him out of bounds. The officials ruled that Pearson would have landed inbounds had Wright not pushed him and awarded him the catch and the spotted the ball first and ten at the fifty-yard line.

With twenty-four seconds left on the clock, Staubach broke the huddle. Pearson ran a similar route to the one before, but this time, he cut back inside and took off down the sidelines. Staubach pump faked, and Paul Krause bit, freeing up Pearson one-on-one with Wright down the sidelines. Then Staubach threw the ball up for grabs.

What happened next depends on who you talk to. Dallas fans claimed that Wright slipped on a muddy field as the ball came down. The most popular opinion is that Pearson pushed Wright to the ground and should have been flagged for offensive pass interference.

Wright fell to the ground, and Pearson caught the ball and backpedaled into the end zone for the controversial go-ahead Dallas touchdown.

With twenty-four seconds left in the game, the crowd quickly turned violent after the noncall and began throwing things onto the field. Armen Terzian, the official who signaled the touchdown, was hit in the head with a half-empty bottle of whiskey thrown from the stands.

Dallas advanced to the NFC Championship Game, winning 17–14 after what newspapers dubbed the Hail Mary Pass.

"Like a good Catholic kid," Staubach said after the game, "I said I closed my eyes and said a 'Hail Mary.'"

Dallas would blow out the Los Angeles Rams, who had the league's best-scoring defense in 1975, 37–7 to advance to the franchise's third Super Bowl.

January 15, 1976

NCAA Sanctions Handed to Mychal Thompson

The "holier-than-thou" schools that say they don't do it,
I'm sure they have alumni do it for them.

—Mychal Thompson

Former Gopher standout Mychal Thompson is one of nine Gophers men's basketball players to have their numbers hanging from the rafters of the Barn. While wearing number 43 for the Gophers, Thompson scored 1,442 points, made 604 field goals, and pulled down 697 rebounds—all school records.

Even after the sanctions handed down in 1976.

Unofficially, Thompson totaled 1,992 points, made 823 field goals, and pulled down 956 rebounds during his four seasons at the U.

Gophers coach Bill Musselman recruited the 6'10" center out of Jackson High School in Miami, Florida, in 1974. With Thompson in the lineup, the Gophers were ranked number 18 to start the season and were looking for their first official (since their 1971–72 bid was vacated) NCAA tournament appearance.

Despite big numbers from Thompson and other players like Mark Olberding, Flip Saunders, Mark Landsberger, and Ray Williams, the tournament bid never came. The Gophers were ranked as high as number 16 in 1974 (finished 18–8, 11–7) and 1975 (finished 16–10, 8–10); but they missed the cut in Thompson's freshman and sophomore seasons.

During his junior year in 1976, Thompson and the Gophers went 24–3 and 15–3 in the Big Ten. He averaged 22 points and nine rebounds a game. However, it was revealed in January 1976 that Thompson had scalped two complimentary Gopher basketball tickets valued at $39 for $180 during his freshman season in 1974–75, and the NCAA placed him on probation. When Musselman continued to play him anyways, the NCAA vacated all the Gophers wins from the 1976–77 season and declared them ineligible for the NCAA tournament.

When Thompson scalped his tickets, the NCAA didn't have a rule regarding the sale of tickets. The league instituted their ticket regulations prior to the 1975–76 season. The Big Ten instituted the rule declaring a player ineligible for selling tickets (even for face value) at the same time.

Thompson returned to Minnesota for his senior season and averaged 22 points and ten rebounds a game for a 17–10 team. He declared for the NBA Draft following the season and was selected by the Portland Trail Blazers with the top pick in the 1978 Draft.

December 10, 1976
Danny Thompson Passes Away

Danny Thompson was a fan favorite while playing utility man for the Twins from 1970 to 1976. The scrappy infielder hit .248 in six seasons, and in his lone season as a full-time shortstop for the Twins in 1972, he finished twenty-third in the AL MVP voting. Two years later, the day before his twenty-sixth birthday, Thompson was called back to the doctor after a routine preseason physical for additional tests and was diagnosed with granulocytic leukemia. Despite the diagnosis, he still played baseball. In 1974, he led all-American league shortstops with a .270 batting average. In 1975, he played in 112 games while undergoing treatment at Mayo Clinic in Rochester. After playing in thirty-four games for the Twins in 1976, he was traded along with friend Bert Blyleven to the Texas Rangers for four players (including Roy Smalley and Mike Cubbage). Thompson was determined to finish the season while undergoing treatment. He played in sixty-four games for Texas, hitting .214 in 216 plate appearances. His final start came against the Twins at Metropolitan Stadium on September 29 in front of a crowd of only 2,444 fans. His final plate appearance came as a pinch hitter against the White Sox on October 2 in the bottom of the ninth. Sixty-nine days later, he died at age twenty-nine.

January 9, 1977

Super Bowl XI versus Oakland

We shut a lot of people up about not being able to win the big game.
—Raiders tight end Dave Casper

A year after the heartbreak in the 1975 playoffs against the Dallas Cowboys, the Vikings were poised for one more push to finally win a Super Bowl. Reigning NFL MVP Fran Tarkenton, now thirty-six years old, returned for his sixteenth NFL season. And he wasn't the only NFL vet whose window was closing. Center Mick Tingelhoff was also thirty-six years old. Carl Eller and Paul Krause were thirty-four, and Jim Marshall was thirty-nine. There was every reason to believe the Vikings reign in the NFC was coming to an end, but they had one more year left.

The defense, despite the age of its stars, finished second in scoring defense in 1976. The Vikings added new offensive weapons for Tarkenton, acquiring former Oregon standout Ahmad Rashad from the Buffalo Bills and drafting 1976 Offensive Rookie of the Year Sammy White out of Grambling State. With Rashad (671 receiving yards, 3 touchdowns); White (906 receiving yards, 10 touchdowns); and Chuck Foreman (career-high 1,155 rushing yards, 13 touchdowns), the Vikings finished ninth in total offense and finished the regular season 11–2–1 and were crowned NFC Central champions for the eighth time in nine seasons. Tarkenton added to his career stats and padded his all-time pass completions, passing yards, and passing touchdowns records.

The Vikings were the top seed in the NFC Playoffs and faced the 10–4 wild card Washington Redskins in the Metropolitan Stadium in the opening round. Washington was coming off an emotional upset win against the Dallas Cowboys to get them into the playoffs, and it showed. The Vikings led 21–3 at the half and 35–6 after three quarters before Washington made it a respectable 35–20 in garbage time. The Vikings ran for a combined 221 rushing yards against the Redskins.

Minnesota's running game looked to stay hot in the NFC Championship Game against the Los Angeles Rams. The Vikings had put up over 200 yards on the ground in their last three games (221 versus Washington, 226 versus Miami, and 218 versus Green Bay).

The Rams had upset the Cowboys in the divisional round and denied the world a Vikings versus Cowboys rematch from the year before. But the Vikings and Rams also had a rivalry brewing, having met twice in the NFC Championship in the previous three seasons. It was the Rams' third straight NFC Championship Game.

For the past decade, it was the stifling defense of the Purple People Eaters that led the Vikings to big wins. This time, it was the special teams. With the ball on the goal line in the first quarter, Rams coach Chuck Knox elected for a Pat Dempsey field goal over challenging Alan Page, Carl Eller, and company for the fourth down conversion. Cornerback Nate Allen blocked the kick, and Bobby Bryant returned it ninety yards for a Vikings touchdown. The Nate Allen block was the fourteenth kick that Minnesota had blocked that season.

A twenty-five-yard Fred Cox field goal in the second quarter after the Vikings blocked a punt gave the Vikings a 10–0 lead despite it only being eighty-nine yards of total offense. The Rams completed a forty-three-yard pass play at the end of the second quarter and went into the locker room trailing by ten points.

The Vikings offense came alive in the third quarter, with Chuck Foreman breaking a sixty-two-yard run that set him up a one-yard touchdown and a 17–0 lead. But just like in Week Two, the Vikings couldn't contain the Rams' running game. McCutcheon, who finished the game with 128 rushing yards, ran and scored a ten-yard touchdown in the third quarter. After LA missed the PAT, the Vikings led 17–6. On the Vikings next offensive series, Fred Dryer blew past offensive lineman Steve Riley and blindsided Tarkenton, causing him to fumble. Jack Youngblood picked up the ball and advanced it to the Minnesota eight-yard line. Hayden connected with Harold Jackson for a touchdown, and just like that, the Vikings' 17-point lead was down to four.

Both defenses battled in the fourth quarter. After a Bobby Bryant interception, the Vikings iced the game on a Sammy Johnson touchdown run after Chuck Foreman hurt his back on a 57-yard pass play. Foreman finished the game with 200 all-purpose yards, 150 of that in the second half. The Vikings won 24–13 and advanced to their third Super Bowl in four years.

Waiting for the Vikings in Super Bowl XI were the AFC champion Oakland Raiders. The Raiders had a similar history as the Vikings—dominant in their respective league but never able to win the big game. The Raiders had won division titles nine times in the previous ten years and recorded double-digit wins seven times but had lost six AFC title games (1968–70, 1973–75) and Super Bowl II to the Green Bay Packers.

The Raiders were 13–1 in 1976, the closest anybody had come to matching the 1972 Miami Dolphins' perfect season from 1972. Their one loss was a 48–17 loss to the New England Patriots in Week 4. Oakland got their revenge in the first round of the playoffs, knocking the Pats out 24–21. Oakland took down the two-time defending Super Bowl champion Pittsburgh Steelers in the AFC Championship Game to advance to their second ever Super Bowl. Since hiring John Madden as the head coach following the 1968, the Raiders were 88–22–7, good for a .772 winning percentage—second only to the Vikings' .781.

The Vikings came into the matchup with the most Super Bowl appearances in NFL history with three but had lost each contest: Super Bowl IV versus Kansas City, Super Bowl VIII versus Miami, and Super Bowl IX versus Pittsburgh. Each team was looking for their first Super Bowl title at the Rose Bowl in Pasadena, California, on January 9, 1977.

The Vikings were four-point underdogs against the Raiders, which was their third Super Bowl in which they were underdogs (they were favored by 13 points in Super Bowl IV against Kansas City and lost by 16 points). They looked to prove the oddsmakers wrong in front of the 103,400 people at the Rose Bowl and the 62 million viewers at home.

The Raiders—with an offense led by future Hall of Famers like quarterback Ken Stabler, wide receiver Fred Biletnikoff, tight end Dave Casper, and offensive linemen Art Shall and Gene Upshaw—drove to the Minnesota eleven-yard line on their first drive of the game. But a missed twenty-nine-yard field goal by Minnesota native (born in Breckenridge) Errol Mann kept the game tied at zero.

As they had done all season long, the Vikings' special teams made another huge play midway through the first quarter. With Hall of Fame punter Ray Guy kicking from Oakland's thirty-four-yard line, linebacker Fred McNeill blocked the punt (the first of only three blocked punts in Guy's fourteen-year career), and Minnesota recovered on the three-yard line. Foreman ran for a gain of yard, then Tarkenton handed off to Brent McClanahan to punch it in. He fumbled, and Oakland recovered the ball.

Oakland drove the ball again with big gains by running back Clarence Davis (thirty-five-yard carry on a third and seven) and a twenty-five-yard pass from Stabler to Casper. Facing a fourth and goal from Minnesota's seven-yard line, Madden sent Mann back out to attempt the twenty-four-yard field goal. This time he made it and gave Oakland a 3–0 lead.

The Raiders would score on their next two offensive possessions: a one-yard touchdown pass from Stabler to Casper and a one-yard run by Pete Banaszak. Oakland led 16–0 at the half, and it was the fourth time in as many Super Bowls that Minnesota had been shut out in the first half.

Oakland added to their point total with a forty-yard field goal to increase the lead to 19–0. The Vikings finally got on the board on the final play of the third quarter with an eight-yard touchdown pass to Sammy White.

In the fourth quarter, the Vikings began moving the ball again before Tarkenton was picked off by linebacker Willie Hall. Three plays later, Biletnikoff reeled in a forty-eight-yard pass that set up Banaszak's second touchdown of the game.

Now trailing 26–7, the Vikings needed a lot of points in a hurry to get back in the game. Tarkenton drove the Vikings down to the Oakland twenty-eight-yard line. But on a pass intended for White, Tarkenton was picked off by Willie Brown, who returned it seventy-five yards for a pick-six and a 32–7 fourth quarter lead.

Bud Grant replaced Tarkenton with backup quarterback Bob Lee for Minnesota's final drive of the game. Lee led the Vikings eighty-six yards in nine plays and threw a fourteen-yard touchdown pass to Stu Voigt with twenty-five seconds left in the game.

Oakland won Super Bowl IX 32–14. As they had done in their previous two Super Bowls, the Vikings game up huge chunks of rushing yards: 137 to Clarence Davis and another 73 to Mark van Eeghen. The 429 yards by the Raiders offense was a new Super Bowl record, as was their 288 yards in the second half.

In their four Super Bowls, the Vikings never had a lead. In fact, the Vikings never scored in the first half. The vaunted Purple People Eaters defense gave up an average of 216 rushing yards in the four games and forced only three turnovers. The offense wasn't much better, turning the ball over fifteen times (three of those in the red zone) and averaging only 57 rushing yards per Super Bowl.

January 1, 1978

1977 NFC Championship Game

Lee is a capable quarterback, but he isn't Fran Tarkenton.
—Dallas defensive end Harvey Martin

The Vikings, one season removed from their fourth Super Bowl loss since 1969, started the 1977 season 5–3 before losing thirty-seven-year-old Fran Tarkenton to a broken leg. Backup Bob Lee led the Vikings to a 9–5 finish and the third overall seed in the playoffs as the Vikings looked to return to the Super Bowl. They beat the LA Rams 14–7 to advance to their fourth NFC Championship Game in five seasons. (The Rams beat the Vikings 35–3 in Week 6 that season.)

Awaiting them in the championship game was a familiar postseason foe: the Dallas Cowboys. This was the fourth playoff matchup with Dallas since 1971, and the Vikings had only won one of those matchups, beating the Cowboys 27–10 in the 1973 NFC Championship Game.

The Cowboys still featured Hall of Fame quarterback Roger Staubach and a high-powered offense. Wideout Drew Pearson led the NFL in receiving yards and yards per game. Dallas also traded up in the 1977 Draft to select runningback Tony Dorsett out of Pittsburgh. Dorsett would win the Offensive Rookie of the Year award and rush for over 1,000 yards that season.

While the Dallas offense led the NFC in scoring with 24.6 points per game, Defensive Player of the Year Harvey Martin and the Dallas defense only allowed 15.1 points per game. Martin led the NFL with an estimated 23 sacks (sacks weren't an official stat yet) and was featured on a defense that allowed the fewest rushing yards (1,651) and total yards (3,213).

The Vikings traveled to Irving, Texas, for the championship game with some bragging rights on the line. They were trying to get to their record fifth Super Bowl, while Dallas was trying to tie the Vikings with their fourth appearance.

Despite winning the NFC Central in 1977, the Vikings struggled mightily with turnovers. They were −18 in the take/give that year: 22 interceptions (14 by Tarkenton in nine games before he got hurt) and 36 fumbles.

The Vikings won the toss and chose to receive the ball, but two plays into the game, running back Robert Miller fumbled at the Vikings' thirty-nine-yard line. Martin recovered the fumble, and two plays later, Staubach threw a thirty-two-yard touchdown pass to Golden Richards. Carl Eller blocked the extra point, and Dallas was up 6–0 ninety seconds into the game.

Chuck Foreman also fumbled in the first quarter (also recovered by Martin), but the Vikings forced a punt after Dallas went three-and-out.

Cowboys coach Tom Landry opened up the playbook in the second quarter, fooling the Vikings defense on a fake punt. Danny White, the passing-threat punter who was also Staubach's backup, picked up a first down with a fifteen-yard run to keep the Dallas drive alive. (White would take over at quarterback when Staubach retired in 1979 and would win sixty-one games for Dallas in the 1980s while still handling punting duties.) Robert Newhouse would score a five-yard touchdown to cap off the drive to extend the Dallas lead to 13–0.

The Vikings offense got a break on the next drive with a forty-four-yard pass interference call on Charlie Waters. But even with the penalty yards, they couldn't score a touchdown on the Dallas defense and settled for a thirty-two-yard Fred Cox field goal to make it 13–3.

The Vikings would get another field goal from Cox, this one from thirty-seven yards out, near the end of the second quarter. It would end up being the final points scored by Cox in his career. (Cox is still the all-time leading scorer in Vikings history with 1,365 points with 519 extra points and 282 made field goals.) Dallas drove sixty-five yards in a minute and a half to get into field goal range. Efren Herrera kicked a twenty-one-yarder with three seconds left in the half to make it 16–6.

The defenses exchanged blows in the second half, each team shutting the other's offense down. The passing attack for Minnesota never found a groove. Lee finished 14-of-31 for 158 yards and an interception. Staubach posted similar numbers to Lee: 12-of-23 for 165 yards, the touchdown to Richards and an interception of his own.

The difference in the game? Turnovers.

The Vikings defense had held the high-powered Dallas offense to two touchdowns over three quarters—something that hadn't been done since these two teams met at Metropolitan Stadium in Week 1 (Dallas won in overtime, 16–10). But the Vikings lost their third fumble in the fourth quarter when punt returner Manfred Moore coughed the ball up at the Vikings' thirty-five-yard line. Five plays later, Dorsett ran the ball to the right side and scored an eleven-yard touchdown to give Dallas a 23–6 lead with four minutes left.

"We gave up too much too early," Bud Grant said. "We thought we still had a chance, but that final fumble was the ball game. It took the punch out of us. Turnovers always hurt you. We've lived with turnovers all year. Today it finally got the best of us."

The Vikings defensive line of Marshall, Page, Eller, and Doug Sutherland bottled up Dorsett for most of the game, except for the eleven-yard run. He finished with seventy-one yards on 19 carries. Fullback Robert Newhouse led Dallas in rushing yards with eighty-one yards on 15 carries.

Foreman carried the ball twenty-one times for only fifty-nine yards. He put the ball on the ground twice, losing one of them.

"We got the idea that Foreman was playing hurt," said linebacker Tom "Hollywood" Henderson. "Lee doesn't use him as much as Tarkenton does. We were waiting for him on those crucial third-down plays."

The 1977 season would be the last gasp for a team that had dominated the league since Bud Grant took over as head coach in 1967: nine division titles in ten years. They had 107 regular season wins and four Super Bowl appearances. But the black mark that hangs over those teams is the empty trophy case with zero Super Bowl wins.

Including the 1977 NFC Championship Game, the Vikings have played in six title games since the 23–6 loss to Dallas. And they've lost all six.

<<BONUS ACHE>>

Les Steckel

Even without their stars of the 1970s, the Vikings stayed competitive in the early 1980s. Until Bud Grant retired, that is. 1984 was the first year since 1967 that the Vikings weren't led by Grant. Les Steckel took the reins, and the Vikings were 3–13—the second-worst record in franchise history. Only the 1962 team (2–11–1) was worse. The 1984 Vikings allowed an average of 30.3 points per game and was the most PPG allowed in the NFL from 1983 to 2000. Steckel was fired after the season, and the Vikings rehired Bud Grant.

September 23, 1978

Lyman Bostock Is Murdered

I don't think you ever get over it. You cope with it, but as far as getting over it, no.
—Thomas Tuner

Lyman Bostock was born in Birmingham, Alabama, in November 1950. His father, Lyman Bostock Sr., played in the Negro Leagues from 1938 to 1954; but Lyman was never really close to him. His parents split when he was young, and he moved with his mother, Annie, to Gary, Indiana, in 1954. Gary had been a steel hub prior to World War II, but its infrastructure began to crumble in the mid-1950s. In 1958, Annie and Lyman moved again, this time to Los Angeles.

He played high school ball at Manual Arts High School, then he attended San Fernando Valley State College in Northridge, California. He decided not to play baseball though. Instead, he devoted his time to fight social injustice against African Americans. In 1970, he was arrested and spent three weeks in jail.

Despite not playing baseball, the St. Louis Cardinals still drafted him in the 1970 MLB Draft. He decided to return to college and play ball for the Matadors. He hit .344 as a junior and .296 as a senior as the Matadors were runners-up in the 1972 Division II College World Series.

Bostock was drafted again, this time by the Twins in the twenty-sixth round of the 1972 MLB Draft. He spent three seasons in the minors before being named the Twins Opening Day center fielder in 1975. His rookie season was cut short after breaking his ankle while crashing into the outfield wall in a game against Oakland. He hit .282 with 52 runs scored in ninety-eight games.

In his second year, he hit .323, which put him fourth in the AL in batting average behind Kansas City's George Brett and Hal McRae and teammate Rod Carew. He also became the fourth Twin to hit for the cycle, accomplishing the rare feat on July 24 in a 17–4 win against the Chicago White Sox.

The next season, he and Rod Carew formed one of the best one-two punches. Bostock's .336 average was second only to AL MVP Carew's .388 in his quest for .400. And with free agency looming, he was due for a big raise.

1977 was the second year of free agency in baseball. Prior to that, with the league's reserve clause, a player didn't change teams unless they were traded or released. Notoriously stingy Twins owner Calvin Griffith didn't offer Bostock a raise until thirteen other teams had made offers to him.

The Twins were in the middle of what would be the longest postseason drought in franchise history. The stars of the 1970 AL West championship team—like Harmon Killebrew, Tony Oliva, Jim Kaat, and Jim Perry—were long gone. The only one left was Carew, who would be traded to the California Angels after the 1978 season. The Twins were near the bottom of the league in attendance (averaged 14,500 fans per game).

Free agency hit the Twins hard in 1977. AL RBI leader Larry Hisle signed a six-year contract with the Milwaukee Brewers, and Bostock signed a five-year $2.25 million contract with the California Angels. When he signed, he donated $10,000 to a church in Birmingham to rebuild its Sunday school.

He started the 1978 season off slowly for the Angels, hitting only .147 in the month of April. He tried to give the money back to Angels owner Gene Autry, saying he hadn't earned it. Autry declined, so Bostock donated his entire April salary to charity. He would find his stride in June, batting .404. He finished the 1978 season with a .296 average.

After a 5–4 loss against the Chicago White Sox at Comisky Park on September 23, Bostock visited family in nearby Gary, Indiana, which is about a half-hour drive from Chicago. Visiting relatives in Gary was a tradition Bostock had every time he played in the Windy City.

He went to his uncle Thomas Turner's house for a meal. Afterward, he and his uncle went to visit Joan Hawkins, who had tutored him as a teenager. After their visit, Lyman and Thomas agreed to give Hawkins and her sister, Barbara Smith, a ride to their cousin's house. Thomas and Joan were in the front seat. Lyman and Barbara were in the back.

Barbara had been living with her sister while separated from her husband, Leonard Smith, who was a serial abuser. Earlier that day, Barbara had told Leonard she wanted a divorce. He immediately thought she was having an affair, but the couple had separated fifteen times since their marriage in 1974 and Barbara had called the police on him on several occasions.

The group didn't know that Leonard was watching them and saw them get into the car. He saw Lyman and Barbara get into the back seat together and assumed that Lyman was the one Barbara was cheating on him with, when in fact the two had only met about twenty minutes beforehand when Lyman had arrived at the Hawkins house.

When Thomas stopped at a red light, Leonard made his move. He pulled up next to their vehicle and fired one blast of a .410-caliber shotgun into the back seat where Lyman and Barbara were seated. The shot was intended for Barbara but hit Lyman in the right temple.

Barbara was able to identify her husband's vehicle as it sped off, but Thomas's concern was getting his nephew to a hospital. He pulled over at a grocery store and called an ambulance.

Then he got a hold of the Angels team hotel in Chicago to tell them what had happened. Angels trainer Freddie Frederico drove to the hospital, then he called the Angels to give them the somber news.

"'Lyman hasn't got a chance,' he told us," said team representative Ken Brett. "'All they can do is make him comfortable before he dies.'"

Lyman Bostock died two hours later, at 1:06 a.m. on September 23.

"The news stories had the police saying Smith was trying to kill his wife," Turner told the *Star Tribune* in 1988. "Smith shot the person he wanted to shoot. He thought he was shooting Barbara's boyfriend. He wasn't, but that's what he thought."

Smith was found not guilty by reason of insanity and was committed to a psychiatric treatment facility. He was released seven months later.

While Bostock didn't play for the Twins when he was murdered, he was a fan favorite while he was a Twin. The entire baseball world mourned the twenty-seven-year-old baseball star who was in the wrong place at the wrong time. The Angels wore commemorative black armbands in 1978, and hundreds of people that Bostock had touched with his philanthropy attended his funeral. Angels manager Jim Fregosi was supposed to deliver a eulogy but couldn't bring himself to do it. So Ken Brett did it.

"When he found the road to success, his first thoughts were to help the people who had helped him," Brett said. "We are all better people for having known Lyman and having him touch our lives."

Bostock's career ended with a .311/.365/.427 line with 305 runs scored and 250 RBI.

February 3, 1979

Rod Carew Is Traded to California

I think the best thing would be for the Twins to trade me. If I got the chance to go to a pennant contender, I would like that.

—Rod Carew

The Twins were in a rough position after the 1978 season. Their star player, Rod Carew, wanted out. He wanted to play for a contending team. Minnesota hadn't made the playoffs since 1970 and hadn't finished higher than third place since. He wanted to distance himself from Twins owner Calvin Griffith, who had recently come under fire for racist comments. In an owner's meeting in Chicago in 1978, Griffith said he lobbied to move the Twins to Minnesota because there were too many black people in Washington and "black people don't go to baseball games." Carew publically stated that he didn't want to play on "Griffith's plantation."

It's no easy task to get compensation for a player that had won seven American League batting titles in twelve seasons, appeared in twelve consecutive All-Star games, and had a career .334 average. After the 1978 season, Carew had the highest active career batting average and trailed only Pete Rose, Lou Brock, Carl Yastrzemski, and Rusty Staub among active players in career hits (2,085).

But with the introduction of free agency in baseball following the 1976 season, the Twins needed to trade him or get nothing in return. They had already had All-Star-caliber players like Lyman Bostock (California Angels) and Larry Hisle (Milwaukee Brewers) walk away after the 1977 season. But unlike Tom Seaver, who was traded/banished by the New York Mets to the Cincinnati Reds in 1977 after a contract dispute, Carew had enough major league service time that he could pick which team he was traded to.

Carew had three teams on his list: the New York Yankees, the Boston Red Sox, and the California Angels and made it known before the 1978 season that he'd like to be moved. Carew also mentioned to the *New York Times* in April 1978 that he would consider the Los Angeles Dodgers as well, but he would need American League waivers to join a National League team. The *Times* also asked him if he'd consider trades to the Kansas City Royals, Texas Rangers, Chicago White Sox, or Milwaukee Brewers. He answered no each time.

The trade deadline came and went, and Carew remained on the Twins. He finished the season with a .333 average, which was high enough to win his seventh batting title and sixth title in seven seasons.

Carew had moved from his natural position at second base to first base in 1976 and had appeared in only fifteen games at second since '76. The Angels needed a first baseman. They had twenty-five-year-old Ron Jackson, who hit a career-high .297 in 105 games in 1978, but he still only had a career stat line of .255/.308/.380 with 22 home runs and 127 in his first three seasons. (The Twins traded Dan Ford to California for Jackson two months before the Carew trade. Jackson was a Twin for parts of three seasons before being traded to Detroit in August 1981.) The Yankees and Red Sox had All-Stars Chris Chambliss and George Scott, respectively, at first base but were reportedly willing to include them in deals for Carew. Reports said that the Yankees were also willing to part with pitching prospect Dave Righetti (who would be the 1981 Rookie of the Year, a two-time All-Star, and two-time Rolaids Relief Man of the Year).

California was Carew's first choice, and that's where the eventual eighteen-time All-Star was traded to. In return, the Twins received outfielder Ken Landreaux, outfielder/catcher Dave Engel, and pitchers Brad Havens and Paul Hartzell.

With Carew going to California, the Yankees traded Chambliss to Toronto for Rick Cerone, Tom Underwood, and Ted Wilborn in November 1979. A month later, he was traded to Atlanta for Barry Bonnell, Joey McLaughlin, and Pat Rocket. He played for the Braves for the next seven seasons (.272/.345/.422 with 366 RBI and 319 runs scored). George Scott struggled for Boston in 1979 and was traded to Kansas City forty-five games into the season, hitting .224 with one home run (he hit a league-leading 36 only four years earlier). He played forty-four games for Kansas City (.267, two home runs) before being cut in August and signing on with the Yankees for the final sixteen games of the season before retiring after the season.

Twenty-four-year-old Ken Landreaux was a Twin for two seasons and was named Twins' lone All-Star in the 1980 Mid-Summer Classic at Dodger Stadium. He hit .294/.341/.435 with 145 RBI and 137 runs in two seasons before being traded to the Dodgers a week before the 1981 season for Mickey Hatcher.

Twenty-one-year-old Dave Engel had just finished his first minor league season for the Single-A Salinas Angels. He had hit .305 with six home runs and 40 RBI in forty-three games before being traded to the Twins. After being traded to the Twins, he made the jump from Single-A to Triple-A as the Twins assigned him to the Toledo Mud Hens. He hit .298 with 124 RBI and 120 runs scored in two full seasons. He made his big-league debut with the Twins in 1981 and spent the next five seasons with the Twins, hitting .268/.316/.400. He was an All-Star in 1984, then he was traded to Detroit for Chris Pittaro and Alejandro Sanchez before the 1986 season.

Twenty-four-year-old Paul Hartzell had three years of major league experience when he was traded to the Twins. He was 21–26 with a 3.27 ERA and 3.2 K/9. He was in the rotation for the Twins in 1979 and started twenty-six games. He was 6–10 with a 5.36 ERA, then he was released in the last round of roster cuts in Spring Training in 1980.

The final piece of the Carew trade was nineteen-year-old pitcher Brad Havens. He pitched seventy-eight innings for the Twins in his rookie season in 1981, going 3–6 with a 3.58 ERA. In 1982, he was a ten-game winner for a Twins team that lost 102 games. He was the opening day starter for the Twins in 1983, but had a disappointing season (5–8, 8.18 ERA). He spent the entire 1984 season at AAA-Toledo (11–10, 2.61 ERA, 9 K/9) before being traded to Baltimore during Spring Training 1985 for Mark Brown.

Carew was an All-Star six more times with the Angels from 1979 to 1985. Although he didn't win any more batting titles in his career, he still hit a respectable .314 in his final seven seasons. He made the playoffs twice with the Angels, losing the ALCS in four games to Baltimore in 1979 and in five games to Milwaukee in 1982. While Carew struggled in the postseason with the Twins (a combined .062 batting average against Baltimore in the 1969 and 1970 ALCS), he hit .412 (7/17) against the O's in the 1979 Championship Series.

"I didn't want to leave," Carew said in 2002. "I would have taken less money to stay with the Twins, but it was still more than Calvin was willing to play. It was enjoyable playing in California for Mr. Autry. You could not find a better person, but if it had been my choice, I would have played in Minnesota my whole career. My heart is still in the Twin Cities."

Carew served as the Angels' hitting coach from 1991 to 1999 but was dropped when Mike Scioscia was hired as manager.

<<BONUS ACHE>>

Calvin Griffith Is Too Cheap to Sign Jim Palmer

Billy Martin was a scout for the Twins in 1963 when he discovered a smooth-throwing pitcher at Scottsdale High School in Scottsdale, Arizona. Martin urged Griffith to sign the eighteen-year-old pitcher. Griffith didn't want to shell out the $50,000 signing bonus (almost $420,000 in 2019), so the Twins passed. That young pitcher signed with the Baltimore Orioles, and between 1965 and 1984, he won three Cy Young Awards, four Glove Gloves, was a two-time ERA leader, three-time wins leader, six-time All-Star, and won six American League pennants and three World Championships. His career 2.82 ERA is the third lowest in MLB history, and in 1990, Jim Palmer was inducted into the Baseball Hall of Fame.

March 28, 1981

NCAA Men's Hockey Championship versus Wisconsin

I really don't care who we play in the finals. I'm pretty confident no matter who we play.
—Gophers head coach Brad Buetow

The 1981 Minnesota Golden Gophers hockey team, arguably one of the best in program history, finished the season with a 33–12–0 record. The thirty-three wins eclipsed the program record of thirty-two wins by the NCAA Championship squad in 1979. All-American Neal Broten, fresh off helping Team USA win gold at the 1980 Olympics in Lake Placid, returned for his sophomore season and won the inaugural Hobey Baker Award. His brother, Aaron, put together one of the greatest seasons in program history, scoring a school-record 106 points (two points shy of the NCAA record) on 47 goals and 59 assists. Steve Ulseth was also an All-American and the WCHA Player of the Year after notching 63 points in thirty-eight WCHA games. Aaron Broten was not named an All-American.

The tournament bracket pitted the top four teams in the east against the top four teams in the west. Clarkson, Providence, Cornell, and at-large Colgate represented the east, while Minnesota, Northern Michigan, Michigan Tech, and at-large Wisconsin represented the west.

The Gophers were the top seed of the NCAA tournament and drew the Colgate Red Raiders in the two-game total-goal series. Colgate also set a program record with twenty-one wins, were scoring 5.5 goals a game and had only lost two of the previous thirteen games. Junior winger Dan Fridgen had 66 points and one was one goal shy of setting a new school record in goals with 37.

The Gophers were without Neal Broten, who was recovering from a dislocated elbow. The Gophers, with Aaron Broten, Ulseth, Jeff Teal, Scott Bjugstad, Butsy Erickson, and company, jumped out to a 6–1 lead; but Colgate battled back to cut the deficit within two goals at 6–4. But the Gophers put it away with three more goals in the final period for a 9–4 final. They won again the next night 5–4 to win the series 14–8.

All four west teams advanced to the final four, with Minnesota playing Michigan Tech and Northern Michigan facing off against Wisconsin.

Minnesota versus Michigan Tech was one of the best WCHA rivalries of the 1970s. The Huskies won the regular season WCHA title in 1974, but the Gophers beat them in the national championship for the program's first NCAA title. The next year, the roles were reversed with Minnesota winning the WCHA, but Tech beat the Gophers for the national championship. In 1976, Tech again won the WCHA and lost to Minnesota in the championship game. Tech had knocked Minnesota out in the quarterfinals the previous season.

The Huskies were riding a hot streak by goalie Frank Krieber. With a 3.11 goals against average, Krieber and Tech had won nine straight games and sixteen of nineteen, losing only to Wisconsin, North Dakota, and Minnesota during that stretch.

Neal Broten returned from his five-week layup with a goal and two assists. Aaron scored two goals and notched two assists as Minnesota won 7–2 to punch their ticket to their NCAA Championship for the fifth time in eight years.

Waiting them was border-rival Wisconsin, who had beaten Northern Michigan 5–1 to advance to their first title game since winning it all in 1977. The Gophers had won three of four games against Wisconsin during the regular season, splitting the series in Madison and sweeping the Badgers at home. Minnesota had a chance to do something they hadn't done before: win the WCHA regular season title, the WCHA playoffs, and a national championship.

Wisconsin jumped out to a 3–0 in the first period, but the Gophers weren't worried. They had overcome a 3–0 deficit to beat Michigan Tech 6–4 in the 1976 NCAA championship game. If they did it then, they could do it again.

Wisconsin increased their lead to 4–0 on Edina native Ted Pearson's goal (Pearson had six goals all season) in the second period. The Gopher's offense, which had been the best in the country, couldn't find the back of the net. The Badgers weren't intimidated by Minnesota's power play, killing three penalties in the first period without a shot allowed on goal.

Steve Ulseth scored the first Gopher goal of the game at 12:37 in the second period to make it 4–1. Fourteen seconds later, Bjugstad was sent to the box for high-sticking, and freshman John Newberry scored on the power play to make it 5–1.

Mike Knocke scored with fifteen seconds left on a power play right away in the third period to cut the deficit to 5–2, and Busty Erickson scored with 3:51 left in the game (also on the power play) to make it 5–3. Goalie Paul Butters came off the ice for the extra attacker, but Wisconsin's Ed Lebler scored an empty netter to push the lead to 6–3. The win for Wisconsin was their third NCAA championship in nine seasons.

<<BONUS ACHE>>

The 2014 NCAA Championship Game versus Union

The Gophers were the number 1 seed in the 2014 NCAA Frozen Four and were looking for their first NCAA Championship since 2002–03. A shorthanded Justin Holl goal against North Dakota in the semifinal with 0.6 seconds left sent the Gophers into the title game against the Union College Dutchmen.

The Dutchman had upset Boston College 5–4 in their semifinal matchup and were red-hot coming into the tournament, having won their final twelve games and going 16–0–1 in their final seventeen games.

The Gophers took a 2–1 lead over Union in the championship game, but things quickly trended toward the Dutchmen. Mike Vecchione, Eli Lichtenwald, and Daniel Ciampini each scored within 1:54 of each other to take a 4–2 lead. Gophers goalie Adam Wilcox had not allowed four goals in a game since a January 25 game against Minnesota Duluth, let alone four goals in one period.

The Gophers would get to within a goal of Union in the third period, but two goals and an empty netter by Union made the final score 7–4, giving Union its first NCAA Championship. Wilcox stopped forty-one shots but allowed six goals on the evening. The eighty-nine combined shots between Union and Minnesota were the second most in tournament history for a game that didn't go to overtime.

May 12, 1981

The Stanley Cup Finals versus New York Islanders

About all we know is that we can't play worse. That is all we learned.
—North Stars GM Lou Nanne

Now in their fourteenth season in the NHL, the North Stars had finally built a contending team.

The 1980–81 North Stars were looking to build off their then-franchise record of 88 points from the previous season. Prior to their 88-point season, they had missed the playoffs five times in six years. With a rebuild beginning with 1978 number 1 overall pick Bobby Smith, Glen Sonmor's 1981 team boasted a lot of young talent (Steve Payne, Dino Ciccarelli, Don Beaupre, Tom McCarthy, Tim Young, Craig Hartsburg, Curt Giles) with a couple of veteran guys sprinkled in (Gilles Meloche, Paul Shmyr, Fred Barrett). General manager Lou Nanne had a team built for the future. And the future was now.

A year after losing in the conference semifinals to Philadelphia 4–1, the North Stars had their eyes set on the next level: the Stanley Cup Finals. They finished one point shy of matching their 1979–80 point total with 87 total points (35–28–17) and made the playoffs for the eighth time in their fourteen-year history. They tied with the Boston Bruins for second place in the Adams division and drew them in the first round of the playoffs for the first and only playoff matchup between the two teams.

When these two teams played the previous February, they combined for 406 penalty minutes. Minnesota won Game 1 at Boston Garden (they were 0–35 all-time in Boston up to that point) in large part to a Steve Payne hat trick. In Game 2, the North Stars blew them out 9–6. In Game 3, back at the Met Center, Minnesota scored four first-period goals in a 6–3 win, sweeping the hated Bruins out of the playoffs.

After reseeding the field, Minnesota drew the Adams Division winner Buffalo Sabres in the quarterfinals. These two teams had met one other time in the playoffs—a two-game sweep by Buffalo in 1977. Minnesota won Game 1 4–3 in OT courtesy of a Steve Payne winner with twenty-two seconds left. Minnesota also won Game 2 at Buffalo Memorial Auditorium. The series shifted back to the Met Center. Minnesota won Game 3 6–4. After trailing in Game 4 3–0, the North Stars scored three quick goals (Ciccarelli, Christoff, Payne) in the second period to tie the game before losing in OT 5–4. Minnesota closed out the series in Game 5 4–3 to advance to the semifinals.

Through the first two playoff series, Minnesota was 6–1. The Calgary Flames were just as much of a surprise in the playoffs as the North Stars were. Entering the tournament as a seven seed, they swept the Chicago Black Hawks and then upset Philadelphia in seven games in the quarterfinals. The teams split the first two games at Stampede Corral. The North Star's offense exploded in Games Three and Four, scoring 13 goals in the two games with Ciccarelli's hat trick in Game 4. Flames goalie Pat Riggin, who had 41 saves (on 47 shots) in the games at the Met calmed down in Game 6, allowing only one goal to the North Stars on 34 shots in a 3–1 Flames win to force a Game 6 back in Bloomington. The North Stars advanced to their first ever Stanley Cup after a 5–3 win at the home.

The Stars were serious underdogs against the defending Stanley Cup champion New York Islanders. They were coached by Al Arbor, who the North Stars knew well from his time coaching the St. Louis Blues in the early 1970s. Arbor had taken over the Islanders in 1973—their second year of existence. After a 19-41-18 season in '73, Arbor's Islanders had now made the playoffs seven consecutive seasons. In 1980, they upset the 116-point Philadelphia Flyers for their first championship. In 1981, they proved their 1980 championship run wasn't a fluke, tallying 110 points and cruising through the first three rounds of the playoffs, sweeping Toronto, beating Wayne Gretzky's Edmonton Oilers in six games, and then sweeping the New York Rangers in the conference championship.

The Stars played the Islanders four times in the regular season and were 0–2–2 and had allowed 17 goals in the four games. So they knew all about the top line of Bryan Trottier, Mike Bossey, and Clark Gillies—three players that would end up in the Hockey Hall of Fame. Goaltender Billy Smith and defenseman and team captain Denis Potvin would also be enshrined in Toronto when their careers were over. Bossey had scored 68 goals and assisted on 51 more in 1981. Trottier, Gilles, Bob Bourne, and Anders Kallur were also 30+ goal scorers for a New York offense that ranked first in the NHL that season with 355, which was the fifth most in NHL history at the time (it now ranks twenty-sixth).

The Stars were also without one of their prime players in the playoffs: center Tim Young was recovering from minor knee surgery after getting hurt in the Boston series. He had the surgery ten days before the start of the finals. And after going through extensive physical therapy to get the knee ready to play, it wasn't at 100 percent yet.

"I think I could play, if they want me on spot duty," he said. "But I don't think I can play a regular shift yet."

In Game 1, the Islanders showed the North Stars that they were the best team in the NHL. They took advantage of Minnesota's youth and inexperience. After Kallur scored the first goal of the game on Gilles Meloche, he and Trottier each scored shorthanded goals within forty-eight seconds of each other to take a 3–0 lead. Kallur's shorthanded goal set a new NHL playoff record with their ninth shorthanded goal of the playoffs.

Early in the second period, in a scrum for the puck along the boards, one of New York's best penalty killers, Butch Goring, dove into the pile for the puck and took Dino Ciccarelli's skate to the face, which cut his lip and tongue. After a dozen stiches, he reentered the game and continued playing.

Billy Carrol made it 4–0 midway through the second period as the Islanders dominated every aspect of the game. The Stars finally broke through the Islanders' defense and scored a goal on Smith at 13:04 in the second (Kent-Erik Andersson). The Islanders retook a three-goal advantage less than a minute later and went on to win 6–3.

"They're going to play their game every night," Sonmor said after the game. "We've got to come up a notch or two to get to their level."

Sonmor started rookie Don Beaupre in the net for Game 2 but saw the same result: a 6–3 loss. But while the final score was the same on paper, the Islanders had to work a lot harder in Game 2 than in Game 1.

"You see this?" winger Bob Nystrom joked after the game while holding a soaked T-shirt. "I got some sweat there. Most times, you get a big lead and the other team says 'We'll pack our bags and leave.' But these guys keep coming at you. Every shift was tough out there tonight."

Ciccarelli gave the Stars their first lead of the Cup Finals with a power play goal 3:38 into the game, but the lead lasted less than a minute. The Isles went on their own power play after a Fred Barrett holding penalty, and Mike Bossey took advantage, tying the game at the 4:33 mark. Nystrom and Denis Potvin would add goals in the period as well, taking a 3–1 into the locker room.

Brad Palmer got the Stars within one with a thirty-five-foot laser past Billy Smith midway through the second period for the only goal in the period. And thirty seconds into the third period, Steve Payne scored the equalizer to tie the game at 3–3. Payne was assisted by Tim Young, who was playing in his first game after having knee surgery only ten days earlier.

On the Payne goal, Smith dove to his left and slammed his elbow into the goal pipe and sprawled on the ice in pain as concern grew around his condition. Smith (who was claimed by the Islanders from the LA Kings in the 1972 Expansion Draft and was a future Conn Smyth winner, Venzia Trophy winner, and Hall of Famer) had only allowed 2.54 goals per game in the playoffs; and his playing injured or Arbor having to substitute him for Glenn Resch or Roland Melanson should have been a huge break for the Stars, who were now riding the momentum at Nassau Coliseum.

Smith took a couple minutes to shake off the pain and returned to the net. "I've been in pain before, but that pain has never been in my elbow. The guys really came to my rescue after I got hurt. It was like they said 'Hey, let's protect Smitty.' It was like they built a cement wall around me the rest of the game."

Captain Denis Potvin skated over to the bench and rallied his defense. "We've got no lead to protect now. Everybody started working harder. When the going gets tough, boy, do we get going."

Povin rifled in a power play goal to retake the lead with twelve minutes for his second goal of the game. Then he assisted on a Ken Morrow goal that went between the legs of Beaupre. Bossy scored his second goal of the game with three minutes left to put the icing on the 6–3 win. Trottier assisted on Bossy's second goal, which gave him a point in fifteen straight playoff games, breaking Bobby Orr's record.

"We're only down 2–0," said Tim Young after the game. "We skated better tonight and passed better. We've still got to go better than this, but we're going home now. They got two wins in their building. But they've got to win two more, and we're not out of it by any means."

The Stars returned home with 15,784 fans filling the Met and jumped out to an early 3–1 lead in Game 3. Steve Christoff scored on the power play three minutes and twenty-five seconds into the game, then Steve Payne scored his fifteenth goal of the playoffs at 14:09. Mike Bossy scored his third goal in two games at 14:47, then Bobby Smith gave the Stars the 3–1 lead.

"We knew the North Stars were going to come out storming," Bossy said. "But I really haven't seen anything that has shaken our confidence to a point where we can't do anything about it."

"The New York Rangers had us down 3–1 in our own building in the semifinals," Butch Goring added. "We just said, 'Hey, let's settle down, get it in their and end and get on 'em.'"

That's exactly what they did:

The same Butch Goring who caught the skate to the face and needed forty stitches to put him back together during Game 1 scored twice in the second period, and Bob Nystrom added another one as the 3–1 Stars lead became a 4–3 deficit at the end of the second period.

But the Stars battled back and rallied to tie the game at 4–4 after Payne scored his second goal of the game at 1:11 in the third. But just fifty-six seconds later, Bossy put the puck past Gilles Meloche for his second goal of the game. It was like Payne and Bossy were having a little competition in Game 3. Steve Payne's first period goal tied him with Bossy at 15, but Bossy scored thirty-eight seconds later to retake the lead at 16. When Payne tied him again in the third, Bossy took the goals lead again only fifty-six seconds later.

"I don't know," Bossy said when asked about it after the game. "I think it's more important to get right back ahead after they tied it 4–4."

Goring completed the Game 3 hat trick (the fourteenth of his career) with his third goal at 6:34 to make it 6–4 Islanders. But the Stars kept fighting. Ciccarelli grabbed the puck behind Billy Smith in the Islanders' net, brought it out to the left side, and went five-hole on Smith to trim the deficit to one. The goal gave Ciccarelli one in each game so far, set the rookie playoff goals record to 14, and tied him for postseason points by a rookie.

Sonmor pulled Meloche late in the period in an attempt to get the equalizer, but an empty netter by Trottier put the Islanders by two with forty-five seconds left as they went on to win 7–5 after trailing 3–1.

"Sometimes I get lucky," Goring told reporters after the game. "And sometimes we play better when we have to come from behind. That's why we're such a great hockey club. We're deep from the goalie on out. Everyone can do their job."

The Islanders won every series-clinching game on the road during their 1981 playoff run: at Toronto, at Edmonton, and at the Rangers, and now they had a chance to do it again in Minnesota.

John Gilbert of the *Star Tribune* described the feeling in the Stars locker room before Game 4 as "eerie."

"Sometimes you can tell when the team is not going to play well and may get blown away," said Al MacAdam. "And sometimes you can tell when we're going to play extremely well too. It was quiet, a funny feeling. I definitely didn't get the feeling we'd come out flying. Looking back on it, maybe it was just a feeling that this could be it."

It was the first time the Stars had faced an elimination game that postseason. It didn't help that the injury report was full of Stars: Tim Young would miss Game 4, not because of his knee but because of an ankle injury. Role players Fred Barrett, Jack Carlson, and Tom McCarthy also didn't suit up for the must-win game. Because of the injuries, rookie center Kevin Maxwell (who only played in six regular season games and had a −1 on the season), started on the first line between Al MacAdam and Steve Payne.

Glen Sonmor tried to break the tension with a rousing pregame speech. "They have to beat us once," he said. "And tonight is not the night."

The Islanders set the tone early in the game with Gord Lane scoring his first goal of the playoffs four minutes into the game. Craig Hartsburg responded by scoring a goal for the Stars at 11:34 to tie the game at 1–1.

Game 4 was the first game back for thirty-five-year-old captain Paul Shmyr. Shmyr had been a healthy scratch since Game 5 against Buffalo in the quarterfinals after falling out of favor with management that has ushered in a youth movement and had watched every game since the semifinals from the press box.

"The way I played tonight," Shmyr said, "was my way of showing management that I can still play."

While Shmyr didn't score a goal or record an assist, he flew around the ice, including lowered his shoulder into Denis Potvin, flattening the Islanders captain late in the first.

The Stars matched the intensity of their captain and rode the momentum from there. Al McAdam scored five minutes into the second period to take a 2–1 lead. But Islanders did what they seemed to do all series: respond with a quick goal after a crucial Stars goal. Mike McEwen scored on a power play goal two minutes later to tie the game at 2–2.

The Stars played their best period of hockey of the finals in the third. Steve Payne deflected a Brad Maxwell shot past Billy Smith at the 12:26 mark, then Bobby Smith clinched the victory with a power play goal with less than two minutes left. Maxwell assisted on all four of the Stars goals in the game. Don Beaupre stopped 33 of 35 Islanders shots as they won their first Stanley Cup Finals game in franchise history.

"It was the best game I've ever seen." Lou Nanne said after the game. "[Islanders general manager] Bill Torrey said the same thing."

The Stars won 4–2 to send the series back to Staten Island for Game 5.

"If we come back to win the Cup," an optimistic Lou Nanne said after the game. "Steve Payne should be awarded the Conn Smyth Trophy [for playoff MVP]. The guy has scored 29 points [17 goals and 12 assists] in playoff games. Only Bossy has more. You can't play any better hockey than what Payne has done for us."

"We got the sleeper in the draft in Mike Bossy [first round, fifteenth overall in the 1977 Draft] in 1977," said Islanders chief scout Jim Devallano. "The Stars got the sleeper in Payne in 1978 [second round, nineteenth overall—the Stars had the top pick in the 1978 Draft and selected Bobby Smith]. They got the same caliber player in Payne that we got in Bossy. We would have taken him if they hadn't."

But dropping one game didn't matter much for the Islanders, who knew they were returning home leading 3–1.

"Worried?" Al Arbor scoffed. "Why should we be worried? We won eight games in a row in the playoffs. It was a heck of a game. Too bad we were on the wrong end of the score."

"We came in here realistically looking for a split, and I guess we accomplished that," said Butch Goring. "It's going to be tough for them on the Island."

When Goring was acquired from the LA Kings late in the 1980 season, he was considered to be the final piece of the championship puzzle in New York. On a team flush with future Hall of Famers, the five-foot-nine and 165-pound center had recorded 19 points in twenty-one playoff games to lift the Islanders to their first Stanley Cup championship in 1980. In 1981, he notched 20 points (10 goals, 10 assists) in the playoffs. Goring, a pretty superstitious hockey player, wore the same long underwear the entire 1981 season and is also credited as creating the "playoff beard," which is when a player doesn't shave for the duration of the playoffs.

"People always talk about us having Trottier, Potvin, and Bossy," Wayne Merrick said. "Maybe the rest of us don't get all the publicity, but we're the type of players who keep digging and digging. You watch Butch out there, and he's such a small guy that you figure that if he can do what he's doing, all the rest of us should be able to do the same thing. We have a lot of depth."

The Islanders would need that depth to knock off the Stars in Game 5. Trottier, the best center in hockey, played sparingly with a shoulder injury he suffered in Game 4. Denis Potvin, the best defenseman in hockey, left the game early in the second period after tearing a tendon in his groin.

"This isn't a two-player hockey team." said Billy Smith. "This isn't a two-line hockey team. The other guys knew they had to pick up the slack."

Butch Goring opened the scoring in Game 5 with a power play goal at 5:12—the first of two goals for him in the first. Twenty seconds after Goring's first goal, Wayne Merrick added a goal to make it 2–0 Islanders. Goring's second goal at 10:03 extended the lead to 3–0. Stars rookie Steve Christoff scored with four minutes left in the first to give the Stars their only goal of the game.

Bob Bourne scored with twenty seconds left in the second period, and Mike McEwen piled another one late in the third for a 5–1 Islanders win and their second consecutive Stanley Cup championship.

Goring, with his 20 points, was awarded the Conn Smyth Trophy. Mike Bossy finished with 35 points (17 goals, 18 assists). Steve Payne led the Stars with 29 points (17 goals and 12 assists).

Despite the Stanley Cup Finals loss, Stars fans were optimistic about their team. Steve Payne broke four team records with his 17 postseason goals, which included two overtime goals. Bobby Smith had a playoff-franchise record of 17 assists. Dino Ciccarelli, who was one of seven rookies the Stars used in the playoffs, set an NHL rookie record with 14 playoff goals.

The North Stars won the Norris Division in 1982 with 94 points, but their quest to return to the Stanley Cup Finals was upended after being upset by the Chicago Black Hawks in the opening round. Meanwhile, the Islanders would win two more titles to extend their run of consecutive titles to four—a run that hasn't been matched since.

April 10, 1982
The Twins Acquire Ron Davis

Sometimes, numbers don't tell the entire story about a player's tenure with the team. For example, Ron Davis pitched for the Twins for about four and a half seasons. His 108 saves rank fifth on the franchise saves list, but to say Davis was consistently inefficient would be an understatement.

Ron Davis was a third-round pick by the Chicago Cubs in the 1976 amateur draft out of Blinn College in Brenham, Texas. He never made it to the bigs in his first stint in Chicago as he was traded to the Yankees while still in the minors in exchange for Ken Holtzman. Davis had struggled as a starter with AA Midland in 1978 (3–3, 6.35 ERA in 11 starts) but was converted to a reliever with the Yankees AA system in West Haven where he excelled (9–2, 1.50 ERA, 5 saves in twenty-one appearances).

In 1979, he made his major league debut with the Yankees out of the bullpen when future Hall of Famer Goose Gossage missed time due to an injury. Davis made his major league debut against the Twins, giving up two runs without recording an out in a 7–3 Yankees win. Davis won 14 games out of the bullpen for the Yankees that season and finished tied for fourth in the AL Rookie of the Year voting, which was a tie between Minnesota's John Castino and Toronto's Alfredo Griffin.

By 1980, Davis and Gossage made up a lethal combination at the back end of the Yankees bullpen as Davis developed into one of the best setup men in baseball. From 1979 to 1981, Davis was 27–10 with a 2.86 ERA, 191 strikeouts, and 22 saves in 140 appearances and was named to the AL All-Star Team in 1981.

He was traded to the Twins five days into the 1982 season in a deal that also sent infielder Greg Gagne and pitcher Paul Boris to Minnesota in for infielder Roy Smalley. Manager Billy Gardner and the Twins moved Davis from setup man to the closer role, although he would often be brought in to get more than three outs. In 1982, Davis averaged 1.2 innings every appearance. He had a rough first season with the Twins, posting a 3–9 record with a 4.43 ERA and five blown saves with 53 games finished for a 102-loss Twins team.

In 1983, Gardner used Davis in four-or-more-out situations less, and Davis's numbers reflected that. His ERA came down to 3.34, and he only saw an average of 1.1 innings every appearance as he finished a career-high sixty-one games.

1984 would be the season most fans remember Ron Davis for. In a bounce-back season for the Twins in which they were involved in a pennant race down the stretch for the first time since winning the AL West in 1970, Davis blew a record 14 saves. His ERA climbed back up to 4.55 as the Twins finished in second place to the Kansas City Royals by only three games.

Despite his struggles, the Twins continued to rely on Davis as their closer. In 1986, the Twins had finally had enough of losses as the result of wild pitches, walk-off walks, and home runs. He was traded to the Cubs midway through the 1986 season for relievers George Frazier and Ray Fontenot.

Davis ended his Twins career with a 19–40 record and a 4.51 ERA and 108 saves in 139 chances. No reliever has lost more games in Twins history.

Davis had short stints with the Cubs, LA Dodgers, and San Francisco Giants to end his career. He didn't close another major league ball game ever again.

<<BONUS ACHE>>

Terry Felton

Terry Felton was a second-round pick by the Minnesota Twins in the 1976 MLB draft. He made his debut in September 1979, throwing two innings of shutout baseball in a 10–1 loss to Milwaukee. From 1980 to 1982, Felton would appear in fifty-five total games for the Twins with ten starts. And he wouldn't win any of them.

Felton holds two MLB records: the most consecutive losses to start a career and the most career losses without a win.

Felton's career stat line reads 0–16 with a 5.53 ERA (he was 0–13 with a 4.99 ERA in 1982). The Twins did win six of the fifty-five games he appeared in.

April 19, 1982

Dick Beardsley and the Duel in the Sun

Beardsley is making a move! It's all come down to this! Beardsley and Salazar! The motorcycle has got to get out of the way!
-WBZ-TV coverage of the 1982 Boston Marathon

Minnesota native Dick Beardsley ran his first marathon in Hurley, Wisconsin, in 1977. In each of his next thirteen marathons, he steadily lowered his times. Beardsley is in the Guinness Book of World Records for running a personal best in thirteen consecutive marathons. He had tied for first in the inaugural London Marathon in 1981, crossing the finish line holding hands with Inge Simonsen (Beardsley later said it was because neither of them had ever won a marathon before so they won it together) and had won back-to-back Grandma's Marathons (Duluth) in 1981–82 and set a course record that would stand for thirty-three years (2:09:37).

Beardsley was one of 7,623 runners that entered the Boston Marathon in 1982 in a field that included four-time Boston Marathon champion Bill Rodgers, Olympian Ed Mendoza, and two-time New York Marathon winner and former NCAA champion Alberto Salazar. Beardsley entered the race as a serious underdog. The day before the race, the Boston Globe referred to him as the Country Bumpkin from Minnesota.

The favorite in the race was Salazar. The former NCAA cross country star from the Boston suburb of Wayland (he was born in Havana, Cuba, but grew up in the US) had the hometown crowd behind him and was one of the fastest men in the world at any distance. The former University of Oregon star owned the world record in the marathon (2:08:13), had the second-fastest American 10K time (27:25), and was a member of the 1980 US Olympic team that boycotted the Moscow Olympics.

Beardsley had run against Salazar once in his career prior to the 1982 Boston Marathon. While Salazar was a senior at the University of Oregon, the two of them were both in the 1980 New York City Marathon. Salazar had never run a marathon before and made headlines by declaring that he would run a sub-2:10:00 race. Beardsley had a great start to the race and led at the eighteen-mile mark as he crossed the Queensboro Bridge. But Salazar caught him and seemed to get stronger as the miles piled up. Salazar cruised to a time of 2:09:41, living up to his sub-2:10:00 promise, the best debut marathon time ever and the first of what would be three consecutive New York City Marathon victories. Beardsley finished ninth with a time of 2:13:55, almost two-thirds of a mile behind Salazar.

Salazar was the best in the world, and he knew it. "There's no other runner here who especially concerns me," Salazar told the reporters before the race. "If [Robert] de Castella or [reigning champion Toshihiko] Seko were competing, it would be different. But looking at the rest of the field . . . I'm the fastest man in the race."

"Alberto wasn't exactly bragging," Beardsley remembered. "He was just extremely confident."

The day of the marathon, April 19, 1982, had a forecasted high of seventy-five degrees. Before the race, Beardsley was making his final preparations: calming his nerves, sipping water, and poking some ventilation holes in the white painter's cap he was going to wear to protect himself from the sun during the race. He made his way to the roped off area where the other pro runners began the race.

And at noon, the gun fired.

Five miles in, the group of pro runners started to separate. But Beardsley stayed in Salazar's back pocket. The large crowds they ran by cheered for Salazar, but Beardsley smiled and waved at them anyways. As the race continued, Beardsley noticed something off about Salazar: he wasn't drinking any water.

There weren't any official water stations at the 1982 Boston Marathon. People in the crowd would hand out cups of water and the runners would grab them, but Salazar always refused. Beardsley would even offer water to him from a cup that he took, but he never accepted.

At the thirteen-mile mark, the race had came down to four runners: Rodgers, Mendoza, Beardsley, and Salazar. By the firehouse at the base of Braeburn Hill just past seventeen-mile marker, thirty-four-year-old Rodgers fell off the pace. Not soon after, Mendoza did the same. Now it was Beardsley and Salazar neck and neck.

Anybody who has ran the Boston Marathon will tell you the toughest part of the race begins at the seventeen-mile mark: Heartbreak Hill. Beardsley had trained in Georgia specifically for the Boston Marathon, not to get away from the brutal winter weather but because of Georgia hilly terrain that was close to what he'd face on Heartbreak Hill. When he'd arrived in Boston in early April to continue his training, he ran the stretch of race in heavy snow and howling wind. Up one side and down the other, eight times.

Heartbreak Hill was where Beardsley planned to open a gap between him and Salazar. His strategy was to run hard for four hundred yards, then back off for two hundred. He'd do that three or four times, but after the fourth one, he would only back off for one hundred yards, hoping to catch Salazar off guard. But Salazar countered every move Beardsley threw at him, and they left Heartbreak Hill in a dead heat.

Around the twenty-two-mile marker, Beardsley could no longer feel his legs. But he kept up the pace with Salazar. He tried to take his mind off the race and think about other things.

"I began to think about a terrible blind date I went on in high school," he says. "I knew it would come in handy, and it did!"

The next thing he knew, he saw One Mile to Go written on the street in gold paint. With one thousand meters to go, Beardsley had the largest lead he had all day—an arm length and a half. The crowds were getting so loud he couldn't hear himself think. The streets were so thick with people that there was barely enough room for Salazar to pass him if he wanted to, let along for the pair to run side by side down Commonwealth Avenue.

But Beardsley knew that Salazar had a kick left him for the stretch. Salazar had a different training regimen than most marathon runners. Usually, runners build up endurance and then speed. Salazar did it the opposite way. He was fast. His 10K time was nearly two minutes faster than Beardsley's career best.

But Salazar was hurting. The decision to not drink any water was catching up to him. His muscles were cramping. He had stopped sweating. His goal at that point was not to lose, especially to some flash in the pan running in a painter's cap. He figured that Beardsley would drop off in the race soon if he kept up his pace.

As Beardsley pushed off with his right leg to start the sprint to the finish, he got a cramp in his right hamstring. He could feel the knot bulging out of his leg. He grabbed his leg and tried to rub the cramp out. Salazar saw that Beardsley was hurting and seized the opportunity to pass him. Salazar's lead increased to about one hundred yards. But Beardsley kept moving on. As he was running along the right side of the road, he stepped in a pothole. He hit the pothole, stumbled, and nearly fell; but when this happened it stretched out his leg and the cramp went away.

Now with about six hundred meters to go, Beardsley had some ground to gain on Salazar. He couldn't see Alberto anymore, but he could see the police motorcade escorting him as he neared the finish line. He picked up his pace.

"I thought to myself, *You could probably walk in from here and get second place*," Beardsley says. "But if you don't give every ounce of energy you have left, you'll regret it for the rest of your life."

Beardsley kicked it into another gear, closing the gap on Salazar. He lowered his head, pumped his arms, weaved his way through the spectators, and was now trailing Salazar by about twenty meters. The final turn of the race was a left-hand turn onto Ring Road, which turned into a straight away for the last hundred yards.

All that stood between Beardsley and Salazar was the fleet of motorcycles surrounding Salazar. Salazar, not the motorcyclists, knew that Beardsley was gaining on them. The first three motorcycles made the left turn onto Ring Road. But the fourth motorcycle didn't make a sharp left turn like the previous three. Unaware that Beardsley was in hot pursuit, the fourth motorcycle veered to the right and cuts off Beardsley.

"Boy, you talk about the perfect excuse," Beardsley recalls. "Everybody would have believed it except the person it mattered to most: me. When it comes down to it, I just plain got outkicked."

Despite the motorcycle mishap, Beardsley continued to close the gap on Salazar, losing by only two seconds and about ten meters. Salazar clocked a new course record of 2:08:52. Beardsley finished second at 2:08:54.

"I remember crossing the finish line and the clock is reading 2:08-something. There was only like one or two other people who had broken 2:09, and I'm thinking, *Wait a minute, I just ran a 2:08, and I finished second!*"

While both men had broken the course record (the current record was set by Geoffrey Mutai in 2011 with a 2:03:02), neither would run a marathon that fast ever again. It was later discovered that the 1982 Boston Marathon course was 150 meters short, so who knows what Beardsley could have done with another 150 meters to work with.

April 7, 1982

Chicago Begins Dominance over Minnesota Hockey

The North Stars and Wild have matched up against the Chicago Black Hawks (renamed the Blackhawks in 1987) in the playoffs nine times, with Chicago winning seven of the matchups. When the North Stars entered the league in 1967, they were placed in the West Division with other expansion teams Philadelphia, Los Angeles, St. Louis, Pittsburgh, and Oakland, while the Original Six (Montreal, New York Rangers, Boston, Toronto, Chicago, Toronto, Detroit) formed the East. The NHL reformatted leagues several times between 1968 and 1982 with the Black Hawks and North Stars popping in and out of each other's division. In 1970 with the addition of the Buffalo Sabres and Vancouver Canucks to the NHL, Chicago joined the West Division with the other expansion teams.

The league added two more teams in 1972: the New York Islanders were added to the East and the Atlanta Flames were put into the West. The Kansas City Scouts and Washington Capitals joined the NHL in 1974, and the NHL split into two divisions within two conference: the Patrick Division and Smyth Division in the Clarence Campbell Conference and Adams Division and Norris Division in the Price of Wales Conference. Vancouver, St. Louis, Kansas City, Chicago, and Minnesota were all in the inaugural Smythe Division. Despite the addition of relocating teams (Kansas City moved to Denver in 1976 then to New Jersey in 1982. The Oakland/California Golden Seals moved to Cleveland in 1976, then they merged with the North Stars in 1978) and new expansion teams (Edmonton Oilers, Winnipeg Jets, Quebec Nordiques, Hartford Whalers in 1979), the rivalry between the North Stars and Black Hawks remained. Before the 1978–79 season, the NHL reformatted their divisions again and shifted the North Stars to the Adams Division of the Price of Wales Conference with Boston, Buffalo, and Toronto, while Chicago remained in the Smyth Division with Vancouver, St. Louis, and the Colorado Rockies.

Divisions shifted again for the 1981–82 season that put Chicago and North Stars in the same division permanently: in the Norris Division with Winnipeg, St. Louis, Toronto, and Detroit. Despite playing in the same division for eight years, they hadn't met in the playoffs until that season.

The 1981–82 North Stars won the Norris Division with 94 points (37–23–20) and were poised to make another run to the Stanley Cup to challenge the New York Islanders for the title. But the 72-point Black Hawks upset them in first round 3–1.

They met again in 1983, this time in the division finals after division champion Chicago had beaten St. Louis 3–1 and Minnesota defeated Toronto 3–1. Minnesota finished second with a franchise record 96 points to Chicago's 104. Chicago knocked the North Stars out of the playoffs for the second straight season 4–1.

A third straight playoff meeting helped stoke the rivalry between the two teams that were located only four hundred miles apart. In 1984, the Black Hawks had fallen from division champs to only 68 points and a fourth-place finish, matching up against division champ Minnesota, who won the division with only 88 points. Chicago took the series to Game 5 of the best-of-five series, but Minnesota won the series for the first time after a 4–1 win at the Met.

Chicago would knock Minnesota out of the postseason two more times in the 1980s: in the 1985 Division Finals at 4–2 and in Game 7 of the 1990 Division Semifinals.

The North Stars did defeat the Blackhawks in the first round (4–2) on their run to the 1991 Stanley Cup Finals in what would be the final time the two teams met in the postseason before the Stars move to Dallas for the 1993–94 season. Chicago won five of the seven playoff series against Minnesota. The Hawks were 90–56–18 against the North Stars, with the Stars winning the season-series only five times in twenty-six seasons.

When Minnesota was awarded an expansion franchise for the 2000–01 season, they were placed in the Western Conference's Northwest Division with Colorado, Edmonton, Vancouver, and Calgary, while the Blackhawks played in the Central with St. Louis, Detroit, Nashville, and Columbus. A lot of fans expected to see the same dominance from Chicago. But instead, the Wild won seventeen of the first twenty-one matchups with Chicago. They didn't meet in the playoffs until 2013 in the first of three consecutive playoff meetings between the two teams. The Wild finished second in their final year in the Northwest Division in 2013 but lost the playoff series with Chicago 4–2. The next season, they joined Chicago in the Central Division. Fans hopes were sky-high after winning a thrilling Game 7 in overtime against Colorado in the opening round, but the Blackhawks beat the Wild 4–2 in the second round. The next season, after the Wild bested the Blues 4–2, Chicago swept them out of the playoffs on their way to the Stanley Cup championship.

After going 17–6 against Chicago from 2000 to 2005, the Wild were 12–26 against them since to drop their overall record to 32–41–1. Chicago is 122–97–19 all-time against the North Stars and Wild combined.

April 27, 1982

The Vikings Draft Darrin Nelson over Marcus Allen

"One play. Nelson. Through his hands. And the Redskins will go to the Super Bowl."
-Pat Summeral during the CBS Broadcast of the 1987 NFC Championship

Nobody in college football had ever put up numbers like running back Darrin Nelson was putting up in 1977. In head coach Bill Walsh's revolutionary West Coast Offense at Stanford, he became the first freshman in PAC-8 history to rush for over a thousand yards in a season. He added fifty receptions out of the backfield and scored 6 touchdowns—3 on the ground and 3 through the air.

In his sophomore season, he ran for another thousand yards with 6 touchdowns and caught another 50 passes for 4 touchdowns.

Nelson missed the 1979 season with a hamstring injury—the same year Bill Walsh left Stanford to become the head coach of the San Francisco 49ers. When Nelson returned to the field for his junior season in 1980, he had future Hall of Fame quarterback sophomore John Elway handing him the ball. That season with Elway, Nelson ran for 889 yards and 4 touchdowns and caught 47 passes for 4 touchdowns. His senior year in 1981 was his best statistical season: 1014 yards and 11 touchdowns on the ground, 846 yards and 5 touchdowns through the air.

He graduated from Stanford as the program's all-time leader in rushing yards, receptions, touchdowns, and scoring, while also setting the NCAA record for all-purpose yards. Nobody had ever run for a thousand yards and caught 50 passes in a single season. Nelson did it three times.

Nelson entered the 1982 NFL Draft as triple-threat running, receiving, and returning back and was the first running back off the board: the seventh overall pick to Bud Grant and the Minnesota Vikings.

Nelson wasn't terrible in Minnesota. He played in 129 games over ten seasons in Minnesota, had 10,377 all-purpose yards, and had scored 23 touchdowns. He was voted as one of the 50 Greatest Vikings during the team's fiftieth anniversary in 2010.

But there are three things that Darrin Nelson is remembered for in Minnesota Vikings lore.

The Vikings finished 8–7 in the 1987 strike-shortened NFL season and backed their way into the playoffs after a 27–24 overtime loss to the Washington Redskins in Week 15. The Vikings found themselves in a rematch with the Redskins in the NFC Championship Game with a trip to San Diego and Super Bowl XXII on the line. The game was a defensive battle, with Vikings quarterback Wade Wilson getting sacked eight times. The Vikings were down 17–10 with fifty-three seconds left in the game, facing fourth down on Washington's six-yard line.

Needing a touchdown to tie, Wilson threw the ball to Nelson, who dropped it in the end zone before being hit by defensive back Darrell Green. Washington would beat Nelson's former Stanford teammate John Elway in the Super Bowl 42–10.

There's always a lot of second-guessing that happens in the years following a draft. At the time, Darrin Nelson was the top running back prospect in the draft. The Vikings needed a running back . . . never mind the fact that Hall of Fame guard Mike Munchak was taken by the Houston Oilers the pick after Nelson. Nelson was the first running back off the board. The second one was selected three picks later out of USC—the 1981 Heisman Trophy winner, 1982 Offensive Rookie of the Year, 1985 NFL MVP, and six-time Pro Bowler Marcus Allen. If the Vikings took Allen instead of Nelson, maybe they wouldn't feel that they needed to trade for Herschel Walker in 1989.

Nelson had a contract dispute with the Vikings prior to the 1989 season and subsequently lost his starting job to D.J. Dozier. He was then packaged with Jesse Solomon, David Howard, Issiac Holt, Alex Stewart, and eight draft picks to the Dallas Cowboys for Herschel Walker. When he refused to report to Dallas, the San Diego Chargers were added as a third team to the deal. Nelson went to San Diego for a fifth-round pick.

June 6, 1983

The Twins Draft Tim Belcher

I'm not going to tell them pointblank not to draft me and I'm not going to say that everything is all right.

—Tim Belcher

The Twins lost a then-franchise record of 102 games in 1982 and were awarded the first pick in the 1983 MLB Draft. It was the first time since the league established the draft in 1965 that the Twins had the first overall pick.

George Brophy, the Twins' farm director, was tasked with choosing the Twins' top draft choice. "There are no clear number ones like Robin Yount, Reggie Jackson, or Dave Winfield," Brophy told the *Star Tribune* in June 1983. The Twins had options with the top pick, including pitchers Stan Hilton from Baylor, Jim Jefferson of Arizona State, Mike Cherry of the Citadel, Darrel Akerfields of Mesa College, and Tim Belcher of Mt. Vernon Nazarene College. Infielders Jeff Kunkel of Rider College, Gary Green of Oklahoma State, Turner Gil of Nebraska, and Chris Sabo of Michigan were also on the Twins' list.

The day before the draft, Twins president Calvin Griffith said that the Twins had narrowed their choice down to two players: Belcher and Kunkel.

Kunkel, the son of AL umpire Bill Kinkel, had hit .399 with 6 home runs, 37 RBI and 12 stolen bases during his final season at Rider College. Belcher only allowed one run in the final 31 innings of his junior season at MVNC, striking out 52 batters along the way. In total, Belcher had a 5–4 record, struck out 93 batters with a 2.86 ERA, and allowed only 33 hits in 66 innings. He had pitched a no-hitter against Kenyon College and threw three straight shutouts.

The issue with whomever the Twins selected was going to be money. Griffith had said that he wouldn't pay more than $100,000 as a signing bonus to the top pick. The Twins had never paid a bonus higher than $70,000 before. Minnesota's top pick in 1982, fourth overall pick Bryan Oelkers, got a Twins-record $69,500 signing bonus.

The Twins drafted Belcher with the first pick in the draft. Future All-Star shortstop Kurt Stillwell went second to Cincinnati. Kunkel was drafted third by the Texas Rangers.

You would think that being the top pick in a draft would be exciting, but Belcher knew he had a battle ahead of him to get paid like one. The price tag that he and his agent, Chicago lawyer Scott Boras, who making his first high-profile signing, set was at $135,000. "What I was asking for wasn't out of line," he later said. "It was what other first-round picks were getting."

The Twins bidding started at $90,000. Boras got Griffith to increase it to a reported $120,500, but he cut the offer when Belcher didn't pitch well for Team USA that summer. Belcher had three options: he could accept the Twins offer and join the team's minor league system, return for his senior season and reenter the draft the next year, or decide not to sign and enter the secondary draft the following January.

He decided not to sign with the Twins and enter the secondary draft. He was taken with the first overall pick by the New York Yankees, but they lost him to the Oakland Athletics due to a loophole in the compensation rules. (The rule allowed teams that lost free agents to draft players who were not on a protected list. Belcher wasn't on the list, so Oakland stole him from New York.) After three years in Oakland's minor league system, he was traded to the LA Dodgers.

He made his debut for the Dodgers in September 1987—the same year the Twins won the World Series without him. It wouldn't take long for him to get a ring though. He finished third in NL Rookie of the Year voting in 1988 after going 12–6 with a 2.91 ERA with 152 strikeouts. He also won three postseason games for the eventual World Series Champion Dodgers that October. He finished sixth in NL Cy Young voting in 1989 after throwing a league-leading eight shutouts.

Belcher pitched in the major leagues for fourteen seasons with seven different teams, compiling a 146–140 record with a career of 4.16 ERA and 1,516 strikeouts in 2,442 career innings.

Prior to Belcher, there had only been one other number 1 pick that didn't sign: catcher Danny Goodwin spurned the White Sox in 1971.

The Twins' draft misfortune didn't end with Belcher in 1981. Second-round pick Billy Swift didn't sign either (he returned to college and reentered the draft in 1984. He was taken second overall by the Seattle Mariners, had a thirteen-year career and won the NL ERA Title with the San Francisco Giants in 1992 and was runner-up for the NL Cy Young in 1993). They drafted Oddibe McDowell with the first pick in the secondary draft, but he didn't sign either (he also returned to school and was taken twelfth overall by the Texas Rangers in the 1984 Draft. He had a seven-year MLB career).

It adds salt to the wound when you mention that 300-game winner Roger Clemens was the nineteenth overall pick to the Boston Red Sox that year.

<<BONUS ACHE>>

Steve Garvey and Mark Grace

The Twins Steve Garvey in the third round of the 1966 amateur draft, but he decided to play football at Michigan State instead. Garvey would decide to play baseball and was drafted thirteenth overall by the Los Angeles Dodgers in 1968. He'd become a ten-time All-Star and two-time All-Star Game MVP. He'd win the 1974 NL MVP, two NLCS MVPs, and a World Series title with the LA Dodgers in 1981. He led the majors in games played six times, finished second twice, and holds the National League record for consecutive games played (1,207). During his nineteen-year career (fourteen with the Dodgers and five with the San Diego Padres), Garvey hit .294 with 272 home runs, 1308 RBI, collected 2,599 hits, and would lead his teams to five World Series appearances from 1974 to 1984. He won four Gold Glove awards and had six 200-hit seasons. He has a career postseason average of .338 with 11 home runs and 31 RBI in fifty-one career postseason games.

The Twins also drafted first baseman Mark Grace out of Saddleback College (Mission Viejo, California) in the fifteenth round of the 1984 Major League Baseball draft, but instead he transferred to San Diego State University. The following season, he was selected by the Chicago Cubs in the twenty-fourth round, where he signed. Grace made his major league debut for the Cubs in 1988, and after a sixteen-year major league career, the three-time All-Star boasted a .303 average with 2,445 hits, four Gold Gloves, and a World Series ring with the Arizona Diamondbacks in 2001.

September 17, 1983

84-13

All we have heard is that Nebraska is going to run all over us, but team-wise and coach-wise, we think we can give them a game.
—Randy Rasmussen, Gopher captain

Most of the Joe Salem coaching era of Minnesota Golden Gophers football is forgettable. The former Gopher backup quarterback had success coaching South Dakota and Northern Arizona, where he was a combined 77–56–2 from 1966 to 1978. During his tenure as head coach with the Gophers from 1979 to 1983, the Gophers were 19–35–1 overall and 12–33–1 in the Big Ten.

There were a couple positive moments during those years: three straight wins against Iowa including a 12–10 win when the Hawkeyes were ranked #6 in 1981, a 31–14 win over a #12 Purdue team in 1979, a 35–31 win over a #18 Ohio State team in 1981, and a 4–0 record against Ohio of the MAC with whom they opened the season with four out of five years during his tenure. And that's scraping the bottom of the barrel.

Salem's teams were 3–12 against ranked teams, but the game that fans haven't been able to erase from their memories was a laugher at the Metrodome against #1 Nebraska in September 1983.

The Gophers were coming off a 3–8 season that saw them ranked #19 before losing eight consecutive games to finish the season. There was optimism in the locker room that they could improve on that record, but it would be tough. At the end of the season, five of the Gophers' eleven opponents would be ranked in the top 11.

It started wiith Nebraska. The Cornhuskers were already 2–0 and had beaten #4 Penn State 44–6 to open the season. Led by 1983 Heisman-winner running back Mike Rozier, wide receiver Irving Fryar, quarterback Turner Gill, and several other future Hall of Famers, Nebraska would average 52 points per game that season.

As they rolled into the Metrodome, Salem had a plan: the Husker Defense. His game plan was to stack the line of scrimmage to stop Rozier and blitz the quarterback on every play to create pressure. The problem? It left a couple players wide open. In the instance the blitz wasn't well timed or happened away from the play, it would create huge plays for the offense.

During the game, the Gophers were showed they were young and inexperienced. The injury bug didn't help them either. Starting running back Alan Reid broke his arm. His backup, Tony Hunter, also got hurt during the game. Starting safety Craig White was also replaced by a freshman after he got hurt. The only points the Gophers would score were on two Jim Gallery field goals and a one-yard David Puk touchdown run. The Gophers ran for 162 yard and had 21 first downs.

Nebraska, on the other hand, figured out the Husker Defense and racked up 790 yards of total offense. The Husker Defense didn't stop the run as Salem had planned. It allowed Nebraska to rack up 595 yards on the ground on 55 carries. They scored 12 touchdowns:

- A 27-yard touchdown run by Mark Schellen
- A 68-yard touchdown pass to Fryar from Gill
- A 70-yard touchdown pass to Fryar from Gill
- A 41-yard touchdown run by Fryar
- A 12-yard touchdown run by Jeff Smith
- A 7-yard touchdown run by Rozier
- A 1-yard touchdown run by Rozier
- A 12-yard touchdown run by Gill
- A 78-yard touchdown run by Rozier
- A 51-yard touchdown pass to Smith from Craig Sundberg
- A 44-yard touchdown run by Sundberg
- A 1-yard touchdown run by Sundberg

At the end of the day, it was an 84–13 Nebraska win. Nebraska's reserves were so tired that head coach Tom Osborne had to bring some of his starters back into the game to rest his backups. The 84 points scored by Nebraska were the most ever against an NCAA Division 1 opponent and the most the program had put up since a 100–0 win over Nebraska Wesleyan in 1917.

All sixty players that Nebraska brought got into the game before the start of the fourth quarter. Irving Frayer broke the NCAA wingback single game receiving yards record with 138 yards on just two catches.

The Gophers would go 1–10 that season, sneaking by Rice 21–17 in the opening week. Joe Salem would lose his job at the end of the year after losing the last four games by a combined score of 204–53.

April 24, 1984

The 1984 Clarence Campbell Conference Finals

In 1984, Wayne Gretzky was on his way to becoming "the great one." In his first four seasons in the NHL, the Hall of Fame center had scored 269 goals and tallied 709 points in 319 career games. He had won four consecutive Hart Memorial Trophies (given to the league's most valuable player), three consecutive Art Ross trophies (given to the league's top scorer), and two consecutive Lester Pearson awards (given to the most outstanding player voted on by the NHL).

The one thing he hadn't been able to do was hoist the Stanley Cup.

Edmonton was swept by Philadelphia in the first round of Gretzky's rookie year in 1979–80. In 1980–81, they swept Vancouver in the first round before losing in six games to the New York Islanders, who were in the middle of their run of four straight championships. In 1981–82, they were upset by a twenty-four-win LA Kings team in five games. In 1982–83, they finally reached the Stanley Cup Finals before being swept by the Islanders for their fourth straight Stanley Cup.

But this isn't a book about Edmonton's playoff woes (they'd win five Cups between 1984 and 1990). This is a book about Minnesota's ineptitude.

In the 1983–84 season, the North Stars won their second Norris Division championship in three years. At 39-31-10 (88 points), the North Stars were the only division winner not to win at last forty-nine games and have fewer than 100 points.

In fact, eight other franchises (Edmonton, Boston, Buffalo, Quebec, NY Islanders, Washington, Philadelphia, NY Rangers) had more points than the North Stars.

During their Stanley Cup Finals run in 1981, the North Stars were an underdog in almost every series as well. Brian Bellows, Neal Broten, and Dino Ciccarelli were up for the challenge.

In the first round of the playoffs, the North Stars drew rival Chicago… the team that had eliminated Minnesota from the postseason the past two seasons.

The 68-point Black Hawks won Game 1 in Bloomington at 3–1. In Game 2, the North Stars needed some late-game heroics. Tied at 3–3 after the second period, Al MacAdam and Willi Plett each scored to give Minnesota a 5–3 lead. A Denis Savard goal trimmed the lead to 5–4 before Neal Brotten scored to make it 6–4. A late Darryl Sutter goal made it a one-goal game before Minnesota's defense locked down to give the North Stars a 6–5 Game 2 win.

Game 3 at Chicago Stadium went to Minnesota 4–1 to give the North Stars a 2–1 series lead. Game 4 saw Minnesota lose a 3–2 midway through the third period to lose 4–3.

The North Stars never trailed in the decisive Game 5 at the Met Center, winning 4–1 to take the series. The semifinal round matched the North Stars up against the St. Louis Blues, who had defeated the Detroit Red Wings in four games. The two teams split the first four games of the series. In Game 5, the North Stars shut the Blues out 6–0. St. Louis responded in Game 6 by shutting Minnesota out 4–0. A decisive Game 7 was played at the Met Center and was tied at the end of regulation. A Steve Payne goal gave Minnesota the series win in overtime and a date with the Edmonton Oilers in the Conference Finals.

After going 2–0 in elimination games, the North Stars were confident into their tough match up against Edmonton. They'd need more than confidence against a team that featured eight 20+ goal scorers (Gretzky had 87 by himself) and six future Hall of Famers (Anderson, Fuhr, Gretzky, Kurri, Messier, and Coffey).

The series wasn't even close. Edmonton outscored Minnesota 22–10 in the four-game sweep. Five of Minnesota's goals came in an 8–5 Game 3 loss with Andy Moog in net. The Oilers would dethrone the New York Islanders in the Stanley Cup finals, winning their first of five Stanley Cups in the 1980s and ending the Islanders streak of Stanley Cup championships at four. And just like in 1981, the North Stars were once again a footnote of one of the greatest dynasties in NHL history.

November 7, 1984

Willie Hernandez wins 1984 AL MVP over Kent Hrbek

I never finished second in the World Series, did I?

—Kent Hrbek

When you look at the retired numbers near the Budweiser Roof Deck at Target Field, you see that there are a lot of individual accomplishments among Harmon Killebrew, Tony Oliva, Joe Mauer, Rod Carew, Bert Blyleven, and Kirby Puckett. There are MVPs, Gold Gloves, Rookie of the Year awards, Batting Titles, Hall of Fame plaques, and 57 combined All-Star Game appearances among the six legends. But there is one number hanging that lacks the individual accolades, and some argue they should have added one in 1984.

The Minnesota Twins weren't on anybody's radar in 1984. Most of Calvin Griffith's young core of Tom Brunansky, Gary Gaetti, Frank Viola, Tim Laudner, and Kent Hrbek were entering their third major league season and had seen a lot of growing pains on the way.

Through his first two seasons, future Cy Young winner Frank Viola had gone 11–25 with a 5.38 ERA. The Twins bullpen was a mess (Twins closer Ron Davis lost seventeen games between 1982 and 1983). The bright spot was the Class of '82 Twins, specifically Kent Hrbek.

Hrbek was an All-Star and finished second in AL Rookie of the Year voting (behind Cal Ripken Jr.) in 1982. Hrbek had signed with the Twins out of high school in 1978 and made the jump from Single-A to the majors in August of 1981. In 1982, he hit .311 with 23 home runs in 140 games. Even though the future Hall of Famer Ripken played in twenty more games than Hrbek, their stats were comparable. The one big difference? Hrbek's Twins lost 102 games. Ripken's Orioles won 94.

The Twins were "better" in 1983, finishing the season with a 70–92 record. But 1984 is when it seemed it was all coming together.

The rotation was solid. Frank Viola broke out, winning eighteen games. Mike Smithson and John Butcher, both acquired from Texas in a trade for Gary Ward, combined to win twenty-eight more.

And Hrbek was lights-out. He hit .311 with 28 home runs and 107 RBI (the only 100+ RBI season of his career). The Twins were leading the AL West by 5.5 games on August 22nd and were still leading the division on September 23 with eight games to play. But the Twins would lose the last six games of the season, including 2 blown saves in the last four games by Ron Davis (who would tie an AL record with 14 blown saves in 1984). After blowing a 10–0 lead in Cleveland down the stretch, Gaetti was questioned about a crucial throwing error in the game and replied, "It's tough to throw to first base with both hands around your neck." The Twins finished 81–81 and four games behind the Kansas City Royals in the AL West.

During those last six games, Hrbek was 4–22 (.182) with no home runs and 3 RBI. Had the Twins finished over .500 and won the division, Hrbek likely would have been the MVP, taking the Twins from fifth place in 1983 to a division title in 1984.

Regardless, people gave Hrbek a lot of credit for the turnaround, and he was considered a legitimate MVP candidate.

Unfortunately, there was a problem. Well, two of them.

There were two dominant relievers in the American League in 1984: Willie Hernandez of the Detroit Tigers (9–3, 1.92 ERA, 32 SV, 112 K) and Dan Quisenberry of the Kansas City Royals (6–3, 2.64 ERA, 41 SV). Hernandez and Quisenberry would finish first and second in the AL Cy Young voting, and baseball writers were going to cast their votes for the relievers for the league MVP as well.

Looking back at 1984, there were a lot of players that put up better numbers than Hrbek. Was he the most dominant first baseman that season? Eddie Murray (.306, 29 HR, 110 RBI, 7.1 WAR); Don Mattingly (.343, 23 HR, 110 RBI, 6.3 WAR); and Rookie of the Year Alvin Davis (.284, 27 HR, 116 RBI, 5.9 WAR) all had equal or better statistical seasons. Cal Ripken had the highest WAR (10.0) out of any player that season. What made Hrbek such an interesting candidate for MVP was the fact that he had led his team from 102 losses in 1982 to the doorstep of an AL West title two years later.

But was it enough?

> Numbers-wise it was my best year. I hit .311 with 27 homers and 107 RBI. But you know how a lot of people don't believe a pitcher should be considered an MVP candidate, being that

> they have their own award—the Cy Young? Well, they gave the MVP award to Detroit reliever Willie Hernandez. My rookie season, when I hit .301 and drove in 92 runs, I finished second to Cal Ripken for Rookie of the Year. I guess I'm just a second-place kind of guy when it comes to awards. But I never finished second in the World Series, did I? (Kent Hrbek from *Tales from the Minnesota Twins Dugout*)

The panel of twenty-eight writers cast their ballots, and when the results came in, it was Willie Hernandez that won the MVP with sixteen first-place votes and a total of 306 points. Hrbek finished second with five first-place votes and 247 points. Quisenberry also got five first-place votes but had a point total of 235. Murray drew the other two first-place votes and finished with 197 points.

Hrbek became the first Twin to finish second in the AL MVP vote (it was won by Zoilo Versalles in 1965, Harmon Killebrew in 1969, and Rod Carew in 1977).

Oddly enough, Quisenberry won the Rolaids Relief Man of the Year, not Hernandez. The Rolaids award is decided by a point system, not a writer's vote. So Hernandez, a reliever that won the Cy Young Award and the MVP, wasn't named the league's best reliever in 1984.

The Tigers acquired Hernandez from the Philadelphia Phillies in a three-team trade during the final weeks of spring training in 1984 and, with Hernandez leading the charge out of the bullpen, won their first American League Pennant since 1968 with Hernandez converting 32 of 33 save opportunities. The Tigers had four players in the top 10 in MVP voting (Hernandez, Kirk Gibson finished sixth, Alan Trammell was ninth, and Willie Wilson placed tenth.)

Since the inception of the Cy Young Award in 1956 to the season prior to Hrbek's should-have-been-MVP season, the AL MVP had been given to a pitcher only three times: Denny McLain in 1968 (31-6, 1.82 ERA), Vida Blue in 1971 (24-8, 1.82 ERA), and Rollie Fingers in 1981 (6-3, 1.04 ERA, 28 SV). Roger Clemens also won one in 1986, and Justin Verlander was the AL MVP in 2014. Prior to the Cy Young Award, Lefty Grove, Spud Chandler, Hal Newhouser (Newhouser won two), and Bobby Shantz also won MVP awards.

The first question to ask is, Who is eligible to win the MVP? This is, according to the BBWAA, the definition of league MVP:

> Dear Voter: There is no clear-cut definition of what Most Valuable means. It is up to the individual voter to decide who the Most Valuable Player in each league to his team. The MVP need not come from a division winner or other playoff qualifier.
>
> The rules of the voting remain the same as they were written on the first ballot in 1931:

1. Actual value of a player to his team, that is, strength of offense and defense.
2. Number of games played.
3. General character, disposition, loyalty and effort.
4. Former winners are eligible.
5. Members of the committee may vote for more than one member of a team.

You are also urged to give serious consideration to all your selections, from 1 to 10. A 10th-place vote can influence the outcome of an election. You must fill in all 10 places on your ballot. Only regular-season performances are to be taken into consideration.

Keep in mind that all players are eligible for MVP, including pitchers and designated hitters.

Even the BBWAA says there is no clear-cut definition of what Most Valuable means. Number 1: value of a player to his team, both offense and defense. Hrbek's offensive numbers speak for themselves, but what people often overlook is his defensive ability. People often discounted Hrbek's defense because he was a bigger guy. During Hrbek's fourteen-year career, the AL Gold Glove at first base was awarded to either Eddie Murray or Don Mattingly thirteen times (Mark McGwire won the other one). Hrbek does have a Gold Glove in his basement, however—one of Gary Gaetti's. Gaetti gave him his 1988 Gold Glove because if it weren't for Hrbek making great plays at first, Gaetti may not have ever won any.

Also, look at number two: games played. In 1984, Willie Hernandez appeared in 80 games. He threw 140 innings (averaging 1.2 IP per appearance). Kent Hrbek played 149 games, 13 of those were extra inning games and only left five games early due to injury or a pinch hitter. You often hear the argument that despite playing in fewer games, pitchers face as many batters in a season as offensive players get plate appearances. Willie Hernandez faced 548 hitters in 1984, meaning hitters had 548 chances to score off him.

Hrbek had 635 plate appearances that season.

The landscape of baseball was changing in the mid-1970s. Pitchers weren't making 40+ starts or throwing 300+ innings anymore. Teams had begun using relief specialists. The save became an official stat in 1969, and the baseball writers were putting too much stock into it. It was around the same time that people started getting the idea that baseball inside domed stadiums was a good idea.

Pitchers should have their award, and hitters should have their award. As it stands right now, pitchers have the Cy Young award (established in 1956), and hitters have the Hank Aaron award (created in 1999). There are also the Silver

Sluggers, which are given to the best power hitter from each position, NL pitchers and AL DHs included.

And while winning the Cy Young establishes the recipient as the best (and most valuable) pitcher, the Hank Aaron award doesn't do that. Subtracting the years that Justin Verlander (2011) and Clayton Kershaw (2014) won the MVP award in their respective leagues, the same player has won both the MVP and Hank Aaron Award in the same season fifteen times (15/34)—only 44 percent of the time. In 2014, Giancarlo Stanton finished second in the NL MVP voting behind Kershaw and won the NL Hank Aaron award, and in 2011 Jacoby Ellsbury finished second in the AL MVP voting. But José Bautista won the AL Hank Aaron. And of those fifteen, Barry Bonds has three, and Alex Rodriguez and Miguel Cabrera each have two.

The award itself is very inconsistent. When it was first awarded in 1999, it was given to Manny Ramirez and Sammy Sosa based on a point system that factored in hits, home runs, and RBI. From 2000 to 2002, a three-name point system ballot was given to MLB broadcasters. In 2003, an online fan ballot was added. From 2004 to 2006, fans voted for each team's top hitter in August, then an MLB panel chose the top six, then fans voted for the best of the final six.

From 2007 to 2008, five finalists from each league were voted on by the fans from thirty nominees from that MLB panel, then fans voted for the winner. Since 2009, fans vote for both the finalists and overall winners of the award.

There are Silver Slugger awards (given to the best hitter at each position), Batting Titles (awarded to the highest batting average), and overall Statistical Champions (RBI champion, home run leader, doubles champion, etc.).

It's a shame that when you think of great first basemen of the 1980s, Kent Hrbek isn't one of the first names to come to mind. He was an All-Star only once in his career. Even with the Twins leading the AL West in 1987, Kirby Puckett was the lone representative for the Twins . . . as a reserve (despite only playing 31 games in centerfield in the first half, Rickey Henderson was voted as the starting centerfielder). Adding an MVP to his resume would have been a great springboard for what was to come for the Twins in the next couple years, would have put the national spotlight on Minneapolis, and would have added another MVP to the resume of retired numbers at Target Field.

November 27, 1985
Lou Holtz Abandons the Gophers

*There isn't a job in the country I'd leave Minnesota for . . .
with the possible exception of Notre Dame.*

—Lou Holtz

The Gophers hired Lou Holtz as their football coach in 1984 after a disastrous 1–10 season in 1983 after five other coaches declined the head coach position. Holtz had spent the previous seven seasons as the head coach of the Arkansas Razorbacks, compiling a 54–16–2 record. The Gophers were 19–35–1 (12–32–1 in conference play) the previous five years under Joe Salem.

Holtz saw his win totals steadily decline in his seven years at Arkansas, beating a Barry Switzer-coached Oklahoma team in the Orange Bowl in 1977 to missing a Bowl game all together in 1983—the first time he had missed a Bowl game with the Razorbacks. While it was initially reported that Holtz had resigned, former Arkansas athletic director later said that he fired Holtz because he lost the fan base.

Prior to his time with the Gophers, Lou spent three seasons as the head coach of William & Mary (13–12), four seasons at NC State (33–12–3), and most of a season with the New York Jets (3–10), having jumped ship for Arkansas with one game left in the 1976 season.

Holtz and the Gophers agreed to a five-year contract prior to his arrival. In 1984, he coached the Gophers to a 4–7 in his first season, with wins against rivals Wisconsin (17–14) and Iowa (23–17). And, he only lost to #1 Nebraska 38–7 (the final score was 84–13 the previous year).

In 1985, Holtz had the program turned around. On October 22, they were the twentieth ranked team in the country—the program's first top 25 ranking since September 27, 1982, a year in which the Gophers finished 3–8 and 1–8 in the Big Ten. In '85, Holtz and the Gophers were 6–5 and finished 4–4 in the Big

Ten; the first time the team didn't have a losing conference record since 1978. It was the biggest two-year turnaround since Murray Warmath took a 1–8 team in 1958 to the Rose Bowl in 1960.

With the 6–5 record, the Gophers were invited to their first Bowl game since 1977. But Holtz wouldn't be there to lead his team to the Independence Bowl.

Although he was under contract, there was a clause in his deal that said he could leave for Notre Dame if offered the head coaching job of the Fighting Irish. When Notre Dame coach Gerry Faust stepped down in following a 5–6 1985 season (one of only five losing seasons since 1899), the door opened. After rumors swirled that UCLA's Terry Donahue, Virginia's George Welsh, Maryland's Bobby Ross, and former UCLA and Philadelphia Eagles coach Dick Vermeil were tied to the legendary position, Holtz was named the new head coach of the Fighting Irish on November 27, 1985.

The Gophers, coached by John Gutekunst, beat Clemson 20–13 in the Independence Bowl.

Holtz's Minnesota legacy wouldn't end with his 10–12 record in 1985. In 1991, the NCAA hit Minnesota with a 1992 bowl ban and two years of probation for a situation in which he gave U of M quarterback Roselle Richardson $200 in 1985 after Richardson had his wallet stolen. Holtz claimed that it was only $20, but he was told that it "doesn't matter whether it's $20 or $200, it's still a rules violation." (The Gophers were 2–9 in 1992 and didn't get a bowl invite anyways).

While at Notre Dame, Holtz went 100–30–2 in eleven seasons, including winning the 1988 NCAA Championship. After he left Minnesota, the two other programs he worked for (Notre Dame and South Carolina) were also hit with NCAA sanctions.

January 23, 1986

Room 308

The way the university and media painted it, we were guilty, and we hadn't even had a day in court yet.

—George Williams

Jim Dutcher took over the Gopher men's basketball program in 1975 following Bill Musselman's departure to the ABA's San Diego Sails, leaving the program with 128 NCAA violations. The Gophers wouldn't have a losing season under Dutcher until 1984–85 (13–15, 6–12 in the Big Ten). They won the Big Ten Title in 1982 and made a run to the Sweet Sixteen.

The Gophers were 13–5 in 1986 after a Todd Alexander jump hook at the buzzer beat Wisconsin 67–65 at the Wisconsin Field House on Thursday, January 23. Next up for the Gophers was last place Northwestern, who had just been drubbed by Iowa 76–43. The Gophers were on a three-game winning streak and had beaten #2 Michigan the week before. There was a real possibility of not only an NCAA tournament berth but another Big Ten title too.

After the Wisconsin game, the team went back to the Concourse Hotel. Some Gophers fans had a party on the tenth floor of the hotel, which was attended by a few Gophers players, including starting forward George Williams. According to eyewitnesses, Williams was at the party from 1:00 to 3:00 a.m., then left.

Meanwhile, players Kevin Smith and Mitch Lee were heading back to the hotel after meeting an eighteen-year-old female art student from Madison Area Technical College at an outside party. At some point that night, all four of them found themselves in Room 308.

Early the next morning, the team was getting ready to fly home to get ready for the Northwestern game coming up that weekend. Mitch Lee called the Concourse around 6:30 that morning to ask if he'd forgotten his wallet in his room—Room 308. A bellhop ran up to the room to look for the wallet but found the door locked from the inside. He called the room, and a woman answered the phone. She said she had been raped for over two hours by three members of the Minnesota basketball team. Assistant Coach Jimmy Williams, who had remained at the hotel after the team had left, was contacted by hotel staff. He tried calming the woman down by talking to her through the door until the police arrived.

Meanwhile, Lee, Smith, Williams, and the basketball team were boarding their plane back to Minneapolis. Dutcher was paged and informed of the allegations from the hotel.

"I was in disbelief," Dutcher told the *LA Times*. "My first thought was that nobody on my team could be that dumb. I just didn't think the guys would jeopardize their future, my future, the program's future with something like that."

Dutcher had his players get off the plane, where they were met on the tarmac by five squad cars. With them was the woman from Room 308 in an unmarked car. Each player was ordered to walk to the darkened windows of the car in a mock police lineup, making half turns and standing directly toward the window.

Each player walked past the car twice, before the woman identified Lee and Smith. They were arrested and taken to the Dane County Jail. Four other players were taken in for questioning, and by the afternoon, Lee, Smith, and Williams were all jailed.

Coach Williams stayed in Madison to act as liaison for the university. He oversaw midnight curfew check that night. He checked the halls and didn't see anybody. He didn't hear anything unusual from the rooms either. He didn't knock on doors to make a sight check like he usually did.

"The next game was three days away," he told the *Star Tribune*. "I just didn't think it was needed. Besides, I saw a lot of the players in the hotel anyway. It bothers me that she could have gotten on the floor without us knowing."

Attorneys for the three players tried to arrange a special bail hearing on Saturday, but the hearing was denied. The three players spent the weekend in jail.

This was the second rape allegation against Mitchell Lee and the program in the last year. In late January 1985, Lee, then a freshman, was charged with raping a twenty-year-old woman in a campus dorm. He had been acquitted in that sexual assault case only a week before being arrested in Wisconsin.

Lee and Smith were charged with first-degree sexual assault, and Williams was charged with second-degree sexual assault.

Details of the alleged sexual assault case began to hit media outlets. According to the victim, she and friend met Smith and Lee at a party at a downtown bar. She was invited by Smith to "continue the party" at their hotel, but she was hesitant because she wouldn't know anybody and might not have a ride home. She rode back to the Concourse Hotel with Smith, Lee, and another couple from the party and assumed the other couple was going to the same party. After arriving back at the hotel around 2:00 a.m., she walked to Room 308 with Smith and Lee. As the other couple continued down the hall, Lee grabbed her, tore off her clothes, and forced her onto the bed. At some point during the next two and a half hours, Williams entered the room and raped her too.

Back on campus, athletic director Paul Giel and university president Kenneth Keller were trying to put out the fire. Having just put Lee's first sexual assault case behind them, the university was now faced with another one involving three of its athletes.

"Sexual assault, rape, is not only a crime but an offense against all of us as human beings," said Keller. "It's not to be excused. It's not to be explained away."

Not only were Lee, Smith, and Williams kicked off the team but they were also expelled from school. Giel announced that Minnesota would forfeit the next game against Northwestern and would contemplate forfeiting the eleven games remaining on the schedule.

Dutcher, who had planned on resigning after the season was over amid the scandal, resigned in protest after the Northwestern game was canceled.

"Who does that punish?" he asked.

Senior center John Shasky agreed. "I still have some personal goals that I'd like to go for. These are my last eleven games. I can't go anywhere else. I can't come back next year. This is it."

Jimmy Williams assumed coaching duties with Dutcher's resignation. In fourteen years at Minnesota, he had filled in once as head coach: when Dutcher was attending the funeral of his father.

With three key players already kicked off the team, the Gophers also suspended Todd Alexander and Terence Woods for violating team rules. That left the Gophers with only six players for their upcoming game at the Barn against 10–7 Ohio State. Williams recruited football players Tim Juneau and Roselle Richardson to add some depth to the roster.

Miraculously, the Gophers beat the Buckeyes 70–65 in front of a raucous Williams Arena crowd that stayed on its feet the entire game. But the Gophers would lose nine of the next ten games, including eight straight to end the season.

Coach Williams wasn't retained at the end of the season as the Giel cleaned house, bringing in Western Kentucky coach Clem Haskins to take over the program.

In July 1986, Smith, Lee, and Williams were all found not guilty of their sexual assault charges.

<<BONUS ACHE>>

Other Gophers Sex Scandals

Sex scandals are nothing new to the University of Minnesota.

Norwood Teague became the athletic director of the University of Minnesota in 2012 after six seasons at the same position at VCU, replacing Joel Maturi.

Teague was a skilled fundraiser and, in 2015, was in the process of raising $190 million for an athletics facility village—a facility viewed as crucial to keep football and basketball teams to gain four- and five-star recruits. He also laid the foundation to return the Gopher basketball teams to prominence with the hiring of men's coach Richard Pitino and Women's coach Marlene Stollings.

But that year, he was forced to resign his position after it was reported that he inappropriately touched two university employees after drinking too much one night at a university group dinner. He got drunk and became verbally and physically aggressive. He asked one employee why she hadn't married her boyfriend yet, then he began rubbing her back and poking her in the waist.

He began texting the second employee, calling her "cute" and saying they should go skinny-dipping together. He followed her into a hallway, asked if she would ever cheat on her husband, and pinched her butt. Both women left the party with a group of people, just in case Teague followed them out.

University president Eric Kaler reached out to Teague to get help for his alcohol abuse. He was ordered not to have any more contact with either of the women and notified that there would be a university investigation. Teague decided to resign, $50 million short of his signature Athletes Village project. The $166 million facility opened in January 2018.

Another slew of sexual assault charges rocked Gopher Nation in 2016.

Tracey Claeys had coached under Jerry Kill for the twenty-one seasons while the two were at Saginaw Valley State, Emporia State, Southern Illinois, Northern Illinois, and Minnesota. With Kill's health, Claeys had filled in as head coach starting in 2005 when Kill had a seizure on the sideline during a Southern Illinois game. When Kill suffered a seizure on the sidelines during a Gophers game against New Mexico State in 2013, Claeys took over again. Kill would have another seizure before the Michigan game that year, and Claeys coached the whole game. Kill took the rest of 2013 off. After returning for the entire 2014 season, Kill stepped down as head coach on October 28, 2015, citing health reasons. Claeys was named interim coach, went 2–5, but led the Gophers to a win in the Quick Lane Bowl against Central Michigan. The interim tag was removed, and he was officially the twenty-ninth head coach in program history.

The Gophers were 9–4 in 2016, but the last few weeks were overshadowed by another black spot on the program. After being invited to the Holiday Bowl, ten players were suspended while the University investigated a claim of a sexual assault. Local law enforcement also investigated and decided not to charge any of the players, saying it wasn't a winnable criminal case. The university review, in a graphic eighty-page investigative report, included details, text messages, and other evidence that the police didn't have in their reports. The university investigation also accused the students of trying to conceal evidence, conflicting reports, and impeding the investigation.

Less than two weeks before the game, the remaining Gophers players, encouraged publicly by Claeys, threatened to boycott the upcoming Bowl game unless the suspended players were reinstated. After filing appeals, five of the players were eventually reinstated. Four players were expelled, and one player was given a one-year suspension. Two days after the details of the assault were released, the team rescinded their boycott and agreed to play in the game. They beat Washington State 17–12.

Two weeks after the game, Claeys was fired, partially for his public support of the players' boycott. A review done by the law firm Dorsey & Whitney found that there was "weak leadership by the football team coaching staff" and a "lack of understanding by student-athletes and Athletics Department personnel of Student Conduct Code disciplinary process"; and there was a "breakdown in trust between the University leadership and the football team due in part to the University leadership's inability to share private student information."

Claeys was replaced with Western Michigan head coach P. J. Fleck, who, ironically, had coached under Kill with Claeys at Northern Illinois from 2008 to 2009. After two years away from coaching, Claeys was hired by Washington State as their defensive coordinator. He served in the position until he abruptly resigned following a 67–63 loss to UCLA in 2019.

August 7, 1987

Joe Niekro's Emery Board

David Letterman: "So you're telling me that you did not doctor the ball that night?"
Joe Niekro: "Do I look like a doctor?"

Joe Niekro is one of the great knuckleball pitchers in the history of major league baseball. An All-Star for the Houston Astros in 1979, Niekro won 221 games over a twenty-two-year career, including a pair of twenty-win seasons. But Twins fans best remember him for a game in California in the summer of 1987.

The Twins were in the thick of the AL West race that August. At the start of the month, the Twins were in first place at 56–48 and had a two-and-a-half game lead over the California Angels. After back-to-back walk-off losses to the Oakland As, they headed south down the coast to Anaheim Stadium to face the Angels. With their division lead trimmed down to one game, Twins manager Tom Kelly turned to pitcher Joe Niekro to pick up a game on California.

The Twins had traded for Niekro in June, sending catcher Mark Salas to New York for the forty-two-year-old knuckleball pitcher. Since coming to Minnesota, he was 2–4 with a 5.43 ERA and thirty-two strikeouts in fifty-three innings, giving up an OBP of .350.

The Angels scored two runs off Niekro in the second inning, but a two-run Gary Gaetti single in the top of the third tied the game at 2–2. Niekro sat down George Hendrick, Mark McLemore, and Bob Boone in the bottom of the third as he settled down into the middle innings.

After getting Gus Polidor to ground out to start the bottom of the fourth, Brian Downing dug into the box to face Niekro. After three pitches, home plate umpire Tim Tschida stopped play and walked toward the mound. He had noticed that the balls Niekro was pitching had a consistent scuff on them.

"Those balls weren't roughed up," Angels manager Gene Mauch said after the game. "Those balls were borderline mutilated."

After not finding anything in his glove, Tschida told Niekro to surrender his glove so he could look for foreign objects that could be used to scuff and mark the ball. Manager Tom Kelly came out to defend his pitcher and was soon joined by the officiating crew and the Twins infielders. First-base umpire Dave Phillips told Niekro to empty his back pockets. As he turned out his back-right pocket, Niekro pulled out an emery board and tried to sneakily throw it behind Phillips. Phillips quickly noticed, picked it up, and threw Niekro out of the ball game. Neikro continued to plead his case, but to no avail. The officiating crew gathered six baseballs and placed them in a plastic bag to send to the League offices for further inspection. Neikro also had a strip of sandpaper in his pocket.

"I'll be honest with you," Niekro said after the game. "I always carry two things out there with me: an emery board and a small piece of sandpaper. I've done that ever since I started throwing the knuckleball. Sometimes I have to file my nails between innings. Sometimes I sweat a lot and the emery board gets wet, so I use the sandpaper as a backup."

Reliever Dan Schatzeder replaced Niekro as the starter for Minnesota, and he pitched Minnesota to an 11–3 win thanks to a 5-RBI night from Gary Gaetti.

Niekro, however, received a ten-game suspension for his alleged doctoring of baseballs. He returned just in time for the playoff stretch but went 2–5 with a 7.83 ERA in eight starts. Despite that, the Twins won the AL West by two games. Niekro pitched two scoreless innings in Game 4 of the 1987 World Series against the St. Louis Cardinals. He was released by the Twins after going 1–1 with a 10.09 ERA in five appearances in 1988.

January 17, 1988

The NFC Championship Game versus Washington

> *I thought it was a touchdown.*
> —Vikings quarterback Wade Wilson

The Vikings ended a four-year playoff drought (their longest since missing the playoffs for the first seven years of their existence) in 1987 and were just three seasons removed from their 3–13 season under Les Steckel. The Vikings began the season 0–3 with the replacement team put together during the strike, but finished the season 8–4 (8–7 overall) and grabbed the sixth and final Wild Card spot in a conference dominated by Joe Montana's San Francisco 49ers (13–2), Rickey Jackson's New Orleans Saints (12–3), Charley Mann's Washington Redskins (11–4), and Walter Payton's Chicago Bears (11–4).

The Vikings faced the New Orleans Saints in the wild card game with the Saints as 6.5-point favorites to win. The Vikings defense—anchored by Chris Doleman, Keith Millard, Henry Thomas, and Doug Martin—held Bobby Herbert and the Saints offense to only nine first downs, 53 rushing yards, and 104 passing yards in a 44–10 drubbing at the Superdome. Steve Freeman, John Harris, Issiac Holt, and Najee Mustafaa each picked off Herbert; and Joey Browner and Doleman each recovered fumbles for a total of six New Orleans turnovers.

The next opponent for the Vikings was Joe Montana, Jerry Rice, and the San Francisco 49ers. In what is still regarded as one of the greatest Vikings wins ever, the Vikings defense battered and bruised Montana to the point that 49ers head coach benched him halfway through the third quarter trailing 27–10—the first time Montana had been benched in his career. The defense limited Jerry Rice, who had 22 touchdowns in 1987, to three receptions for 28 yards and kept him out of the end zone. Anthony Carter, on the other hand, broke a thirty-seven-year-old playoff record with 227 receiving yards on ten receptions. Although Steve Young came in and mounted a vicious comeback, the Vikings won 36–24.

The Vikings advanced to their first NFC Championship since the 1977 season. Waiting for them was a Washington Redskins team that had been in four NFC Championship Games and two Super Bowls in the previous seven years. Washington had beaten the Vikings 27–24 in overtime in the final week of the regular season after overcoming a ten-point deficit in the final five minutes.

The two headlines heading into the game was the Battle of the Backups matchup between the Vikings Wade Wilson (replacing an injured Tommy Kramer) and the Redskins Doug Williams (taking snaps for Jay Schroeder). Both Wilson and Kramer were healthy for the championship game, but head coach Jerry Burns decided to go with the hot hand in Wilson.

"I thought about Tommy," he said. "My feeling was, Wade was doing a pretty good job. We were moving the ball. If we weren't moving the ball, I would have gone with Tommy."

Williams, the journeyman who was drafted in the first round by Tampa Bay in 1978, also played in the USFL. When the USFL folded in 1986, he signed with Washington, where he was reunited with his offensive coordinator in Tampa Bay, Joe Gibbs. Gibbs had been the only NFL scout to come watch Williams's pro day at Grambling State. Under the recommendation of Gibbs, Tampa Bay drafted him seventeenth overall, making him the first black quarterback to be drafted in the first round.

The other key matchup was the Vikings explosive defensive line versus the Redskins offense line, which featured All-Pros Russ Grimm and Joe Jacoby, Pro Bowlers Mark May, Jeff Bostic, and RC Thielemann, plus Raleigh McKenzie and Ed Simmons, who were both named to the 70 Greatest Redskins team in 2002.

The Vikings defensive line had their hands full against the great Redskins offensive line and Doug Williams, who had one of the quickest releases in the league. Vikings defensive coordinator Floyd Peters was going to focus on bringing pressure with Hall of Fame pass rusher Chris Doleman.

"If he can't see a sack coming," Peters said, "he can't unload the ball."

The offensive game plan was to continue to utilize the NFL's best deep threat in Anthony Carter, then run the ball with Darrin Nelson, who was averaging 4.9 yards per carry in the playoffs. The issue there was the Redskins had only given up 6 rushing touchdowns all season. The good news was the three of those came at the hands of the Vikings in Week 17, in addition to 204 rushing yards. Plus, the Redskins best cover guy in Hall of Famer Darrell Green was nursing a rib injury from a play against the Chicago Bears the week before, in which he hurtled a defender on a punt return for a touchdown in a 21–17 win at Soldier Field (which also turned out to be Walter Payton's final game).

The NFC Championship Game was played at RFK Stadium in Washington, DC, a site where the Redskins had won twenty-six of their last thirty-one games and were an NFL best 41–9 at home since 1982. It also didn't make Vikings fans feel better that the Redskins were 8–1 in home playoff games and that the Vikings hadn't beaten Washington since 1980. The last team to beat the Vikings in the playoffs (in 1982) was the Washington Redskins, also in a strike-shortened season.

The Vikings had seen just seen Doug Williams lead the Redskins back from a 24–14 deficit at the Metrodome to beat them in overtime 27–24. He kept the hot hand in the NFC Championship Game, connecting with running back Kelvin Bryant on a forty-two-yard touchdown pass to give Washington a 7–0 lead in the first quarter.

As much attention as the matchup between the Vikings defensive front and the Redskins Front Five got, it was the Redskins defense that was all over the Vikings offense. Wilson would be sacked a total of eight times in the game. The Vikings were expecting four or five defensive formations, like they'd seen three weeks earlier, but instead Gibbs used six to eight.

"They didn't give us the same defense twice," said offensive lineman Gary Zimmerman after the game.

But Wilson still found a way to make his throws. He found a wide-open Leo Lewis in the end zone in the second quarter for a twenty-three-yard touchdown pass to tie the game at 7–7 at halftime. And while Wilson would make his throws, his receivers would let him down time and time again. Dropped passes would haunt the Vikings in the second half of the game.

"We dropped five or six balls," head coach Jerry Burns said after the game. "You just can't do that and win a game."

At the end of the game, there were a total of eight dropped passes by the Vikings. On a third and seven deep in their own territory, running back D. J. Dozier dropped a pass at midfield that would have given the Vikings a first down with great field position.

But Williams was keeping the Vikings in the game, at one time only completing four of his seventeen passes for sixty-seven total yards. Doleman and Millard began getting pressure on him, but even when he had time in the pocket, his receivers were dropping passes or watching errant throws sail over their heads.

The Washington defense forced the only turnover of the game: a third quarter interception by linebacker Mel Kaufman that was tipped at the line of scrimmage by nose tackle Dave Butz. Washington didn't score a touchdown on the pick, but they did get a twenty-eight-yard field goal from Ali Haji-Sheikh and a 10–7 lead.

The Vikings had no turnovers in the game, a complete opposite from a team that had grabbed fourteen interceptions in their last four games.

The Vikings offense had an excellent chance to take the lead early in the fourth quarter. They had first and goal from the Washington three-yard line. Rookie running back Ricky Fenney gained two yards on first down, then he was stuffed on second down. On third down, Dozier replaced him Fenney in the huddle. Dozier had five rushing touchdowns for the Vikings in 1987 and tried leaping into the end zone on third and goal.

He was grabbed from behind by Washington linebacker Neal Olkewicz and stopped short of the goal line. The Vikings had to settle for a Chuck Nelson field goal.

Williams finished the game 9-for-26 with 119 yards, but he burned the Vikings with three big plays: the big touchdown to Bryant on the big touchdown and two big throws to Gary Clark.

Washington had the ball with 9:57 left. Williams got some pocket protection and found a wide-open Gary Clark for a huge forty-three-yard gain to get the Redskins inside the Vikings ten-yard line. The drive resulted in a touchdown with Williams escaping a sack by Keith Millard and throwing a strike to Clark in the end zone, just out of the reach of free safety John Harris. Haji-Sheikh's extra point was good, and Washington led 17–10.

The Vikings began their final drive on their own thirty-three-yard line with 5:04 to play . . . plenty of time for Wilson and Carter to do their jobs. Wilson hit Carter and tight end Steve Jordan for some big plays, but the offense stalled in the red zone. At the Washington ten-yard line, the Vikings gained four yards on the next three plays, setting up fourth and four from the six-yard line with 1:03 remaining in the game.

With one shot at a touchdown, Jerry Burns called the play Smoke 83 Option. The play was designed to use Carter as a decoy in the back of the end zone then throw underneath to Darrin Nelson.

"Short yardage situations haunted us all year," Wade Wilson said. "What it takes to correct it, I don't know."

Nelson beat Darrell Green to the front corner of the end zone, and Wilson saw it. He threw the ball to Nelson. The ball hit Nelson in the hands then rolled harmlessly to the ground as he was hit by Green and linebacker Monte Coleman.

"I got hit right when I grabbed it," Nelson said. "I got my fingertips on it."

TV replay showed that Green and Coleman didn't hit Nelson until after he dropped the pass. Also shown in TV replay was Carter, standing ten feet away from Nelson, waiting for the pass. Carter, who finished with seven catches for eight-five yards, said he would have been able to catch the pass had Nelson not touched it first.

"They just didn't call my play none in the second half and in the third quarter, not any time." Carter said. "I don't know what the deal was. But they coach, and I play."

With fifty-three seconds left, the Redskins ran out the clock and advanced to their third Super Bowl in the 1980s.

"We just didn't want it," a frustrated Joey Browner said after the game. "We had opportunities to get ahead and do what we do. We just didn't do it. No ifs, ands, or buts about it. We lost."

Washington beat the Denver Broncos 42–10 in Super Bowl XXII for their second Super Bowl victory in six years.

The Vikings wouldn't return to the NFC Championship Game until 1998.

April 22, 1988

The Twins Trade Tom Brunansky for Tom Herr

In 1988, the Twins were the defending World Series Champions. Despite only winning eighty-five games in the regular season (the second lowest win total of any World Series Champion), the Twins were able to upset the mighty Detroit Tigers in the ALCS then beat the St. Louis Cardinals in seven games in the World Series.

While some fans only know the big names from that '87 squad like Hall of Famers Kirby Puckett and Bert Blyleven or all-time great Twins like Kent Hrbek and Frank Viola, there is one name that doesn't usually garner a lot of attention: Tom Brunansky.

And in 1988, they traded him to St. Louis for what they thought would be a rock in the middle infield: Tom Herr.

The Twins aquired Bruno from the California Angels one month into the 1982 season in exchange for All-Star pitcher (because somebody had to represent the Twins in 1981...) Doug Corbett and second baseman Rob Wilfong, who led the American League in Sacrifice Hits in 1979.

The Twins, coming off a 41–68 record during the strike-shortened 1981 season, were looking still looking for new face of the franchise. The glory days of Harmon Killebrew, Rod Carew, and Tony Oliva smacking the ball around the Met were long over. The Twins opened the state-of-the-art Metrodome in 1982. In fact, since winning the AL West pennant in 1971, the Twins hadn't finished higher than third in the division. A new era of Twins baseball had begun.

In 1982, Brunansky joined a core of Twins players including Kent Hrbek, Tim Laudner, Gary Gaetti, and Frank Viola among others. As a team, the Twins lost a then franchise record of 102 games, but Brunansky was a bright spot. As a rookie, he hit .272 with 20 home runs and drove in 46 runs. Bruno would hit 20+ home runs every year for the next nine seasons.

He was an All-Star in 1985 and had solidified himself as the everyday right fielder while seeing some occasional playing time in left (by 1985, center field was being held down by a pudgy, undersized player named Kirby Puckett). In 1987, the Twins made the playoffs for the first time in sixteen years despite only winning eighty-five games.

The Twins were huge underdogs in the 1987 ALCS, facing a ninety-eight-win Detroit Tigers team. Brunansky would hit .412 with 9 RBI as the Twins won the series in five games.

Similar story in the World Series. The Twins were matched up against a ninety-five-win St. Louis Cardinals team making their third World Series appearance in six years. Although it wasn't Bruno that killed the Cards, individually (he was 5-for-25 with 2 RBI), the Twins wouldn't have been in position to win the World Series without him on the roster.

In 1988, the Twins brought back the entire starting roster, except for DH Don Baylor. But the Twins felt there was one position they could upgrade if the opportunity presented itself: second base.

Steve Lombardozzi was a ninth-round pick by the Twins in 1981 and had been part of the revolving door at second base for the Twins since Rod Carew moved to first base. Ironically enough, the St. Louis Cardinals got off to a slow start in the 1988 campaign. With a 4–11 record, GM Del Maxvill was desperate for a power hitter after All-Star right fielder Jack Clark (who finished third in the NL MVP voting in 1987) left the Cardinals for the New York Yankees in free agency. He put Tom Herr, a vital piece of the three NL pennant teams, on the trade block.

Twins GM Andy McPhail thought the opportunity was too good to pass up. He traded Brunansky to St. Louis on April 22 straight up for Tom Herr.

At the time, the deal made sense for both teams. The Twins had a lot of outfield depth. Along with starters Dan Gladden and Kirby Puckett, the Twins felt like players like Randy Bush and Mark Davidson were ready to be the everyday right fielder. They were looking for a left-handed batter for the top of the lineup (Herr is a switch hitter), and McPhail said that he thought "Tom Herr was one of the four or five best second baseman playing today."

The Cardinals, on the other side, thought they had Herr's replacement in Luis Alicia (they were wrong); and they thought Herr, who was in the final year of his contract, would leave via free agency (he had stated that he wouldn't have).

Herr spent one season in Minnesota, hitting a respectable .263, but he only knocked in 21 runs in 80 games—way off his 83 RBI the previous season. At the end of the 1988 season, he became a free agent and signed with Philadelphia.

Tom Brunansky, on the other hand, had success in St. Louis. He belted 42 home runs in two seasons for the Cardinals and led the team in home runs both seasons, but the end of the 1980s Cardinals dynasty was nigh and the team wouldn't make the playoffs again until 1996. Bruno then floated around the league, playing for Milwaukee and Boston (twice) before retiring in 1995.

The Twins were able to rebuild from the bad trade, however, signing RF Shane Mack in 1990 and having second baseman Chuck Knoblauch (the 1991 Rookie of the Year) waiting in the wings.

<<BONUS ACHE>>

Vance Worley

The Twins traded outfielder Ben Revere to the Philadelphia Phillies for Trevor May and Vance Worley in December 2012 in a move to bolster their starting rotation. The Twins were ranked twenty-eighth in team ERA (4.77) in 2012 featuring guys like Sam De Vris, Scott Diamond, Jason Marquis, Liam Hendricks, and Sam Deduno. The Twins revamped their rotation in 2013, adding Worley and free agents Kevin Correia and Mike Pelfrey. Worley was the Opening Day starter against the Detroit Tigers on April 1, 2013. He only lasted 10 starts with the Twins, going 1–5 with a 7.21 ERA before being demoted to AAA Rochester as the Twins lost 90+ games for the third straight season and ranked twenty-ninth in the majors in team ERA (4.55). Worley was purchased by the Pittsburgh Pirates the following March after failing to make the team out of spring training. He had a great year for Pittsburgh in 2014, going 8–4 with a 2.85 ERA in 17 starts.

October 12, 1989

The Vikings Trade for Herschel Walker

The 1989 Dallas Cowboys were terrible. They hadn't been to the playoffs in four years and hadn't won a playoff game since advancing to the NFC Championship Game in 1982. It was time for a change. Bum Bright, who had purchased the team from Clint Murchison Jr. in 1984, sold to Jerry Jones. Jones fired the only coach the franchise had ever had in Tom Landry as well as General Manager Tex Schramm. He hired an old teammate from his college football days at Arkansas, University of Miami head coach Jimmie Johnson.

The Cowboys finished a league-worst 3–13 in 1988, so the rookie owner and NFL head coach had the first overall pick in the draft. They decided to build around UCLA quarterback Troy Aikman.

The Cowboys were shut out by the New Orleans Saints 28–0 to begin the season, only gaining 174 yards of total offense. Over their first four games, the Cowboys only averaged 188 yards passing and 67 yards rushing. Jimmie Johnson later said that he felt the Cowboys were so terrible that year that the only thing that could save them would be stockpiling draft picks in exchange for one of their big pieces. But who? The Cowboys only had three players that could be traded in exchange for a haul of draft picks: Aikman, 1988 first-round pick wide receiver Michael Irvin, and former Heisman winner running back Herschel Walker.

Trading Aikman was out of the question. Johnson did have a deal in place that would have sent Irvin to the Los Angeles Raiders until Raiders owner Al Davis talked him out of it by telling him, "Who is going to catch passes for you?" The remaining piece that was made available to move was Walker.

Herschel Walker was an all-world running back in college. The three-time All-American and 1982 Heisman winner left the University of Georgia after his junior year and signed with the New Jersey Generals of the USFL because, unlike the NFL, underclassmen could turn pro and join the league. Walker led the USFL in rushing in 1983 and 1985, rushing for 2,411 yards in '85 and averaging over 5 yards per carry. He also had 2,100 yards of total offense in 1984.

The Cowboys selected Walker in the fifth round of the 1985 NFL Draft while he was still playing for the Generals. When the USFL folded after the 1985 season, he joined his teammates in Dallas. He would share the backfield with another former Heisman winner in Tony Dorsett.

Walker quickly established himself as a dual threat back. In 1987, he had 891 rushing yards, 715 receiving yards, and 8 touchdowns. After losing touches and starts to Walker, Dorsett requested a trade to the Denver Broncos after the 1987 season. That move gave Herschel the opportunity to be the featured back in 1988. That season, he became the tenth player in NFL history to amass 2,000 combined rushing and receiving yards in a season. He was elected to the Pro Bowl in both 1987 and 1988.

Johnson decided that Walker was the expendable piece in the Cowboys' plans to rebuild the team. He wanted an elusive back to fit his offensive game plan and wanted to get away from smashmouth football. Several teams called Dallas to inquire about a trade after Johnson made his intentions to trade Walker publicly. In the eyes of the NFL, the fan base, and the media, the trade was crazy. The Cowboys were 0–5 after five weeks in 1989, and they were now shopping the only proven player on their roster.

The New York Giants wanted him, but Dallas didn't want to trade him to a division opponent. Walker's hometown Atlanta Falcons were also interested but balked out of fear of Walker's future contract demands. The one serious offer that Johnson considered came from the Cleveland Browns.

The Browns were two years removed from back-to-back AFC Championship Game losses to the Broncos and were looking for a player to get them over the hump. They offered one player and a couple first- and second-round draft picks. Johnson liked the deal, but he and Jones decided to call other NFL general managers and try to create a bidding war and create some leverage in the deal.

Vikings GM Mike Lynn had called Johnson earlier in the summer to inquire about Walker. Johnson called him back to let him know he had gotten an attractive offer from Cleveland and gave him an ultimatum: he was going to trade Walker to the Browns at 6:30 that evening unless he got a better deal from the Vikings.

The Vikings were also in a similar situation as the Browns. The Vikings were two years removed from their NFC Championship Game loss to the Washington Redskins in the 1987 strike year. They had lost to the San Francisco 49ers in the second round of the playoffs in 1988 and felt that Darrin Nelson and D. J. Dozier weren't the running backs they needed to get back to their first Super Bowl in over a decade.

On paper, Walker was that player. A dynamic offensive weapon to pair with Anthony Carter, Steve Jordan, and Wade Wilson. And the Vikings wouldn't have to give up any major pieces of their current team to get him? For Lynn, it was too good to be true.

He bet the farm on Walker: five players, three draft picks, and five conditional draft picks (the Cowboys would get the five picks if they cut or traded any of the five players in the deal). In exchange, the Vikings got Walker and three mid- to late-round picks.

The key to the deal was the conditional picks. Jimmie Johnson had no intention of keeping any of the five players in the deal. "The Vikings thought they were one player away from the Super Bowl," Johnson told ESPN in 2014. "I knew we were fifty-three players away."

The original proposal he received from Lynn included five players: LB Jesse Solomon, LB David Howard, CB Issiac Holt, RB Darrin Nelson, and DE Alex Stewart. The deal also included Minnesota's first, second, and sixth-round pick in the 1990 NFL Draft. Lynn later said in an interview that he felt he gave Dallas five guys that could start and help the team out right away. Johnson had no interest in that.

What he was interested in was the conditions tied to each of the players. If he cut Jesse Solomon, he would get a first-round pick in 1991. If he cut David Howard, he would get a second-round pick in 1991. If he cut Issiac Holt, he would get a first-round pick in 1992. If he cut Darrin Nelson, he would get a second-round pick in 1992, and if he cut Alex Stewart, he would get a third-round pick in 1992.

Nelson refused to report to the Cowboys. So the San Diego Chargers were added as a third team in the trade. The Chargers got Nelson, Minnesota got San Diego's fifth-round pick, and Dallas got Minnesota's second rounder in 1992 for dealing Nelson.

There was one holdup in the deal: Herschel Walker. He heard about the trade and threatened to retire instead of becoming a Viking. Jerry Jones gave him a $1 million exit bonus.

The trade was finalized in October 1989. Walker had an immediate impact for the Vikings. In his first game as a Vikings against the Green Bay Packers, he ran for 148 yards on 18 carries. It was the first 100+ yard game for a Vikings running back since 1983 as the Vikings beat the Packers for only the fourth time in the last eighteen meetings.

Walker's numbers dropped exponentially after the opening game. While the Vikings were 7–4 with Walker (10–6 overall in 1989), he wouldn't run for 100+ yards again that season. The Vikings did make the playoffs but were blown out by San Francisco 41-13. Walker had nine carries for 29 yards and two catches for 14 yards in the game.

Walker would play two and a half seasons for the Vikings. They missed the playoffs at 6–10 in 1990 and at 8–8 in 1991. He ran for 2,264 yards and 20 touchdowns, caught 86 passes for 681 yards and five touchdowns, and won zero Super Bowls.

Things went a little better for the Cowboys. A month after the trade went down, Johnson waived Stewart and got the Vikings' third-round pick in 1992. Jesse Solomon, who led the Vikings with 121 tackles in 1988, walked out of the Cowboys facility after being demoted to the second team. He was traded to New England for a sixth-round pick, and Jimmie got Minnesota's first-round pick in 1991.

David Howard played in sixteen games as a backup for the Cowboys in 1990. He was eventually traded to the New England Patriots in a package for the Patriots first-round pick.

Issaic Holt was the only player to see Johnson's gamble pay off. He was the only player in the trade to have a starting role with the Cowboys but was cut by Johnson in 1993 after questioning how many voluntary off-season workouts were required.

Jimmie Johnson had his picks. But what would he do with them? You can blame Mike Lynn and the Herschel Walker trade all you want, but if Dallas didn't pick the right players in the draft, they were making a lateral move.

The funny thing about Johnson getting all those picks from the Vikings is, he never made selections in those slots. He used the picks to move up in drafts to grab players that he wanted. He used the Vikings first and second-round pick in 1990 to trade up with the Pittsburgh Steelers to take Florida running back Emmitt Smith. He also traded the Vikings sixth-round pick for DB Stan Smagala. In 1991, he packaged the Vikings first-round pick (which he got for trading Solomon) to New England for the first overall pick in the draft, which they used on DT Russell Maryland. He traded his additional second-round pick (for trading Howard) to trade with Houston for RB Alonzo Highsmith. In 1992, he traded his additional first-round pick (for cutting Holt) and the third-round pick (for waiving Stewart) to New England for their first and second picks in the Draft, then traded New England's first to Atlanta to move up again. He took corner Kevin Smith with Atlanta's pick and safety Darren Woodson with New England's second. He used the Vikings second-round pick (for trading Nelson) in a deal to acquire two picks from Kansas City.

Altogether, Jimmie Johnson made fifty-one trades to build the Cowboys team that he wanted. The Cowboys were 1–15 in 1989 but won back-to-back Super Bowls in 1992 and 1993 and another one in 1995 due, in large part, to the draft picks sent to them in the Walker deal.

The Vikings still haven't played in a Super Bowl since 1976.

March 25, 1990

The 1990 Elite 8 versus Georgia Tech

I thought they wanted it more than we did. I felt like they almost gave us the knockout punch.
—Georgia Tech coach Bobby Cremins

In 1989–90, Clem Haskins was in his fourth season as head coach of the Gophers men's basketball team and was putting together one of the best regular seasons in school history. The team's twenty-three wins was one shy of the school's now-vacated record set by Jim Dutcher's 1976–77 team.

The Gophers were 23–9 (11–7 in the Big Ten) and finished tied for fourth in the conference, which was their best Big Ten finish since winning the regular season title in 1981–82. Led by senior forward Willie Burton and his 20 points per game, there were six future NBA players on Haskins' roster: Burton, Melvin Newbern, Kevin Lynch, Walter Bond, Richard Coffey, and Bob Martin.

They finished twentieth in the AP Polls and made it to back-to-back NCAA tournament appearances for the first time in school history. They were given the sixth seed in the Southeast Regional. Their first opponent was 11-seeded University of Texas–El Paso. The Gophers were ice-cold from the floor, only hitting a third of their shots (22 of 66), but took 19 more shots than the Miners, thanks in large part to 23 forced turnovers. The Gophers led 24–23 at the half but trailed 47–42. Two quick Newbern and Coffey steals sparked an 8–1 Gophers run. With the game tied at 50, Newbern hit a three-pointer to give the Gophers the lead with fifty-five seconds remaining. UTEP's Henry Hall responded with a three of his own with thirty-three seconds left, and the game went to overtime tied at fifty-three. The Gophers did just enough to avoid the upset in overtime, winning 64–61.

Next up was 14-seed Northern Iowa, who had upset the 3-seed Missouri 74–71 in their opening round matchup. This time, it was Willie Burton's time to shine. Burton scored a career high 36 points and was 9 of 12 from three-point land. The Gophers led 71–62 with 8:41, but the Panthers cut the deficit to three points three times with a minute and a half left in the game. UNI center Jason Reese scored 29 points (12–15 shooting) and pulled down 10 boards, but it wasn't enough for the Panthers as the Gophers won 81–78 to send them to their second consecutive Sweet 16.

Minnesota's tallest task would come in the Sweet 16 against 2-seed Syracuse, led by Derrick Coleman, who would be the top pick in the upcoming NBA Draft. Coach Haskins's strategy was to double team Coleman: first with Richard Coffey, then whoever could help. The Orange led at the half, 39–35. The Gophers would shoot 79.2 percent (19/24) from the floor in the second half, pouring in 47 points. Coleman didn't get a shoot up in the final eight minutes of the game. The Gophers knocked off Syracuse 82–75 to advance to their first ever Elite Eight.

Their opponent in the next round was on a Cinderella run too. 4-seed Georgia Tech had just survived Shaquille O'Neal and the LSU Tigers and had beaten top-seeded Michigan State in overtime to advance to the Elite Eight.

The Yellow Jackets were led by a three-headed scoring attack: Dennis Scott, Brian Oliver, and Kenny Anderson. Nicknamed Lethal Weapon III, the trio was responsible for 77 percent of Georgia Tech's points that year.

The game was tight with three minutes left. Anderson hit a jumper to extend the lead to 89–84, then Burton came down the court and hit a three to cut the deficit to two points. After each team exchanged misses, Coffey drew a charge call on Oliver to give Minnesota the ball. Lynch was fouled on the other end with thirty-five seconds left, but he only made one of his two free throws to make the score 89–88.

Two made free throws from Oliver after Minnesota intentionally fouled gave Tech a 91–88 lead. Newbern missed a jumper on the other end, and Anderson made both free throws after Minnesota fouled again.

Now with seven seconds left in the game, and trailing 93–88, Burton hit a three-pointer to bring the Gophers within two again. Minnesota intentionally fouled Anderson again, and he missed the front end of the one and one.

With no time-outs left, Lynch flew up court and threw up a three-point prayer from the corner while he was double-teamed.

It was an air ball. Georgia Tech won 93–91 to advance to the final four. Scott, Oliver, and Anderson took 52 of the team's 56 shots and would combine for 89 of the team's 93 points.

Georgia Tech would lose to Stacey Augmon, Larry Johnson, and the eventual-champion UNLV Runnin' Rebels 90–81 in the Final Four.

The Gophers would miss the Big Dance each of the next three seasons, before five consecutive appearances that were all vacated due to the academic fraud scandal.

May 15, 1991

The Stanley Cup Finals versus Pittsburgh

*Maybe Norm Green wasn't being greedy when he refused to put
Game 6 on free TV. Maybe he was just being kind.*

(Dan Barreiro, *Star Tribune*)

At the beginning of the 1990–91 NHL playoffs, the Minnesota North Stars had a 1 in 10,000 chance of winning the Stanley Cup. They snuck into the playoffs anyways with 68 points (27–39–14)—38 points behind Norris Division champion Chicago.

The North Stars had a new head coach in 1990–91, after Pierre Page left to become the general manager of the Quebec Nordiques, in Bob Gainey. Gainey, a rookie head coach, would be elected into the NHL Hall of Fame as a player in 1992 with an impressive resume on the ice: four Frank J. Selke trophies and five Stanley Cups with Montreal in a sixteen-year NHL career.

Minnesota struggled out of the game, only winning five of their first twenty-six games. Fans at the Met Center began "Lindros! Lindros!" chants, figuring their team would be in a good position to draft the prospect the hockey world was calling The Next One: Eric Lindros (who would be drafted first overall by the Quebec).

Dave Gagner scored 40 goals for the North Stars that season, Mike Modano tallied 64 points, Neal Broten added 56 assists, and Jon Casey notched 21 of the team's 27 wins with a 2.98 GAA. While the North Stars were average on home ice at the Met Center (19–15–6), they were abysmal on the road with an 8–24–8 record.

But the Stars snuck into the playoffs as the sixteenth team in the sixteen-team field, even though they lost six of their last eight regular season games. Their first opponent in the playoffs would be the Chicago Blackhawks.

Historically, the North Stars didn't a great record against Chicago in the postseason. The North Stars had won only one of five playoff series against

Chicago since 1982. In 1991, the Blackhawks were the top seed in the Clarence Campbell Conference with 106 points. Minnesota was 2–5–1 against Chicago during the regular season.

Surprisingly, the Stars took the Blackhawks to overtime, tied 3–3, in Game 1 at Chicago Stadium. A Brian Propp rebound put past Chicago's Calder Memorial Trophy–winning goalie Ed Belfour gave Minnesota a 1–0 lead in the series. Game 2 was a slugfest, with a combined 145 penalty minutes. Chicago's defense allowed only six shots on goal in the first period and seven in the second. Trailing 4–0 in the second period, Jon Casey was benched for Brian Hayward in the second period in an eventual 5–2 Chicago win, evening the series at 1–1.

Minnesota came out strong in Game 3 at the Met Center, leading 5–2 after the first period. But four unanswered Chicago goals the rest of the way gave the Blackhawks a 6–5 win and a 2–1 series lead. Things got chippy at the end of Game 3 after Chicago forward Mike Hudson slammed Hayward into the crossbar at 6:15 in the third period as Jeremy Roenick scored the game winner. Things stayed chippy before Game 4, with a fight nearly breaking out before the game at Chicago Stadium. The Stars even the series at 2–2 with a 3–1 in a game that had 113 penalty minutes in the second period alone.

Jon Casey shut out the Blackhawks on the road (the Stars only had five shutouts the entire regular season) in a 6–0 win in Game 5 win as the Stars score five power play goals. In the decisive Game 6 back at the Met, Casey stopped 26 of 27 shots in a 3–1 win. The sold-out Met Center crowd danced in the aisles as the North Stars became the first team in twenty years to knock the tournament's top seed out of the playoffs in the first round as the Stars tied an NHL record with 15 power play goals in a single series.

Next up for the Stars: the St. Louis Blues, who had finished second in the Norris Division with 105 points. After knocking Detroit out in the first round, the Blues welcomed the Stars to St. Louis Arena. The Stars had a little better playoff history against the Blues, but St. Louis had knocked them out in two of their last three playoff appearances.

Jon Casey's hot streak continued in Game 1 against the Blues, stopping 31 of 32 shots in a 2–1 win. Casey was helped by defensemen Stewart Gavin and Gaetan Duchesne, who held that season's leading scorer Brett Hull (86 goals in 1990–91) to one shot, no goals and no assists. St. Louis ended the Stars' three-game winning streak in Game 2 with a 5–2 win to even the series at 1–1.

The Stars' offense erupted in Game 3, scoring four goals (Curt Giles, Stew Gavin, Brian Bellows, Neil Wilkinson) in the first period, then one more in the second. The defense held Brett Hull scoreless for the third straight game, which was his longest scoring drought of the season. The Blues went 0-for-7 on the power play and had only one goal in their last twenty-eight opportunities.

Things didn't go much better for St. Louis at the Met Center in Game 4. Trailing 3–1 after the first, they got locked out of their locker room during the first intermission and had to wait for a janitor to come unlock the door. As terrible as their power play had been in the regular season, the Stars were electric in the playoffs. In an 8–4 Minnesota win, the North Stars converted four of eight power plays. After Brett Hull finally scored his first goal of the series to make it 4–2 in the second, Minnesota rattled of four straight goals to take a 3–1 series lead.

St. Louis found their groove in Game 5, staving off elimination with a 4–2 win. After the game, Stars center Bobby Smith said the second period of Game 6 was the worst period Minnesota had played the entire post season, getting outshot 18–5 and allowing three goals. Jon Casey was pulled, trailing 4–0 in the third period and giving up four goals on 29 shots in a 4–2 St. Louis win.

Game 6 came back to the Met Center, with a chance for the North Stars to win their second playoff series in front of the home fans. The game was scoreless into the third period until Chris Dahlquist scored his first goal of the playoffs nineteen seconds into the period. Bobby Smith added some insurance at the 3:50 mark to give Minnesota a 2-0 lead with seventeen minutes left in the game. Brett Hull scored his eleventh goal of the playoffs to bring the Blues within one with three minutes left. Bobby Smith would add some insurance with an empty netter before St. Louis scored again with the extra attacker with seventeen seconds in the game. The Stars won 3–2 to advance to their first Conference Finals since 1984.

The 1991 Campbell Conference Finals was a rematch of the 1984 Conference Finals that saw the Edmonton Oilers sweep the North Stars. Despite trading Wayne Gretzky to the LA Kings after the 1988 Stanley Cup Finals, the Oilers won the 1990 championship behind the play of Mark Messier, Jari Kurri, Glenn Anderson, and Esa Tikkanen and the goalie combo of Grant Fuhr and Bill Ranford.

Edmonton finished third in the Smyth Division in 1991 with 80 points (37–37–5). The Oilers were without Kurri, who was playing in Italy during a contract dispute with Oilers management, Glenn Anderson's output had decreased dramatically, Fuhr was dealing with an injury and was suspended for a year for cocaine issues, and reigning Hart Memorial Trophy winner Mark Messier played in only fifty-three games and scored the fewest goals since his rookie year with 12. They knocked out the Calgary Flames in seven games in the semifinals, then they took out Gretzky and the Kings in the Division Finals to match up against Minnesota in one of the most unlikely Conference Finals matchups in the history of the game.

Coming into the game, Edmonton had never lost in the Conference Finals (6-for-6), and the North Stars hadn't won at Edmonton's Northlands Coliseum in more than a decade. But Jon Casey's magical run in the playoffs continued. After giving up a goal to Steve Smith in the first three minutes of Game 1, Casey shut out the Oilers the rest of the way. Goals by Neal Broten, Dave Gagner, and Gaetan Duchesne gave Minnesota a 3–1 win and a 1–0 series lead.

Minnesota's streak of poor Game 2s continued as well. Casey allowed four goals on 11 shots in the first period, with Edmonton's Petr Klima scoring three of them in less than five minutes. The Oilers won 7–2, and evened the series heading back to Bloomington.

The Stars returned the favor in Game 3, hanging a seven-spot on Edmonton. Minnesota led 3–1 after the first period and chased goalie Bill Ranford after he gave up his fourth goal. He was replaced Grant Fuhr, who allowed three goals on eight shots.

The Oilers, who were built on speed and finesse, changed their strategy in Game 4 by trying to outmuscle the North Stars. The Oilers struck first and took a 1–0 lead on Craig MacTavish's goal in the first, but Minnesota responded by scoring five unanswered goals the rest of the way, including two power play goals (Gagner and Broten) in the second period. Minnesota won Game 4 5–1.

Minnesota had a chance to clinch their first Stanley Cup Final berth since 1981 in Game 5 at Northlands Coliseum. Mark Tinordi scored the first goal for the Stars two minutes into the first period, and Marc Bureau added another one to give the Stars a 2–0 lead. But an Esa Tikkanen goal in the second and a Mark Messier goal in the third tied the game 2–2 late in the third period. Bobby Smith deked Fuhr to score the game winner with five minutes left in the game. The Stars won 3–2 and became the first sub-.500 team since the 1948–49 Toronto Maple Leafs to make it to the championship.

> *The Stars and Penguins have a rich history. It's just that many of their fans have spent lifetimes trying to forget it.* (*Star Tribune* writer Jerry Zgoda)

The 1991 Stanley Cup Finals featured two franchises each looking for their first NHL championship. The North Stars had lost the finals to the New York Islanders in 1981, and the Pittsburgh Penguins were making their first ever finals appearance. In fact, since their inaugural season in 1967, Pittsburgh had never made it past the second round of the playoffs.

A lot like the Stars, Pittsburgh had seen some lean years, unwise trades and draft choices, near bankruptcy, and rumors of relocation. Then came Mario Lemieux, the first overall pick in the 1984 NHL Draft. And the trade offer from then-Stars GM Lou Nanne, offering all twelve Minnesota draft picks for the first pick in the draft, which Pittsburgh declined.

Despite missing Lemieux for fifty games in 1990–91 due to complications from back surgery, the Penguins were 41–33–6 under Minnesota native Bob Johnson largely in part to trading for players like Ulf Samuelsson, Ron Francis, Joe Mullen, and Larry Murphy (from the North Stars) and the play of rookie Jaromir Jagr (27 goals, 30 assists, 57 points), Mark Recchi (40 goals, 73 assists, 113 points), and Kevin Stevens (40 goals, 46 assists, 86 points). Despite his injury,

Lemieux scored 45 points in only 26 games (19 goals, 26 assists) as the Penguins went 14–9–3 to finish the regular season.

Pittsburgh trailed their opening round series 3–2 before dispatching the New Jersey Devils in Game 7. After losing the first game in round 2 against the Washington Capitals, Pittsburgh won the next four games to win the series, and after losing the first two games of the Wales Conference Finals to the Boston Bruins, Pittsburgh won the next four games to advance to their first Stanley Cup final in franchise history.

Just as they had done in Game 1 against Chicago, St. Louis, and Edmonton, the Stars won on enemy ice at Pittsburgh Civic Arena. It was also the fourth straight Game 1 loss for Pittsburgh. Pittsburgh took an early 1–0 lead on an Ulf Samuelsson goal, but Minnesota took a 2–1 lead (Neal Broten and Ulf Dahlen) before the first intermission. The two teams exchanged goals in the second, including Broten's second goal of the game in what was a bit of a breakout game for the Roseau native.

"I had a lot of goals at Christmas," Broten said. "Somebody said I only have three goals since Christmas. I had a frustrating second half of the season." (Broten had 10 goals on December 23 but only finished the season with 13.) "The first goal was lucky, and I deserve some lucky goals. Thirteen goals for the season is horse manure for me. I didn't get one lucky goal all year."

Leading 4–3 in the third period, Bobby Smith scored a quick goal at the 1:39 mark. It would be the eventual game winner, with Joe Mullen putting the puck past Jon Casey to cut the deficit to one. The Stars defense would lock down for the final ten minutes in a 5–4 Game 1 victory.

"Start blocking off the streets, folks," Patrick Reusse wrote in the *Star Tribune* the next morning. "There is going to be a Twin Cities parade to remember."

The Stars were now 4–0 in Game 1, but were 0–3 in Game 2.

"We know that when we win the first game, the home team is going to feel a lot of pressure," Bob Gainey said. "Pressure to come back and win on their home ice. We know what we'll see from Pittsburgh."

What they saw was playoff heroics from Mario Lemieux and Tom Barrasso and the return of Hall of Fame defenseman Paul Coffey, who had missed the previous ten games after getting a metal plate put in his face to repair a broken jaw. Pittsburgh scored two goals in the first period before Mike Modano got the Stars on the board with a power play goal fifty-five seconds into the second period. Fifteen minutes later, Lemieux scored a now-legendary goal in the second, getting Casey to commit to the forehand before going backhand and tucking the puck into the net before crashing into it to extend the Penguins lead to 3–1.

As phenomenal as the Stars power play attack had been during the playoffs, they were only 1-of-9 in Game 2, including 0–4 in the first period. Barrasso stopped 39 of 40 shots in a 4–1 win.

Another huge loss for the Stars in Game 2 was forward Brian Bellows getting banged up with an unnecessary knee injury. Ulf Samuelsson, known as the Bad Swede of the NHL, was known for cheap hits. He knocked Boston star Cam Neely out of the Conference Finals with the same move (Neely, a 2005 Hall of Fame inductee, missed all but twenty-two games the next two years due to complications from the injury).

"You're always going to take Bellows out of the game," Samuelsson said after the game. "He's a good player, and we watch him closely. I want to take him out of the play, and if I can take him out of the game, that's even better."

When Ulf hit Bellows, the puck was nowhere near them and should have been called interference, but the officials missed the call.

While Bellows suited up for Game 3 at Met Center, Mario Lemieux and his playoff-leading 13 goals was a scratch from the lineup after having back spasms after warm-ups. A sold-out crowd of 15,378 was ready, knowing that their home team was 7–1 at home in the playoffs and hadn't lost at the Met since their first home game of the playoffs.

The Stars strategy in Game 3 was to get a quick lead to invigorate the crowd, but the game was scoreless after the first. In the second, the Stars got the quick scoring they were looking for. Dave Gagner scored at the 7:21 mark, and while the PA announcer was announcing the goal, Bobby Smith scored another one . . . thirty-three seconds after Gagner. Phil Bourque cut the lead to 2–1 with a goal in the third period, but Gaetan Buchesne re-extended the Stars's lead to 3–1 with a goal only forty-six seconds later. With the 3–1 win, Minnesota was now 8–1 at home in the playoffs (eight straight wins) and had outscored their opponents 37–19.

"It didn't happen like we wanted it to," Gagner said after the win. "But to get that first goal was a big relief for everybody."

"I was actually pretty happy it was tied after the first," Neal Broten commented. "They came out pretty strong, and we were a little overanxious. We were a little more patient in the second period, and that's when we finally got the goal. You've got to be patient in a situation like that. You can't get frustrated or upset about it."

With the Game 3 win, the Stars were only two wins away from the first Stanley Cup in franchise history.

Mario Lemieux was back for Game 4 at the Met Center, and Pittsburgh responded in a big way by scoring three goals in the first three minutes of the game (Kevin Stevens, Ron Francis, and Lemieux). It was the first time in Stanley Cup history that a team led 3–0 that quickly. Dave Gagner put Minnesota on the board with a goal at 18:22 in the first. Pittsburgh and Bryan Trottier made it 4–1 midway through the second period before the Minnesota offense got on a roll. Brian Propp and Mike Modano each scored power play goals to cut the deficit to 4–3 to set up one of the most exciting third periods in hockey history: the Stars trying to come back from a three-goal deficit and the Penguins trying to beat an unbeatable team on their home ice.

Things got physical late in the third period, with both teams getting chippy. Eventually, Pittsburgh's Troy Loney was called for a high-sticking penalty on Mark Tinordi, which resulted in a five-minute power play for the Stars. With the home crowd roaring and momentum on their side, the Stars looked to tie the game. But Tom Barrasso locked down, and Jon Casey was called for an interference penalty four minutes into the power play. An empty netter for Pittsburgh with fifteen seconds left sealed the Game 4 win for Pittsburgh, evened the series at 2–2, and sent the series back to Pittsburgh for Game 5.

Game 5 started similarly to Game 4, with quick Pittsburgh goals in the first period. They scored three goals early in Game 4, but put up four goals in the first thirteen minutes of Game 5 (Mario Lemieux, Kevin Stevens, Mark Recchi scored twice in less than two minutes). Bob Gainey benched Jon Casey (allowed four goals on 13 shots) fourteen minutes into the game. The blame shouldn't be placed entirely on Casey for the Game 5 start: the Stars defense was beaten in the neutral zone, allowed breakaways and open shots, turned the puck over in their own zone, and did not get to loose pucks.

With the Pittsburgh organist playing "Do You Know the Way to San Jose" (a dig at the rumors the North Stars were going to be relocated), fans holding signs that read "Remember Super Bowl IX" (a 16–6 Steelers win over the Vikings), a 4–0 lead, and Minnesota's playoff-hero goalie removed from the game, the fans packed inside the Igloo were fired up.

Casey, who had started all twenty-two Stars playoff games with a 2.76 goals-against average, was replaced by Brian Howard. Howard made a couple terrific saves after entering the game, including a phenomenal save on a Lemieux breakaway. The Stars seemed invigorated by Howard and got on the board with a Neal Broten shorthanded goal with just under six minutes left in the first.

Another golden opportunity presented itself for the Stars at the beginning of the second period: Barrasso had to be substituted after pulling a groin muscle. He was replaced by former Gopher goaltender Frank Pietrangelo (played for the Gophers from 1982–86), who was immediately swarmed by desperate North Stars.

"You just can't be as sharp as you'd like to be," said Pietrangelo, who hadn't played in thirty-four days. "You just try to go in there and get the job done."

Dave Gagner scored another shorthanded goal for the Stars at 6:54 in the second to cut the deficit to a 4–2. After setting a playoff record with thirty-five power play goals, the Stars had equaled their total power play goals (3) with shorthanded goals (3) in the Pittsburgh series.

Ron Francis scored a goal for at 16:26, giving Pittsburgh a 5–2 lead heading into the second intermission.

Ulf Dahlen scored his second goal of the postseason little over ninety seconds into the third period, and Gagner scored at 7:42 to bring Minnesota to within a goal.

What Stars fans likely remember most from Game 5 was the questionable officiating from referee Kerry Fraiser during the last ten minutes of the third period. After the Stars went on the power play after crosschecking penalty against Pittsburgh's Peter Taglianetti, Fraiser called two soft penalties against Minnesota following the Dahlen goal that killed momentum—Gagner (tripping at 9:49) and Brian Glynn (cross check at 10:05). Not only did it eliminate the North Star's power play chance but it also gave Pittsburgh a two-man advantage for just under 1:09.

"There were some questionable things that happened," said Coach Bob Gainey. "The first penalty was just a push behind the net. I think all players should be treated equal, but sometimes it doesn't seem that way."

The Stars were able to kill the two penalties while only allowing one shot on goal and began frantically looking for the equalizer against Pietrangelo.

With two minutes left in the third period, Neal Broten tried to wrestle Troy Loney away from the net. Larry Murphy fired the puck toward Hayward. The puck bounced off the back of Broten's skate and snuck past Hayward for a 6–4 lead. Loney was awarded the goal.

"I didn't feel anything," Loney said of the goal. "I went to the net and I didn't see what happened, and I never felt the puck hit me or anything."

"He [Fraiser] gives 'em a 5-on-3 and then a goal like that," an angry Gaetan Duchesne said after the game. "Loney didn't even try to get his stick on the puck on that last goal."

Gainey argued, to no avail, that the puck was kicked in (replay showed the puck deflecting off Broten's skate) and that Loney was in the crease. Fraiser awarded the goal anyways.

The Stars were heading back to Bloomington with their back against the wall in their first elimination game of the playoffs, but they knew they were 8–2 at the Met Center that postseason. Brian Hayward was one of the few optimistic Stars after the game. "Maybe we can get something out of coming back so hard."

The North Stars headed into Game 6 in a blur of what-ifs: What if they hadn't spotted the Penguins a 3–0 lead in Game 4 and a 4–0 lead in Game 5 and hadn't given up seven goals in the first seventeen minutes of the last two hockey games?

The Stars came into Game 6 looking to become the first team since the 1971 Montreal Canadiens to come back from 3–2 deficit to win the championship, but a lot of Stars fans wouldn't have the opportunity to watch the game at home. Owner Norm Green decided not to put Game 6 on local TV for free, but instead, he elected to black out the game and put it on cable-access pay-per-view for $12.95 (Green waned $460,000 from KMSP-Channel 9 and their sponsors to air the game on their station—up from the $250,000 for Game 5).

The big question for Bob Gainey was who his starting goaltender would be. Casey had set a team record by starting all twenty-two playoff games (winning fourteen) but had given up seven first-period goals in the previous two games. Casey had been pulled in favor of Hayward five times in the playoffs, but Gainey went right back to him the previous game. And it had been paying off. Casey was 3–1 in games after he had been benched.

But it was Hayward that helped keep the Pittsburgh offense at bay after relieving Casey less than fourteen minutes into Game 5, stopping 16 of 18 shots on net. Minnesota outscored Pittsburgh 4–2 after Casey had left.

Gainey went with Casey to start the elimination game. While Casey had gone ice-cold, so had the power play. In the first three series, the North Stars scored on 26.8 percent of their power play opportunities. Against Pittsburgh, they only converted on 9.1 percent.

Nine seconds into the game, Neal Broten was penalized for interference, and the Penguins scored on their first shot of the power play (Ulf Samuelsson) two minutes into the game. The Stars had a two-man advantage with Kevin Stevens and Gordie Roberts in the penalty box together for ninety seconds, but Lemieux stole the puck and scored a shorthanded goal on the breakaway for a 2–0 lead. Joey Mullen scored for Pittsburgh less than a minute later, and the Penguins led 3–0 13:14 into the hockey game. Casey was pulled for Hayward in the first period again after giving up the three goals on only eleven shots.

Hayward didn't do much better. Bob Errey put the puck past Hayward midway through the second period, and after breakaway goals from Ron Francis and Joe Mullen (his second of the game), Pittsburgh extended the lead to 6–0.

Hayward was pulled in the third after giving up a goal to Jim Paek (a rookie who had only played in three games that season), who was set up beautifully by Lemieux. Gainey sent Jon Casey back out to finish the game with 18:31 left as disappointed fans began filing out of the Met.

Larry Murphy scored on the power play at 13:45 (Lemieux's third assist of the game) to make it 8–0.

"We just ran out of gas," said Dave Gagner. "You can't blame us as much as give credit to them. They had the better team."

The eight-goal defeat is the largest margin of defeat in an elimination game in Stanley Cup history.

Lemieux played in only five games in the series, but still scored 12 points (he led the NHL with 28 postseason assists) and was named the Conn Smythe Trophy winner as playoff MVP. The city of Pittsburgh was undefeated in the championship round of any sport dating back to 1960. (The Pittsburgh Pipers won the inaugural ABA Championship in 1968, the Pittsburgh Steelers won four Super Bowls in the 1970s, and the Pittsburgh Pirates had won the three World Series they had been in since 1960.)

The Pens would repeat as Stanley Cup Champions in 1992. Minnesota improved their record to 32–42–6 in 1992 but lost in the opening series to the Detroit Red Wings (they lost Game 7 after leading the series 3–1). It would be their last postseason appearance before relocating to Dallas.

May 17, 1992
The 1992 NBA Draft Lottery

The lottery was created to eliminate the perceived incentive to lose games. Obviously, the Rockets became the team on which most people focused. Even if teams were not losing on purpose to better their position, the perception did exist.

-David Stern, NBA commissioner

The Minnesota Timberwolves were still in their infancy in 1991. Through their first three years in the league, the baby NBA franchise had only won 66 of their first 246 games, including a 15-67 (.183) season in 1991. Following the season, the team was ready for as fresh a start as a third-year franchise can get by dealing Tony Campbell to the New York Knicks and Pooh Richardson and Sam Mitchell to the Indiana Pacers.

The Timberwolves finished with the worst record in the NBA, and prior to the 1991-92 season, only three teams had finished with fewer wins in NBA history: the 1972-73 Philadelphia 76ers (9), the 1986-87 LA Clippers (12), and the 1982-83 Houston Rockets (14).

Two of those teams had the top picks in the upcoming drafts. In 1973, the 76ers took Doug Collins (who, with Julius Erving, would eventually lead Philadelphia to the NBA Finals in 1977); and in 1983, the Houston Rockets, one year removed from the NBA Finals, had the first of back-to-back first overall picks (they took the Twin Towers—Ralph Sampson in '83 and Hakeem Olajuwon in '84).

The Timberwolves, who were the only team to win fewer than twenty games in 1991, were ready for their turnaround.

Back to the Houston Rockets for a second, because the Rockets had a huge impact on the Wolves draft position woes.

In 1981, the Rockets were in the NBA Finals for the first time in franchise history and were matched up against Larry Bird, Kevin McHale, Cedric Maxwell, Robert Parrish, and the legendary Boston Celtics. The Celtics had been a thorn in the side of the Rockets forever. A year after relocating from San Diego in 1971, Houston moved from the Western Conference to the East, and the Celtics had knocked them out of the playoffs in two of their four appearances (1975 and 1980). Prior to the 1981 NBA season, Houston had moved back to the Western Conference and, despite a 40–42 regular season record, found themselves matched up against the familiar Celtics in the Finals.

The Celtics won the series in six games for their fourteenth NBA championship.

The Rockets won forty-six games in 1981 behind an MVP season from Moses Malone, but they lost to Seattle in the first round of the playoffs.

That is when the floor drops out.

Malone signed a six-year deal with the Philadelphia 76ers, who had just lost the NBA Finals to the Los Angeles Lakers. Houston went from a forty-six-win team in 1982 to a fourteen-win team in 1983. Some attribute the negative thirty-two win differential to Moses Malone signing with Philadelphia during the off-season. Some attribute it to a seven-foot-four prospect out of Virginia.

Ralph Sampson, a three-time Naismith Award winner and two-time Wooden Award winner, declared for the draft after graduating from Virginia in 1983. He considered going pro after his junior season, but the top overall pick came down to a coin flip between the LA Lakers and the San Diego Clippers. Rather than risk playing for the Clippers (the Lakers won the top pick and selected James Worthy, and the Clippers took journeyman Terry Cummings second), Sampson returned for his senior season.

After being selected number 1 overall by Houston in 1983, Sampson averaged 21 points and 11 rebounds. Houston started the season 20–29—not great but respectable considering they had fourteen total wins a season prior. But the real red flag that stands out is their 9–27 record the last thirty-six games.

The reason? The Rockets decided to "evaluate other talent on the team." I guess practice wasn't enough time to evaluate the guys on the bench. What they were really had their eye on was the 1984 draft class.

In 1983, the top pick was determined by a coin flip between the worst two teams in each conference. So if you had the worst record you had a 50/50 shot of getting the top pick in the draft.

That is when league officials began setting new rules in motion to dissuade tanking, which is when a team intentionally loses games to have better draft position. The Rockets were obviously doing it. It was a no-brainer with some of the top talent of the decade ready to come into the NBA: John Stockton from Gonzaga, Charles Barkley from Auburn, Alvin Robertson from Arkansas, Hakeem Olajuwon from Houston, Sam Bowie from Kentucky and Michael Jordan from North Carolina.

The Rockets finished with the second-worst record in the league at 29-53, but won the coin flip against the 26-56 Indiana Pacers, who had traded their first-round pick to Portland.

Houston had their pick out of everybody in what is considered by many to be the greatest draft class in NBA history. The Rockets decided to pass on the top guard in the draft (Michael Jordan) and double down on the big men, selecting the seven foot center Olajuwon from the University of Houston.

The reloaded Rockets would return to the NBA finals in 1986, only to lose again to the Boston Celtics.

After the 1984 Draft, the NBA had had enough of the tanking rumors clouding the game and affecting the quality of their product. Beginning in 1985, the league went to a lottery system, where teams with the worst record still had the best chance to land the top overall pick but weren't guaranteed anything.

However, the first NBA Draft Lottery is surrounded in a dark cloud as well. Many people believed that the NBA and David Stern rigged the 1985 NBA Draft in favor of the large-market New York Knicks, who had the third-best odds of being awarded the top pick. New York selected coveted big man Patrick Ewing out of Georgetown.

Over the next six seasons, only two of the worst teams earned the top pick.

Now, we catch up to the 1992 NBA Draft. The Timberwolves had the best chance to land the top overall pick, and there was a can't-miss player at the top.

Shaquille O'Neal was a monster like the NBA hadn't seen before. The powerful seven-foot-one 325-lb center from LSU had NBA teams salivating, including Timberwolves head coach Jimmy Rodgers.

The consolation prize was the second pick and the opportunity to draft another big man to build around, Georgetown's Alonzo Mourning.

The Orlando Magic (21–61) won the top pick and drafted Hall of Famer Shaquille O'Neal. The Charlotte Hornets (31–51) won the second pick and drafted Hall of Famer Alonzo Mourning. The Wolves (15–67) were awarded the third pick in the draft and picked Christian Laettner.

Despite being the third overall pick in the draft, Laettner is still defined by his college days and is remembered for his game-winning shot against Kentucky in the 1992 NCAA tournament. He would put up decent numbers during his time in Minnesota (17 points per game), but the Wolves only won sixty games over the next three seasons with Laettner on the team. He developed a reputation as a locker-room distraction on losing teams (the guy had never played on a losing team before coming to Minnesota) and was eventually traded to Atlanta for Andrew Lang and an old Spud Webb.

Shaq would win four championships over his career and established himself as the premier center of the twenty-first century. Mourning was an elite defender and would win a ring [with Shaq] in Miami in 2006. Laettner was a one-time All-Star [with Atlanta] and never advanced past the second round in the five times his teams made the playoffs [zero with Minnesota].

March 10, 1993

The North Stars Announce the Move to Dallas

Why would you move a hockey team from Minnesota to Dallas?
—Neal Broten

The NHL was expanding in the early 1990s. After absorbing the final four WHA teams in 1979 (Hartford, Edmonton, Quebec, and Winnipeg), the NHL was looking to expand to warmer climates. And the Minnesota North Stars would be a huge part of it. The North Stars had played at the Met Center in Bloomington since their inception in 1967, but owners wanted to move the team out of small-market Minnesota into a larger, untapped market.

The first attempt to do this was by George and Gordon Gund in 1990. George Gund had a previous venture with NHL hockey on the West Coast with the California Golden Seals and, as a minority owner, was an integral part in convincing owner Mel Swig to relocate the Seals to the Gunds' hometown of Cleveland in 1976. Swig had purchased the Seals in 1975 with the intention of moving them across the bay to San Francisco. Despite attendance and team play improving, the team relocated to Ohio.

Renamed the Cleveland Barons, the team continued to lose money. The Barons wouldn't have been able to finish the 1977 season had it not been for a $1.3 million loan. Swig sold his majority share of the Barons to the Gunds following the season.

After two more down seasons, the Gunds' decided to fold. It was the first time since 1942 that an NHL team had folded.

The North Stars were in rough shape in the late 1970s as well. The placement of the WHA's Minnesota Fighting Saints had the two teams fighting for attendance dollars. The Fighting Saints folded after three and a half seasons, but the North Stars were hanging on by a thread. Things were so bleak that NHL president

Clarence Campbell was worried that the North Stars would go bankrupt too. By 1978, the North Stars had missed the playoffs five of the last six seasons. The Gunds' had a solution to the problem: merging the North Stars and the Barons. New NHL president John Ziegler agreed.

The Stars absorbed the Barons in 1978 and brought a few talented players over in the merger: goaltender Gilles Meloche and forwards Al MacAdam and Mike Fidler.

With the two franchises merged, the North Stars would make the playoffs each of the next seven seasons, advancing as far as the Stanley Cup Finals in 1981. However, the 1984 season would be the last winning season while the team was in Minnesota.

With attendance numbers starting to fall, the Gunds began their second NHL relocation project. After being instrumental in moving the NHL from Oakland to Cleveland, George wanted to return hockey to the West Coast. There hadn't been any new teams to enter the league since absorbing the rest of the WHA in 1979, and no expansion franchises had been created since the league expanded to twelve teams in 1967.

The Gunds were fed up with the Minnesota Sports Commission. They tried to buy land around the Met Center but were unable to secure the property and started exploring options to move the team to the West Coast.

In 1990, the Gunds applied with the league to relocate the North Stars to the Bay Area. Their initial request was denied because the NHL had bigger plans.

There was already a group trying to form a new expansion franchise in California led by former Hartford Whalers owner Howard Baldwin. A new arena was being built in San Jose to house a new team beginning in 1991. The Gunds weren't happy that their relocation request was denied by the other owners, but they all struck an agreement: the Gunds would sell the North Stars to Baldwin's group that included Rent-a-Car chairman Morris Belzberg and Calgary Flames minority owner Norm Green for $31.5 million and would then take ownership of the new San Jose franchise. As part of the deal, the North Stars would be able to participate in the expansion draft with the new San Jose Sharks franchise and cover the $50 million expansion fee.

Following the 1989–90 season, the NHL held a dispersal draft before the expansion draft. Before the dispersal draft, the North Stars protected fourteen players and two goaltenders. From the remaining players, the Sharks selected fourteen players and two goaltenders to balance out the players acquired in the North Stars/Barons merger in 1978.

After the dispersal draft, the Sharks and North Stars selected ten players each from the other NHL teams.

Only an idiot could lose money on hockey in Minnesota. -Norm Green

In 1979, Norm Green was part of a group that purchased the Atlanta Flames and moved the franchise to Calgary. He was co-owner when the Flames won the Stanley Cup in 1989. In 1990, the NHL asked him to sell his shares with the Flames in order to be a part of the North Stars purchase.

Green purchased 51 percent controlling interest in the North Stars, with Baldwin and Belzberg splitting the other 49 percent. But by October 1990, after feuds with the other men, Green purchased the rest of the shares and became the sole owner of the North Stars.

Despite the team's surprise run to the 1991 Stanley Cup Finals with a record of 27–39–14, Norm Green was already planning on moving the team west. While the Gunds had initially been denied their franchise in California, he was trying to pull a Bob Short and move a beloved Minnesota team to Los Angeles to become the LA Stars. A deal was all but done, but just like in San Jose, there were already plans in place and a group of investors, this time the Walt Disney Company, to create an expansion team (the Mighty Ducks of Anaheim were one of two teams introduced in 1993, alongside the Florida Panthers). Again, the league asked a favor from Green. They told him that if he didn't fight the Anaheim expansion team, they would let him move the North Stars to any new market of his choice.

Green explored nontraditional hockey markets like Phoenix, where he would have a monopoly on the market instead of having to share it with other California teams in San Jose, Los Angeles, and Anaheim; but a deal couldn't be reached.

Midway through the 1992–93 season, Green still didn't have a place to move the team. With his top locations ruled out, he turned his attention to another large traditional market that didn't have an NHL team: Texas. He reached out to the only Texan he knew, Roger Staubach. Roger vouched for Dallas and said it would be a great city to relocate to.

The decision to move the North Stars to Dallas was announced to the fans on March 10, 1993, with sixteen games left in the '93 season. He cited a couple reasons for his decision to move the team: poor attendance, losing seasons, the inability to attract corporate sponsorships, and lost revenue. Norm also wanted to move out of the Met Center and into a new stadium. There were also sexual harassment allegations from employees that he wanted to distance himself from, including a $50,000 lawsuit from a former executive assistant.

Green had a brand-new arena (Reunion Arena, which they shared with the NBA's Dallas Mavericks), and had over ten thousand requests for season tickets in Dallas. Green lost three thousand season ticket holders in Minnesota after raising ticket prices (which, at the time, were the lowest in the league) following the team's 1991 Stanley Cup Finals run. He also was welcomed to share the new Target Center with the Wolves but didn't want to share the $77 million price tag with Wolves owners Marvin Wolfenson and Harvey Ratner. As for corporate sponsorships, Pepsi was a sponsor of the Met Center and the North

Stars. Coca-Cola had advertising and pouring rights for the Timberwolves and the Target Center.

"Can you blame Green for refusing to give in to the political pressure to move his team to the arena next to the Minneapolis garbage burner?" *Star Tribune* writer Patrick Reusse said in an April 1992 column.

"My franchise is worth more if it can be moved," Norm Green said. "If the stadium commission wants me to give up that right, it is going to have to pay for it. If I would sell out of town—which I won't—I could walk away with a $10 million profit."

Another reason Green said it didn't work was the amount of hockey in Minnesota. "If you did a survey in Minnesota that asked if the people there had to keep just two out of these three—pro hockey, college hockey, high school hockey—the answer wouldn't be surprising. The NHL would lose easy," Green said in a 1993 interview with the *Chicago Tribune*.

The North Stars played their last game at the Met on April 13 in a 3–2 loss to the Chicago Blackhawks. Their final game as Minnesota's team was a 5–3 loss in Detroit. Despite it being their seventh consecutive losing season (36–38–10), Minnesota missed the playoffs for the first time since 1989. Russ Courtnall scored the last North Stars goal at the Met, and Ulf Dahlen scored the final goal in the franchise's Minnesota history on the road in Detroit. The North Stars departed with a 758–970–334 record in twenty-six seasons that included seventeen trips to the postseason.

Green took everything to Dallas with him except the "North"—head coach Bob Gainey, Neal and Paul Broten, Andy Moog, and Mike Modano. He took the logo, the name, and the color scheme. He hung Bill Goldsworthy and Bill Masterton's numbers from the rafters. From the outside looking in, it looked like the Stars had created and written their history in North Texas.

After moving to Dallas, the team made the postseason seven of its first eight seasons. Gainey coached two and a half seasons before stepping down from his coaching duties (he stayed with the Stars as the general manager) midway through the 1995–96 season and promoted the coach of their IHL affiliate, Ken Hitchcock. The year after taking over for Gainey, Hitchcock coached the team to the first of five consecutive Central Division titles. In 1997, only five years after leaving Minnesota, the Dallas Stars beat the Buffalo Sabres in the Stanley Cup Finals. The same year, NHL commissioner Gary Bettman announced that Minnesota would get an expansion franchise for the 2000–01 season.

Green wasn't there to see the success of the Stars, however. Due to more financial trouble, he was forced to sell the team to Tom Hicks in December 1995—exactly two years after announcing the team's move to Dallas.

April 30, 1992

Game 7 versus Detroit: the Final Playoff Game

It's very frustrating to be up 3–1 and not be able to finish them off.
—Neal Broten

One year after their Cinderella run to the Stanley Cup Finals, the 1992 North Stars were geared up for another playoff run. They were the fourth seed with 70 points in the Norris Division and drew the division champion Detroit Red Wings—a team they had never faced in the playoffs.

The Red Wings tallied 98 points (43–25–12), finishing ahead of Chicago (87 points) and St. Louis (83 points). Toronto finished in last with 67 points—only three behind Minnesota for the final playoff spot. Winnipeg, which finished in fourth in the Smyth Division, had 81 points. Calgary finished in fifth with 74. Only Toronto and the expansion San Jose Sharks and their 39 points had fewer points than Minnesota.

The Stars had four 30 goal scorers in 1992: Mike Modano (33), Brian Bellows (30), Dave Gagner (31), and Ulf Dahlen (career-high 36). The next highest goal total was Mike Craig with 15. The hero from the 1991 Stanley Cup finals run, Jon Casey (19–23–5, .882 save percentage, 3.40 GAA), split time at goalie with Darcy Wakaluk (13–19, .881 save percentage, 3.28 GAA) after Brian Hayward was selected by the San Jose Sharks in the 1991 Dispersal Draft.

Detroit was at the beginning of their dynasty, making the playoffs in the second year of what would be a string of twenty-five consecutive playoff appearances—a run that would include four Stanley Cup Championships. But in 1992, they were still looking for their first title since 1955.

Detroit featured future Hall of Famers Steve Yzerman (103 points), Sergei Federov (86 points), and defenseman Nicklas Lidstrom plus Tim Cheveldae and his league-leading 38 wins in 72 starts between the pipes.

Despite the division title, Detroit had struggled against the North Stars. They were 3–4–1 against Minnesota that season, but they still liked their chances in a seven-game series.

The North Stars won the first two games of the series at Joe Lewis Arena 4–3 and 4–2. After a 5–4 overtime loss in Game 3, they won 5–4 in Game 4 and were one win away from upsetting the number 1 seed in the first round of the playoffs for the second year in a row (they beat a 106-point Blackhawks team in 1991).

But Minnesota's offense disappeared in Games Five and Six, losing 3–0 and 1–0 in overtime. After scoring 17 goals in the first four games, they couldn't buy a goal against Cheveldae, who stopped all 56 shots he faced in the two games and hadn't allowed a goal in his last 145 minutes on the ice. Cheveldae, who was on the verge of embarrassment after allowing 13 of the 17 goals in those four games (backup goaltender Vincent Riendeau gave up 4 goals in the Game 4 loss) to one of the worst offensive teams in the NHL (the Stars ranked twentieth of twenty-two teams in goals scored). But now, after back-to-back shutouts, Cheveldae was transforming into the series hero.

Cheveldae had stood on his head in overtime of Game 6 to keep the Stars out of the back of the net. Tinordi hit the post in the opening minutes. Sergei Fedorov's goal at the 16:11 mark of overtime, which hit the top of the net just behind the crossbar, was reanalyzed by video replay after the goal light didn't turn on; and it was ruled good. It was the first game-deciding goal in playoff history that was subjected to video replay (video replays were implemented the same season). The home Met Center crowd littered the ice with beer and soda cups. Modano was hit by a whiskey bottle while sitting on the bench (the man who threw the bottle was arrested after other fans in the stands held him down until police arrived). Fans tore cushions off the seats and threw those on the ice too.

The Stars hadn't scored since Todd Elik's goal at 11:27 in the third period of Game 4.

With the series now tied at 3–3 after leading the series 3–1, the Stars needed to regain the offense they had in the first four games as they headed back to Detroit for Game 7.

The Red Wings had been on both sides of the situation in previous seasons. In 1987, they came back from a 3–1 deficit to beat the Toronto Maple Leafs. In 1991, they led the St. Louis Blues 3–1, but they lost the next three games to lose the series.

Game 7 was played on April 30, 1992. The winner would face Chicago, who dispatched the St. Louis Blues in six games. Coming into the game, Stars head coach Bob Gainey knew that would have to rely on the team's depth to win the game.

"I can't expect players like Mike Modano, Mark Tinordi, Neal Broten, or Gaetan Duschesne to play any better than they have," he said. "Jon Casey and Derian Hatcher have played great defense. They've brought this team to the edge of winning or losing by one goal the last two games. We have to look at other players who haven't had their names written so far—Dahlen, Bellows, Elik, and [Dave] Gagner. We need more from them. I can't go to Broten and Casey and ask them for more."

Tinordi knew the game plan for Game 7. "We have to get one by Cheveldae. We're not going to win by not scoring goals. We've hit a couple crossbars and three or four posts. That's the difference in this series."

Another difference in the series was NHL vice president Brian O'Neill's ruling on a Steve Yzerman spearing penalty from Game 5. Yzerman only received a minor penalty in the game, and the Stars asked the NHL to review the call, especially since they had suspended Derian Hatcher for three games after a high stick broke Kevin Miller's jaw in Game 4. O'Neill stated that Yzerman should have been assessed a major penalty, but a suspension wasn't warranted.

Game 7 started like the other six did—great puck movement by both teams. Casey stopped the first nine Wings shots, including a couple on a power play. The Wings were 0–15 on the power play at home during the series but finally broke through on Federov's power play goal at 11:04 in the second to give Detroit a 1–0 lead. Three minutes later, it was 2–0 when Alan Kerr scored. Gerard Gallant made it 3–0 with just over two minutes left after he stole the puck in the Stars zone and beat Casey on a wraparound goal.

The Stars peppered Cheveldae, but he stopped the first 18 shots. With a two-man advantage in the third period after a Ray Sheppard interference penalty and a penalty on Cheveldae for having too little tape on the shaft of his stick, Brian Bellows ended the Stars' scoreless streak at 118 minutes and 36 seconds with a power play goal 4 minutes into the third period.

"After we lost Game 6, the first goal was going to be a momentum builder," Bellows said. "We had four solid chances to score in the first period but didn't. When it was 3–1, we thought we were in pretty good shape."

Detroit restored their three-goal lead at 7:35 when Bob Probert popped a rebound past Casey. Shawn Burr added another goal at 16:53 to make it 5–1. Minnesota scored a goal at 19:09 courtesy of Mike Craig. Forty-nine seconds later, octopi littered the ice as Detroit completed the comeback and eliminated the North Stars.

The Wings became the ninth team in NHL history to win a series after trailing three games to one, and it's only the third one to come back after losing the first two games at home.

June 3, 1993
Twins Can't Sign Jason Varitek

There were some great players taken in the 1993 MLB Draft: a player with 700 home runs and more than 3,100 hits in Alex Rodriguez, a Cy Young winner in Chris Carpenter, and a closer with 422 saves in Billy Wagner. Twenty-three of the top 30 picks made it to the major league.

The Minnesota Twins had the twentieth and twenty-first overall picks, the first coming from Cincinnati as compensation for the Reds signing John Smiley. The Twins used that pick on nine-time Gold Glove winner Torii Hunter.

With the twenty-first pick in the draft, the Twins selected catcher Jason Varitek out of Georgia Tech.

Varitek is one of only three players to play in the Little League World Series, College World Series, and Major League World Series. He was a three-time All-Star, a Gold Glove winner, a Silver Slugger winner, and a two-time World Series Champion. He caught a record four no-hitters from four different pitchers.

And he did it all with the Red Sox.

Varitek, who was named the fourth captain in Boston Red Sox history in 2004, did not sign with the Twins after being drafted. Instead, he returned to Georgia Tech to play for first year coach Danny Hall, who had never had a losing season at Georgia Tech (1994–2018). With Varitek and teammates pitcher Brad Rigby, outfielder Jay Payton, and shortstop Nomar Garciaparra, Georgia Tech finished runner-up to Oklahoma in the 1994 College World Series.

He was drafted again in the first round of the 1994 MLB Draft, making him one of only three players to have been selected in the first round of the MLB Draft, along with catcher Charles Johnson (Montreal in 1989 and Florida in 1991) and outfielder JD Drew (Philadelphia in 1997 and St. Louis in 1998). He was drafted fourteenth overall by the Seattle Mariners. (The Twins had the eighth overall pick, but they drafted infielder Todd Walker over Varitek and other future

All-Stars Garciaparra and Paul Konerko, who were taken twelfth and thirteenth, respectively).

The Twins did get a compensatory pick for failure to sign Varitek in 1993. They drafted pitcher Travis Miller (7–18, 5.05 ERA in seven seasons) thirty-fourth overall. And they got their catcher of the future, drafting A. J. Pierzynski in the third round.

Varitek almost didn't sign with the Mariners either. He signed with the Independent League St. Paul Saints, then agent Scott Boras declared his MLB contract void since he signed with a non-MLB affiliate. MLB said that under its Rule 4 draft that any player who hasn't signed with a major or minor league team is eligible to be drafted the following year. Varitek did eventually sign with the Mariners and never played with the Saints.

Varitek never played for the Mariners big league club either. After three seasons at AA Port City and AAA Tacoma, he was traded to the Red Sox with pitcher Derek Lowe for closer Heathcliff Slocumb in what is seen as one of the most lopsided trades in baseball history.

<<BONUS ACHE>>

Failed Twins First Round Picks

Varitek wasn't the only first-round miss for the Twins. Pitcher Bryan Oelkers was the fourth pick overall in 1982 (0–5, 8.65 ERA) and taken before one pick ahead of Dwight Gooden. Pitcher Tim Belcher was the first overall pick in 1983, but the Twins weren't able to sign him. Catcher Derek Parks was the tenth pick in 1986 and only played forty-five games over three seasons with the Twins. Outfielder Dave McCarty was the third overall pick by the Twins in 1991 but only played parts of three seasons in Minnesota. He was drafted ahead of All-Stars Dmitri Young, Manny Ramirez, Cliff Floyd, and Shawn Green. First baseman Travis Lee was the second overall pick in 1996 and used a loophole to become a free agent and signed a four-year $10 million contract with Arizona. Pitcher Ryan Mills was the sixth pick in 1998, but he never made it to the majors and was picked ahead of Felipe Lopez, Carlos Pena, Brad Lidge, and C. C. Sabathia. Outfielder B. J. Garbe was the fifth pick in 1999. He never made it to the majors and was taken before Barry Zito, Ben Sheets, and Alex Rios. Pitcher Adam Johnson was the second pick in 2000 (1–3 with a 10.25 ERA in nine games for the Twins). From 1976 to 2011, the Twins had fourteen top 10 draft choices, and only two of them became impact players: Michael Cuddyer (ninth overall in 1997) and Joe Mauer (first overall in 2001).

April 22, 1995

The Vikings select Derrick Alexander over Warren Sapp

Before the 1994 season, the Vikings traded future Hall of Fame defensive end Chris Doleman along with their 1994 second-round pick to the Atlanta Falcons in exchange for their 1994 second-round pick (David Palmer) and their first-round pick in 1995.

Without Doleman and his pass rush ability on the outside, the Vikings saw their sack total drop from 45 to 36 (Roy Barker and James Harris combined for 6.5 whereas Doleman had 12.5 by himself the previous year). The 10–6 Vikings made the playoffs as a wild card team before losing to the Chicago Bears in the opening round of the playoffs. They recognized their need to find an elite pass rusher to pair with John Randle to replace not only Doleman but also Pro Bowl defensive tackle Henry Thomas, who had signed with Detroit after the season. With Atlanta's pick they had gotten in the Doleman deal, the Vikings had the eleventh and twenty-fourth picks in the NFL draft.

There were several good pass rush prospects in the draft: Kevin Carter from Florida, Mike Mamula from Boston College, Hugh Douglas from Central State (Ohio), Warren Sapp from Miami, and Derrick Alexander from Florida State.

Warren Sapp was the best defensive player available in the draft. Sapp filled his trophy case in 1994: the Bronko Nagurski Award (best overall defensive player), the Lombardi Award (best defensive lineman or linebacker), the Bill Willis Award (best defensive lineman), was named first-team All-American and the Football Writers' Association of America Defensive Player of the Year.

Sapp should have been one of the first players off the board on draft day, but rumors of character issues and drug use began to surface. Executives weren't sure if he was work the risk. The first five players taken (Ki-Jana Carter to Cincinnati, Tony Boselli to Jacksonville, Steve McNair to Houston, Michael Westbrook to Washington, and Kerry Collins to Carolina) were all offensive players. St. Louis and Philadelphia each decided to pass on Sapp and took Kevin Carter and Mike Mamula, respectively. Three more offensive players (Joey Galloway, Kyle Brady, and J. J. Stokes) came off the board with picks eight, nine, and ten. Then it was Minnesota's turn. Unbeknownst to Denny Green and the Vikings, Warren Sapp would become a Hall of Fame pass rusher. Could you imagine him paired up the middle with John Randle?

Denny Green and his staff elected to take Derrick Alexander. Sapp was taken by the Tampa Bay Buccaneers with the next pick.

Alexander was a serviceable player for the Vikings. The 1994 ACC Defensive Player of the Year started twelve games at right defensive end during his rookie season, combining for 34 tackles and 2 sacks. His numbers steadily increased every year, and he had a career year in 1998: 42 combined tackles and 7.5 sacks.

Alexander left Minnesota via free agency after 1998 and signed with the Cleveland Browns. He played there for one season before retiring.

Sapp, meanwhile, was a four-time All-Pro and seven-time Pro Bowler for the Buccaneers. The 1999 Defensive Player of the Year racked up 96.5 sacks (second most by a defensive tackle behind John Randle's 137.5) and helped lead Tampa Bay to a win in Super Bowl XXXVII.

June 18, 1995

Tom Lehman Loses the First of Three Straight US Opens

I let it slip through my fingers.

—Tom Lehman

Minnesota fans have a special place in their hearts for homegrown talent. We love the "one of us" stories.

Pro golfer Tom Lehman was born in Austin, Minnesota, and moved up north to Alexandria at a young age. He golfed collegiality at the University of Minnesota and went pro in 1982. At age thirty-six in 1995, he was still looking for his first major tournament win. He finished as the runner-up at the 1994 Masters Tournament behind José María Olazábal.

Lehman was tied atop the leader board with Greg Norman at the 1995 US Open at Shinnecock Hills (New York) after three rounds after firing a third-round 67.

Norman was sitting −5 after Day 2 of the event, but a +4 on day 4 brought him to −1 for the tournament, tied with Lehman and one shot ahead of Phil Mickelson and Bob Tway. Corey Pavin, Nick Price, Steve Stricker, Scott Verplank, and Ian Woosnam were all tied for fifth place a +2.

Norman and Lehman both pared Hole 1, but a Norman bogey on 2 and a Lehman birdie on 3 gave Lehman a two-stroke lead. Norman played par golf through Hole 12. Meanwhile, Lehman bogeyed 4, 10, and 11 and double bogeyed 7 to fall two shots back. Corey Pavin, who started the day at +2, was now tied with Lehman for second place and was two shots behind Norman for the lead.

Pavin and Lehman each shot a birdie on 12, and Norman bogeyed the hole to tie the group at +1.

Hole 13 resulted in pars for Pavin and Lehman and another bogey for Norman to move him one shot back.

The group of three each pared 14. Pavin and Norman recorded birdies on 15, while Lehman shot par. With three holes left, Corey Pavin had a one-shot lead at even par.

Lehman's drive on the par 5 sixteenth hole ended in the rough. Lehman had to aim left and play a fade or aim right and hook it back toward the short grass. He chose the hook, only it didn't hook. He then had to chip out of the rough onto the fairway. He later missed a five-foot bogey putt. The double bogey on the hole to move to +3. Norman would bogey 17 to move to +2.

Pavin, meanwhile, was still even thru 17 before his second shot from the fairway on Hole 18. Pavin's legendary shot from 209 yards out with his four-wood came to rest within ten feet of the hole. He would par the hole to win his first major. Norman finished +2, and Lehman finished +3 after having a two-shot lead over Pavin after nine holes.

Norman, who was 5 under after thirty-six holes, was +7 over his last two rounds. He went to thirty-two consecutive holes without a birdie. For Lehman, there were numerous missed opportunities with two double bogeys on the final day, and he was unable to overtake a plummeting Norman yet unable to hold off a surging Pavin.

It wouldn't be the last time Lehman would struggle in the US Open. In 1996, he had a three-stroke lead over Steve Jones after eight holes in the final round but lost to by a stroke after bogeying 18. In 1997, he had a two-stroke lead heading into the final round but bogeyed two of the final three holes to finish in third behind Ernie Els and Colin Montgomerie. He led after fifty-four holes in three straight US Opens—something that hadn't been done since Bobby Jones in 1928–30. Jones won two of three. Lehman didn't win any.

July 12, 1996

Kirby Puckett Retires

It was a pleasure for me and every other Twins' fan, and baseball fans, to be able to sit and watch every game he played. How lucky am I? – Twins manager Tom Kelly

Ten All-Star Games. Six Gold Glove Awards. Batting Champion. Six Silver Slugger awards. Four-time hits leader. Seven top 7 MVP finishes. All-Star Game MVP. Postseason Hero. Hall of Famer. Kirby Puckett did it all for the Twins from his four-hit major league debut in 1984 to that final at-bat at the Metrodome in September 1995.

Puckett hit .314 with 23 home runs and 99 RBI in his last season with the Twins. He was voted to his tenth consecutive All-Star Game and was the only player left from the two World Series teams in 1987 and 1991.

On September 28, 1995, the Twins were finishing their final home stand against the Cleveland Indians. Facing Dennis Martinez in the first inning and down 0–2 in the count, Martinez hit Puckett in the face with a fastball, breaking his jaw and ending his season. Nobody would have imagined that it would be Puckett's final at bat.

The 1996 season was full of optimism for the Twins. Puckett was back and healthy, and the team had signed future Hall of Famer Paul Molitor as their DH. Puckett and Molitor were supposed to bring the Twins back to relevancy after three losing seasons.

Puckett was on fire in spring training. He lit up the Grapefruit League with a .344, including getting two hits off Atlanta Cy Young winner Greg Maddux. But one day after facing Maddux, Puckett woke up with a black dot in his right eye. When the dot eventually went away, he still couldn't see out of the eye.

Four laser surgeries later, Puck's eyesight hadn't returned. Six hours after his last surgery, Puckett was at a press conference at the Metrodome, sunglasses over the patch on his right eye, announcing that his sight wouldn't return and that he was immediately retiring from baseball. At the age of thirty-six, he was done.

He finished his career with a .318 batting average (the highest career average for an AL batter since Joe DiMaggio), a .360 OBP, 207 homers, 414 doubles, and more than 1,000 runs and RBI each. He is the only player in Twins history to hit .300, get 200 hits, score 100 runs, and knock in 100 RBI in two different seasons (1988 and 1992).

Without Puckett, the Twins would finish 79–83 in 1996 despite big years from Molitor (.341, 113 RBI), Chuck Knoblauch (.341, 45 stolen bases) and Marty Cordova (.309, 111 RBI). A huge what-if in Twins history is what that team could have accomplished with Puckett in the lineup instead of rookies Rich Becker and Matt Lawton.

After he retired, the Twins hired him as an executive vice president. He would also receive the 1996 Roberto Clemente award for his community service.

Kirby Puckett had his number 34 retired by the Twins in 1997 and was elected into the Baseball Hall of Fame in 2001 on his first ballot. Eight months later, he was hiding from the public as his reputation took several hits. In 2002, a woman filed a restraining order against his wife, Tonya, after she threatened to kill her over an alleged affair with Puckett. She later asked for a protective order from Puckett, claiming that he assaulted her. Later that year, Puckett was accused of groping a woman in an Eden Prairie restaurant bathroom. He was charged with false imprisonment, fifth-degree criminal sexual misconduct, and fifth-degree assault. He was found not guilty on all counts, but the damage to Puck's reputation was done.

He stepped back from his annual pool tournament that had raised $4 million for Children's HeartLink and his University of Minnesota scholarship program. He pulled himself from the Twins Winter Caravan lineup. He decided not to help the team lobby for a new downtown ballpark.

In March 2003, *Sports Illustrated* columnist George Dohrmann published an article about Puckett, documenting his darker private life and revealing a new side of the heavily revered star: extramarital relationships with several women during his playing days, claims of sexual harassment, and threats of physical harm to his wife whom he later divorced.

After the incident and the article, Kirby faded out of the public eye and moved to Arizona. His close friends started to worry about Kirby and his health, as his weight had climbed to an estimated three hundred pounds.

On the morning of March 5, 2006, Puckett suffered a massive stroke at his home in Arizona. He underwent surgery to try to relieve the pressure from his brain, but it was unsuccessful. Kirby Puckett was dying. Friends and former coaches and teammates flew to Arizona to say their goodbyes. The next day, Kirby Puckett passed away at the age of forty-five. He was the second youngest Hall of Famer to die after being inducted (only Lou Gehrig, age thirty-seven).

Twins fans were shocked at the news of the loss of their former superstar. The afternoon of March 12 was declared Kirby Puckett Day. A public ceremony was attended by fifteen thousand fans during a blizzard at the Metrodome. In 2010, a statue was unveiled in the plaza of Target Field commemorating Puckett and his game-winning home run in Game 6 of the 1991 World Series.

June 26, 1996

The Timberwolves trade Ray Allen for Stephon Marbury

I'm just looking forward to being there forever. I'm just going to be at Minnesota with Kevin Garnett.

—Stephon Marbury

The 1996 Draft is considered one of the best draft classes in NBA history, with one third of first-round picks becoming All-Stars. That draft saw three MVPs, eight All-NBA players, and two Defensive Player of the Year recipients. The consensus number 1 pick in the 1996 Draft was Georgetown's Allen Iverson. Other first-round elections included Shareef Abdur-Rahim, Antoine Walker, Peja Stojakovic, Jermaine O'Neal, Steve Nash, Zydrunas Ilgauskas, and Kobe Bryant.

The Timberwolves had the fifth pick in that draft and selected guard Ray Allen out of UConn. During his nineteen-year career, Allen was a ten-time NBA All-Star, two-time NBA Champion, and All-time leader in made three-point field goals (both regular and postseason). In 2018, he was elected into the Naismith Memorial Basketball Hall of Fame.

He was a member of the Minnesota Timberwolves for nineteen minutes and thirty-seven seconds.

Kevin McHale was promoted from assistant general manager to vice president of basketball operations in 1995. In 1996, he traded troubled guard J. R. Rider and his East Bay Funk Dunk to the west coast Portland Trail Blazers for James Robinson, Bill Curley, and a first-round pick (twentieth overall pick in 1997, Paul Grant). With Rider gone, the Wolves needed an electric guard to pair with Kevin Garnett.

The guard McHale had his eye on was Stephon Marbury of Georgia Tech. Marbury was regarded as the best pure point guard in the draft. He averaged 19 points and five assists for a 24–12 Yellow Jackets squad that made it to the Sweet 16 in the NCAA tournament.

Before Rider was dealt to Portland, there was nearly a deal in place to trade him and the Wolves' first-round pick to Toronto for the second overall pick. With the Philadelphia 76ers likely to take Georgetown's Allen Iverson number 1 overall, it would all but guarantee Marbury would end up in Minnesota.

But the deal stalled, and Minnesota stayed at the number 5 spot in the draft. All he could do was hope that the teams ahead of Minnesota in the draft; Philadelphia, Toronto, Vancouver, and Milwaukee didn't take him.

After Philadelphia took Iverson, Toronto took future Defensive Player of the Year Marcus Camby out of UMass. With the third pick, the expansion Vancouver Grizzlies took Pac-10 Freshman of the Year Shareef Abdur-Rahim out of Cal.

And with the fourth pick, Milwaukee took Marbury. Minnesota settled for UConn guard Ray Allen.

Before the draft, Milwaukee general manager Mike Dunleavy and McHale had agreed to a trade if the situation arose: Milwaukee would draft Marbury then trade him to Minnesota for Allen and a first-round pick.

Wolves fans were ecstatic to get Marbury. The duo Garnett and Marbury established themselves as the best young duo in the NBA and immediately began garnering comparisons to Karl Malone and John Stockton. Marbury was runner-up to Iverson in the Rookie of the Year voting, and he helped lead the Wolves to the playoffs for the first time in franchise history. After getting swept by Houston in the first round, Marbury improved in every major statistical category in his sophomore season. More points, steals, assists, rebounds, field goal percentage, minutes, and played in eighty-two games. In the playoffs, they took Seattle to five games, but they lost in the first round for the second consecutive season.

The following off-season, Garnet signed a six-year, $126 million contract extension that prompted a lockout. Owners renegotiated the collective bargaining agreement to limit maximum player salaries. Marbury saw his maximum earnings drop to $71 million, a little over half what Garnett would make.

Marbury, who was entering the final year of his rookie contract, repeatedly declined the Wolves' extension offers. Instead, he demanded a trade to either New York or New Jersey. Media reports narrowed it down to three reasons: he was jealous of Garnett's massive contract, he wanted to play in a larger market for the endorsement opportunities, and he wanted to play closer to his home in Brooklyn, New York.

Eighteen games into the 1999 season, he got his wish. He was traded to the New Jersey Nets in a three-team deal that brought Terrell Brandon to Minnesota from Milwaukee and sent Sam Cassell from New Jersey to Milwaukee. Garnett signed the big extension to stay, looked up, and his wingman was gone.

Ray Allen, on the other hand, joined a Milwaukee Bucks team that was rebuilding with Glenn Robinson and Vin Baker. The Bucks would miss the playoffs the first two years Allen was there. After the lockout, they hired George Karl and acquired Sam Cassell in the Stephon Marbury–to–New Jersey trade. Milwaukee made the playoffs in the lockout-shortened season at 28–22—Milwaukee's first playoff appearance since 1991. After the season, Allen signed a six-year $70.9 million extension.

In 2001, Allen, Robinson and Cassell had the Bucks one win away from the NBA Finals. In Game 7 of the Eastern Conference Finals, Allen scored a team-high 26 points in a 108–91 loss to Iverson and the 76ers. The following season, the Bucks were pegged as Eastern Conference favorites, but they finished 41–41 and missed the playoffs by one game. The next season, he was traded to Seattle.

Marbury bounced around the league. After three seasons in New Jersey, he was traded to Phoenix Suns for Jason Kidd. In 2003, he was traded back east to the New York Knicks. After five abysmal seasons in New York, he was released, then he signed with the Boston Celtics in 2009—a Boston team that boasted both Kevin Garnett and Ray Allen, who had just come off a championship season together.

But Minnesota fans will always wonder what would have happened if Marbury had stayed more than two-plus seasons or if McHale never would have traded for him at all.

<<BONUS ACHE>>

Adreian Payne

Flip Saunders became the general manager of the Timberwolves in May 2013. After taking a year to access the talent he had on the team, he began building. He traded a protected future first-round pick to the Atlanta Hawks for forward Adreian Payne in 2015. Payne was the fifteenth overall pick out of Michigan State in 2014 but had bounced between the NBA and the D-League in his first couple months as a pro. He played ninety-nine games for the Wolves between 2015 and 2017, starting twenty-four of them while averaging 4 points and 3 rebounds per game. He was released following the 2017 season. The future first-round picked ended up being shooting guard Kevin Huerter (nineteenth overall pick in 2018). Huerter averaged 10 points per game in his rookie season and was named to the All-Rookie Team.

April 24, 1997

The NBA Playoffs versus Houston

When they made runs at us, we panicked, but when we made runs at them, they just retaliated even more.

—Tom Gugliotta

For the first time in their eight-year history, the Minnesota Timberwolves were headed to the postseason. Finishing 40–42 and third in the Midwest Division behind the eventual Western Conference champion Utah Jazz and Houston Rockets, twenty-year-old Kevin Garnett and the Wolves were ready to make a run in the playoffs.

Also leading the charge with Garnett was rookie standout Stephon Marbury, whom Wolves general manager Kevin McHale had made a draft-day deal for. Forward Tom Gugliotta earned his only career All-Star Game appearance that year and led the Wolves in scoring with 20 points per game. Garnett and Gugliotta were both named to their first All-Star team that season, giving the Wolves their first ever All-Stars. The Wolves also traded for James Robinson and Cherokee Parks and signed free agents Dean Garrett and Chriss Carr.

Even though they finished the season two games under .500, the Wolves earned the sixth seed with a tiebreaker over the Phoenix Suns (the 36–46 LA Clippers were the eighth seed). They drew division opponent Houston in the opening round of the best-of-five series.

The Rockets had won the second of back-to-back NBA championships two years before and still featured their star player since 1984, center Hakeem Olajuwon. Rockets GM Carroll Dawson had traded four players to the Phoenix Suns for future Hall of Famer Charles Barkley to give the Rockets a dual big threat in the front court. Throw in another future Hall of Famer in shooting guard Clyde Drexler. Eighth-year player small forward Mario Elie, who played a vital bench role in the two Houston titles in the mid-90s, was a regular starter for the first time in his career, and Coach Rudy Tomjanovich went with Vanderbilt rookie Matt Maloney as his point guard. Maloney would start all eighty-two regular season games for the Rockets that year.

In Game 1, it wasn't one of the three guys you'd expect to have a big game: it was Elie and Maloney. While the Wolves held Barkley, Drexler, and Olajuwon to a combined 22 points in the first half, Elie scored 13 and Maloney was 4 of 5 from three-point range in the first half. Marbury led the Wolves with 26 points, and Garnett added 21 in his first career playoff game. But the Rockets outrebounded the Wolves 58–36 as Dream and the Round Mound of Rebound had eleven boards each as the Rockets cruised to a 112–95 Rockets win.

Game 2 was closer, with the Wolves taking a 79–78 lead on a Marbury three with just under six minutes left in the game. Houston responded with free throws from Elie and Barkley and a bucket by Olajuwan to go on an 11–2 run, then Drexler sealed the win with a three-pointer with about a minute left. Despite the Wolves' best effort and 22 points from Marbury and 26 rebounds from Garnett, the Wolves dropped Game 2 of the series 96–84.

The Wolves hosted their first ever postseason game at the Target Center on April 29, 1997, in a must-win elimination Game 3. Just like Game 2, the game was close the whole way. The game was tied 59–59 at the half. Just like he was in Game 1, Maloney kept Houston in the game with the three-ball, scoring a career-high 26 points and making 6 of 8 three-pointers. As a team, the Rockets shot 53 percent from beyond the arc (15 for 28) to keep the hungry Wolves at bay. Along with Maloney's 26, Barkley added 20 points; and Hakeem chipped in 19 en route to a 125–120 win. Coming into the matchup, Houston was 15–0 when winning Game 1 of a five-game series. Marbury averaged 21 points and 8 assists in the series, and Gugliotta scored 18 points per game. Garnett added 17 points and 9 rebounds a game.

For Houston, Barkley and Olajuwon each averaged 18 points and 10 rebounds, and Elie and Malone's numbers weren't that off those of the future Hall of Famers with Elie also scoring 18 points per game and the rookie Maloney scoring 17.

Minnesota's first-round playoff exit would turn out to be the first of seven consecutive postseason appearances without a series win. Houston would beat the Seattle SuperSonics in seven games in the next round before losing to Utah in six games in the Western Conference Finals.

March 10, 1999

The Gophers Vacate Their 1997 Final Four Appearance

In the two years I was there, I never did a thing. Either Jan or Jeanne did everything.
—Former player Russ Archambault

The 1997 Minnesota Golden Gopher men's basketball team may have been the best team in the history of the program. A 31–4 record, a Big Ten Championship, a number 1 seed in the NCAA tournament, and a Final Four appearance with a team loaded with NBA talent (Bobby Jackson, Sam Jacobson, John Thomas, Quincy Lewis, and Trevor Winter).

But if you look in the history books or in the rafters of Williams Arena, you'll find nothing.

After their exciting NCAA tournament run that included wins against Texas State, Temple, Clemson, and UCLA before falling eventual-champion Kentucky, expectations were high for the 1997–98 squad despite losing Big Ten Player of the Year Bobby Jackson (round 1, pick 23 by Seattle) as well as John Thomas (round 1, pick 25 by New York) to the NBA Draft). The Gophers finished 20–15 overall but finished eighth in the Big Ten with a 6–10 conference record and missed the NCAA tournament; however, the Gophers did win the NIT Tournament 79–72 over Penn State.

The Gophers returned to the Big Dance the next season, finishing 17–11 and 8–8 in conference play. But the day before the Gophers were scheduled to face Gonzaga in the first round of the NCAA tournament, the *St. Paul Pioneer Press* published an article accusing U of M office manager Jan Gangelhoff of doing coursework for more than twenty men's basketball players since 1993. In the article, George Dohrmann wrote that Gangelhoff was completing coursework, taking exams, and being paid $3,000 in cash by Gophers' head coach Clem Haskins to tutor his players. In 1996, she was caught doing a take-home exam with former player Kevin Loge. Two players, Russ Archambault and Courtney James, were driven to Gangelhoff's home for tutoring sessions. Gangelhoff also said that she gave the same paper to different players for different classes.

As soon as Dohrmann's article was published, the U of M and the NCAA began an investigation. The school suspended four players (Kevin Clark, Miles Tarver, Antoine Broxsie, and Jason Stanford) for the tournament. Minnesota was upset in the first round by 10-seed Gonzaga, who would advance to the Elite 8.

Gopher Nation was outraged by the timing of the article. The *Pioneer Press* received angry letters and hostile phone calls. Minnesota Governor Jesse Ventura was upset too and accused Dohrmann and the press of sensationalism journalism. After the article came out, two more people came out claiming to have done schoolwork for U of M basketball players: Gangelhoff's sister Jeanne Payer and sociology major Alexandra Goulding.

In October 2000, the NCAA released their findings in a public infractions report. In the report, they found the university guilty of academic fraud. It was found that Gangelhoff prepared nearly four hundred pieces of coursework for about twenty different men's basketball players between 1993 and 1998. The whole thing was organized by academic counselor Alonzo Newby, and Haskins knew about Gangelhoff doing coursework for his players. Newby and players intimidated staff into changing grades for student-athletes to remain eligible. In addition, the NCAA found that Haskins and his athletic program had gave cash and other benefits to student-athletes in the basketball, football, and men's hockey programs. The investigation cost the U of M $2.5 million.

The NCAA and the university came down hard on the men's basketball program. The university gave themselves a self-imposed postseason ban for the 1999–00 postseason, reduced their scholarships, and forfeited 90 percent of the money the school made for their 1994, 1995, and 1997 NCAA tournament appearances (an estimated $350,000). Minnesota president Mark Yudof bought out the contract of Clem Haskins for $1.5 million and accepted the resignations of vice president McKinley Boston and athletic director Mark Dienhart. Three years later, Haskins was ordered by a Hennepin County District court to return $815,000 of his buyout for committing fraud by lying to the NCAA.

A month after releasing Haskins, the U of M hired Dan Monson away from Gonzaga to take over the program one month after his Bulldogs eliminated the Gophers from the tournament.

> If we could go back and do it again everybody would do it totally different. And you try to teach your kids how not to make the same mistakes you made as a young man. (Former player Bobby Jackson)

The NCAA acted too. They placed the university under probation for four years, took away five more scholarships, reduced paid recruit visits, and issued show-cause penalties to Haskins, Newby, and Gangelhoff.

In addition to all that, the NCAA also vacated all the Gophers postseason wins as well as records and awards from 1994 to 1998. In total, the Gophers vacated three NCAA tournament appearances (including their Final Four appearance), two NIT tournament appearances (including the 1998 NIT Tournament Championship), Bobby Jackson's Big Ten Player of the Year award (1997), and Clem Haskins' Big Ten and National Coach of the Year awards (1997).

George Dohrmann, meanwhile, won the 2000 Pulitzer Prize for beat reporting for his reports on the scandal.

April 24, 1998

The Wolves blow a 2–1 lead versus Seattle

We feel awful good about coming back from 1–2.
—Seattle coach George Karl

The season after leading the Timberwolves to their first playoff appearance, Kevin Garnett and Stephon Marbury continued to blossom into one of the league's best duos. Garnett's 18 points and 10 rebounds per game, plus Marbury's 18 points and 9 assists led the Wolves to their first winning season (45–37) and their second straight playoff berth. And they had done it without All-Star Tom Gugliotta, who missed the entire second half of the season with an ankle injury.

In addition to singing veteran bench piece Tom Hammonds and trading Stojko Vrankovic to the Clippers for center Stanley Roberts, the Wolves also traded Doug West to Vancouver for Anthony Peeler midseason.

The Timberwolves had an explosive offense in 1997–98. Their 101.1 points per game average was the second highest in the Western Conference behind Shaquille O'Neal and Kobe Bryant's Los Angeles Lakers. But they also gave up a lot of points: 100.4, good for fourth worst (the teams below them were 19–63 Vancouver with 103.9, 17–65 LA Clippers with 103.3, and 11–71 Denver with 100.8). At 45–37, the Wolves entered the playoffs as the number 7 seed in the West and matched up against Gary Payton, Vin Baker, and the 61–21 Seattle SuperSonics.

The Sonics won their third straight Pacific Division title in 1998. The had lost to Michael Jordan's Chicago Bulls in the 1995 NBA Finals, and had lost a close Game 7 to Houston in 1996 after being down 3–1 in the series. Longtime Sonic Shawn Kemp signed with Cleveland before the season started, but Seattle signed three-time All-Star Vin Baker to replace him in the lineup. Baker started all eighty-two games for Seattle in 1997–98 and averaged 19 points, 8 rebounds, and a block per game.

Game 1 was at KeyArena in Seattle. The Wolves, having been swept in the opening round by Houston the year before, was still looking for the franchise's first playoff win. And it didn't come in Game 1. Minnesota only shot 33 percent from the field, including an abysmal 3 of 24 in the second quarter, where they trailed 53–32 at the half. They were only outscored by four points in the second half, but the game had pretty much been decided. In his first career playoff game, Vin Baker (who didn't make the playoffs in four seasons with the Milwaukee Bucks) scored 25 points and had 12 rebounds. Garnett led the Wolves in scoring with 18 points and pulled down a Wolves playoff record of 18 boards.

In Game 2, the Wolves broke their four-game playoff losing streak. Led by 25 points from Marbury and 21 points from Terry Porter, the Wolves beat the Sonics on their home floor 98–93 for the franchise's first playoff win. Gary Payton scored 32 points in the loss but needed 25 shots to do it (12 of 25, 48 percent).

In Game 3 back at Target Center, midseason acquisition Anthony Peeler was the star. Peeler scored a career playoff-high 20 points, including 4-for-7 from beyond the arc as the Wolves stunned Seattle with a 15–4 fourth quarter run to win Game 3 at home, 98–90.

The Wolves had a chance to clinch their first postseason series in Game 4 at the Target Center, but being down 2–1 in a five-game series wasn't anything new to coach George Karl and the Sonics. The previous year, they were down 2–1 to the Phoenix Suns but came back to win the series. If they wanted to continue their quest for their first NBA title since 1979, they'd have to do it again. Seattle hadn't lost three straight games the entire season.

Hersey Hawkins for Seattle scored the first bucket of Game 4; a three. Seattle started the game on a 7–0 run and led after the first quarter 28–21 as Minnesota closed the quarter on a 10–3 run, the last five points of the run coming from Michael Williams. Hawkins had 16 points after the first quarter and hit three of four threes. Minnesota kept the run going in the second quarter, outscoring Seattle 13–5 and taking a 34–33 lead with 4:51 left in the half. Seattle would bounce back and finish the quarter strong and led 46–43 at halftime.

Garnett would tie the game at 58–58 with a turnaround jumper in the third. KG would finish the game with a team-high 20 points and 10 rebounds. Peeler would put the Wolves in front with his fifth three of the night with just over three minutes to play in the third. But again Gary Payton, Detlef Schrempf, and Sam Perkins responded again, scoring the next nine Seattle points while taking advantage of seven consecutive misses by Minnesota. Williams ended Minnesota's scoring drought with a little leaner after ending the third period with a bad turnover with less than a second left. After three quarters, Seattle led 67–63.

As much as Minnesota fought back, Seattle responded every time. The Sonics extended the lead to 10 points, 77–67, with 8:30 left to play in the game on a deep

Payton three ball—his only made three of the game. He'd finish with 24 points, 8 assists, and 6 rebounds.

Trailing 84–78, Porter was fouled on his way to the basket and went to the line for two shots with the chance to get the Wolves to within four points with a minute left in the game. He'd miss both free throws. On the other end, the Wolves fouled Hawkins to send him to the line. He made both shots to extend the lead back to a six-point game.

After a quick Garnett make on the other end, Hawkins went back to the free throw line and made two more free throws. A quick Marbury three with thirty seconds left cut the lead to 88–83. Once again, Hawkins was fouled on the inbound, and once again, he made both of his free throws.

Trailing by seven in the closing seconds, Marbury drove the lane, made the shot, and was fouled to send him to the free throw line. After completing the three-point play, the Wolves trailed by four points with ten seconds left. The Sonics inbounded the ball to Hawkins, and he was fouled again, sending him to the line. He only made one of two free throws to give Seattle a 91–86 lead with eleven seconds left. Quick back on their own end, Marbury found Garnett under the basket for a quick layup to cut the deficit to three points, 91–88.

On the inbound, the Wolves began face-guarding Hawkins to keep the ball away from him. Instead, Nate McMillan got the ball to point guard Greg Anthony, who was fouled instead. Anthony was 63 percent from the free throw line that season and missed the first in front of a now-raucous Target Center, feeling that they were destined for a big bucket to end the game and send it to overtime.

Anthony made the second. With no time-outs, Marbury streaked up the court and shot a three while trying to draw contact. He hit the back iron and didn't draw the foul call as the Sonics escaped Game 4 with a 92–88 victory and a decisive Game 5 in Seattle. Hawkins finished with 24 points—16 in the first quarter and was eight of nine from the free throw line.

In the Game 5, the Wolves were lights out from beyond the arc in the first half, hitting ten of fifteen three-point shots. Peeler had 17 first-half points, and Minnesota had a 47–44 lead at halftime.

But the Wolves went ice cold in the second half, hitting only one of ten threes. Payton, who played all forty-eight minutes of Game 5, took advantage. He opened the third quarter with a three-pointer, followed by three threes by Hawkins (Seattle would sink seven third-quarter threes). Seattle would end the third quarter on a 10–2 run with Payton scoring six of the ten points. Sam Perkins put Seattle in the lead for good, putting his team up 63–62 in the third.

In the fourth, who else but Hawkins hit a crucial three-point shot with under four minutes left to give Seattle a nine-point lead, but it was Schrempf who stole a pass and slammed the ball home with under a minute to give Seattle a 95–82 lead.

Seattle won Game 5 97–84.

Anthony Peeler had another good game for Minnesota, scoring a franchise playoff record 28 points. Garnett and Marbury did not. The two stars combined for only 14 points, were 5 of 21 from the field, and had a combined 15 turnovers, 10 by Garnett.

Seattle completed the 2–1 series comeback two years in a row and advanced to the next round to face the LA Lakers, a team they had beaten three out of four times in the regular season.

The Lakers won the series 4–1.

<<BONUS ACHE>>

More Wolves Playoff Woes:
1999 NBA Playoffs versus San Antonio

The Timberwolves finished an even 25–25 in the lockout shortened season in 1999. It would also be the final playoff run for Kevin Garnett and Stephon Marbury, who would request a trade after KG signed his record-breaking six-year $126 million contract. The Wolves snuck into the playoffs as the eighth seed, where they met top-seeded San Antonio. The Wolves and Spurs split the first two games, before San Antonio won the next two to win the best-of-five series 3–1. It was Avery Johnson, not Tim Duncan or David Robinson, that led the Spurs in scoring over the four games with nearly 20 points per game. Garnett averaged 22 points, 12 rebounds, 4 assists, and 2 blocks per game in the losing effort as the Timberwolves lost in the first round of the playoffs for the third consecutive season. The Spurs would win their first NBA title in franchise history and the first of five titles for Tim Duncan.

2000 NBA Playoffs versus Portland

The 2000 Timberwolves won a franchise record of fifty games, but even fifty wins wasn't enough to secure home court advantage in a stacked Western Conference. They matched up against the fifty-nine-win Portland Trail Blazers, led by Rasheed Wallace, Steve Smith, Damon Stoudamire, and Scottie Pippen. The Wolves lost by three points in Game 1 and four points in Game 2 at Rose Garden Arena, but won Game 3 94-87 at Target Center. Portland took Game 4, 85-77, to eliminate the Wolves in the first round. Scottie Pippen led the Blazers in scoring and rebounding with 19 points and seven boards per game. Terrell Brandon led Minnesota in scoring with 20 points and 9 assists per game. Kevin Garnett nearly averaged a triple double for the series: 19 points, 10 rebounds, 9 assists in the four-game series as the Wolves were eliminated in the opening round for the fourth straight season.

2001 NBA Playoffs versus San Antonio

The Timberwolves made their fifth straight playoff appearance after finishing 47–35 in 2001 and opening the playoffs against top-seeded San Antonio, just as they had done two years earlier. Tim Duncan averaged 22 points and 13 rebounds, and David Robinson averaged 17 points and 12 rebounds as the Spurs defeated the Wolves in four games. It was the fifth consecutive first-round playoff exit for the Wolves.

2002 NBA Playoffs versus Dallas

The Wolves tied a franchise-best fifty wins in 2002. The Wolves were 28–9 before Terrell Brandon hurt his knee and missed the rest of the season. They made the playoffs for a sixth straight time and this time matched up against Dirk Nowitzki's Dallas Mavericks. Dirk averaged 33 points and 15 rebounds in the three-game sweep of the Wolves. Michael Finley put up 24 points a game, and Steve Nash averaged 21 points and 9 assists as the Mavs beat the Wolves by an average of 10 points per game. It was the sixth consecutive first-round playoff exit for the Wolves.

May 17, 1998

Twins at New York Yankees: The David Wells Game

I'm going to cherish this for the rest of my life.

—David Wells

On May 17, 1998, pitcher David Wells was three days away from his thirty-fifth birthday. The journeyman pitcher had signed with the New York Yankees before the 1997 season after prized free agent pitcher Roger Clemens elected to sign with the Toronto Blue Jays (Wells was included in a trade in 1999 that brought the eventual seven-time Cy Young Winner to New York).

The Twins were 18–23 and on their way to a sixth consecutive losing season (they'd finish 70–92). The Yankees, meanwhile, were 27–9 and on their way to a 114-win season and their second World Series title in three seasons.

Wells had been less than stellar in his first eight starts. Although he had a 4–1 record, his ERA coming into the game was 5.23. Two starts before his matchup with the Twins, he had given up seven runs in 2.2 innings of work against the Texas Rangers (the Yankees still won the game 15–13).

Wells arrived at Yankee Stadium on May 17th after only an hour of sleep the previous night after partying with SNL actors Jimmy Fallon and Seth Meyers. According to his 2003 autobiography, he got to work "half-drunk with bloodshot eyes, monster breath and a raging, skull-rattling hangover."

Luckily for Wells, he was facing a horrendous Twins lineup that would finish eleventh in the American League in scoring. Missing from Tom Kelly's lineup that Sunday afternoon was David Ortiz, who was hitting .306 and leading the Twins with a .531 slugging percentage. Ortiz was on the disabled list with a broken bone in his hand. Second baseman Todd Walker, who was hitting .359 at that point, was also on the bench for the unfavorable lefty-lefty matchup. In his place and batting second was Brent Gates and his .179 average.

The Twins' starting lineup that day featured Matt Lawton, Gates, Paul Molitor, Marty Cordova, Ron Coomer, Alex Ochoa, John Shave, Javier Valentin, and Pat Meares with LaTroy Hawkins on the mound.

Wells only needed nine pitches in the first inning to cut through the Twins lineup, and only thirteen in the second. The Yankees took a 1–0 lead in the bottom of the second on a wild pitch that scored Bernie Williams from third base. Williams also hit a solo home run off Hawkins in the fourth for a 2–0 lead.

Wells struck out Shave, Valentin, and Meares in the third inning. After striking out Cordova and Coomer in the fifth, the nearly fifty thousand fans at Yankee Stadium for Beanie Baby Day started to realize what was happening.

The only real trouble Wells ran into was in the seventh inning. After getting Lawton to fly out to center to start the inning, first baseman Tino Martinez may have saved the perfect game. Brent Gates hit a hot grounder to first, but Martinez was able to beat Gates to the bag. The next batter Wells faced was future Hall of Famer Paul Molitor.

Molitor was playing his final season of pro baseball. The forty-one-year-old with well over three thousand hits at this point was still one of the most respected hitters in baseball, despite only hitting .250 during the first six weeks of the season.

Wells got behind Molitor 3–1. Home plate umpire Tim McClelland had given both Wells and Hawkins a pretty wide strike zone all day.

"I had a pretty good at bat working and took some close pitches," Molitor said. "He threw that 3–1 pitch, then came back with a pitch maybe 1–2 inches further away."

Baseball fans may remember McClelland best as the home plate umpire in the George Brett Pine Tar game (nine years later, McClelland worked the game in which Brett recorded his three thousandth hit and was the first person to congratulate him) and for his safe call of Matt Holliday in the bottom of the thirteenth inning of the 2007 NL Wild Card tiebreaker between the Colorado Rockies and San Diego Padres.

Molitor didn't swing, and McClelland called strike 2. Wells targeted the outside corner with a fastball that Molitor swung through for strike 3, retiring the Twins in the seventh.

The Yankees offense put another two runs up in the bottom of the inning. After Bernie Williams doubled for his third hit of the day (he finished 3-for-3 with two doubles and a solo home run and three runs scored), Darryl Strawberry hit him in with a triple. Chad Curtis knocked in Strawberry with a single to give the Yankees a 4–0 lead.

In the top of the eighth, Chuck Knoblauch almost cost Wells a perfect game. 1998 was Knoblauch's first season with the Yankees after being traded by the Twins. He was still considered one of the best fielding second basemen in the game, having won a Gold Glove Award the previous season. Ron Coomer hit a scalding line drive right at Knoblauch at second base. Knoblauch went down to a knee to field the grounder but dropped the ball. He was able to recover and throw out Coomer by a step and a half.

"Coomer's ball was the only one that was hit solidly," Wells told reporters after the game. "It was the only one that gave me a scare. When he hit it, I thought, *That's going to center field.*"

In the ninth, Wells got Shave to fly out, struck out Valentine for his eleventh strikeout, then induced Meares to pop up to Paul O'Neill in right field, who caught the ball a couple feet from foul territory for the final out.

"I've never been on a team that's been no-hit," Molitor said after the game. "As a fan of the game, it's a good thing for baseball and a good thing for the Yankees."

For the Yankees, it was their first no-hitter since Doc Gooden no-hit the Mariners in May 1996, and it was the tenth no-hitter in franchise history.

It was the fifteenth perfect game in Major League history, and the first for the Yankees since Don Larsen's masterpiece against the LA Dodgers in Game 5 of the 1956 World Series (David Cone would throw a perfect game against the Montreal Expos in July 1999 to give the Yankees three, which is the most of any baseball franchise).

It was the fourth no-hitter pitched against the Twins since relocating from Washington in 1961 (Catfish Hunter threw a perfect game in May 1968, Vida Blue in September 1970, and Nolan Ryan in September 1974). Of those fifteen perfect games through May 1998, two of them have been thrown against the Twins.

January 17, 1999

The NFC Championship versus Atlanta

*It's a pretty good bet. If you think that Gary Anderson will
make this field goal, the answer should be yes.*
—John Madden, FOX Broadcast

The Vikings were perennial playoff contenders in the 1990s. They had a .500 record or better every year that decade except 1990 (when they were 6–10 and trying to recover from the Herschel Walker trade) and made the playoffs seven out of nine times. The most exciting of those years was 1998. The 1998 Minnesota Vikings were a team destined to win the Super Bowl. After starting quarterback Brad Johnson injured his ankle in week 2, Randall Cunningham rejuvenated his career as the Vikings quarterback. With the high-octane passing attack featuring Cris Carter (78 receptions, 1,011 yards, 12 touchdowns) and 1998 Rookie of the Year Randy Moss (69 receptions, 1,313 yards, 17 touchdowns) the Vikings set a new NFL record with 556 points scored.

The Vikings finished the regular season 15–1 and were the top seed in the NFL playoffs. They were the third fifteen-win team in NFL history. The other two (San Francisco in 1984 and Chicago in 1985) both won the Super Bowl, so expectations were high. After their first-round bye, the Vikings dismantled Jake Plummer and the Arizona Cardinals 41–21.

Meanwhile, on the other side of the NFC bracket, the 14–2 Atlanta Falcons were having a miracle season. After failing to make the playoffs the previous two years, new head coach Dan Reeves had completely retooled the roster. Thirty-eight of the Fifty-three players on the 1998 Falcons were on the team for the first time, including quarterback Chris Chandler, who had a career year for Atlanta (career high 3,154 yards, and 25 touchdowns). The 1994 seventh-round pick Jamal Anderson had a career-high 1,846 rushing yards (second only to Terrell Davis's

2,008) and 14 touchdowns (second to Davis's 21). Reciever Terance Mathis led the team with 64 catches for 1,136 yards and 11 touchdowns.

For years, the NFC West (then consisting of Atlanta, San Francisco, New Orleans, Carolina, and St. Louis) was ran by San Francisco. From the time Joe Montana became the full-time starting quarterback in 1981 up until Steve Young's final full season in 1998, the 49ers won 13 NFC West Division titles, made the playoffs sixteen times, and won five Super Bowls. Even though San Francisco was 12–4 in 1998, Atlanta finished 14–2 (the two teams split their season series) and locked up the second seed in the NFC. Their divisional round matchup was against the 49ers after San Francisco held on to beat Green Bay 30–27.

Despite not scoring a touchdown in the second half, Atlanta held on to beat San Francisco 20–18 to knock of the Niners and head to Minneapolis as eleven-point underdogs in their NFC championship matchup with the Vikings.

During the 1998 season, the Vikings were dominant at the Metrodome. They averaged 35 points per game and beat opponents by an average of 23 points per game, and the lowest margin of victory was a 31–24 win against the New Orleans Saints. The Vikings hosted the Falcons on Sunday, January 17, in front of a sold-out Metrodome crowd of 64,060 fans looking for the team's first NFC Championship in twenty-two years.

Atlanta got the ball first and took their opening drive seventy-six yards into the end zone on a five-yard touchdown pass from Chandler to Anderson. A Morton Anderson field goal gave Atlanta an early 7–0 lead. The Vikings responded right away, going eighty yards in five plays that was aided by a thirty-yard defensive pass interference play, while Ray Buchanan was covering Moss. Cunningham hit Moss in the back of the end zone on a thirty-one-yard touchdown on the next play.

The Vikings defense did their part on Atlanta's next drive, with LB Ed McDaniel recovering a Harold Green fumble at the Minnesota forty-one-yard line. Minnesota took the ball to the Atlanta 11, where Gary Anderson hit a twenty-nine-yard field goal to make the score 10–7 Minnesota.

On the first play of Atlanta's next possession, O. J. Howard caught a thirteen-yard pass from Chandler before Orlando Thomas forced him to cough up the ball. Robert Griffith recovered it to give the ball back to the Vikings offense. Six plays later, he was in the end zone after a one-yard quarterback sneak to give the Vikings a 17–7 lead.

The Falcons went three-and-out after consecutive sacks by Tony Williams and John Randle. Dan Stryzinski punted the ball back to the Vikings.

The Falcons defense committed back-to-back penalties (facemask on Jessie Tuggle and unnecessary roughness on Michael Booker) to give the Vikings a free thirty yards. With the ball now on the Atlanta nineteen-yard line, something odd happened. Randy Moss dropped a pass in the end zone with just over three minutes left to go in the half that would have put the Vikings up 24–7. Instead, the Vikings settled for another Gary Anderson field goal to lead 20–7.

After the Vikings' defense forced another Atlanta punt, another uncharacteristic thing happened: the Vikings offense lost a fumble. At their own eighteen-yard line, Cunningham was strip-sacked by Chuck Smith. It was the first fumble the Vikings offense had lost in eleven games.

Chandler found Mathis in the end zone on the first play from Minnesota's fourteen-yard line for the score to cut the deficit to 20–14 with a minute left in the half.

The Vikings got the ball to start the third quarter but couldn't move the ball on their first possession of the second half. The Falcons put together a six-minute drive that got down to Minnesota's seven-yard line. On third and goal, cornerback Jimmy Hitchcock blitzed and tackled Anderson in the backfield for a three-yard loss. Morton Anderson kicked a field goal to bring the Falcons within four points.

Now, with 5:36 left in the third quarter and a 20–17 lead and the offense having trouble moving the ball in the second half, Cunningham and the Vikings offense started the drive at their own eighteen. The Vikings, usually reliant on their explosive offense, only had one play of 20+ yards the entire game, which was Moss's thirty-one-yard touchdown. Cunningham was able to pick apart the Falcons defense and kill clock as well—eighty-two yards in fifteen plays and taking nearly seven minutes off the clock before hitting WR Matthew Hatchette for a five-yard touchdown and a 27–17 lead with 13:41 left in the game.

Mitch Berger's kickoff was taken in the end zone for a touchback. The Vikings' defense held strong on the first two plays, forcing an incomplete pass intended for Mathis and giving up a one-yard run to Tim Dwight. But on third and nine from their twenty-one, Chandler and reciever Tony Martin connected for a seventy-yard gain to the Minnesota nine setting up first and goal. Again, with their backs against the wall, the Vikings' defense held strong and forced another Morten Anderson field goal to make it 27-20.

Each team went three-and-out on their next possessions. With the Vikings up seven and looking to ice the game with 8:42 left, Cunningham fumbled for a second time in the game. Atlanta;s Shane Dronett recovered the ball at the Minnesota thirty-yard line.

Atlanta couldn't pick up a first down and, needing a touchdown to tie the game, threw a pass intended for Mathis on fourth down; but it was defended well by Corey Fuller. No damage done.

At least not on the scoreboard. The Vikings hadn't struggled like this in a game all season. Missed opportunities, mental mistakes, and mounting injuries were taking their toll. All Minnesota needed to do was score one more time and kill clock while doing it.

With 6:07 left and the ball at the Minnesota twenty-five-yard line, the Falcons began to see a heavy dose of Pro Bowl running back Robert Smith and Leroy Hoard. They worked the ball down to Atlanta's twenty-one-yard line. On third and seven, Cunningham targeted TE Greg DeLong with a pass to keep the drive alive. Incomplete. Now fourth and seven, Minnesota sent Gary Anderson out to attempt a thirty-eight-yard field goal and give the Vikings a ten-point lead with just over two minutes left.

It's also important to note that Gary Anderson was the first kicker in NFL history to make every kick during the season. He was 35-for-35 on field goals and 59-for-59 on extra point attempts during the regular season and had made both of his kicks and five extra points in the Arizona playoff game the week before. And because the game is indoors, weather wasn't going to be an issue.

"On third down, I looked at Denny and was like, 'What do you want me to do? Want me to take a shot here?'" The Vikings' offensive coordinator Brian Billick recalled to *Sports Illustrated* in 2018. "He says 'No. Get in position to kick the field goal, kick the field goal and we go to the Super Bowl.' I turned my back to the field because I figured we're going to the Super Bowl. Gary hadn't missed one all year long. He was 100 percent. Had not missed a field goal all season, so I'm going back to the Gatorade thinking it's over."

But it wasn't over. At the snap, the Vikings faced a heavy rush from defensive backs Buchanan and Ronnie Bradford. They ran into Anderson and knocked him to the ground after the kick.

> Here's the snap, the kick is up, and it is . . . no good! No good! Gary Anderson has missed a field goal for the first time in two years! -Atlanta Falcons Radio Broadcast

Anderson missed the kick by about a foot wide left.

The Vikings still led by seven points and had to hold Atlanta out of the end zone in the final two minutes. The Falcons got the ball back on their own twenty-nine-yard line where Anderson had missed and quickly moved the ball downfield against the Vikings defense. Chris Chandler led the Falcons down to the Vikings sixteen-yard line. On first down, safety Robert Griffith dropped a deflected pass that would have ended the game. The easy interception went in and out of his hands, and instead of sealing the win, it gave Chandler a second chance at tying the game.

And he did with a sixteen-yard pass to Mathis with under a minute left in regulation.

Minnesota would have to work quickly to get into field goal position. At their own twenty, Cunningham scrambled for a seven-yard gain before an incomplete pass to Randy Moss on second down. It was third and three from their own twenty-seven-yard line. Denny Green could get aggressive and try for the deep pass, knowing he had the offensive weapons to do it. Or he could play it safe and hope for the best in overtime.

In a move that has been widely criticized in the years following the game, he told Cunningham to kneel the ball, run out the clock, and send the game into overtime.

In 1998, overtime in the playoffs meant the first team to score wins the game. The Vikings won the coin toss and chose to receive the kickoff but were only able to convert one first down before Mitch Berger pinned Atlanta inside their own fifteen-yard line.

After picking up a pair of first downs of their own, Atlanta was forced to punt the ball back to Vikings. Again, the Vikings were only able to convert one first down and were unable to get the ball into scoring position. On third and ten, Cunningham threw the ball just out of the reach of Randy Moss that would have likely ended the game with a long touchdown. Berger had to punt the ball back to the Falcons.

The Falcons drove to the Vikings' twenty-one-yard line—the same place that Gary Anderson had missed from. Morton Anderson didn't miss as his field goal split the uprights. The Falcons defeated the Vikings 30–27 and advanced to their first Super Bowl in franchise history.

"I don't think that city has ever rebounded from it" -Brian Billick

The football world was shocked. The game was playing on the JumboTron at Mile High Stadium in Denver before the AFC Championship Game between the Broncos and the New York Jets. Terrell Davis said after the game that the distraction of not having to face the Vikings, their biggest threat to a second consecutive Super Bowl victory, almost cost them the game.

Meanwhile, in the Vikings locker room, the team was inconsolable. There were NFC Champion banners up in the locker room when the team got off the field. Vikings athletic trainer Fre Zamberletti said that he had never seen so many athletes openly sobbing after a game. In the weeks following the upset, Cris Carter mulled retiring because he was so downtrodden.

Then the second-guessing began. Should the Vikings have kneeled to run out the clock at the end of regulation? Or should they have been aggressive and try to get the ball back into field goal position to give Anderson a chance to win it? The Vikings were aggressive near the end of the first half. Up 20-7 with just over a minute left, Cunningham fumbled inside the 20 and Atlanta scored a touchdown on the next play. And even if the Vikings were able to get the ball into field goal range, what was Anderson's mental state like after missing his first kick in two years? Would they throw to Carter? Or Moss, whom the Falcons held to one catch for four yards in the second half? Was the low-percentage play worth risking another uncharacteristic mistake?

Historians and analysts all agree that the Vikings are the best team in the history of the NFL not to make the Super Bowl. The Vikings became the first 15+-win team not to play in the Super Bowl (later joined by the 2004 Pittsburgh Steelers and the 2011 Green Bay Packers).

Atlanta lost Super Bowl XXXIII to John Elway and the Denver Broncos 34–19.

April 17, 1999

The Vikings Draft Dimitrius Underwood

We did our homework. That's all I can say.
—Vikings scout Roger Jackson

In the 1995 NFL Draft, Coach Denny Green and the Vikings passed on defensive tackle Warren Sapp due to character issues and drug problems. Sapp went on to become a Hall of Fame defensive tackle for the Tampa Buccaneers and Oakland Raiders. In 1998, they took a risk on a talented-yet-troubled wide receiver with the twenty-first overall pick in the NFL draft. It paid immediate dividends. Randy Moss caught a rookie record of seventeen touchdowns and led an NFL record-setting offense to a fifteen-win season.

In 1999, they didn't want to make another Sapp mistake.

After losing to Atlanta in the NFC Championship Game, the Vikings held the twenty-ninth overall pick in the upcoming draft. They also had the eleventh overall pick acquired in a trade with Washington that sent quarterback Brad Johnson to DC.

There was a talented-yet-troubled defensive player for Nick Saban's Michigan State Spartans named Dimitrius Underwood. During his junior season, Underwood had fifty-seven tackles (12 for loss), eight sacks, and two forced fumbles in eleven games. He missed his entire senior season with what was diagnosed as an ankle injury, but there was more going on behind the scenes.

Underwood hurt his ankle before the 1998 season but was medically cleared to return a few weeks into the season. He told Coach Saban that he wanted to wait a couple of weeks to return to the field. Saban recognized some underlying issues with Underwood and wanted him to sit out the entire year to get the mental aspect of his game together then return to the lineup the following season. Underwood, who had NFL plans, responded by walking away from the team and stopped showing up to class.

He declared for the NFL draft—another decision that Saban didn't agree with. Saban told him that he was going to be honest with any NFL scouts that called. Saban ended up raising a lot of red flags around the league with warnings about his mental instability.

Underwood was a projected mid- to late-round pick in the upcoming draft. His physical tools (six feet seven, 280 pounds) and great combine (4.8 40-yard dash) had him ranked as the ninth best defensive end prospect in the draft. He was big, he was fast, and if he could stay healthy, he could develop into an elite pass rusher.

The football world was shocked when he was taken twenty-ninth overall by the Vikings—one pick ahead of All-Pro (and 2007 NFC Defensive Player of the Year) DE Patrick Kearney and with other Pro Bowlers Al Wilson, Mike Rucker, and Dre Bly still on the board. (The Vikings used the eleventh overall pick on QB Daunte Culpepper.)

Ironically, fourteen teams called Nick Saban to inquire about Underwood. The Vikings were not one of them.

"I just have to laugh," said Roger Jackson, the Vikings scout who tracked Underwood through the NFL draft. "We did our homework. That's all I can say. If he fooled us, then he fooled everybody in the league." Apparently, the Vikings did about as much homework as Underwood did during his senior year, because Nick Saban was flat out telling teams not to draft him.

Underwood barely lasted one day as a Viking. He signed a five-year $5.3 million contract on August 1, 1999. After his first practice in Mankato the next day, he went AWOL. Apparently, he hitched a ride to MSP Airport. He flew to Cleveland and, after not having any contact with the Vikings or family members, was found four days later sleeping in a car in his hometown of Philadelphia with eight dollars in his pocket. He says he was conflicted about becoming a professional athlete or his personal obligation to ministry. After another week away from the team, he received a call from Philadelphia Eagles' great defensive end Reggie White, also ordained minister. White convinced him to return to the Vikings. He forfeited his $1.75 million signing bonus and was waived.

After being cut by the Vikings, he said he would retire from pro football, but he signed a one-year contract with the Miami Dolphins two weeks later. He played in one preseason game for the Dolphins, where he dislocated his shoulder. He made the team out of training camp but was inactive the first two games due to his shoulder. That month, he flew to Lansing, Michigan, and got into an argument with his ex-girlfriend, to whom he was paying child support. He attempted suicide by cutting his throat with a sword and was found walking down the street. The Dolphins placed him on the non-football injury list on September 28. He then spent two months in protective care, where he was diagnosed with bipolar disorder. That December, he checked himself into a mental health center in Florida. A week later, he attempted to escape by jumping a fence and fleeing none more emotional than a huge windmill dunk under Sealy's new banner. He lifted two fingers to the sky as he ran back down the court.

<<BONUS ACHE>>

Eddie Griffin

Eddie Griffin was the seventh overall pick by the New Jersey Nets in the 2001 NBA Draft, and he was traded to Houston on draft night. He was named to the NBA All-Rookie Team in 2002, but after two seasons in Houston, he was released after alcohol issues. He signed with the Nets, only to miss the entire 2003–04 season in a rehab center. The Timberwolves signed him to a one-year contract for the 2004–05 season, and he averaged seven points and six rebounds off the bench while keeping his alcohol use in check. After the season, the Wolves signed him to a three-year contract. His numbers declined over the next two seasons as his alcoholism plagued him. He was released by the Wolves after playing in thirteen games in the 2006–07 season.

On August 17, 2007, Griffin was killed when his car collided with a moving train in Houston, Texas. His body was mangled and burned so badly that he had to be identified by dental records. His BAC was .26. Griffin was spending the summer getting into basketball shape to play in Europe the next season. He was twenty-five years old.

June 23, 2000

The Wild Pass on Martin St. Louis in the Expansion Draft

We all missed him and we all should be ashamed that we missed him because all the signs were there.
—Calgary Flames GM Craig Button

Hindsight is twenty-twenty, especially when it comes to drafting. Even drafing for an expansion franchise (unless you're the Las Vegas Golden Knights and make the Stanley Cup Finals in your inaugural season...). In 2000, the new Minnesota Wild had a chance to select an unprotected future superstar and missed.

Minnesota and Columbus had just been granted expansion franchises to grow the league to thirty teams for the 2000–01 season. In similar fashion to the 1993 Expansion Draft that welcomed the Florida Panthers and Mighty Ducks of Anaheim to the league, Columbus and Minnesota would snake draft and select three goaltenders, eight defensemen, thirteen forwards, and two wild card players from twenty-six other teams. (Nashville and Atlanta were exempt from the expansion draft as they were also both new to the league. Nashville joined in 1998 and Atlanta joined in 1999.)

While the Wild would select some impact players for their inaugural season like Filip Kuba, Sean O'Donnell, and Darby Hendrickson, there was one player that both Minnesota and Columbus missed on.

The Calgary Flames had an undrafted five-foot-six twenty-year-old winger named Martin St. Louis. After leaving him unprotected in the draft, he was released by Calgary and was signed by Tampa Bay. St. Louis appeared in sixty-nine games over two seasons with the Flames, scored 4 goals, 20 points, and had a +/− of −7.

At the time, the decision not to take St. Louis was a no-brainer. He was an undersized college player who had only been in the league a season and a half.

Each team losing players in the expansion draft would lose two players. If a goalie was selected, it could not lose a defenseman. If a team had a defenseman taken, it couldn't have another one taken. The Wild took Calgary Flames defenseman Filip Kuba with the fifteenth overall pick in the draft, so Calgary couldn't lose a goalie or another defenseman in the draft.

Sergei Krivokrasov was a 1992 first-round pick that had a reputation of being able to score at the minor league level but not in the NHL. He was picked up by the new Nashville Predators in 1998 and saw career highs in goals (25), points (48), and assists (16). His numbers tailed off the next season, and he was traded to Calgary.

St. Louis had a similar reputation. He could score at an alarming clip while at the University of Vermont. He scored 51 points as a freshman for the Catamounts with 15 goals. Paired with Eric Perrin, they were an unstoppable force. St. Louis led the team in scoring his sophomore year with 71 points. As a junior, he scored 29 goals.

He caught on with Calgary after playing a year in the IHL with Cleveland in 1997–98.

After not being selected in the 2000 NHL Expansion Draft and being cut by Calgary, he signed a contract with the Tampa Bay Lightning, believing it to be his final chance to play in the NHL.

During his first four seasons in Tampa Bay, he would score 105 goals and 239 points, including his Hart Memorial Trophy season of 2003–04 when he led the league in assists, points, and shorthanded goals. He also led the Lightning to their first-ever Stanley Cup Championship that season.

The Wild would struggle out of the gate offensively. While St. Louis was scoring goals and winning awards in Tampa, the Wild ranked thirtieth, twenty-fifth, twenty-fourth, and twenty-third in scoring during their first four seasons. St. Louis was inducted into the NHL Hall of Fame in 2018 after scoring 365 goals and 368 assists (953 points in 972 career games over seventeen NHL seasons. He was a five-time All-Star, a three-time Lady Byng winner, got two Art Ross trophies, a Hart and Pearson trophy, and the 2004 Stanley Cup.

November 6, 2000

Vikings at Green Bay Packers: the Antonio Freeman Catch

What are they going to rule it? He caught it? He did WHAT?!?
— Al Michaels, MNF Broadcast

The Vikings started the 2000 season 7–0 in Daunte Culpepper's first year as the team's starting quarterback. The twenty-three-year-old quarterback had some great weapons in his arsenal, including Cris Carter, Randy Moss, and Robert Smith. After averaging 28 points per game the first seven games, they lost to the Tampa Bay Buccaneers 41–13 for their first loss of the year and, at 7–1, were tied for first place with Tampa Bay atop the NFC Central Division.

The following week, they traveled to Lambeau Field to take on the struggling Green Bay Packers. The Packers missed the playoffs for the first time in six seasons the year before (a welcome change for a franchise that had only made the playoffs twice between 1968 and 1992) and got off to a slow start in the Mike Sherman era, winning only three of their first eight games.

After forcing a Packers three-and-out on their first drive, the Vikings drove to the Green Bay 11-yard-line but had to settle for a Gary Anderson field goal on their opening drive. Brett Favre and Packers ate more than eight minutes of clock on their next drive, and Ryan Longwell kicked a twenty-four-yard field goal on the second play of the second quarter to tie the game.

The Vikings scored a touchdown on their second drive, set up by a forty-two-yard completion to Randy Moss. Culpepper found Cris Carter in the end zone for a 10–3 lead. Favre and the Packers answered right back with an amazing underhand flip touchdown to tie the game on a five-yard catch by Ahman Green.

Two plays later, Darren Sharper picked off Culpepper on a pass intended for Moss at the Minnesota forty-three-yard line, but the Packers couldn't capitalize on the turnover. On the next Vikings drive, Sharper picked Culpepper off again on a deep pass for Moss, this time in the end zone. Again, the Vikings defense held the Packers offense, allowing thirty-two yards on the drive before Josh Bidwell punted the ball back to David Palmer.

Minnesota had the ball at their own thirteen-yard line with one minute and eleven seconds left, and Offensive Coordinator Sherman Lewis decided to stay aggressive. A thirty-three-yard pass to Moss and a twenty-two-yard Robert Smith run had the ball at the Packers' thirty-yard line. After three straight incompletions, Gary Anderson kicked another field goal, this one from forty-eight yards away, to give the Vikings a 13–10 as the first half expired.

The Vikings got the ball to start the second half. After being sacked by David Bowens for a thirteen-yard loss, Culpepper threw his third pick of the game, this time to cornerback Mike McKenzie, who returned it to the Minnesota 34. The Vikings defense held the Packers to another three-and-out, and they settled for another Ryan Longwell field goal.

With three picks in the game, the Vikings started their next drive with a heavy dose of the running game. Robert Smith and Mo Williams combined for five carries to start the next drive, then Culpepper got in on the action with a nine-yard pickup on a bootleg. After a loss of thirteen yards on a sack by Cletidus Hunt, Culpepper threw a swing pass to Smith on third and seventeen. Smith made Tod McBride and LeRoy Butler miss tackles in the open field and took the ball forty-five yards into the end zone for his first receiving touchdown in two years.

The 20–13 lead lasted all of twenty-eight seconds after Allen Rossum returned the kickoff ninety yards to the Minnesota two-yard line. Two plays later, the Packers were in the end zone, courtesy of a two-yard Green run—his second touchdown of the evening.

In a tie game once again, Minnesota was forced to punt after five plays, pinning Green Bay at their own eight-yard line. The Vikings forced another three-and-out, but David Palmer muffed the punt return, and Rob Davis recovered at the Minnesota thirty-five-yard line for Minnesota's fourth turnover of the game. Again, the Vikings forced Green Bay to punt. Despite forcing four turnovers, Green Bay only had three points to show for it.

A Favre pass intended for Bill Schroeder went through his fingertips on fourth down, and Ryan Longwell came out to kick a forty-eight-yard field goal. But instead, Longwell took the direct snap and punted it, attempting to catch the Vikings off guard and pin them deep in their own territory. Instead, the ball rolled into the end zone for a touchback.

Minnesota got the ball back with 10:40 left in the game, and while they took over six minutes off the clock, they were unable to score and punted the ball back to Rossum and the Packers.

After a thirteen-yard completion to Antonio Freeman, Favre was sacked by John Randle. Green got the yardage back on a six-yard carry, before Frank Winters lost it on a false start penalty. An incompletion to Antonio Freeman brought up another fourth down and another Josh Bidwell punt back to the Vikings with 2:35 left in a tie game.

The Vikings and Packers would exchange punts after both teams went three-and-out with the game on the line. Bidwell's twenty-five-yard punt from the Green Bay 23 left the door wide open for the Vikings to steal the win and move to 8–1. With fifty-two seconds left, Culpepper found Moss for an eight-yard completion to move the ball to the Green Bay forty. After firing incomplete to Matthew Hatchette, Culpepper scrambled for a six-yard gain to the Green Bay 34. Culpepper found Moss again on first down for an eighteen-yard strike, and Moss was tackled by McBride and Butler at the fifteen-yard line. Minnesota called a time-out with eight seconds left.

Green Bay called a time-out of their own to ice Anderson, but Gary never got a chance as Berger couldn't handle the poor snap by Mitch Palmer. Berger threw a desperation pass intended for Andrew Jordan but was picked off in the end zone by Tyrone Williams to send the game to overtime. Minnesota outgained the Green Bay offense 407 yards to 216 but committed 11 penalties for 129 yards.

Green Bay won the coin toss heading into overtime and elected to receive the ball as the rain started coming down in Green Bay. Rossum returned the ball to the Green Bay 18 and let the offense get to work. Green bulled the ball to the twenty-nine-yard line before Favre found Schroeder for a twenty-two-yard gain to move the Pack into Vikings territory. Green picked up seven more yards on the ground, before being tackled in the backfield on a blitz by Robert Griffith.

Now facing third and three and facing a heavy blitz from the Vikings defense, Favre took a shot for the end zone. Antonio Freeman was in single coverage with Cris Dishman, who had perfect position to intercept the ball. Freeman slipped on the wet Lambeau Field grass at the twenty-yard line as Dishman deflected the pass. The ball bounced off the back of Freeman's left shoulder as he was facedown on the ground, then the ball slid into his right hand and never touched the ground. Dishman, and everybody in the stadium, thought the pass was incomplete and gave up on the play. But Freeman popped up, juked Robert Griffith, and beat Dishman to the goal line for the game-winning forty-three-yard touchdown.

Wayne, it was meant to be. It was meant to be. -Larry McCarren
to Wayne Larrivee on the Packers' radio broadcast

The 26–20 final was the only time the Packers led during the game. They finished 9–7 (they beat the Vikings twice in 2000) but missed the playoffs for the second straight season.

January 14, 2001

The NFC Championship Game versus New York

There's nothing that took place out there today that we were prepared for.
—Denny Green

Even though it was two years ago, the Vikings (and their fans) were still looking for redemption for the end of the 1998 season.

Daunte Culpepper broke out in his first season as a starter at quarterback, throwing for nearly 4,000 yards with 33 touchdowns: 15 to Randy Moss and 9 to Cris Carter. Culpepper accounted for 40 touchdowns in his first full season (33 passing and 7 rushing.). The only other quarterbacks to accomplish that were Dan Marino, Steve Young, Kurt Warner, and Brett Favre.

The Vikings started the season 7–0 and finished 11–5. With home field advantage on the line throughout the playoffs, they lost their last three games to finish as the number 2 seed. The New York Giants at 12–4 were the top seed in the tournament.

The Vikings had a bye in the first round, then they rolled through New Orleans 34–16 to advance to their second NFC Championship Game in two seasons. They would head to the Meadowlands to take on the New York Giants, who had beaten their division rival Philadelphia Eagles 20–10 to advance to their first conference championship in a decade.

A lot of analysts favored the Vikings in the championship game, solely based on their offense. "Last week, all (the Giants) had to do was stop Donovan McNabb," said Fox Studio analyst Terry Bradshaw. "This week, they must try and contain Randy Moss, which is impossible, Cris Carter, Daunte Culpepper, running and throwing, and Robert Smith, who runs behind a very good offensive line. They can't rely on their defense and special teams to score points for them because it's not going to happen. That offense has to put points on the board."

Fellow analyst Howie Long saw how great Minnesota's offense was but had questions about the defense. "The defense does not play well when it has to play from behind. They play well when they seem to be up emotionally, and they were relieved when St. Louis was upset by New Orleans." Long was right. The Vikings did dodge a bullet by not having to play the Rams. St. Louis was the defending Super Bowl champions, averaging 33.8 points per game. They beat the Vikings 40–27 in Week 15. New Orleans upset them 31–28 in the wild card round.

The Giants featured a heavy rushing attack from Tiki Barber and Ron Dayne, who combined for 1,176 rushing yards and 13 touchdowns. Quarterback Kerry Collins played every offensive snap for the Giants that seasons, throwing for 3,610 yards and 22 touchdowns, eight of them to Ike Hilliard and seven to Amani Toomer. The Giants defense—anchored by Michael Strahan, Keith Hamilton, Jessie Armstead, Michael Barrow, and Jason Sehorn—only allowed 15.4 points per game, only gave up 284 yards per game, led the league with 66 sacks, and forced 31 turnovers. Meanwhile, Minnesota's offense averaged 372 yards per game and the offensive line of Korey Stringer, Todd Steussie, Corbin Lacina, Matt Birk, and David Dixon only allowed 34 sacks of Culpepper.

In their playoff win against Philadelphia, the Giants hadn't scored an offense touchdown. Ron Dixon returned the opening kickoff for a ninety-seven-yard touchdown, Jason Sehorn had a thirty-two-yard pick-six, and Brad Dalusio kicked two field goals. Head coach Jim Fassel, offensive coordinator Sean Payton, and defensive coordinator John Fox had their hands full.

"We're not going to win with field goals this week," Coach Fassel said during a press conference.

The Giants game plan was to attack the Vikings through the air and hit their weak cornerbacks. With Orlando Thomas and Kenny Wright out with injuries and Cris Dishman released, defensive coordinate Emmitt Thomas had to rely on Robert Tate and Waswa Serwanga as his starting corners.

The Vikings were –1.0 favorites to win the game, but it didn't take long for Kerry Collins to exploit the Vikings' weakness. The Giants won the coin toss, elected to receive, and less than two minutes later, were in the end zone after Ike Hilliard burned cornerback Keith Thibodeaux for a forty-six-yard touchdown and a 7–0 lead.

On the ensuing kickoff, Moe Williams fumbled the ball on the eighteen-yard line, and it was recovered by Giants defensive back Lyle West. One play later, the Giants were in the end zone again after a Collins to fullback Greg Comella touchdown and a 14–0 lead with 12:53 left in the first quarter.

The Vikings did pick off Collins twice in the first quarter—one by Robert Tate and one by Dan Morgan—but the Vikings weren't able to convert the turnovers for points. Culpepper returned the favor with an interception in the end zone to end the lone scoring threat the Vikings had and went three-and-out on the other one.

Brad Dalusio kicked a twenty-one-yard field goal on the first play of the second quarter to push the Giants lead to 17–0. The Vikings offense responded with an incompletion and back-to-back sacks by Strahan and Michael Barrow. Mitch Berger punted the ball back to New York.

Kerry Collins continued to light up the Vikings with the passing attack, driving seventy-one yards in five plays, highlighted by a forty-three-yard bomb to Ron Dixon and an eight-yard touchdown to Joe Jurevicius to open a 24–0 lead.

Vikings fans, some who paid up to $800 for their ticket, began leaving Giants Stadium shell-shocked. At halftime, the lead had grown to 34–0.

"All of our losses have been because we were too cocky or not up for the challenge," said Randy Moss after the game. "All week, we've been hooting and hollering, talking this and talking that. Nobody ever talked about going out there and smacking them in the mouth . . . I guess for us, as a whole team, we ate our words today."

At the end of the bloodbath, the Giants won 41–0 and advanced to their first Super Bowl in ten years. The Vikings lost their second NFC Championship Game in three seasons as Kerry Collins threw for 381 yards and 5 touchdowns. The Giants amassed 518 yards of total offense and forced five Minnesota turnovers.

Culpepper was 13-for-28 passing for only 78 yards, three interceptions, and was sacked four times. The Giants held the Vikings to only 114 yards of offense, held them to 1-of-8 on third down conversions, and only allowed Minnesota to have the ball for 17:28. Robert Smith ran seven times for 44 yards and caught two passes for minus-two yards in his final game as a pro, deciding to retire from football at age twenty-eight. The loss was so devastating for Cris Carter that he mulled retirement too, just as he had done following the loss to Atlanta. He did come back for one final year before signing with the Miami Dolphins for one final shot at a championship.

The loss to the Giants was the second worst loss in Vikings history, shadowed only by a 51–7 loss to San Francisco on December 8, 1984. The Vikings' worst playoff loss also came at the hands of the 49ers: a 41–13 loss in 1990. It was also the first time Minnesota had been shut out in a game since 1991. The Giants would lose to the Baltimore Ravens in Super Bowl. The Vikings were 5–11 in 2001 and would only make the playoffs once in the next seven seasons.

May 2, 2001

Twins versus New York Yankees: the Chuck Knoblauch Game

If the trouble in left field does not end, the game will be forfeited, and the Yankees will win. NOW QUIT THIS!
—Twins' public address announcer Bob Casey

Every fan base has a moment they try to distance themselves from, or take back, completely. Most of them involving throwing something onto the field: Philadelphia Eagles fans throwing snowballs at Santa Claus in 1968, a New York Yankees fan throwing a knife at Wally Joyner in 1986, and a Detroit Pistons fan throwing a beer at Ron Artest in 2004. And yes, even Minnesota fans have something to be ashamed of.

The 2001 season was an exciting year for Twins fans. For the first time in nearly a decade, they were in a pennant race. A red-hot April saw the team win eighteen games, the team's first +.500 April since 1996 (13–12), the best start to the season in franchise history, and the best record in baseball. The team's rebuilding years of the mid and late 1990s was finally paying off.

While most of the stars of those Twins teams had retired, some players from the 1991 World Series team still played in the majors in 2001: Scott Erickson was pitching for Baltimore, Mark Guthrie was a reliever for Oakland, Kevin Tapani was in the rotation for the Chicago Cubs, and Danny Neagle was pitching for Colorado. There was only one remaining position player however: Chuck Knoblauch.

After Kirby Puckett and Kent Hrbek retired in the mid-1990s, Knoblauch was the star for the Twins. Knoblauch, the 1991 AL Rookie of the Year, was a four-time All-Star for the Twins from 1991 to 1997, batting .304/.391/.406 with 276 stolen bases, 391 RBI, and 713 runs scored. He had three Top 20 MVP finishes, two Silver Sluggers, and a Gold Glove award.

Knoblauch saw the lean years of Twins baseball in the 1990s. He saw players like Greg Gagne, Dan Gladden, and Jack Morris become Pat Meares, Rich Becker, and Scott Stahoviak. His relationship with manager Tom Kelly and the front office became strained. Despite signing a new contract with the Twins in 1996, he demanded a trade a season later.

The Twins found a trade partner in the New York Yankees and dealt the All-Star second basemen in exchange for Christian Guzman, Eric Milton, Brian Buchanan, Danny Mota, and $3 million. Knoblauch joined the Yankees at the beginning of their dynasty. Alongside Derek Jeter, Bernie Williams, Jorge Posada, and Tino Martinez, Knoblauch and the Yankees won the World Series for three consecutive years from 1998 to 2000.

After the trade, Knoblauch's defensive game had completely fallen off the map. The former Gold Glove winner developed a serious case of the yips, which is an unexplainable mental plague that throws off a player's game. There is nothing wrong physically, but it's a mental hurdle that a lot of players can't overcome.

Knoblauch was one of those players. His errors doubled from 13 in 1998 to 26 in 1999. By 2000, he had trouble making accurate throws to Martinez at first base. Despite changing his mechanics, his defensive game wouldn't improve. He made 15 errors before the All-Star Break, including a three-error game (in five chances) against the White Sox. In 2001, Yankees manager Joe Torre moved him from second base to left field in favor of star rookie Alfonso Soriano.

Fast forward to April 30, 2001. The 18-6 Minnesota Twins welcomed the three-time defending World Series champion New York Yankees to town for a three-game series. The two teams split the first two games, Brad Radke shutting down the Yankees offense 2-1 in the first game and Mike Mussina shutting out the Twins 4-0 in the second.

Wednesdays at the Metrodome meant one thing: Dollar Dog night. As many as you wanted. General admission seats in left field in 2001 were only $10 apiece. A total of 36,825 fans showed up that night for a great pitching matchup between two young standout pitchers: Joe Mays of the Twins and Orlando "El Duque" Hernandez of the Yankees.

The Twins took a 1-0 lead in the bottom of the fifth on a Torii Hunter home run. New York tied the game in the top of the sixth when Paul O'Neill singled in Soriano. The Twins rallied in the bottom of the frame. After loading the bases, Torii Hunter was hit by a pitch to bring Luis Rivas home. Mike Stanton replaced Hernandez and immediately gave up a two-run single to Doug Mientkiewicz for a 4-1 lead. That's when things started getting crazy.

The left field crowd behind Knoblauch was getting unruly. There had been a minor incident in left field during the Monday game, and the Twins doubled their normal security for a Wednesday night game. A Twin Cities radio station called for fans to show up and give Knoblauch the business, which stirred the pot.

Another issue was that 16,000 fans walked up to the box office that night. It was their largest midweek May attendance since 1988.

A group of fans in the left field seats, wearing shirts that spelled out "Watch Your Back Chuck," began throwing hot dogs, golf balls, batteries, and coins at the Yankee left fielder. It became so unruly that third base umpire Angel Hernandez signaled to Torre to pull his players off the field. Tom Kelly came out of the dugout and headed to left field in an attempt to calm the chaos. Even public address announcer Bob Casey began pleading with fans, telling them if the trouble in left field didn't stop, the Twins would forfeit the game.

The instigators in the incident were removed from the game, and play resumed after a twelve-minute delay. But another incident flared up again in the eighth inning, which prompted another delay. The umpires met at home plate and seriously considered a Minnesota forfeit. More fans were ejected, and the game was completed. Minnesota won 4–2.

At the time, Chuck shrugged it off, recognizing it was just a small demographic of the crowd. "Even after all this, I won't say anything bad about the city," he said. "It's probably a bunch of sixteen-year-olds who don't have a clue who Chuck Knoblauch is."

The New York media, however, was very bitter about the incident. When the Twins traveled to the Bronx the next week, the *New York Times* published an article chastising the "dangerous and destructive louts in Minnesota" and accused the fans of being frustrated that they were facing contraction and taking it out with a jealous rage on the most successful baseball franchise in the league. And they made a point of mentioning a sign in left field for Jacque Jones that read "Don't Worry . . . You're Safe Here. This is New York."

More than a decade later, Knoblauch changed his tune too. In 2013, he told the *Star Tribune* that "it hurt. It really meant that much? To try and intentionally hurt me? It's twisted. It made me bitter about Minnesota. They need to turn the page."

Since the Chuck Knoblauch incident, the Twins are 38–103 against the Yankees, including 2–16 in the playoffs in four ALDS series and a wild card play-in game.

August 1, 2001

Korey Stringer Dies of Heat Stroke

There is nothing you go through in life that prepares you for something like this.
—Vikings wide receiver Cris Carter

Korey Stringer was a first-round draft pick by the Vikings in the 1995 NFL Draft, the second of two first-round picks that year (Derrick Alexander was taken eleventh overall). Stringer was an All-American at Ohio State, blocking alongside future Hall of Famer Orlando Pace and clearing the way for Heisman Trophy winner Eddie George and future teammate Robert Smith.

Stringer was a starter right out of the game in 1995, starting all but two games he played in. While anchoring the offensive line at right tackle, he helped pave the way to four Robert Smith thousand-yard seasons, and the Vikings made the playoffs every year except his rookie year, including trips to the NFC Championship Game in 1998 and 2000.

Stringer was one of seven pro bowlers for the Vikings in following the 2000 season: Smith, quarterback Daunte Culpepper, recievers Randy Moss and Cris Carter, center Matt Birk, and safety Robert Griffith.

The Vikings had high expectations heading into the 2001 season. They were 11–5 the previous season and, coming off a 41–0 loss to the New York Giants in the NFC Championship Game, were hungry to take the next step.

The first Tuesday of training camp was a hot day, with a heat index of 99 during practice.

"It was hot," center Matt Birk recalled. "But hot days in Mankato in the summer are nothing new."

Coaches had the offensive line put in some extra work after practice, which had already lasted over two hours. Everybody was hot and tired but continued to put in the work.

"Korey was tired just like everybody else," Birk said. "And then, one time, he slowly went down to the ground. He went down to one knee and then rolled over. I asked him if he was okay, and he calmly asked for a trainer."

Stringer was helped to the air-conditioned trainer's tent, where he lost consciousness. He was rushed to Immanuel St. Joseph's Hospital in Mankato. A team of doctors worked around the clock to save him. When he arrived in the emergency room, paramedics couldn't get a blood pressure reading, but he still had a pulse. He was exhibiting signs of heat stroke. His skin was warm and dry, and he had a temperature of 108.8 degrees. Stringer's kidneys began to fail, and he was moved from the ER to the ICU. Doctors attempted to bring down his body temperature using icy cold towels. Stringer's treatment continued into the night, and he appeared to make some progress.

But Stringer's kidneys failed, and he was placed on dialysis. Then he developed a condition where his blood wouldn't clot. He needed help breathing and was put on a respirator. Then his heart began to fail.

"We thought we had turned a corner," said Dr. David Knowles, a Mankato physician who worked with the Vikings while they were in Mankato. "But once his heart gave out, there was nothing we could do."

Korey Stringer died at 1:50 a.m. on August 1 from complications of heat stroke. He was twenty-seven years old.

"We are devastated," said wide receiver Cris Carter. "There was not a more well-liked player on our football team. There was not a player that anyone enjoyed spending more time with than Korey."

Stringer's death was the first in an NFL training camp since J. V. Cain died of a heart attack during St. Louis Cardinals training camp in 1979. With Stringer's death came immediate changes in how both the NFL and NCAA handle hot practices, and the changes trickled all the way down to youth levels and opened a conversation about other player health and safety issues.

The Vikings retired Stringer's number 77 on November 19, 2001, during a Monday night game against the New York Giants.

OCTOBER 13, 2002

Twins versus Anaheim in the ALCS

The Twins don't need a Rally Monkey. They need a Rally Gorilla.
—*Star Tribune* writer Dan Barreiro

2002 was the year Twins fans had waited a decade for. Since winning the World Series in 1991, the Twins had missed the postseason for ten straight seasons. In 2001, the Twins had their first winning season since 1992 but still finished six games behind the Indians for the Central Division championship and seventeen games behind the 102-win Oakland Athletics for the Wild Card (the Seattle Mariners won the West with 116 wins). Following the 2001 season, Tom Kelly, who had managed the Twins since 1986, retired. Terry Ryan hired third-base coach Ron Gardenhire to take the helm.

But the 2002 season was a court order away from never happening at all.

After the 2001 World Series, baseball owners voted 28–2 to eliminate two teams (the Twins and Montreal Expos were the two teams that voted no) due to economic struggles. The teams would either relocate or be contracted. A team hadn't changed cities since the Washington Senators moved to Texas to become the Rangers in 1972. A team hadn't been contracted since 1899, when the National League axed the Baltimore Orioles, Cleveland Spiders, Louisville Colonels, and Washington Senators (Baltimore, Cleveland, and Washington would form teams in the rival American League in 1901).

Things didn't look good for the Twins. Relocation rumors began to swirl, with the most popular destination being the Durham, North Carolina, area. North Carolina was a blossoming sports market. The Hornets were testing the waters in the NBA, and the newly formed Panthers of the NFL were a hit. But Don Beaver, who was leading the charge to bring the Twins to Charlotte or the Piedmont Triad (Greensboro, Winston-Salem, and High Point), couldn't get public funding secured for a new ballpark and the deal fell through.

Amid contraction talk, Carl Pohlad would get a reported $250 million to shut down the Twins, which, after buying the team for $17 million in 1984, wasn't a bad return.

The hero in all this was Hennepin County District Judge Harry Crump. Ten days after MLB owners voted to eliminate the Twins, Crump ruled that the Twins couldn't be contracted or relocated until they fulfilled their lease in the Metrodome, which ran through the 2002 season. The MLB appealed the ruling, but their request was denied. On February 5, 2002, Commissioner Bud Selig begrudgingly announced that the Twins were safe for the 2002 season; but contraction talks would resume once the 2002 season concluded.

The Twins played under a cloud of uncertainty for the first five months of the season, but you wouldn't be able to see it. They built off their 2001 season and had a 7.5-game lead at the All-Star Break with a 50–39 record.

But the season was almost lost, just like it was in 1994. Baseball was nearing their second strike in eight years that would again eliminate the post season. But on August 30, the MLB avoided the strike at the eleventh hour and agreed to a new deal with the MLBPA by agreeing to a new deal, which included an agreement that there would be no contraction talks until 2006.

The Twins won their first division title since winning the AL West in 1991 with a 5–0 win over the Cleveland Indians on September 15. The Twins finished the year 94–67—their highest win total since winning ninety-one games in 1988. The Twins were led into the playoffs with their young core of outfielders Jacque Jones and Torii Hunter, third baseman Corey Koskie, reliever J. C. Romero, and catcher A. J. Pierzynski and the veteran pitching of Rick Reed, LaTroy Hawkins, Brad Radke, and Eddie Guardado.

The Twins matched up against the Oakland Athletics in the ALDS and one of the best playoff rotations of all-time: AL Cy Young winner Barry Zito (23–5, 2.75 ERA, 182 K), Mark Mulder (19–7, 3.45 ERA, 153 K), and Tim Hudson (15–9, 2.98 ERA, 181 K). The Twins were heavy underdogs against the 103-win A's. On the other side of the American League bracket, the wild card Anaheim Angels (99–63) took on the AL East champion New York Yankees (103–58).

The Twins trailed 5–1 in Game 1 but shut out the A's the rest of the game. After Koskie's two-run home run in the top of the third, the Twins scored three more in the sixth to take the lead and went on to win Game 1 7–5 for their first playoff win since Game 7 of the 1991 World Series.

Oakland won games 2 and 3 to take a 2–1 lead in the five-game series. The Twins jumped all over Tim Hudson and Ted Lily in the fourth inning of Game 4, scoring seven runs in front of raucous Metrodome crowd and forced Game 5 back in Oakland with a 11–2 win.

The Twins had the A's on the brink of elimination in Game 5, leading 5–1 after scoring three insurance runs in the top of the ninth with a Pierzynski two-run home run and a David Ortiz RBI double, all off closer Billy Koch.

Closer Eddie Guardado served up a three-run home run to Mark Ellis in the bottom of the frame, pulling Oakland to a run at 5–4. After getting Terrance Long to fly out to center, Randy Velarde singled to right. Ray Durham stepped into the box representing the series-winning run at the plate and lifted a foul pop-up down the first base line. Gold Glove first baseman Doug Mientkiewicz lost the ball in the California sun, but Denny Hocking ran in from second base to secure the out and win the series for the Twins. Players piled onto Hocking after he made the game-winning play. During the scrum, Jacque Jones accidentally stepped on Hocking's middle finger and split the nail in two places, forcing him to miss the upcoming American League Championship Series.

The Anaheim Angels had ended the Yankees' run of four consecutive AL pennants by upsetting them in four games to advance to their first ALCS since 1986. The Angels had been to the ALCS three times ('79, '82, '86) but had never punched their ticket to the World Series. The last time the Twins were in the ALCS (1991), they beat the Toronto Blue Jays in five games.

"Hopefully, Anaheim kicks the tar out them," an upset Koch said the day after giving up the three runs in Game 5.

Despite finishing the season with five fewer wins than the Angels, the Twins were given home field advantage in the ALCS because they were a division winner. Game 1 against Anaheim was played in front of 55,561 excited fans ... and Bud Selig, who watched most of the game from Cal Pohlad's private suite. Selig was never announced to the fans, who likely would have stormed the box had they known he was there.

"I understand people's anger," he said among the twelve security guards assigned to him at the game. "I know I'm the lightening rod. It's over. It's done. You're sick of listening to it, and frankly, I'm sick of talking about it. Everything has a way of working out for the best, and it certainly has. I'm grateful the Twins are here; I'm grateful they have a team. If it happens that I present the World Series trophy to the Minnesota Twins, that'd be great."

Joe Mays (4–8, 5.38 ERA, 38 K in 17 starts) got the ball in Game 1. Mays won seventeen games for the Twins in 2001, but had struggled in 2002, including Game 2 of the Oakland Series when he was tagged for six runs in three and two thirds of an inning.

Torii Hunter hit a leadoff double in the bottom of the second off Angels starter Kevin Appier. Hunter advanced to third on a wild pitch then scored on a Pierzynski sacrifice fly for a 1–0 lead.

The Angels got the run back in the top of the third. Adam Kennedy and David Eckstein hit back-to-back singles, then Christian Guzman let a Darin Erstad ground ball go through his legs, which scored Kennedy from second base.

Mays was brilliant in Game 1, pitching eight innings and not allowing an earned run. After Brad Fullmer got an infield single in the fourth inning, Mays retired the next thirteen Angels hitters.

"I got the opportunity to go out there and establish myself early," Mays said.

Koskie knocked a double off the baggie in right field, plating Luis Rivas to take a 2–1 lead. Mays gave way to Guardado in the ninth, who had a much smoother ninth than he did in Game 5 in Oakland. He struck out Erstad but walked the tying run in Tim Salmon. Angels manager Mike Scioscia subbed the speedy Chone Figgins to pinch-run for Salmon. Guardado got Garrett Anderson to fly out, then he struck out Troy Glaus to end the game.

Gardenhire started Rick Reed (15–7, 3.78 ERA, 121 K) in Game 2. The Twins had traded All-Star outfield Matt Lawton to the New York Mets for Reed in 2001, and he had established himself as a reliable starter in the rotation. The thirty-seven-year-old Reed hoped that his regular season success would carry over into the playoffs.

It hadn't in Game 3 against Oakland (four runs in six innings), and it didn't in Game 2 against Anaheim.

Erstad hit a first inning home run off Reed for the Angels' first lead of the series. The Angels added three more in the second for a 4–0 lead, thanks to some uncharacteristic errors from the Twins. Troy Glaus singled, Brad Fullmer doubled, and then Scott Spiezio hit a pop-up down the right field line. Michael Cuddyer sprinted up for the ball but misplayed the ball off the Metrodome turf. Glaus scored easily on Spiezio's double, and Fullmer advanced to third. Bengie Molina flew out to right, but it was too shallow to score Fullmer. Adam Kennedy hit a comebacker to Reed. Figuring Reed would get the easy out at first, Fullmer took off for home. Reed threw to Pierzynski behind the plate, who tagged Fullmer out at home.

Reed now had runners on the corners with two outs and looked poised to get out the inning with minimum damage after getting Kennedy caught in a rundown. Mientkiewicz and Rivas almost had Kennedy out, when Spiezio took off for home. Mientkiewicz saw him take off and threw home. Pierzynski tried to make the tag, but Spiezio's thigh hit him in the arm. The ball flew back to the backstop. When the dust settled, Spiezio was safe, Kennedy was standing at third, and Pierzynski was charged with an error.

"We had him," Mientkiewicz said. "I should have thrown sooner. It's not AJ's fault. I could have made a better throw."

Eckstein hit an RBI single to right to make it 4–0 Angels.

Reed would settle down and not allow another run until giving up a two-run homer to Brad Fullmer in the top of the sixth. Now trailing 6–0, Gardenhire pulled Reed for spot-starter Johan Santana. With the bases cleared, Santana retired the side.

"I have a lot of redeeming to do," said Reed, who was 0–2 with a 6.97 ERA and six home runs allowed in two playoff starts. "I haven't been too happy with my outings. But it's a seven-game series, and anything can happen."

The Twins had a tough time breaking through on Angels starter Ramon Ortiz in the sixth. The Twins had gotten the leadoff man on base in the third, fourth, and fifth innings but hadn't scored. Rivas led off the bottom of the third with a single then was picked off by Ortiz. After David Ortiz singled to lead off the fourth, Ramon Ortiz got Hunter to hit into a double play. Pierzynski's single in the fifth was followed by another double play ball, this time from Rivas.

Guzman led off the bottom of the sixth with a double to center field, then he was knocked in by Koskie who had his second RBI in as many games. Hunter doubled to left, which advanced Koskie to third base. Doug Mientkiewicz then singled in both runners with a single to short center field. The Twins had cut the deficit to 6–3.

Scioscia turned to the bullpen and Brendan Donnelly with one out in the sixth. After Donnelly got out of the sixth, Scioscia subbed in the blossoming twenty-year-old rookie Francisco Rodriguez. K-Rod had just beaten the Yankees twice in the ALDS and became the first major league pitcher to record his first two career victories in playoff games. He struck out three of the first four Twins he faced.

"I hope I never see him again," said Mientkiewicz, who singled off Rodriguez. "He's got some of the best stuff I've ever seen."

With two outs in the eighth, in came Twins killer Troy Percival. In thirty-six career innings against the Twins, Percival had never allowed an earned run. And that didn't change in Game 2 as he struck out Bobby Kielty, Dustan Mohr and Jacque Jones to end the game.

"We wouldn't be here if f it wasn't for our bullpen, and I'm not just taking about Percival," said Scioscia.

With the series tied at 1–1, the ALCS shifted to Edison International Field of Anaheim: the home of the Rally Monkey.

Anaheim's Rally Monkey was born by accident in a game against (ironically) the San Francisco Giants. Trailing 4–1 in the seventh, the videoboard operator played a short video clip of Spike, the monkey from *Ace Ventura: Pet Detective*, to try and get the crowd into the game. The crowd loved it. They put it up again. The Angels rallied to tie the game in the bottom of the ninth. With slugger Mo Vaughn up with runners on second and third, the videoboard operator played the clip one more time, this time with the words "Rally Monkey" superimposed on top. Vaughn hit the game-winning RBI single, and Rally Monkey was born.

The Angels had a league-leading eighteen comeback wins in which they trailed in the seventh inning or later. And the Rally Monkey was paying attention in Game 3.

Eric Milton squared off against Jarrod Washburn for seven innings. The only run Milton allowed was a leadoff home run to Garret Anderson in the bottom of the second. Washburn kept the Twins bats quiet until the seventh, when Jones broke out of a 0–18 slump with an RBI double.

In the eighth, Troy Glaus stepped into the box against Minnesota's best reliever: J. C. Romero. Romero had his best pro season in 2002, boasting a 9–2 record with a meager 1.89 ERA and only three home runs allowed in eighty-one appearances. The Angels videoboard operator played the Rally Monkey, and Glaus took Romero deep for a 2–1 lead.

"I didn't think he hit it well." Romero told reporters after the game. "Trust me, the last thing I expected was to give up a home run in that inning."

"All I was trying to do was get on base," Glaus said.

Blame the Rally Monkey.

Francisco Rodriguez struck out two more batters in the eighth before Percival game in and threw seven pitches to retire the Twins in the ninth.

Now down 2–1 on the road, Brad Radke (9–5, 4.72 ERA) was scheduled to make his first appearance of the ALCS. In his career, Radke had been brilliant against the Angels, boasting an 11–4 record and a 1.72 ERA, including a 6–1 record and 1.38 ERA at Edison International Field.

"It worked out that this will be my only start of the series." Radke when asked why he wasn't moved up in the rotation despite his career numbers. "I just have to go out there and try my best."

"It looks like we've got Milton lined up for Game 7 if it gets that far," Gardenhire said. "I don't like to mess with my pitching staff."

"Hopefully," Radke added, "this will be my only start of the series."

Radke did his job, shutting out the Angels until the seventh inning. Unfortunately for the Twins, rookie starter John Lackey (9–4, 3.66 ERA, 69 Ks) was just as good.

Radke, known for his pinpoint control, threw 77 pitches in the game—54 of them for strikes. In the seventh, he gave up a hit to Erstad. The videoboard played a Rally Monkey clip. Erstad stole second, but a bad throw by Pierzynski moved him up to third. Tim Salmon walked to put runners on first and third. Glaus, the hero from Game 3, hit an RBI single to right to score the game's first run and give Anaheim a 1–0 lead. Former Twins utility man Alex Ochoa came into pinch run for Salmon at second base.

The videoboard flashed Rally Monkey. Scott Spiezio hit a double to right field, which scored Ochoa to make it 2–0 Anaheim. After Radke hit Bengie Molina with the first pitch of his next at bat, Gardenhire relieved him in favor of Santana, who got out of the inning.

Scioscia went to his bullpen in the eighth inning . . . back to Rodriguez. Mientkiewicz continued to hit well against him, raking a leadoff double to center field. But two more strikeouts for Rodriguez and a groundout ended the Twins threat and sent them back into the field.

That's when the wheels fell off for the Twins.

Santana got Eckstein to hit a pop fly to first base. With the Rally Monkey watching from the videoboard, Erstad hit a single then advanced to second when a Santana pickoff throw got past the glove of Mientkiewicz. With a 1–0 count on Alex Ochoa, Santana was pulled for LaTroy Hawkins. Ochoa grounded out to short, which advanced Erstad to third base. After facing just one batter and throwing only two pitches, Hawkins was replaced by Romero to get Garret Anderson out. Anderson singled on a 2–2 count, scoring Erstad and making it 3–0 Anaheim.

Gardenhire went back to the bullpen, lifting his best reliever after only four pitches for Mike Jackson. Glaus singled on Jackson's first pitch. On a 1–0 count, Fullmer doubled and picked up two RBI with both Glaus and Anderson scoring. Jackson intentionally walked Spiezio to set up the force at any base, then Bengie Molina tripled to score two more runs.

Eight pitches (four on the intentional walk). Four Anaheim runs. Bob Wells was the fifth reliever of the inning and struck out Adam Kennedy to mercifully end the inning.

The Twins were able to scrape one run across in the top of the ninth, but not against Troy Percival. Ortiz hit a two-out RBI single that scored Koskie to make the final score in Game 4 7–1.

"I can promise you that the Minnesota Twins will show up tomorrow," Gardenhire said. "We've had our backs against the wall, been in holes all year long."

And now, after facing contraction, labor negotiations, and an elimination game in the ALDS against the best pitching staff in baseball, the season hung on a must-win Game 5. If the Twins were going to stand a chance, they needed a jolt of offense from somewhere, having scored two runs in the past twenty-one innings.

The Twins wasted no time getting on the scoreboard in Game 5. Ortiz laced an RBI double that scored Koskie to give them their first lead since Game 1. Pierzynski added another run in the second with an RBI single that scored Dustin Mohr. The two-run lead was the largest for the Twins in the series. Joe Mays, who won Game 1 at the Metrodome, only allowed two hits in the first three innings. Adam Kennedy led off the bottom of the third with a solo home run. Spiezio led off the bottom of the fifth with a solo shot, and two batters later Kennedy hit another solo homer to give the Angels a 3–2 lead.

Momentum shifted back to the Twins in the seventh inning—the inning they had fallen apart the previous two games. Brendan Donnelly loaded the bases with one out and was replaced by Francisco Rodriguez. Bobby Kielty walked to score a run and tie the game. A wild pitch allowed Dustin Mohr to score from third to give the Twins a 4–3 lead, and Jacque Jones had a sacrifice fly to deep center field to score Pierzynski to put the Twins up 5-3.

But the Twins still had to play the bottom of the seventh, and bullpen issues would again doom the Twins. With the Rally Monkey jumping and shrieking on the video board and the thunder sticks of Angels fans booming in the stands, Johan Santana gave up back-to-back singles before giving up Kennedy's third home run of the game to put Anaheim back in front 6–5. LaTroy Hawkins came in and gave up three straight singles to load the bases. J. C. Romero came in and walked Garret Anderson for another run. Six straight hits and seven consecutive Angels reached base; Romero struck out Troy Glaus. Shawn Wooten hit a single to make it 8–5 Anaheim. Romero threw a wild pitch to allow another run to score, then he gave up a two-run single to Spiezio.

It was 11–5 Anaheim.

Bob Wells relieved Romero and gave up two more hits: one to Chone Figgins and one to Adam Kennedy. With the bases loaded again, Wells hit Eckstein to score another run, then Erstad grounded out to first as Figgins scored from third. Alex Ochoa struck out to finally end the inning. Ten runs on ten hits for Anaheim, setting the LCS record for runs and hits in an inning and consecutive hits.

Just for good measure, Troy Percival came out to close the game in the ninth, setting the Twins down in order and eliminating them from the playoffs.

Adam Kennedy was named the ALCS MVP, mostly for his three-homer performance in Game Fve. He hit .357 (5-for-14) with three home runs and five RBI. The Angels scored twenty-nine runs in the series—eighteen of them in the seventh inning or later. They were trailing or tied in all three games at home and won all three.

The Angels would win their first World Series against the San Francisco Giants—the team the Rally Monkey was born against.

<<BONUS ACHE>>

2003 Western Conference Finals against Anaheim

Less than a year later, Anaheim stuck it to Minnesota in another conference championship . . . this time in hockey. The 2003 Minnesota Wild were a team of destiny. They were down 3–1 in the playoffs twice: first to Colorado (Andrew Brunette's series-winning goal in overtime of Game 7) then to Vancouver (Minnesota outscored the Canucks 16–7 in the final three games).

Unfortunately, so were the seventh-seeded Mighty Ducks of Anaheim. In the Western Conference Championship against Anaheim, they ran into the goaltending of Conn Smyth winner Jean-Sébastien Giguère. Giguère only allowed one goal in the four-game sweep of the Wild, shutting them out three times and stopping 122 of 123 shots (Andrew Brunette in Game 4) in 268:04 minutes of ice time. The conference championship loss to the Mighty Ducks would be one of four in four-year span for Minnesota sports fans (Vikings lost the NFC Championship Game to New York in 2000, the Twins lost the 2002 ALCS to Anaheim, and the Timberwolves were beaten by the Los Angeles Lakers in the 2004 Western Conference Finals).

December 16, 2002
The Twins Release David Ortiz

Ok, I screwed it up.

—Twins GM Terry Ryan

There are very few full-time DHs worthy of a Hall of Fame nod. Paul Molitor (3,319 hits), Frank Thomas (521 HR), Jim Thome (612 HR), and Edgar Martinez (two-time Batting Champion, five-time Silver Slugger, .312 career average) are in. Tony Oliva (three-time Batting Champion) will likely eventually get in (we hope). Then there's a pretty significant drop-off to guys like Brian Downing, Harold Baines, Chili Davis, Don Baylor, Mike Sweeney, and Hal McRae.

And somewhere near the top of all-time great DHs is David Ortiz. Fans remember David Ortiz (AKA Big Papi) for his clutch hits in the playoffs for the Red Sox and his towering home runs out of Fenway Park.

Ortiz hit .290 with 483 home runs and 1,530 RBI over a fourteen-year career in Boston. He was a ten-time All-Star and finished in the top 5 in AL MVP voting four times in four seasons. He helped end the Red Sox's eighty-six-year World Series championship drought in 2004. And for good measure, he led them to championships in 2007 and 2013.

He is the all-time leader in home runs (485), RBI (1,569), and hits (2,192) by a DH. His career batting average in the World Series is .455.

And once upon a time, he was a Minnesota Twin. And they released him. Flat out cut him.

It was 2002. The Twins had just made the playoffs for the first time since winning the World Series in 1991. Ron Gardenhire had taken over managerial duties after Tom Kelly stepped down after the 2001 season and had inherited a lot of strong, young talent. Guys like Torii Hunter, A. J. Pierzynski, Doug Mientkiewicz, Corey Koskie, and Jacque Jones. These guys had come up through the minors together and would help lead the Twins to back-to-back-to-back AL Central titles in the early 2000s.

The Twins had acquired Ortiz via trade from the Seattle Mariners in 1996, while Tom Kelly was still manager. He got his call-up to the Twins in September 1997 after batting .317 with 31 home runs and 124 RBI combined in the minors (High A, AA, and AAA).

As odd as it would seem, Ortiz's bat did not fit TK's baseball philosophy or the Twins Way. Kelly preferred small-ball tactics and solid defense in his lineup, two things that Ortiz needed to improve on. After getting his feet wet in the big leagues in 1997, Ortiz had his eyes set on the starting first baseman job out of spring training in 1998. But a fractured wrist landed him on the disabled list, and the job went to future Gold Glove winner Doug Mientkiewicz. Ortiz was limited to ten games that season.

In 1999, he was the everyday designated hitter, appearing in 130 games. He hit a respectable .282, but with only 10 home runs . . . due in large part to the Twins Way: make plays in the field, don't give away scoring chances with dumb base running or consistently fail to advance base runners, and slap outside pitches to the opposite field.

The Twins Way attributed to Ortiz's light hitting and lack of power during his Twins years: a .266 average with 58 home runs over six seasons. Ortiz wasn't a fan of Tom Kelly's strategy. In an interview with Tom Powers of the Pioneer Press in 2004, Ortiz said "I'd take a big swing and [Kelly] would be screaming at me: 'Hey, hey, hey, what are you doing?' Are you kidding me? You want me to swing like a little girl? I'll swing like a little girl."

Ortiz's best season as a Twin was 2002—a breakout year for the Twins. Despite battleing knee injuries, Ortiz hit 20 home runs and knocked in 75 runs for the 2002 AL Central Champion Minnesota Twins. In the nine playoff games for the Twins (3–2 series win versus Oakland in the ALDS and a 4–1 series loss versus Anaheim in the ALCS), he had 8 hits in 29 at bats (.275) with only 4 RBI and no home runs.

Ortiz was eligible for arbitration following that season. The Twins could either pay him $1.5 million or release him.

Remember, this time, Kelly was no longer the manager. Ron Gardenhire had taken the reigns prior to 2002, but Gardy had been a coach under Kelly since 1991. And the Twins Way had been instilled in him, as well as general manager Terry Ryan, who was the ultimate decision maker.

Terry Ryan and the Twins decided to release Ortiz in December of 2002. Ortiz finished his career with the Twins with a .266 average with 58 home runs and 238 RBI over parts of six seasons. Ryan decided to cut Ortiz for a few reasons: he didn't want him to take the Twins to arbitration, he felt Matt LeCroy would make an adequate DH over the next handful of seasons, and he wanted a roster spot for the upcoming Rule 5 draft.

Ortiz signed a one-year $1.25 million contract with the Boston Red Sox in January 2003—less than the $1.5 million he was expected to get in arbitration with the Twins.

Matt LeCroy became the full-time DH for the 2003 season. He appeared in 107 games for the Twins, hitting .287 with 17 home runs and 85 RBI—numbers that were comparable, if not better, than Ortiz during his time with the Twins (Ortiz hit .288 with 31 HR, 101 RBI, and finished top 5 in the MVP voting for Boston, so there's that.)

In limited action for the Twins from 2003 to 2005, LeCroy hit .273 with 43 home runs and 153 RBI. Ortiz hit .300 with 47 home runs and 148 RBI . . . in 2005 alone.

The player the Twins coveted in the Rule 5 draft was shortstop José Morban. They selected him from the Texas Rangers for $50,000.

Morban didn't work out for the Twins. He was placed on waivers in spring training and claimed by Baltimore. He had 71 at bats for the Orioles in 2003, batting .141 with two home runs and 5 RBI, then he never appeared in a major league game ever again.

> Obviously, it's a situation that I watched, and I've observed, and I see what he's done, and I see what he's meant to the Boston Red Sox. Ok, I screwed it up. -Terry Ryan

The justifications/excuses to cut Ortiz were there: He was below average in the field as a first baseman, limiting him to the designated hitter role. He hit only .205 against left-handed pitching and .240 with runners in scoring position. He also went on the disabled list for a second consecutive season with writs and knee issues.

But mostly, it was a money thing to keep the Twins ballooning salary from exceeding a wild $50 million per year.

August 11, 2003

Herb Brooks Dies in a Car Accident

Herb was one of those people who believed in the task. Whether or not there was any glory was unimportant . . . the miracle of 1980 was really the miracle of character.
—Former Minneapolis governor Arne Carlson

Few coaches are as revered and respected in the game of hockey as Herb Brooks. The St. Paul native led Johnson High School to the 1955 state hockey championship before he joined the University of Minnesota's hockey program. He was a member of the 1967 and 1968 Olympic teams before turning to coaching in 1970.

His first job was as an assistant for Minnesota before taking over the program in 1972. He coached the Gophers to national championships in 1974, '76, and '79.

His most famous achievement, however, was coaching the 1980 Olympics "Miracle on Ice" game in Lake Placid, New York. In a tournament game against Russia, who had won five of the previous six gold medals in hockey, Brooks's handpicked team of college students upset the hockey superpower on their way to the USA's first Olympic Gold medal since 1960.

After the Olympics, he found his way into the NHL. He coached the New York Rangers from 1981 to 1985. After being fired by the Rangers, he returned to the college ranks in 1986, coaching then-Division III St. Cloud State (he led the Huskies to a 25–10–1 record) before becoming the head coach of the Minnesota North Stars from 1987 to 1988. He became a scout for the Pittsburgh Penguins in 1995, as well as managed the team for the 1999–00 season. He won a silver medal with Team USA in the 2002 Winter Olympics in Salt Lake City. He then stepped away from coaching to become the director of player development for the Pittsburgh Penguins.

During his coaching career in the NCAA and NHL, Brooks only had four losing seasons in sixteen years as a head coach.

But he was taken from this world too soon. Six days after his sixty-sixth birthday, Brooks fell asleep behind the wheel of his minivan as he was driving home from an Olympic hockey fundraiser in Biwabik on the afternoon of August 11, 2003. Eyewitnesses say his van slowly veered to the right and went partly off the road. It overcorrected, crossed four lanes of traffic, and rolled into the ditch.

The Minnesota State Patrol quickly ruled out drug, cell phone, or alcohol use and said Brooks didn't have a medical emergency while driving. Weather and road conditions were also ruled out as contributing factors. They also reported that he wasn't wearing a seat belt and was thrown from the vehicle. He likely would have survived the crash if he had been buckled up.

Numerous awards, tributes, and honors have been given to Herb posthumously. Disney released the film "Miracle" starring Kurt Russel as Brooks in 2004. St. Cloud State and the Olympic ice arena in Lake Placid, New York, bear his name. A statue of Herb was placed outside the RiverCenter in St. Paul as well as the Herb Brooks National Hockey Center in St. Cloud. He was also inducted into the Hockey Hall of Fame builders' category in 2006. The Minnesota State High School League also gives the Herb Brooks Award at the end of the State Hockey Tournament to "the most qualified hockey player in the tournament who strongly represents the values, characteristics and traits that defined Herb Brooks."

<<BONUS ACHE>>

Billy Martin Dies in a Car Accident

The fiery and combative Billy Martin, who would become known for fighting with his players, umpires, owners, random marshmallow salesman, and whomever he could get his hands on, was traded to the Twins by Milwaukee in June of 1961. He became a scout for the Twins the following season, and in 1965 was promoted to third-base coach and is widely credited for helping 1965 **AL MVP** Zoilo Versalles with his swing and working with a young Rod Carew to make him one of the best baserunners in baseball history. In 1968, after failing to win Calvin Griffith over for the vacant Twins manager position, he took the manager's job with the Twins AAA affiliate Denver Bears to prove to Griffith he could manage. He took over the Bears when they were 8–22, and they finished the season 65–50 under Martin. He was promoted to Twins manager in 1969 and led them to the AL West title. Despite that, Griffith fired him after the season. Martin would manage the Detroit Tigers from 1971 to 1973, the Texas Rangers from 1973 to 1975, then had numerous stints with the Yankees from 1975 to 1978, 1979, 1983, 1985, and 1988 in which he was fired by Yankees owner George Steinbrenner four times and resigned another time after leading the Yankees to the 1977 World Series title. He also managed Oakland from 1980 to 1982. In 1989, he was a special advisor to the Yankees. While home for Christmas, he was the passenger in a pickup when the vehicle swerved off an icy road. Martin, age sixty-one, was killed in the accident on Christmas Day. The driver, William Reedy, was charged with driving while intoxicated.

April 20, 2003

The Wolves Lose Their Seventh Straight Playoff Series

I feel bad for Flip Saunders.
—Lakers head coach Phil Jackson

The Timberwolves won a franchise-record fifty-one games during the 2002–03 season. Kevin Garnett took another giant leap forward, averaging new career highs in points per game (23.0) and rebounds per game (13.4). He was runner-up in the NBA MVP award behind Tim Duncan.

The Timberwolves, led by Garnett and free-agent acquisitions Troy Hudson (career-high 14.2 points, 5.7 assists per game after Terrell Brandon was lost with a knee injury) and Kendall Gill plus double-digit scoring averages from Wally Szczerbiak and Rasho Nesterovic and other contributions from Joe Smith, Anthony Peeler, and Rod Strickland, earned the fourth seed in the Western Conference playoffs.

Awaiting them was the three-time defending NBA champion Los Angeles Lakers. All-Stars Kobe Bryant (averaging 30 points per game), Shaquille O'Neal (27 points, 11 rebounds) got off to the slowest start in ten years—winning only eleven of their first thirty games as Shaq recovered from off-season foot surgery. They got hot at the end of the season, winning eleven of their last thirteen games to get to the fifty-win plateau and the number 5 seed in the West.

In the week leading up to the playoff series with the Lakers, Wolves fans attentinos weren't on Shaquille O'Neal. They were on his wife, Shaunie. Shaq and Shaunie were expecting their third child during the first round of the playoffs, and Shaq said he wouldn't rule out missing at least one game to be there for the birth of his son. Shaqir O'Neal was born on April 19—the day before the playoffs started, guaranteeing that Shaq would suit up for Game 1.

Making their seventh consecutive playoff appearance, the Timberwolves were 0–6 in first-round Game 1s (all on the road), but this time the Wolves were at home. They were 33–8 at Target Center (the Lakers were 19–22 on the road); Wolves fans liked their chances. The game plan involved shutting down the three-time defending NBA Finals MVP O'Neal, who came into the series averaging 30 points, 14 rebounds, and 2 blocks over the previous three playoffs.

The 2003 NBA Playoffs also changed from a five-game series in the opening round to a seven-game series, so the Wolves would need to beat the Lakers four times to advance past the first round for the first time in franchise history.

While attempting to shut down O'Neil, Rick Fox, and Derek Fisher went a combined 5/6 from beyond the arc in the first half. But the story was Kobe Bryant's 28 first-half points on 12 of 16 shooting with seven assists and no turnovers.

The Lakers jumped out to a 17–6 lead midway through the first quarter and extended that lead to 20 points with just over a minute left in the half. But Garnett, who finished with 23 points, 14 rebounds, and 7 assists in forty-six minutes, willed the Wolves to within four points with after a 24–14 Minnesota run in the first 9:11 of the third quarter.

But as good as Bryant in the first half, O'Neil took over the second. In an attempt by Wolves to contain Bryant, Shaq scored 20 of his 32 points.

"I don't have an answer for that," Wolves head coach Flip Saunders said after the game. "Nobody does. That's why they're the defending champions."

The Wolves bench, with 11 points from Marc Jackson and 10 from Rod Stickland, outscored the Lakers bench 30–11, but the 79 combined from Shaq and Kobe were too much to overcome as the Lakers took Game 1 117–98.

After their sluggish start in Game 1, the Wolves offense took off in Game 2. They led 8–0, then 21–11. Troy Hudson, who would earn the nickname Laker Killer after the series, finished with a career-high and franchise-record 37 points. Garnett added a playoff-best 35 and Sczczerbiak chipped in 21.

Even with the onslaught from Hudson and Garnett, the Wolves only led 39–38 midway through the second quarter. The Wolves went on an 18–5 to close out the half, highlighted by a Hudson buzzer-beating three as the half expired.

The Wolves extended their lead to 23 late in the third quarter before winning by 28 points, 119–91. Having won only six of their previous twenty-five postseason games, the 28-point victory was easily the largest playoff win for the franchise, besting their previous record of nine.

"That's as good a game as we probably have played since I've been here," Coach Saunders said.

Shaq and Kobe each had 27 points (Bryant was just 9-of-28 shooting), but no other Lakers finished in double figures.

"We're a team that fights," said Garnett after the game. "You can knock us out and we'll get back up and start throwing haymakers."

Game 3 shifted to LA with the series tied 1–1. The Lakers jumped out to an early 9–4 lead, but the Wolves responded quickly, outscoring the Lakers in each of the first three quarters. Lakers guard Jannero Pargo hit a three with two seconds left in the third quarter to cut the Laker deficit to nine points, 80–71, heading into the fourth quarter.

Kobe and Shaq had both been contained through the first three quarters, combining for only 30 points.

Lakers coach Phil Jackson sat O'Neil to start the fourth quarter. With O'Neil on the bench, the Lakers opened the quarter on a 9–4 run (all nine points were scored by Bryant and former Augsburg Auggie Devean George). When O'Neil reentered with 8:30 in the game, the Wolves lead was 84–80. Shaq scored the next seven points for the Lakers, tying the game at 87–87. The Wolves missed six of their first nine shots of the quarter to let LA back in the game. Even more critical for the Wolves, Garnett picked up two fouls during that stretch, giving him five. His fifth sent Rick Fox to the line for two free throws. Fox made them both for an 89–87 lead.

Garnett stayed in the game, down by two with five minutes left. He dished an assist to Szczerbiak at the rim to tie the game. Then after an offensive foul by Derek Fisher on the other end, he retook the lead on a fourteen-foot jumper. The Wolves rebuilt their lead to 101–96 with twenty-two seconds left.

Kobe made a three-pointer and was fouled by Szczerbiak. After making the free throw to complete the four-point play, the Lakers were only down by one, 101–100. After a time-out, Anthony Peeler inbounded the ball to Szczerbiak while trying to tiptoe down the sideline. He drew contact and was nudged out of bounds by Rick Fox. The turnover put the ball back in Kobe's hands with seventeen seconds left.

With seconds second left, Kobe drove to the basket, but he was sent to the line after a Rasho Nesterovic shooting foul. With a chance to take the lead, Kobe missed the first attempt. The second attempt was good, tying the game at 101. Troy Hudson had a good look at the buzzer but missed from twenty-seven feet as Game 3 headed to overtime.

As rough as the final twenty-two seconds of regulation was for the Wolves, it got a lot worse twelve seconds into overtime when KG picked up his sixth foul after Robert Horry flopped while KG tried to work around a screen. With Garnett (33 points, 14 rebounds) out of the game, Saunders went with a line-up of Troy Hudson, Marc Jackson, Wally Szczerbiak, Gary Trent, and Anthony Peeler.

Peeler scored the first four points of OT, giving the Wolves a 105–101 lead. LA missed their first four shots before a pair of Shaq free throws with three minutes left. After a Szczerbiak offensive foul, the Lakers tied the game with a Shaq layup at 105-105.

Szczerbiak was called for a technical foul after getting tangled up with Rick Fox with 2:00 left. Kobe hit the free throw to give the Lakers the lead, 106–105.

Troy Hudson intercepted a bad Kobe Bryant pass and was fouled by Robert Horry. T-Hud made both free throws to retake a one-point lead.

With forty-seven seconds to go, officials called another foul on Szczerbiak, this time as Pargo attempted a fast break layup, even though video replay shows that Wally never touched Pargo. The rookie from the University of Arkansas hit both free throws to put the Lakers up 108–107. The foul on Pargo was Szczerbiak's fifth.

After a Hudson layup was sent six rows in the stands by Shaq, Gary Trent pulled a veteran move on Kobe. He pump-faked, got Kobe in the air, and drew contact and the foul. Trent, who entered the game for Garnett at the beginning of the OT period, made both free throws to put the Wolves up for good. The Wolves survived overtime without Garnett and took a 2–1 series lead.

The Lakers were reinvigorated in a critical Game 4 by Shaquille O'Neal. "Get me the ball," Shaq told his teammates before the game. "Get me the ball, and get out of the way."

Shaq had 15 points and 8 rebounds in the first quarter. He finished Game 4 with 10 offensive rebounds and, as a result, the Lakers outscored the Wolves 29–2 in second-chance points.

Somehow, despite this, the Wolves had an eleven-point lead (74–63) with 1:53 left in the third quarter. But turnovers and missed shots sparked an 11–0 Lakers run, capped off by a Kobe three to tie the game.

The Wolves would have three more leads of five points or more, but Shaq and the Lakers kept fighting back. Shaq finished Game 4 with 34 points, 23 rebounds, and 6 assists. Wolves center Rasho Nesterovic was virtually helpless (Shaq outscored him 172–42 and outrebounded him 92–30 in the series). As was Marc Jackson. So was Garnett. Each of those three players racked up five fouls, all while guarding O'Neal. Joe Smith was tasked with guarding Shaq to give those players a rest and racked up four fouls over a four-minute span.

While Shaq missed seven of his fifteen free throws, he hit a big one with fifty seconds left to give LA a four-point lead. A Garnett ended a 6:30 scoring drought with a three ball and got the Wolves back within one with thirty-five seconds left—one of a franchise-record twenty-seven threes attempted by Minnesota.

O'Neil tipped in a Kobe miss with nineteen seconds for his tenth offensive rebound (the Wolves had eight as a team), to give the Lakers a 98–95 lead. Down by three, KG missed both of his free throws (he was 7-for-7 for the game) after being fouled in the pain by Shaq. Kobe, however, made all four of his free throws in the final twelve seconds as LA took Game 4 102–97.

Minnesota started the game 13-for-13 from the free throw line but was only 3-of-7 down the stretch. The Wolves only made two field goals in the last seven minutes of the game. After blowing the eleven-point lead and being up 3–1 with three shots to close out the Lakers, the Wolves were now essentially in a best-of-three series with the three-time defending NBA champions.

The Wolves had a lead in Game 5 for a grand total of forty-two seconds—when they led 2–0 (eighteen seconds) and 40–39 (twenty-four seconds). The Wolves committed 17 turnovers, were outscored 16–2 in fast-break points, outmatched in steals 13–3, and lost by 30 points 120–90. All five Lakers starters were in double figures: Bryant with 32 (23 in the second half), Shaq with 27, Derek Fisher with 24 (5-of-7 from three-point land), while Robert Horry and Devean George each had 12.

"You can't play like that at this time of year," Anthony Peeler said. "We just played terrible."

"When you get up 14 or 16 points, you play a lot looser," Flip told the *Star Tribune* after the game. "We never put them in a situation where they felt any pressure."

The do-or-die Game 6 shifted back to Staples Center in LA. The Wolves led after the first quarter, 30–25, and led 33–27 in the second when things began to fall apart. A Kendall Gill turnover and a Marc Jackson charge helped an 8–0 LA run. Joe Smith lost the basketball on back-to-back possessions that were two of seventeen turnovers forced by LA (eight in the second quarter). Minnesota was outscored in the second quarter 22–13 and trailed 47–43 at the half.

Shaq was an assist shy of a triple-double (24 points, 17 rebounds, 9 assists), but Kobe was the star with 31 points, 20 of those coming as the Lakers pulled away in the third quarter. Kobe also scored the first 10 points of the fourth.

Garnett ran out of gas, finishing with 18 points. Troy Hudson had 16 points at halftime, but only finished with 18 as the Lakers won Game 6 101–85 to take the series 4–2.

The series win was Phil Jackson's twenty-fifth consecutive playoff series win. The Wolves had a 7–22 record in the playoffs, lost the last two games of the Lakers series by a combined 46 points, and lost their seventh consecutive playoff series.

September 30, 2003

The Yankees Begin Postseason Dominance over Twins

Damn Yankees. They do this every year it seems like, at least to us.
—Jason Kubel

The Minnesota Twins won their first postseason series since the 1991 World Series in 2002, ending a decade of futility by upsetting the Oakland Athletics 3–2 in the ALDS before bowing out to the eventual World Champion Anaheim Angels in the ALCS.

In 2003, the Twins defended their AL Central crown with a 90–72 record, four games ahead of the Chicago White Sox. But despite winning the division, they would be serious underdogs in the playoffs with the 101-win Yankees taking the AL East, the 96-win Athletics returning to the postseason, and the 95-win Boston Red Sox taking the Wild Card. The Seattle Mariners had 93 wins (three more than the Twins) but missed the postseason.

The Twins drew the Yankees in the ALDS in the first ever playoff matchup between the Twins and Bronx Bombers.

The Twins, who were used to the underdog role, got off to a surprising start in the series with a Game 1 win, beating future Hall of Famer Mike Mussina at Yankee Stadium. Eddie Guardado made it interested in the ninth. Leading 3–0, he gave up a single to Bernie Williams. Hideki Matsui hit a long fly ball to Shannon Stewart (who was acquired at the trade deadline and finished fourth in the AL MVP voting after hitting .322 with the Twins and sparking an offense that went 46–23 after getting him from Toronto), who made a leaping catch at the fence to rob Matsui of extra bases. Aaron Boone doubled to Stewart in left field, but a great throw by Stewart kept Williams at third base. Alfonso Soriano plated Williams with a single to second base to make it 3–1. Nick Johnson, representing the winning run, grounded out to Corey Koskie at third base to end the game.

The Twins' offense would equal their Game 1 total over the next three games, getting mowed down by Andy Pettite, Roger Clemens, David Wells, and Hall of Fame closer Mariano Rivera as the Yankees outscored the Twins 15–3 over the next three games. Derek Jeter killed the Twins' pitching, hitting .429 in the series with a .556 OBP. Bernie Williams scored three runs, knocked in three, and batted .400, while Alfonso Soriano recorded seven hits and four RBI. For the Twins, Torii Hunter hit .429, Shannon Stewart hit .400, and no other Twins had an average higher than .250.

In 2004, both teams repeated as champions of their respective divisions with the Yankees once again winning 101 games and the Twins improving to 92–70 to win their third consecutive AL Central title. Once again, they drew each other in the postseason, with the Boston Red Sox and Anaheim Angels matching up on the other side.

The Twins had Cy Young winner Johan Santana, who hadn't been tagged with a loss since before the All-Star Break, on the hill in Game 1; and just like in Game 1 of 2003, the Twins beat Mike Mussina. Santana struck out five Yankees over seven innings as he, Juan Rincon, and Joe Nathan combined to shut the Yankees out 2–0 at Yankee Stadium.

Then, just like in 2003, the Twins couldn't win a game the rest of the series. Trailing Game 2 5–3 in the eighth inning, the Twins scored two runs of Mariano Rivera on a Justin Morneau RBI single and a Corey Koskie ground-rule double to tie the game at 5–5. In extras, the Twins took a 6–5 lead in the top of the twelfth on Torii Hunter's go-ahead home run. All-Star closer Joe Nathan, who replaced Juan Rincon in the bottom of the tenth, was beginning his third inning of work. He had three strikeouts over his first two-and-a-third innings and was cruising through the Yankee lineup. But with one out, he walked Miguel Cairo and Derek Jeter. Alex Rodriguez, who was added after a trade with the Texas Rangers in the off-season, hit a ground-rule double that plated Cairo and tied the game. Nathan intentionally walked Gary Sheffield to load the bases. J. C. Romero replaced Nathan and served up a fly ball to Hideki Matsui that was deep enough to right field that Jeter scored the winning run on the sacrifice fly.

The Twins took an early 1–0 lead in the bottom of the first in Game 3 back at the Metrodome in support of Carlos Silva, who then gave up three runs in the top of the second. The Yankees added four more in the sixth and would win Game 3 8–4.

In another win-or-go-home Game 4, the Twins again took a 1–0 lead in the first, this time on a Torii Hunter sac fly off Javier Vazquez. After the Yankees tied game in the third, the Twins added another run in the fourth on a sac fly by Corey Koskie and three more in the fifth on a solo home run from Henry Blanco and a two-run double by Lou Ford. Johan Santana, in his second start of the series, pitched even better than he did in Game 1: one run and seven strikeouts over five innings, even on just three days' rest. He left with his team leading 5–1 after throwing 87 pitches. Grand Balfour pitched two scoreless innings, facing the minimum in both innings. Juan Rincon, who was 11–6 with a 2.63 ERA in 2004, entered the game in the eighth to preserve the four-run lead.

And minutes later, it was gone. After giving up a single to Gary Sheffield then walking Hideki Matsui, Bernie Williams singled in Sheffield. Rincon struck out Posada then gave up a three-run home run to Ruben Sierra to tie the game at 5–5. After giving up a double to John Olerud, Twins manager Ron Gardenhire pulled Rincon after allowing four runs and only one out. Joe Nathan, who was in his first full season as a closer, got Miguel Cairo and Derek Jeter to end the inning.

Nathan pitched two scoreless innings, and the combo of Esteban Loaiza, Tom Gordon, and Mariano Rivera out of the Yankees bullpen had held the Twins scoreless since the fifth. Kyle Lohse relieved Joe Nathan in the tenth inning, trying to keep the Yankees at bay and force a winner-take-all Game 5. He retired the Yankees in order in the top of the tenth, and Rivera responded in the bottom of the innings. Lohse struck out Jeter to start the eleventh, then he gave up a double to Alex Rodriguez, who stole third base with Lohse napping on the mound. Lohse threw a wild pitch to Gary Sheffield, which scored the go-ahead run in Rodriguez, which would be the series-winning run. The Yankees won the series 3–1 and eliminated the Twins for the second time in as many seasons.

The Twins saw their run of AL Central Division titles end in 2005 and missed the playoffs for the first time in three seasons. In 2006, they were swept by the Oakland Athletics. The Twins wouldn't meet the Yankees in the playoffs again until 2009, which was the final season in the Metrodome.

Both teams had quite a bit of turnover in the four years since their last playoff series. While players like Justin Morneau, Joe Mauer, Michael Cuddyer, Jason Kubel, and Nick Punto were on the team in 2004, they weren't full-fledged stars yet. The only pitchers from 2004 that was still on the team were closer Joe Nathan and reliever Matt Guerrier, who had only pitched in nine games in 2004. Mauer and Morneau had two of the best seasons in Twins history, with Morneau hitting 30 home runs and knocking in 100 runs, and Mauer taking home AL MVP honors with a .365 average, 28 home runs, and 96 RBI.

The Yankees were still anchored by Derek Jeter, Jorge Posada, Alex Rodriguez, Andy Pettite, and Mariano Rivera and had bolstered their team with a massive off-season spending spree by signing pitchers C. C. Sabathia (seven years, $161 million), A. J. Burnett (five years, $82 million), and first baseman Mark Teixeira (eight years, $180 million).

The Twins started the 2009 playoffs early with the classic Game 163 walk-off win against the Detroit Tigers to win their first division title in three years. They flew to New York to face the Yankees in the inaugural playoff game at the new Yankee Stadium.

The Twins hadn't had much success against the Yankees since their last playoff matchup in 2004. They were 0–7 against New York in 2009 and 12–24 since 2005. The silver lining heading into the 2009 ALDS was that of the seven losses to New York, six of them were by two runs or fewer.

The Twins came into the game red-hot, having won seventeen of their last twenty-one games; but fans knew that Ron Gardenhire's Twins were 5–25 against the Yankees in New York.

The Twins got to their New York hotel room around 4:15 a. m. the morning after Game 163. Then, surprisingly, they grabbed a 2–0 lead in the top of the third inning. Michael Cuddyer knocked in shortstop Orlando Cabrera, then Joe Mauer scored on a C. C. Sabathia passed ball. Derek Jeter tied it in the bottom of the frame with a two-run homer. Nick Swisher put the Yankees in front with a two-out RBI double in the fourth against Twins starter rookie Brian Duensing (5–2, 3.64 ERA), but things fell apart in the fifth.

Jeter drew a leadoff walk, and after Duensing got quick outs from Johnny Damon and Mark Teixeira. Alex Rodriguez, 0-for-29 in his career with runners in scoring position in the postseason, knocked Jeter in for a 4–2 lead. Gardenhire lifted Duensing after 79 pitches for Francisco Liriano to face Hideki Matsui. Matsui was 0-for-4 lifetime versus Liriano. Matsui launched a two-run home run, and New York went on to win Game 1 7–2.

The Twins squandered more chances to steal a game in New York in Game 2. The Twins led 3–1 in the bottom of the ninth with Joe Nathan on the mound. Nathan's struggles against the Yankees is well-documented: he was 0–4 with a 3.28 ERA with 11 saves in 27 appearances.

Teixeira roped a single to right, then Alex Rodriguez blasted a two-run home run to center field, tying the game. Nathan got the next Yankees in order and the game went to extras.

The Twins stranded two runners on base in the top of the ninth. Nathan struggled in the bottom of the ninth again. After getting Melky Cabrera to ground out to short, he gave up a single to Jorge Posada. Yankees manager Joe Girardi pinch-ran Brett Gardner for Posada. After Gardner stole second, Nathan had him dead-to-rights and picked off second, but Nathan threw the ball away and Gardner advanced to third. Nathan intentionally walked Derek Jeter to set up the force at second base before Gardenhire pulled his All-Star closer for José Mijares. Mijares got Johnny Damon to line into a double play to end the threat.

The play that drives fans crazy from the 2009 ALDS happened in the top of the eleventh inning. Facing Damaso Marte, Joe Mauer laced a ball down the left field line that glanced off the tip of Melky Cabrera and hit the dirt eight to ten inches in play then bounced foul then into the stands for a ground-rule double. Leftfield umpire Phil Cuzzi, who was watching the play from ten feet away, called a foul ball that took a guaranteed double from the reigning AL MVP.

Mauer did finish his at bat with a single to center, then Jason Kubel hit a ground ball into right field. Girardi pulled Marte for David Robertson, and Michael Cuddyer singled to load the bases with nobody out.

Robertson only threw five more pitches the rest of the inning: Delmon Young lined out to first on the first pitch he saw and Carlos Gomez grounded to first (Yankees forced Mauer at home) on the first pitch he saw. Then on a 1–1 count, Brendan Harris flew out to center to end the inning, stranding three.

In the bottom of the eleventh, Mark Teixeira ended it with a walk-off home run off Mijares for a 4–3 Yankees win.

Facing elimination again, the Twins turned to their midseason pickup Carl Pavano, a name familiar to Yankees fans. Pavano had signed with the Yankees in 2005 after an All-Star season with the Florida Marlins. In his four injury-plagued seasons that saw him miss time from everything from broken ribs from a car accident to a bruised buttock to an elbow strain that eventually required Tommy John surgery. At the end of his contract, he had made $39.5 million for only 26 starts over four seasons. He signed a one-year deal with the Cleveland Indians in 2009 before being traded to Minnesota for Yohan Pino at the trade deadline. Pavano was 5–4 with a 4.64 ERA for the Twins since the August 7 trade, and Yankees fans were licking their chops over facing Pavano at the Metrodome in Game 3.

But Pavano returned to All-Star form, only allowing three hits over his first six innings of work. The Twins took a 1–0 lead on a Joe Mauer RBI single off Yankees starter Andy Pettitte in the bottom of the sixth. But the Yankees jumped on Pavano in the top of the seventh. Solo home runs by Alex Rodriguez and Jorge Posada put the Yankees in front 2–1.

The Twins nearly tied the game in the bottom of the eighth. After a double to center field, Nick Punto tried scoring on a Denard Span single to short but was thrown out at home. In the top of the ninth, Joe Nathan inherited a one out, bases loaded were a mess created by Ron Mahay, Jon Rauch, and José Mijares walks. After back-to-back RBI singles from Posada and Robinson Cano, Nathan struck out the side to give the Twins offense one final chance in the bottom of the ninth.

Mariano Rivera, who would become the first unanimous Hall of Fame selection in 2019, shut down the Twins and gave the Yankees a 4–1 win in Game 3 and a sweep of the Twins. The Yankees would go on to win their first World Series since 2000.

In 2010, the Twins opened Target Field and repeated as AL Central champions at 94–68 six games ahead of the Chicago White Sox despite losing closer Joe Nathan to Tommy John surgery and Justin Morneau to a concussion. Behind AL MVP Josh Hamilton, the Texas Rangers won the West at 90–72. Joe Maddon's Tampa Bay Ray's won the AL East with a record of 96–66, finishing one game ahead of the wild card-winning Yankees (95–67).

That set up yet another ALDS matchup with the Yankees. But this time, for the first time ever, the Twins had home field advantage. Fans hoped it would come in handy, since the Twins were 15–54 against the Yankees since 2002, including 2–9 in the playoffs. (The Yankees won four of six meetings in 2010.)

Game 1 of the 2010 ALDS was October 6, 2010, in what was the first outdoor playoff game in Minnesota since October 4, 1970, in the ALCS against Baltimore.

Francisco Liriano (14–10, 3.62 ERA, 201 strikeouts) was the Game 1 starter for the Twins and dominated the Yankees for the first five innings of the game. The Twins gave him some run support: Michael Cuddyer hit a two-run home run off Yankee starter C. C. Sabathia in the second and Orlando Hudson scored on a Sabathia passed ball in the third.

Then Liriano fell apart. After retiring ten consecutive Yankees batters, he allowed four runs in the sixth inning for a 4–3 Yankees lead. The Twins did tie the game in the sixth when Sabathia issued a four-pitch walk to Delmon Young with the bases loaded. But the Twins left them loaded when J. J. Hardy struck out to end the threat.

Gardenhire turned to Jesse Crain to keep the game tied in the seventh, but a two-run Mark Teixeira home run gave the Yankees a 6–4 lead. Mariano Rivera converted the four-out save as the Yankees erased the three-run deficit to take Game 1. The loss was Minnesota's tenth straight playoff loss.

Game 2 featured Carl Pavano in what was arguably his best season as a pro. From May 29 through August 13, he was 11–2 with a 2.79 ERA. He was 17–11 with a 3.75 in 2010 and was tasked with evening the series with the Yankees.

Just as they had in Game 1, the Twins took an early lead in the second inning, leading 1–0 after Danny Valencia's sacrifice fly off Andy Pettitte scored Delmon Young from third base. The Yankees tied the game on an Alex Rodriguez sac fly in the fourth and took the lead on a Lance Berkman solo home run in the fifth to lead 2–1. Orlando Hudson hit a solo shot for the Twins in the sixth to tie the game.

But just like in Game 2 of the 2009 series, the game was overshadowed by a poor call by an umpire. Lance Berkman dug into the box against Pavano with Jorge Posada on first. A 1–2 ninety-one-miles-per-hour fastball appeared to split the plate in half for strike 3. But home plate umpire Hunter Wendelstedt called it a ball. Berkman ripped the next pitch over the head of Denard Span in center field for the go-ahead RBI double. Ron Gardenhire went out to calm Pavano down then. When Wendelstedt came to break up the mound meeting, Gardy began ripping into him. Wendelstedt tossed Gardenhire out of the game. The Twins stuck with Pavano, who gave up a bunt single to Brett Gardner that moved Berkman to third and an RBI single to Derek Jeter for a 4–2 Yankee lead. Pavano came out of the game after allowing four runs on ten hits. José Mijares and Jon Rauch got out of the inning without allowing any more damage.

Andy Pettitte set the Twins down in order in the seventh. Kerry Wood struck out two Twins in the eighth before Mariano Rivera completed his fifteenth consecutive scoreless postseason inning against the Twins as the Yankees took a 2–0 series lead.

The Twins turned to Brian Duensing in Game 3 to save their season and avoid their twelfth consecutive postseason loss. Duensing was 10–3 with a 2.62

ERA that season, and the Twins had high hopes for the twenty-seven-year-old, so much so that they refused to include him in a deal that would have brought Cliff Lee to Minnesota at the trade deadline.

The Twins had a lead in each of the nine previous postseason losses to the Yankees, but not in Game 3. Duensing only lasted three and a third innings, giving up five runs on seven hits: RBI singles to Jorge Posada (second inning), Mark Teixeira (third inning), and a two-run home run to Marcus Thames in the fourth. After the Thames homer, Denard Span made a gesture to the Bleacher Creatures in the outfield seats, who mocked him with chants of "Tor-ii Hun-ter!"

The Twins had a chance to make it a game in the eighth. After Girardi pulled Phil Hughes (seven shutout innings) for Kerry Wood, the Twins pushed a run across with Orlando Hudson's RBI single. Boone Logan inherited the bases loaded with one out and the Twins down by five. He got Jason Kubel to pop out to third. Giradi then subbed in David Robertson, who got Delmon Young to fly out to center and end the threat.

The Yankees won the game 6–1, swept the Twins again, and saddled them with their twelfth consecutive playoff loss, which was good for the second longest playoff losing streak in baseball history (the Boston Red Sox lost thirteen straight from 1986 to 1995).

The Twins wouldn't make the playoffs again until 2017 when they were the second wild card team. Their opponent? The Yankees.

The Twins scored three runs in the top of the first, chasing ace Luis Severino from the game after one third of an inning. Brian Dozier led off the game with a home run, then Eddie Rosario hit a two-run shot to make it 3–0. But the Yankees Didi Gregorius hit a full-count, three-run homer that run off Ervin Santana in the bottom of the first to tie the game. The Yankees beat the Twins 8–4 for their tenth straight postseason win over the Twins, and it was the Twins' thirteenth straight postseason loss since 2004.

Things looked to be different in 2019. The Twins had a rejuvenated lineup, featuring the most prolific home run–hitting squad of all time. They set a new major league record with 307 home runs in a single season, shattering the Yankees' record of 267 from 2018. The Twins won the AL Central for the first time since 2010 and posted the second 100-win season in franchise history. They became the first team to boast a lineup with five 30–home run guys: Nelson Cruz (41), Max Kepler (36), Miguel Sano (34), Eddie Rosario (32), and Mitch Garver (31). Eleven Twins had double-digit home runs.

Not far behind them in the home run race were the Yankees, who hit 306. The Yankees won the AL East with a 103–59 record and matched up with the Twins with home field in the ALDS.

"I think the fans and everyone who has followed the Twins for a long time have many thoughts about these types of games," said new manager Rocco Baldelli. "But I don't think any of our guys care one bit about what has happened here previously. And I think our guys are about as confident going into this series as you can be."

In addition to 307 home runs, the Twins also won a league-leading fifty-five road games that season.

The Twins flashed their home run power early in Game 1, with All-Star shortstop Jorge Polanco taking James Paxton deep in the top of the first. Nelson Cruz hit another solo home run in the third to take a 2–0 lead. José Berríos allowed three Yankee runs in the bottom of the third as the Yankees took the lead. The Twins tied it in the top of the fifth, but New York would score seven runs over the next three innings and would take Game 1 10–4. Utility man D.J. LeMahieu was 2–3 with two home runs and 4 RBI.

The loss tied the Twins with the 1986–1995 Boston Red Sox for the most consecutive postseason losses in league history. Eleven of the fourteen losses came at the hands of the Yankees. The Twins had scored first in ten of the eleven losses.

The Yankees scored first in Game 2 then hung a seven-run third inning on the Twins. Four runs were charged to starter Randy Dobnak, then Tyler Duffey (who had a 2.50 ERA with eight home runs allowed in 58 appearances) served up a grand slam to Gregorius. With the eventual 8–2 loss, the Twins passed Boston for the longest postseason losing streak of all-time with fifteen straight losses.

Game 3 returned to Target Field—the first playoff game in Minneapolis in nine seasons. Baldelli looked to the veteran Jake Odorizzi to end the losing streak and get Minnesota back in the best-of-five series.

Odo struck out three of the first five Yankees batters he saw (LeMahieu, Brett Gardner, and Giancarlo Stanton) before serving up a solo homer run to Gleyber Torres in the second inning. Gardner had an RBI single in the third. Odorizzi wouldn't allow another run for the rest of his outing, which lasted five innings. Severino, who missed all but three starts in 2019 due to rotator cuff inflammation, started Game 3. The Twins loaded the bases against Sevy with nobody out, but a pop fly and back-to-back strikeouts ended the threat. The Twins had two baserunners on in the third, but again failed to score. Severino gave way to Tommy Kahlne, Chad Green, Adam Ottavino, Zach Britton, and Aroldis Chapman the rest of the way. The Twins only run in Game 3 was a solo home run by Rosario in the bottom of the eighth inning (off Britton), but it was too little too late. The Yankees won 5–1, swept the Twins again, and advanced to the ALCS. The Twins have lost sixteen straight playoff games since 2004 . . . thirteen of them at the hands of the Yankees.

December 28, 2003

Vikings at Arizona Cardinals—McCown to Poole

Noooooooo! The Cardinals have knocked the Vikings out of the playoffs!
—Paul Allen, KFAN

The 2003 NFL season began and ended with two of the biggest blunders in team history. On Draft Night 2003, the Vikings were trying to trade their seventh overall pick and move back in the draft, but the clock expired before a deal was done. Jacksonville (QB Byron Leftwich) and Carolina (OT Jordan Gross) quickly submitted their picks before the Vikings were ultimately able to draft DT Kevin Williams ninth overall.

The Vikings were looking to return to the postseason for the first time since losing the NFC Championship Game in 2000 and hadn't missed the playoff's three consecutive years since the mid-1980s.

At the beginning of the season, it looked like the streak was going to end. The Vikings won the first six games (including division games against Green Bay, Chicago, and Detroit) to spring out to a 6–0 record.

But the Vikings would lose six of their next nine games, with five of those six loses coming at the hands of losing teams. Now 9–6 and tied with Green Bay atop the division, the Vikings needed to beat a 3–12 Arizona Cardinals team on the road to win the NFC North and advance to the postseason.

Daunte Culpepper, Randy Moss, and the Vikings offense move the ball quickly on their first drive, going seventy-two yards in seven plays to get to the Cardinals one-yard line. On third and goal, running back Moe Williams was stuffed at the line of scrimmage by Fred Wakefield. Instead of taking the early field goal, head coach Mike Tice stayed aggressive and went for it on fourth down. Culpepper rolled out of the pocket and threw an incomplete pass out of the back of the end zone, intended for Hunter Goodwin.

"I liked the decision to go for it," Williams said. "You want to set the tempo. We hadn't been stopped at the one-yard line all season. Why not go for it?"

Arizona quarterback Josh McCown, starting from his own one-yard line, orchestrated a ninety-five-yard drive, highlighted by a thirty-six-yard Emmitt Smith scamper. With a first and ten from the Minnesota eleven, the Vikings defense held firm, only allowing six yards to set up fourth down. Neil Rackers kicked it through the uprights from twenty-two yard out for a 3–0 lead.

Vikings kicker Aaron Elling missed a forty-four-yard field goal (he was 72 percent that season, and only five of ten from forty-plus yards) on the next drive, giving the ball back to McCown with excellent field position.

The two team exchanged punts, until three minutes left in the second quarter when Brian Williams picked off McCown at midfield. He fumbled when he was tacked by tight end Freddie Jones, but he was able to recover the fumble. It looked like Minnesota ball, but an "illegal use of hands" penalty on defensive back Ken Irvin negated the play. Arizona couldn't take advantage of the penalty and punted four plays later.

With the ball at their own ten-yard line, Culpepper and the Vikings had ninety-one seconds to put points on the board before halftime. Instead, a deep pass intended for wide receiver Kelly Campbell was intercepted by Dexter Jackson and returned to the Minnesota 13. The Cardinals couldn't punch it in and settled for another Rackers field goal and a 6–0 halftime lead.

The Vikings offense finally woke up on the second drive of the third quarter, with Moe Williams getting the first points on the board for Minnesota with a one-yard touchdown. In the fourth quarter, Culpepper and Moss connected for Moss's seventeenth touchdown of the season, which tied a career high. Moss became the first player in NFL history to average over a hundred yards and one touchdown per game (1,632 yards, 17 touchdowns on 111 receptions) in a single season.

On the Cardinals first play of the fourth quarter, McCown was intercepted by rookie Kevin Williams. Elling kicked a forty-six-yard field goal to extend the lead to 17–6 after 17 unanswered Vikings points.

The Vikings defense had held the Cardinals to minus-13 yards in the second half, and with 6:42 left in the game, a win and a playoff berth appeared to be a lock for the Vikings.

But then things began to unravel. The Vikings defense had Arizona fourth and six from their own forty-four-yard line. Cardinals coach Dave McGinnis elected to go for it, and it paid off. McCown hit rookie Anquan Boldin for a six-yard gain and a first down to keep the drive alive.

Kevin Williams sacked McCown for an eleven-yard loss, then McCown was sacked again, this time by Lance Johnstone. But Billy Lyon was called for defensive holding on the second sack. It turned a third and twenty-five into a first and ten on Minnesota's forty-five-yard line.

After McCown was sacked again, this time by Chris Hovan and Fred Robbins, the Cardinals got in the red zone on a thirty-seven-yard reception to Nate Poole (who had been cut by the Cardinals four times in two seasons). On fourth and goal from the two-yard line, McCown threw to tight end Steve Bush for the touchdown. After the two-point conversion failed, the Vikings lead 17–12.

With only two minutes left, the Cardinals attempted the onside kick to try and get the ball back. A high bouncing kick from Neil Rackers hit Vikings tight end Jim Kleinsasser in the hands as he was hit by a wave of Cardinals. The ball popped out and was recovered by Damien Anderson.

McCown led the Cardinals offense and looked to orchestrate the game-winning drive from his own thirty-nine-yard line. He threw a deep pass intended for rookie wide receiver Bryant Johnson, and Vikings defensive back Denard Walker was called for pass interference, moving the ball to the Vikings thirty-one-yard line.

The Cardinals got the ball to the Minnesota nine-yard line. On second down, Kevin Williams recorded his third sack of the game for an eight-yard loss, giving him 10 ½ sacks on the season. With seventeen seconds and seventeen yards to go, McCown was strip-sacked by Lance Johnstone, but offensive tackle Reggie Wells recovered the fumble. McCown had four of Arizona's five fumbles on the day, but the Vikings didn't recover any of them.

Now fourth and twenty-five from the twenty-eight-yard line and no time-outs left, the Cardinals had to take a shot to the end zone. Poole got behind Walker's coverage as McCown stepped up in the pocket to avoid being sacked by Kenny Mixon, rolled to his right, and fired a prayer to the corner of the end zone as time expired. Safety Brian Russell had coverage over the top, saw Poole break free of Walker's coverage and came over to assist. Poole leapt and made the catch, but he only got one foot in bounds as Russell knocked him (and Walker) out of bounds before getting the second foot inbounds. The official immediately ruled touchdown and said that Poole would have gotten both feet down had Russell not pushed him out.

"It's a judgment call," Russell said after the game. "But that game really didn't come down to the last play."

After a booth review, it was ruled a touchdown. The Cardinals won 18–17. With Green Bay's 31–3 over a Denver Broncos team that had already clinched a playoff spot and had nothing to play for, the Packers were the 2003 NFC North champions.

The force-out rule was eliminated in 2008.

"You were asking officials in a split second to make a judgment call that's not reviewable," Russell said in 2008 after the rule change. "Now the rule is simple, and it's reviewable. What happened to us in 2003 shouldn't happen to another team again."

The Vikings had eight sacks compared to Arizona's one, and while the Cardinals were only 3-of-14 on third down conversions, they were three-for-three on fourth down conversions, including two for touchdowns.

Poole had thirteen receptions that season: his longest catch of the season was the thirty-seven-yard reception in the fourth quarter, and his only touchdown that season came in the Cardinals final seconds of the season. His five receptions and eighty-six yards in the game were both career highs.

The Packers hosted the Seattle Seahawks in the first round of the playoffs the next week, and they invited Nate Poole to attend the game. While at the game, the city of Green Bay gave him the key to the city. The Packers beat Seattle in overtime in the Matt Hasselbeck "we'll take the ball and we're gonna score" game.

It doesn't help, but the Packers also lost to the Cardinals at Sun Devil Stadium that season.

With the loss, the Vikings joined the 1978 Washington Redskins as the only teams in NFL history to miss the playoffs after starting 6–0. The Vikings were in first place from the first week of the season until the final seconds.

November 4, 2004

Sergei Zholtok Dies from Heart Failure

Sergei Zholtok was a fan favorite with the Minnesota Wild from 2001 to 2004. Although he wasn't a member of the inaugural team in 2000, his impact was felt during the early days of the franchise.

Zholtok was drafted fifty-fifth overall by the Boston Bruins in the 1992 NHL Entry Draft. He appeared in twenty-five games over two seasons with the Bruins before being picked up by Ottawa. He had his breakout season with the Montreal Canadians in 1999–00, scoring twenty-six goals. He was traded to Edmonton in December 2000 during a down year in which he scored five goals in sixty-nine games between Montreal and Edmonton.

With his value at a low point, he was acquired by the Minnesota Wild for just a seventh-round draft choice. The move gave Zholtok increased playing time on the second-year franchise, including playing the point on the Wild's first power play unit.

Zholtok averaged just over sixteen minutes of ice time with the Wild during his three seasons with the Wild with 48 goals and 62 assists in 210 career games with Minnesota. He shared the *C* with Brad Bombadir and Matt Johnson during the 2002–03 season in which Wild broke out, won forty-three games, and made the playoffs for the first time in franchise history.

He was a key contributor as the club made a run to the Western Conference Finals, including recording the assist on Andrew Brunette's legendary overtime goal in Game 7 against Colorado. Zholtok had 13 points in 18 playoff games that year.

He was traded to Nashville along with Bombadir for draft picks in March 2004 and appeared in eleven regular season games and six playoff games for the Predators.

Throughout his career, Zholtok had a weird medical history. He was sent to a St. Paul Hospital after he hyperventilated during a game. After a similar incident in 2003, he was diagnosed at Mayo Clinic with a heart arrhythmia but was cleared to play.

Friend and former Wild teammate Darby Hendrickson told the Pioneer Press in 2004 that Zholtok wouldn't have kept playing if he knew his health was at risk.

With the NHL lockout in 2004-05, Zholtok elected to play in his native Latvia and signed with Riga 2000 (Latvia). He convinced Hendrickson to join him on the team in Latvia.

On November 3, 2004, Zholtok left a game with five minutes remaining and collapsed, gasping for air in the hallway.

Paramedics performed cardiopulmonary resuscitation. They attempted to shock his heart. Hendrickson saw what was going on and called Wild physician Sheldon Burns, who was familiar with Zholtok's medical history and joined Zholtok as he lay on the floor.

But nothing could be done.

> As difficult as it was, I'm glad I was there. I know he would have wanted me there. I know he would have wanted his father there. He's a guy I loved. I don't relive my final moments with him. I relive the unbelievable moments I shared with him. -Darby Hendrickson

An autopsy determined cause of death was heart failure. The hockey world mourned the loss of Zholtok. During a game against Minnesota and Nashville, he was honored at center ice in front of a sellout, misty-eyed Xcel Energy Center.

<<BONUS ACHE>>

Derek Boogaard

Minnesota Wild fans loved their enforcer while he skated with the team from 2005 to 2008. And while he only scored two goals and had 12 assists with the Wild, fans loved to see him beat the crap out of other players. Whether he was delivering a huge hit or dropping gloves with Trevor Gilles, Brian McGrattan, Raitis Ivanans, Todd Fedoruk (who had to have his face repaired with metal plates after a fight with the Boogeyman), David Koci, or D. J. King fans loved to see number 24 on the ice. And at six feet seven and 265 pounds, he was one of the most respected, yet most feared, players in the NHL. While with the Wild, Boogaard became addicted to painkillers as a result of the beating he took on the ice every night. When Boogaard missed training camp before the 2009-10 season, the injury report said he was out with a concussion when he was secretly at a drug treatment facility in California. When he became a free agent after the season, he signed a four-year $6.5 million deal—unheard of for an enforcer—with the New York Rangers. He reported to Rangers training camp weighing 300 pounds.

He played twenty-two games for New York before being shut down with postconcussion syndrome. While he was away from the ice, his prescription medication usage increased. He returned to workouts for the Rangers in March, but they sent him to rehab in California. Two months later, he spent a couple days in Minneapolis with his brother, Aaron. After a night of partying with friends, he complained the room was spinning and went to bed. He never woke up. The doctor said with the mixture of alcohol and oxycodone in his system, he probably died as soon as he closed his eyes. Two months after Boogaard's death, his autopsy revealed that he had an advanced form of chronic traumatic encephalopathy (CTE) with significant damage to his brain tissue. That season, the Wild paid tribute to Boogaard by presenting a framed jersey to his family at center ice.

May 21, 2004

The Western Conference Finals versus LA Lakers

We've come a long way after losing seven straight times.
—Flip Saunders

The 2003–04 season is easily the greatest season in Timberwolves history. General manager Kevin McHale revamped the roster with only four players returning from the previous season: Kevin Garnett, Troy Hudson (who missed most of the season with an injury), Wally Szczerbiak, and Gary Trent. Through trades and free agent signings, McHale added Sam Cassell, Latrell Sprewell, Trenton Hassell, Fred Hoiberg, Mark Madsen, Ervin Johnson, and Michael Olowokandi. There was an adjustment period for the Wolves to begin the season, finishing the first month of the season 9–8; but the Wolves—featuring their Big Three of Garnett, Sprewell, and Cassell (all of whom were All-Stars that season)—turned it on in December with an 11–2 record. The Wolves finished the season 58–24, winning their last nine games to clip San Antonio for the top seed in the Western Conference. Garnett would be named NBA MVP after averaging 24 points, 14 rebounds, and 5 assists per game. KG would also win the NBA Defensive Player of the Year.

The Wolves made quick work of rookie Carmelo Anthony's Denver Nuggets, winning the best-of-seven series in five games for the Wolves' first postseason series victory in franchise history. The Sacramento Kings took the Wolves to seven games in the semifinals, with the Wolves escaping with an 83–80 Game 7 victory when Chris Webber missed a game-tying three as time expired. Garnett put the team on his back in the series, averaging 24 points, 15 rebounds, 4 assists, 2 steals, and 3 blocks per game in the series, including a 32-point 21-rebound effort in Game 7. The Wolves were headed to the Western Conference Finals for the first time in team history.

Matching up against the Wolves were the Los Angeles Lakers—the team that had knocked the Wolves out of the playoffs the previous season. Kobe Bryant and Shaquille O'Neal had been joined by two aging future Hall of Famers: Karl Malone (who took a $17 million pay cut to join the Lakers) and Gary Payton, both in search of their first championship (both had been beaten in the finals by Michael Jordan's Chicago Bulls in the 1990s). Despite the off-the-court distractions of Bryant's sexual assault trial in Colorado, the feuding between Bryant and O'Neal and trying to find a balance between four future Hall of Famers on one of the first "super teams" in the NBA, the Lakers won the Pacific Division with a 56–26 record, which was good for the number 2 seed in the West. They had beaten the Houston Rockets in five games, then the San Antonio Spurs in six games to reach the Conference Finals for the fourth time in five years. When the Lakers' Big Four all played in the same game, they were 33–9.

Game 1 was at Target Center and was a rare off-night for the reigning NBA MVP. Garnett would shoot 46 percent from the field (7/15) and finish with 16 points.

"You could tell he didn't have his normal energy," Lakers head coach Phil Jackson said after the game.

"Fatigue is not an issue," said Garnett. "This is the Western Conference Finals. Suck it up or go home."

Sam Cassell wasn't much better (5/14 for 16 points). Sprewell led the Wolves with 23 points, but the Wolves defense couldn't contain Shaq. Olowokandi had the pleasure of guarding Shaq for most of the game. Shaq stuffed the stat sheet while being guarded by Ervin Johnson, but despite Olowokandi's stifling defense (Michael also had 10 points and 11 boards off the bench), Shaq finished with 27 points and 18 rebounds. Bryant added 23, and sixth-man Derek Fisher scored 11 of his 14 points in the second half.

The game was tied 67–67 with 7:13 left in the third quarter before an 11–0 Lakers run opened it up. The Wolves fought back to get within two points at 88–86 with 4:03 to go, but LA hit their free throws and clutch shots to take Game 1 97–88.

"We have to take care of the ball," said Garnett, whose team turned the ball over fifteen times, including nine times in the second period. "We've been here before. We've been down 1–0 before. Now it's time to regroup."

Things looked rough for the Wolves early in Game 2. Sam Cassell left the game after only forty-three seconds with a hip injury.

"I thanked him for a great forty-five seconds," Flip Saunders said. "I suppose if you look at it like he didn't play tonight, it's a positive for us. He has four days rest before Game 3."

Everybody knew Garnett (24 points, 11 rebounds) would stuff the stat sheet after his underwhelming Game 1. The Wolves also got 17 points from Sprewell, and Szczerbiak (who had only played in twenty-eight games due to injuries) scored

16 points off the bench. But it was the player who came in for Cassell that stole the headlines the next day.

Journeyman Darrick Martin, who began his career on a ten-day contract with the Wolves in 1995, was playing for the Wolves for the third time in his career. He spent the previous season playing in Italy and Russia, then he signed a pair of ten-day contracts with the Wolves in the middle of the 2003–04 season before signing a contract for the remainder of the year. He had played in sixteen games, averaging ten minutes and three points per game.

After replacing Cassell at point guard, Martin played 36:45, and while he only shot 4-of-11 from the floor, he finished with 15 points, 6 assists, and no turnovers. He was also 6-for-6 from the free throw line.

Whatever off-night bug had plagued Garnett in Game 1 found Shaquille O'Neal in Game 2. He was contained by Johnson, Olowokandi, and Mark Madsen, who hung on him defensively wherever he went. The three Wolves centers combined for 15 points, outscoring Shaq, who finished with 14.

The Wolves led 32–24 after the first period, with Szczerbiak scoring nine of his sixteen points that quarter. He stayed hot in the second with Wally, Spree, and KG combining for 32 points (while Shaq was held to only four) to take a 51–37 lead into the half.

Frustration began to set in for the Lakers in the second half. Even with a guy who had been playing for the Sioux Falls Skyforce three months ago, they couldn't stay with the Wolves. Karl Malone put an elbow into Martin's sternum, was called for a flagrant 2, and was ejected from the game. At the end of the night, seven technical fouls were handed out.

"When you play a team two times in three days, you start to not like each other," Saunders said. "We play hard, not dirty."

The Lakers had two separate 8–0 runs in the third to trim the score to 63–56, but Garnett (after missing four straight jumpers) drilled a three with .04 seconds left to extend the lead to 68–56.

Bryant would finish with 27 points in the game, but Shaq's 14 would be the only other Laker in double figures (Payton had eight, Malone had five, Devean George had three, and Fisher led the Lakers bench in scoring with four points). The Wolves won Game 2 89–71 to even the series at a game apiece. The 71 points matched a playoff low for the franchise as they shot 36 percent from the floor.

"They played with desperation," Bryant said. "And we didn't match it."

"Our guys are upset," added O'Neal. "It'll be different in Game 3. It was nothing I'd never seen before. It was just one of those games for me. I was missing chippies. I don't usually go 4-for-10. I won't go 4-for-10 in Game 3."

Game 3 shifted to Staples Center in Los Angeles, where the Lakers were nearly unbeatable, going 34–7 at home that season.

As was typical with every home Lakers game, the stars came out for Game 3. But oddly, some of the familiar faces in the crowd were wearing blue and green instead of purple and gold. While the elite of the elite sat courtside, Randy Moss sat in the second row next to Snoop Dogg. Prince was also at the game, sitting two rows behind them.

Sam Cassell was back in the lineup and played nearly twenty-seven minutes, dropping 18 points. Darrick Martin didn't have nearly as good a game in Game 3 as he did in Game 2, splitting time with Cassell at point, going 0-for-2 from the floor. Szczerbiak had another great game off the bench, finishing with 21 points. Sprewell had 18, and Garnett had 22 points and 11 rebounds. But after that, there wasn't much offense with only seven Wolves recording points: Trenton Hassell had six, Ervin Johnson and Fred Hoiberg each had two. Michael Olowokandi was 0-for-4 from the field.

The Wolves resorted to the highly debated Hack-a-Shaq rule, which is where players would intentionally foul O'Neil to send him and his horrendous free throw shooting (only made 49 percent of his free throws that season) instead of letting him dominate from the paint. Garnett, Johnson, Olowokandi, Madsen, and fourth-string center Oliver Miller combined for twenty-two fouls. After missing eleven of his first thirteen free throws, Shaq would finish 8-of-22 (36 percent). In the game, Shaq passed Michael Jordan for most postseason free throw attempts in NBA history, despite playing in twenty-nine fewer games (150 to 179).

Gary Payton, who had 16 total points in the first two games of the series, took advantage of the still-hobbled Cassell, scoring 14 first-quarter points to lead the Lakers to a 24–17 first-quarter lead. In the second quarter, Devean George shined with two long three-pointers and a breakaway steal and dunk. Payton didn't score at all in the second quarter. Despite eight points from Shaq and zero by Kobe Bryant on 0-of-2 shooting, the Lakers led at half 44–35.

"When you're defending things and trying to prevent Shaq from getting the ball as much as possible, those are guys you leave open at times," said Saunders. "The difference in the three games, in Game 2, those guys didn't make those shots. In games 1 and 3, they came through and made big shots for them."

Cassell led the Wolves with 15 first half points, then Wally Szczerbiak stole the show for the Wolves in the third quarter. After scoring only 2 points in the first half, Szczerbiak scored 14 consecutive points for the Wolves to get back within 2 points, 64–66. Kobe would heat up too, scoring 13 of the 26 Lakers points in the quarter, including 4 points in the final fifty-two seconds to increase the Wolves deficit to 65–70 after three quarters.

With the Wolves bigs in foul trouble from playing Hack-a-Shaq, O'Neil began to do his thing. After posting one of his worst playoff games, he put up one of his best: 22 points, 17 rebounds (10 defensive, 7 offensive), 4 assists, and 4 blocks, including draining six of his last nine free throws to help the Lakers down the stretch.

"Shaq is used to it by now," Kobe Bryant said after the game. "[Former teammate] Mark Madsen has been hacking him for the last couple years in practice. Flip normally doesn't go to the Hack-a-Shaq. Tonight, he tried it, and Shaq did a pretty good job."

The aching Cassell sat on the bench most of the second half. Sprewell led the Wolves with 14 points in the quarter as Garnett played sparingly with foul trouble. He would foul out after hacking Luke Walton with forty-three seconds left, but with the Wolves down eight points, it didn't matter much. Walton hit both of his free throws to push the lead to 10 as the Lakers went on to win 100–89.

The Lakers shot an amazing 43 free throws in the game, the most the Wolves had ever allowed in the playoffs. The Wolves only shot 14. Flip Saunders cried conspiracy.

"I think it's ironic," Saunders griped after the game, "that in forty-two minutes, Kevin got six fouls. In two games at home, he had two fouls. I've never been one to overreact to those situations, but that's ironic. And he only shot two free throws. Two years ago, we changed the rules where you weren't allowed to put your hands on a guy. Just because Kevin is seven-foot tall doesn't mean Karl Malone can put two hands on him."

After the loss, the Wolves dropped to 1–4 when giving up 100 points in the 2004 playoffs.

Hours before Game 4, Kobe Bryant was in a courtroom in Eagle, Colorado. The previous July, he had been arrested in connection with a sexual assault case filed by a nineteen-year-old employee at the Lodge and Spa at Cordillera the day before undergoing off-season surgery. Bryant had gone back and forth from the courtroom in Colorado to the basketball court with his teammates. On four occasions, Bryant had appeared in court in the morning, then he played on the court that night. And all four times, the Lakers had won.

There was speculation that Bryant would be late for Game 4 or even miss it entirely for a pretrial hearing, but court adjourned early enough for him to get to Los Angeles for the game. He walked into Staples Center seventy-five minutes before the opening tip.

Flip Saunders put Darrick Marin in the starting lineup for the Sam Cassell, who was still dealing with his hip and back injury. Cassell would come off the bench, but he only logged five minutes in the game. Trenton Hassell and Latrell Sprewell combined for 14 points in the first half as the Wolves led 24–23 at the end of the first period.

But the Wolves offense went ice-cold, and the Lakers used a balanced attack in the second, with six different players scoring points and out rebounded the Wolves 17–5 in the quarter. Derek Fisher led the Lakers in scoring with six points, and Shaq pulled in twelve boards in the first half as they fought to turn a one-point deficit into a five-point halftime lead.

"When you put bodies on Shaq, that opens up rebounds for other people." Saunders said at halftime. "He's very difficult to defend . . . both with the ball and without the ball."

Kobe had made two free throws in the first, chipped in five in the second, and then exploded in the third quarter. After Szczerbiak hit two technical free throws to bring the Wolves to 56–54, Bryant scored 11 points in a row in a 19–6 Lakers run. Bryant scored 18 in the third quarter alone. Meanwhile, Shaq continued to control the glass and had 19 rebounds at the end of the third (the Wolves had 24 as a team).

Meanwhile, the Wolves offense was so terrible that Saunders sent Cassell in the game—the only game he played in that he didn't start that season. He had started 387 of his last 390 games (he would only start 211 of his next 305). Sam hit a three right away but couldn't move up and down the floor very well or defend at all. He only played about five minutes before asking to be taken out. The Wolves shot 34.2 percent (13-for-38) from the floor as a team in the second and third period as the Lakers opened a 75–60 lead.

The Wolves outscored the Lakers 25–17 in the fourth quarter, and Garnett would finish on assist shy of a triple double (28 points, 13 rebounds, 9 assists). But the Wolves never got back within seven points, dropping Game 4 92–85. Kobe poured in 31 points and helped the Lakers improve to 5–0 on days he spent time in the courtroom. Shaq had 19 points and 19 boards and hit seven of his fifteen free throws.

"It's down to one game for us," Saunders said after the game.

"I just feel so bad," Martin told reporters. He had gotten his first start for the Wolves since March 20, 1996. "All of us want to win. But Kevin? You can see it. He plays with so much passion."

"We got to win at home," said Garnett, who played 47:29 seconds of the forty-nine-minute game and led the Wolves in points, rebounds, assists, and blocks for the second straight game. "That's the focus. In my book there was no tomorrow. I think that phrase applies even more now."

Only six teams in NBA history had managed to overcome a 3–1 deficit, and the Lakers had won eleven consecutive closeout games since 2000.

Game 5 returned to Target Center, and Garnett and Sprewell answered the call. After finishing just short of a triple-double in Game 4, KG scored 30 points and hauled in 19 rebounds.

"You can't flatly state that Garnett's overall performance equaled what Puckett did for the Twins with a game-winning home run in 1991," Patrick Reusse of the *Star Tribune* wrote the next day. "But it was right there."

"He did a lot, didn't he?" Trenton Hassell smiled after the game. "Ran the point. Guarded Shaq. Guarded Malone. Guarded Kobe. Guarded Fisher. He's a tired man in that locker room."

Flip Saunders tweaked his starting lineup, replacing Ervin Johnson with Michael Olowokandi and starting Martin for the injured Cassell for the second straight game. The Wolves struggled out of the game, trailing after the first quarter 21–14. The Wolves shot a measly 27 percent from the field.

"We knew that if we didn't win this game, summer vacation started." Garnett said.

Garnett and Sprewell took over the second quarter, combining for 28 of the Wolves 32 points and hitting 60 percent of their shots. Sprewell scored 11 of the team's first 13 points in the quarter, helping the Wolves take a 46–40 halftime lead. The Wolves were on cruise control in the fourth, leading 86–70 with 6:07 left. Garnett had added 12 points to his total in the third and the defense had clamped down on Bryant, limiting him to three points in the quarter.

Flip Saunders called a time-out with his team leading by sixteen points, which brought the record crowd of 20,109 to its feet. Even Sam Cassell, dressed in street clothes, hobbled onto the court to congratulate his teammates.

Then the Kobe Show started. Coming out of the time-out, Bryant scored 6 straight points to fuel a 10–0 Lakers run. In the 2000 conference finals, Kobe led the Lakers back from a 15-point deficit to stun the Portland Trail Blazers in Game 7. The Wolves only made four field goals in the quarter (4–16, 25 percent), but hit 16 of 19 free throws—none bigger than Fred Hoiberg's completion of an and-one. Shaq had just been called for a three-second violation. Leading by 6 points, Hoiberg was fouled by Bryant and made the difficult twenty-foot jump shot. He hit the free throw to extend the lead to 9. Garnett hit four foul shots down the stretch to make it 93–80, but Derek Fisher and the Lakers weren't done yet. The Lakers went on a 12–5 in the final eighty seconds to close the gap to 98–93 after a jumper from Fisher with six seconds left. An O'Neil foul of Szczerbiak after the inbound sent Wally to the line for two free throws. He missed both. Luke Walton corralled the rebound and passed the ball off to the red-hot Fisher, who sank a three as the clock expired. The Wolves won 98–96 as the Lakers just ran out of time.

"The clock was definitely our ally tonight," said Saunders.

In addition to Garnett's 30/19 forty-six-minute effort, Sprewell poured in 28 points. Fred Hoiberg, who had been limited for the first five games with injuries, scored 14 points off the bench to provide offense in lieu of the injured Cassell.

"We didn't want to go home," said Sprewell. "I think we played that way."

Starters Trenton Hassell, Michael Olowokandi, and Darrick Martin combined for nine points on 3-of-13 shooting.

Despite the win, the Wolves still needed to win two more games to advance to their first ever NBA Finals beginning with Game 6 in Los Angeles—a place where the Lakers rarely lost and had won eight straight postseason games.

The only thing that could stop Garnett with his back against the wall was foul trouble and sloppy play. Saunders had to bench KG with 5:07 left in the first quarter. Garnett finished the first quarter with one point (on a technical free throw), was 0-of-2 from the floor with four turnovers. The Wolves had six turnovers in the quarter that turned into 13 Lakers points and a 28–17 lead.

In the second quarter, the Lakers got into foul trouble. Kobe had two quick fouls and sat a good chunk of the second half, then Shaq went to the bench after picking up his third of the quarter with a minute left. As a team, the Lakers committed eleven fouls as the Wolves hit 16 of their 17 free throws in the quarter to pull within two points at the half, 48–46. The Wolves cut way down on their turnovers, giving the ball back to the Lakers only once.

"We were right there," Saunders said.

The officials swallowed their whistles in the third period with three of the league's biggest stars in foul trouble. After shooting a combined 40 free throws in the first half, the Lakers shot four and the Wolves didn't have any. Garnett and Sprewell scored a combined 14 points, and the Wolves led by as many as four points in the quarter. Despite six more turnovers in the quarter, the Wolves lead 68–67 at the end of the third. Now all the Wolves had to do was hold on. They were only twelve minutes away from forcing Game 7.

Phil Jackson turned to an unlikely hero: Kareem Rush. Rush was averaging twelve minutes and just under three points per game in the series, but with Kobe in foul trouble and Derek Fisher banged up after spraining his knee late in Game 5, Jackson had to turn to Rush.

Rush responded by making his first six three-pointers of the game. His fourth broke a 68–68 tie with 10:33 left. The Lakers wouldn't trail in the game the rest of the way. The Wolves had one final chance to get back in the game with 7:42 left. Technical fouls were called on Malone and Bryant, and Shaq was on the bench with five fouls with the Wolves trailing 77–74. But Garnett turned the ball over with an offensive foul. Kobe immediately scored. After Szczerbiak missed a wide open three in the corner, Rush hit his fifth three-pointer and pushed the Lakers lead to 82–74. Rush would finish with 18 points as the Lakers bench outscored the Wolves reserves 30–20.

"You can't defend that," said Trenton Hassell about Rush's career game. "If their role players step up, that's the ball game."

Despite 27 points from Sprewell and a 22-point, 17-rebound night from Garnett, the Wolves couldn't overcome the 19 turnovers that turned into 33 Lakers points as Los Angeles advanced to their fourth NBA Finals in five seasons with a 96–90 win.

"I got a taste of the Western Conference finals," Garnett said afterward. "But it doesn't mean a thing if you don't win it all. I'm a person who always tries to grab some sort of positive out of a negative. It's a nice foundation for the future. We've just got to add a couple of pieces."

For Garnett, Game 6 would be his last playoff appearance in Minnesota. After starting next season 25–26, Flip Saunders was fired and replaced by GM Kevin McHale. While the team did improve under McHale, the Wolves missed the playoffs for the first time since 1996. The Wolves began a rebuild that off-season, electing to let Latrell Sprewell walk away and trading Sam Cassell and a first-round pick (which ended up being Austin Rivers) to the LA Clippers for Marco Jaric and Lionel Chalmers.

The Wolves missed the playoffs again the following season, which led to the team trading Garnett to the Boston Celtics in July 2007. The Wolves wouldn't make the playoffs again until the 2017–18 season.

<<BONUS ACHE>>

Latrell Sprewell Can't Feed His Family

The Timberwolves acquired Latrell Sprewell from the New York Knicks prior to the 2003–04 season, and he, along with Kevin Garnett and Sam Cassell, helped lead the Wolves to the deepest playoff run in franchise history that ended in the Western Conference Finals. After the season, the Wolves offered Sprewell a three-year $21 million contract extension. He declined, saying that he "had a family to feed." The Wolves withdrew their offer, and Sprewell had the worst season of his career as the Wolves missed the playoffs for the first time in eight seasons. The 2004–05 season was the last time the Wolves would have a winning record for thirteen years.

FEBRUARY 25, 2005
The Vikings Trade Randy Moss to Oakland

Randy Moss is, hands down, the most physically gifted man to play wide receiver in the NFL. The six-foot-four, 210-pound receiver from Rand, West Virginia, had over 9,100 yards and scored 90 touchdowns . . . in his first seven seasons in the NFL.

He had fallen into the Vikings lap with the twenty-fourth overall pick in the 1998 NFL Draft due to character concerns and, on the field, he was well worth it (most of the time).

The Vikings were 36–12 during Moss's first three years with the team, including two NFC Championship Game appearances in 1998 and 2000, but a 5–11 record in 2001 led to the firing of head coach Denny Green as the reigns of the franchise were handed over to Mike Tice.

The Tice era was underwhelming: four consecutive runner-up finishes in the NFC North and 32–32 record. The Vikings did back into the playoffs with an 8–8 record in 2004 with Randy Moss providing an all-time Randy moment when he fake-mooned the fans in Green Bay after catching his second touchdown of the game.

2004 was a rare off year for Moss. He missed three games with a hamstring injury, and despite 13 receiving touchdowns in thirteen games, he failed to reach the thousand-yard mark for the first time in his career.

Some of Moss' antics and off-field issues were creating problems too. In September 2002, Moss was driving in downtown Minneapolis and bumped a traffic control officer trying to prevent him from making an illegal turn. A search of his vehicle revealed a gram of marijuana.

The reason that twenty NFL teams passed on Moss was beginning to show, and in March 2004, the Vikings officially moved on from Randy Moss by trading him to the Oakland Raiders for linebacker Napoleon Harris and Oakland's first-round pick in the upcoming draft.

Mike Tice got his defensive piece with Harris, and with the seventh overall pick in the 2005 NFL Draft, the Vikings selected WR Troy Williamson out of South Carolina to replace Moss in the lineup.

Harris, a first-round pick by Oakland in 2002, was brought in to help shore up a defense that gave up over 24 points per game in 2004 (twenty-sixth in the league). Harris played in 15 games (starting three) in 2005 and finished with 18 tackles as he was hampered with injuries. The 2005 season was better with three interceptions, 2.5 sacks, and 96 tackles in fourteen games. Harris signed a six-year deal with the Kansas City Chiefs after that season. After being released one year into his contract, he re-signed with the Vikings after an injury to E. J. Henderson. He finished that season with 32 tackles and one sack in ten games.

With the seventh overall pick in the 2005 NFL Draft, the Vikings selected WR Troy Williamson out of South Carolina to replace Moss.

Williamson had all the tools to be the deep threat to replace Randy Moss: the size, the speed, and the smarts. The one thing he couldn't do was catch the dang ball. He blamed bad depth perception for his poor hand-eye coordination that resulted in eleven drops in 2006, none worse than the one week 17 against the Denver Broncos.

The Vikings started 3–6, but after five straight wins were sitting at 8–7 and on the verge of an unthinkable playoff spot. A win over Denver, who had a playoff spot in the AFC locked up, would put them in the playoffs for the first time in three years.

Then Troy Williamson happened. First, with the Vikings down 7–3, Williamson dropped what would have been a guaranteed seventy-three-yard touchdown from Tarvaris Jackson. The second drop was on a crucial first down later in the game. The game would head to overtime tied at 19–19 before a Jackson fumble at the Vikings' thirteen-yard line set up a thirty-yard Jason Elam field goal to win the game. The Vikings were officially eliminated with Washington's 27–6 win over Dallas as the Redskins grabbed the sixth and final playoff spot in the NFC.

Williamson's Vikings career ended with 1,067 yards and three touchdowns in three seasons. He averaged two catches per game. He was traded to the Jacksonville Jaguars for a sixth-round pick in 2008.

Moss, meanwhile, was having a career resurgence. After some disgruntled time in Oakland, he was traded to the New England Patriots, where Bill Belichick sorted him out. Moss scored an NFL record 23 touchdowns for the Pats in 2008, helping lead the way to the first 16–0 regular season in NFL history. Meanwhile, the Vikings have only had four thousand-yard seasons since Moss was traded: Sidney Rice (2009), Adam Thielen (2017 and 2018), and Stephon Diggs (2018).

April 21, 2005

Onterrio Smith and the Whizzinator

Fact: There is a bar in Mankato with a fake penis on the wall.

In 2009, Buster's Sports Bar and Grill's $750 bid at an auction won arguably the most famous fake penis in Vikings history.

Vikings running back Onterrio Smith had issues with marijuana before the team drafted him out of Oregon in 2003. Smith had been kicked off the University of Tennessee football team in 2000 before transferring to Oregon, where he graduated with the seventh most rushing yards in school history.

Smith played in twenty-six games for the Vikings (nine starts) over two seasons, rushing for 1,123 yards and 7 touchdowns and catching 51 passes for another 523 yards and two more scores. He had also already been hit with two substance abuse violations. A third one and he'd be suspended for an entire year. With a relatively ineffective rushing attack with Smith, Mewelde Moore, and Michael Bennett, a suspension to a running back was the last thing the Vikings needed.

While he was flying out of MSP in April 2005, Smith was caught with several vials of dried urine and a contraption called a Whizzinator when his bags were searched. A Whizzinator is a strap-on device with a heated external bladder that can be filled with clean or synthetic urine to beat drug tests.

While there are other methods of trying to beat a drug test (herbal tea, flushing your system, pills, etc.), the Whizzinator was an odd choice for trying to beat an NFL drug test. While the device is efficient at dispensing clean urine, it's not good enough to fool the chemical analyst that watches NFL players pee in the cup. NFL spokesperson Greg Aiello told *USA Today* in 2005 that "players are visually observed from the front giving the sample with their shirts off and pants and underwear pulled down to their knees."

Smith said the device was for his cousin, and even though he was caught with the Whizzinator, he wasn't suspended for a third failed drug test.

That occurred less than a month later when he, to no one's surprise, failed a third drug test and was suspended for an entire year.

Smith was cut by the Vikings one month before his suspension was up.

April 23, 2005
The 2005 NFL Draft

The Minnesota Vikings had a terrible 2005 NFL Draft. Two first-round picks, seven picks total, and none of them lasted more than four years on the team.

Coming off an 8–8 season and their first playoff appearance since 2000, the Vikings dealt receiver Randy Moss to Oakland for the seventh overall pick in the draft.

The Vikings needed a wide receiver to replace Moss. The Vikes were left with Nate Burleson, Kelly Campbell, Marcus Robinson, Keenan Howry, and Ben Nelson; and they desperately needed a big-play receiver.

With the seventh pick, the Vikings selected Troy Williamson of South Carolina. Williamson, a two-time 100- and 200-meter dash state champion in high school, was a surprise pick to go this high; and he was selected because of his breakaway speed.

The Vikings also needed to bolster their defense, so they selected defensive end Erasmus "the Eraser" James out of the University of Wisconsin. James accumulated 124 tackles, 18 sacks, forced 7 fumbles, and was named to the All Big-Ten Team during his time at Wisconsin.

Troy Williamson only lasted two seasons in Minnesota, where he became notorious for dropping passes. In 2006, he tied for second in the league with eleven drops. In his last game as a Viking in 2007, with the Vikings needing a win to get to the postseason, he dropped two crucial passes in the game against Denver, one for a TD and one for a crucial first down late in the game. The Vikings lost the game and missed the playoffs. He was dealt to the Jacksonville Jaguars for a sixth-round pick and is highly regarded as the worst draft selection in Vikings history.

Erasmus James didn't last long either. Although he had 28 tackles and 4 sacks during his rookie campaign, his next two seasons were full of injuries. He was traded to the Washington Redskins for a seventh-round pick. He appeared in five games for the 2008 Redskins before they cut him.

The Vikings took tackle Marcus Johnson out of Ole Miss. Johnson in the second round. He played in forty-seven games (18 starts) in three seasons. He signed with Tampa Bay after his rookie contract expired.

Cornerback Dustin Fox was taken in the third round with the eightieth overall pick. He was a four-year starter at Ohio State, and he won the BCS championship with the Buckeyes in 2002. During full-contact drills, he hurt his left arm and it was cut soon after.

Runningback Ciatrick Fason was drafted in the fourth round out of Florida. He only lasted two seasons with the Vikings, rushing for 161 yards and 5 touchdowns, and was cut during training camp of the 2007 season.

The Vikings didn't have a fifth-round pick (they used it to trade up for Fason), but they took defensive tackle C. J. Mosley out of Missouri in the sixth round. He showed some promise in his one season with the Vikings. He appeared in twelve games, recording 15 tackles and 3 sacks. He was traded to the New York Jets during the off-season in exchange for quarterback Brooks Bollinger.

Cornerback Adrian Ward of UTEP was the Vikings' final pick in the draft. He was released before training camp.

The only successful player from the 2005 NFL Draft was undrafted punter Chris Kluwe out of UCLA. The part that probably stings the most is that twenty-one NFL teams passed on a quarterback out of California named Aaron Rodgers, who was taken twenty-fourth overall. Both the Cowboys and Vikings (who each had multiple first-round picks) passed on him twice.

October 6, 2005

The Love Boat

The 2005 season was a rough one for the Minnesota Vikings.

A year after sneaking into the playoffs at 8–8 and winning a playoff game at Lambeau Field, the Vikings started the season 1–4. They had traded Randy Moss to the Oakland Raiders the previous off-season. Daunte Culpepper got hurt in Week 7 as the Vikings saw their pass offense drop from second with Culpepper and Moss to twentieth with Brad Johnson and Travis Taylor.

While things did eventually turn around midseason with a six-game winning streak, that's not what media outlets and fans were talking about.

The Vikings were 1–3 heading into their bye week. Newly signed defensive back Fred Smoot allegedly coordinated a group outing on Lake Minnetonka. He rented two houseboats from charter company Al & Alma for the get-together of an estimated one hundred guests. Prostitutes were flown in from Atlanta and Florida.

The first call came into police around 9:20 on the evening of October 6 to report that "seven black men" had exited a "big shuttle bus limousine" and had urinated in her front yard. Once the boats left the docks, it became a floating orgy. The cleaning crew found used condoms, lube, and wrappers for sex toys all over the boats.

Seventeen key members of the Vikings were charged in their role in the party, including Smoot, Culpepper, Mewelde Moore, Pat Williams, Bryant McKinnie, Nate Burleson, Ralph Brown, Troy Williamson, Travis Taylor, Jermaine Wiggins, Kevin Williams, Lance Johnstone, Willie Offord, and Moe Williams. Four of those players were eventually charged with misdemeanors while the other cases were dismissed.

When the Love Boat Scandal hit the media, the Vikings became the object of national ridicule from sports channels to late-night TV. Owner Zygi Wilf allegedly yelled at the team for forty-five minutes in a profanity-laced tirade and threatened to cut any and all players who were involved. Wilf, who was seeking state funding for the new US Bank Stadium, publicly apologized to Governor Tim Pawlenty and other state officials before instituting a new team code of conduct.

November 3, 2005

Bartolo Colon Wins the Cy Young over Johan Santana

Bartolo Colon is a fan favorite. The smirking overweight seemingly ageless pitcher has somewhat of a cult following across baseball, especially later in his career. While with the Mets from 2014 to 2016, the baseball world seemed to stop every time Colon came up to bat for New York's National League franchise.

Colon has been around a long time. He was the last active player to pitch for the Montreal Expos. After being released by the Braves on July 4, 2017, he signed a deal with the Minnesota Twins. When he played for the Twins in 2017, he played for a manager that had ten career plate appearances against him (Paul Molitor was 2-8 with two walks and a strikeout against Colon). But as Bartolo-mania swept across the country, Twins fans still remember him for one thing: winning the 2005 Cy Young award over Johan Santana.

In the mid-2000s, there was no pitcher in the world better than Johan Santana. After becoming a regular in the Minnesota Twins' starting rotation in 2003, Santana won 122 games for the Twins and Mets over the next seven years. The height of Santana's dominance was 2004–2006. Over those three years, Santana was 55–19 with a 2.75 ERA and averaged nearly 250 strikeouts. Johan won the AL Cy Young in 2004 and 2006, and he should have won it in 2005 as well.

Johan finished third in the AL Cy Young Voting in 2005 behind Colon and Yankee closer Mariano Rivera. Looking back on the numbers, there is only one reason that Colon was voted for over Santana. The only major stat category that Santana didn't lead Colon in was wins. Colon's Anaheim Angels won ninety-five games and made the playoffs. Santana's Twins won eighty-three and finished third in the AL Central. Other than only winning sixteen games, 2005 was arguably the best season of Santana's career. And he finished third because the Angels were a better team than the Twins.

It's not that Colon had a bad year for Anaheim in 2005. But Santana was better. Santana led the majors in strikeouts (he had 80 more than Colon), allowed 35 fewer hits, and 12 fewer runs despite pitching nine more innings. An even more telltale stat of their seasons is wins above replacement (WAR), which didn't exist in 2005. Santana had a 7.2 WAR compared to Colon's 4.0. And it's not recognized as an official stat by MLB or Elias, so there's that.

What traditionalist baseball writers saw was that Colon was 10–2 in his last 14 starts for the Angels, who needed every single one of those wins to hold off Oakland in the AL West. It also helps Colon's win total that his bullpen blew zero saves for him, and his offense gave him run support (6.02 runs per game).

Santana left the game with the lead nineteen times and saw the bullpen give three of those away. The Twins only scored 121 runs for him, compared to Colon's 149. Santana's stats in his last three no-decisions that year were 23 innings pitched, 9 hits, 3 runs. And 0 wins.

Another mind-blowing stat from 2005 is, Colon's opponent average was .254. Santana's *on-base percentage* was .250.

To make things worse, after injuries ended his career, there is little chance that Johan Santana will be elected to Baseball's Hall of Fame. Every other pitcher to win three or more Cy Young Awards (except for Rogers Clemens, Clayton Kershaw and Max Scherzer) have been elected into the Hall: Tom Seaver, Jim Palmer, Pedro Martinez, Sandy Koufax, Greg Maddux, Steve Carlton, and Randy Johnson.

There are four two-time winners in (Bob Gibson, Gaylord Perry, Tom Glavine, Roy Halladay), and one who will get in (Justin Verlander) compared to two who aren't in (Denny McLain and Bret Saberhagen), one who won't get in (Tim Lincecum), and one who is still building his resume (Jacob deGrom).

While Santana's stats likely aren't enough to get him into the Hall (139–78, 3.20 ERA, 1988 strikeouts over a twelve-year career), that third Cy Young on his resume may have put him over the top. But instead, it went to Colon. The rare Cy Young three-peat for Santana never happened. A three-peat has never happened in the American League.

Minnesota fans still aren't sure what was worse that season: Santana getting screwed out of history or watching the White Sox win the World Series that year.

March 24, 2006

Gophers versus Holy Cross

> *Do you believe in miracles?!?*
> *Yes! Yes, I do!*
> —WCHC 88.1, College of Holy Cross student radio

The 2005–06 Golden Gopher men's hockey team was one of the best in program history. The team featured four first-round picks in the 2009 NHL Draft: defenseman Erik Johnson (first overall to St. Louis), center Phil Kessel (fifth overall to Buffalo), forward Kyle Okposo (seventh overall to New York Islanders), and defenseman David Fischer (twentieth overall to Montreal). Ryan Potulny was an All-American, Kessel was also the WHCA Rookie of the Year, and Don Lucia was named WCHA Coach of the Year. Danny Irmen, Chris Harrington, and Alex Goligoski were also key contributor for the 27–9–5 Gophers.

The Gophers were a number 1 seed (second overall) heading into the NCAA tournament, and heavy favorites against number 15 Holy Cross, who were making their second tournament appearance in school history (their first was a 3–0 loss to North Dakota in 2004).

In the first three-plus years of the sixteen-team NCAA format, the number 1 seeds were 15–0 against number 4 seeds.

Despite winning at least a share of the WCHA regular season championship for the first time since 1997, the Gophers limped into the tournament on a two-game losing streak and finishing fourth in the WCHA Final Five tournament, losing to St. Cloud State in overtime 8–7 and getting shut out by Wisconsin 4–0.

The Gophers outshot the Holy Cross Crusaders 13–10 in the first period but didn't score. The two teams were a combined 0–5 on the power play (Minnesota was 0 for 2).

Holy Cross struck first in the second period at 8:49 on a Dale Reinhardt goal from Blair Bartlett and Tyler McGregor. At 13:15, Minnesota tied the game on a shorthanded goal by Mike Howe. The tie lasted only forty-one seconds; however, as the Crusaders regained the lead on a 5-on-3 power play goal by McGregor from James Sixsmith and Jon Landry. Phil Kessel scored the equalizer at the 15:45 mark from Evan Kaufmann and Chris Harrington. The Gophers outshot Holy Cross 14–6 in the second period.

The Gophers took their first lead of the game at 2:17 in the third on an Alex Goligoski goal from Blake Wheeler. The Crusaders struck back at the 7:53 mark when a Sean Nappo hit the pipe, and the puck landed in the crease behind Gopher goalie Kellen Briggs. Pierre Napert-Frenette got behind Briggs and knocked the puck in to tie the game at 3–3. Minnesota outshot Holy Cross for the third consecutive period. The game headed to sudden death overtime.

Just fifty-three seconds into overtime, Tyler McGregor (who already had a goal and an assist) streaked down the left side and had his attempted pass deflected by a Gopher skate. It popped right back to him, and he fired the game-winning shot to Briggs' stick side to complete the biggest upset in college hockey history.

"I saw a side open net" McGregor told NCAA.com after the game. "That's when it becomes a blur."

To make matters worse, the game was played at the Ralph Engelstad Arena in Grand Forks—home of the rival North Dakota Fighting Sioux.

JUNE 28, 2006

The Wolves Trade Brandon Roy for Randy Foye

The 2006 NBA Draft class was underwhelming. Besides number 2 overall pick LaMarcus Aldridge (who was drafted by the Chicago Bulls then traded to Portland for fourth overall pick Tyrus Thomas and Viktor Khryapa), there was only one All-Star selected in the first twenty picks. While some role-players have stuck around the NBA (Rudy Gay, J. J. Redick, Thabo Sefolosha) most of the top 20 players didn't work out. Andrea Bargnani was the top overall pick by the Toronto Raptors, followed by players like Adam Morrison, Sheldon Williams, Patrick O'Bryant, Mouhamed Sene, Cedric Simmons, and Quincy Douby.

The other All-Star was selected sixth overall by the Timberwolves: Brandon Roy.

Roy had averaged 20 points per game as a senior at the University of Washington, shot 50.8 percent from the floor, 40.2 percent from beyond the arc, and helped lead the 26–7 Huskies to the Sweet 16. He was named Pac-10 Player of the Year and was a finalist for the Wooden, Naismith, Oscar Robertson, and Adolph Rupp awards.

He fell to the Timberwolves, who had the sixth overall pick. The Wolves had just missed the playoffs for the second year in a row and needed a star guard to pair with Kevin Garnett, who led the Wolves with 21.8 points per game in 2005–06. Roy's scoring ability fit that mold. Their 2005 first-round pick, Rashad McCants, only averaged 7.9 points per game in 17.2 minutes on the court. Danny Granger, Monta Ellis, and Lou Williams were all selected after McCants.

But the player Wolves GM Kevin McHale liked in the draft was Villanova senior Randy Foye. The 2005–06 Big East Player of the Year put up similar numbers to Roy: 20.5 points per game, but he only shot 41.1 percent from the floor and 35 percent from three. McHale had a verbal agreement with the Houston

Rockets to select Roy at six then trade him to Houston for Luther Head and Randy Foye if Foye fell to the Rockets at eight.

The Portland Trail Blazers selected Foye with the seventh overall pick.

McHale traded Roy to Portland for Foye and cash. Roy would win the Rookie of the Year and earn three All-Star trips for Portland, averaging 18.8 points per game over the next five seasons, and he would help the Blazers reach the postseason after a five-year absence (Portland missed the playoffs one time between 1976 and 2002 before their five-year drought).

Degenerative knee issues would cut Roy's career short, and he was forced to retire in 2011. But he was one of the best players at his position during those five seasons.

Meanwhile, Randy Foye averaged 13 points per game over three seasons in Minnesota before he was traded to Washington in 2009.

Brandon Roy would eventually play five games for the Wolves, coming out of retirement to play for Minnesota in 2012. He averaged 5.8 points per game in those five games before another knee injury forced him to retire a second time.

October 3, 2006
The ALDS versus Oakland

It's the worst feeling in the world.
—Torii Hunter

On June 7, 2006, the Minnesota Twins were 25–33. They had just been walked off by the Seattle Mariners, had lost four straight games, and were now 11.5 games behind the first place Detroit Tigers in the AL Central. With the black "34" on their uniforms honoring the late Kirby Puckett, who had suddenly passed away at the end of spring training, the Twins were in danger of missing the playoffs for the second straight season.

The Twins began a midseason roster overhaul: releasing third basman Tony Batista (.236, 5 HR, 21 RBI in 50 games), trading shortstop Juan Castro (.231, 14 RBI in 50 games) and pitcher Kyle Lohse (2–5, 7.07 ERA in 22 appearances), and replacing them with younger players like Nick Punto, Jason Bartlett, and Francisco Liriano.

After their loss to Seattle, the Twins began to play some of the best baseball the franchise had ever seen. They went 16–2 in interleague play against the NL West and 71–33 overall. The Twins' "Piranhas" lineup, as Chicago White Sox manager Ozzie Guillen called them, led the majors with a team average of .287 at the end of the season.

"All those piranhas," Guillen said. "Blooper here, blooper here, beat out a ground ball, hit a home run, they're up by four. They get up by four with that bullpen? We'll see you at the national anthem tomorrow. When I sit down and look at the lineup, give me the New York Yankees. Give me those guys because they've got holes. You can pitch around them. You can pitch to them. These little guys? They're on base all the time."

The "little guys" that Guillen was talking about were Jason Tyner (batting eighth), Jason Bartlett (batting ninth), Luis Castillo (leadoff), and Nick Punto (batting second). The four players all hit between .290 and .312 and were essentially four leadoff hitters surrounding the power of the lineup. A lineup that featured Justin Morneau, who became the first Twins since 1987 to hit 30 home runs in a season. Torii Hunter also hit 30 home runs that season. Michael Cuddyer, who wasn't an everyday player at the beginning of the season, took Jason Kubel's spot in right field and had a career year with 109 RBI. And of course, there was catcher Joe Mauer and his .347 average.

The bullpen Guillen mentioned was All-Star closer Joe Nathan (7–0, 1.58 ERA, 36 saves, 95 Ks in 68 innings), Juan Rincon (3–1, 2.91 ERA in 75 games), Dennys Reyes (5–0, 0.89 ERA in 66 games) and Pat Neshek (4–2, 2.19 ERA in 32 games).

The Twins featured a dynamic 1–2 punch of All-Stars Johan Santana (19–6, 2.77 ERA, 245 strikeouts) and rookie Francisco Liriano (12–3, 2.16 ERA, 144 strikeouts). Liriano started the season in the bullpen but changed spots with the struggling Carlos Silva that May. His 1.96 ERA led the majors at the end of July and put him in both Cy Young and Rookie of the Year conversations, but a trip to the disabled list in August left him short of the ERA title. He hit the disabled list for the Twins on August 7 with elbow inflammation and only pitched two more innings for the Twins the rest of the regular season. He would undergo Tommy John surgery on November 6 and would miss the entire 2007 season.

The Twins clinched a playoff spot on September 25, and with three games left, the Twins were tied atop the AL Central with Detroit—the latest a team had ever had a share of first place for the first time that season. Since Detroit had won the season series, the Twins had to win the division outright. A tie would put them in the wild card. The New York Yankees and Oakland Athletics had also wrapped up playoff spots. A division title meant Oakland would come to the Metrodome. A wild card berth meant the Twins would have to head to New York to face the Yankees again—a team that had beaten them in their previous two playoff appearances.

The Tigers had three games against the hundred-loss Kansas City Royals, while the Twins played the Guillen's White Sox. After the Tigers and Twins each lost the first two games of the series, it all came down to game 162 for the AL Central.

The Royals completed the sweep of Detroit. The Twins won 5–1 to give them their ninety-sixth win and the AL Central crown. It was the first time the Twins were in first place all season.

At the end of the season, the Twins had the AL Cy Young winner in Johan Santana (and the AL's first pitching Triple Crown since 1999), the AL MVP in Justin Morneau (34 home runs and 130 RBI), the AL Batting Champion in Joe Mauer (the first catcher to win a batting title)—the first team in the American League to win all three awards (the 1962 LA Dodgers had batting champion Tommy Davis, Cy Young winner Don Drysdale, and NL MVP Maury Wills).

Torii Hunter won his sixth Gold Glove in center field. Liriano would finish runner-up in the Rookie of the Year voting to Detroit's Justin Verlander.

The Twins welcomed the 93–69 Oakland Athletics to the Metrodome for Game 1 of the ALDS in a rematch of the 2002 series—the last time the Twins had won a playoff series. The Tigers played the Yankees as the wild card.

"After Johan, it's pretty much open," said A's third baseman Eric Chavez, talking about the Twins rotation. And he was right. With Liriano shut down for the season, the Twins second option was Boof Bonser, who was 7–6 with a 4.22 ERA. Johan had not lost a game at the Metrodome since August 1, 2005: 16–0 with a 1.93 ERA. The A's had also had their struggles in the first round, having made the playoffs every year from 2000 to 2003, but never having advanced past the first round.

"It's a completely different team," said pitcher Barry Zito. "I don't think many of us feel some kind of first-round jinx or anything like that." Oakland had replaced stars Miguel Tejada, Jermaine Dye, Mark Mulder, and Tim Hudson with former Rookie of the Year Bobby Crosby, Nick Swisher, Dan Haren, and Joe Blanton. The A's had also added Twins killer Frank Thomas in the off-season. Thomas had 39 home runs and 114 RBI for the A's that season, and he finished his career with 52 home runs and 142 RBI in 186 games against the Twins.

Game 1 featured two of the games' best pitchers: Santana versus Zito. Zito's legendary curveball helped him win sixteen games and led the AL with thirty-four starts. His 3.38 ERA ranked in the top 15 in the American League.

Santana struck out Jason Kendall and Mark Kotsay to start the game, then he got Milton Bradley to ground out. In the second, he ran into Frank Thomas, who led off the second with a home run. After Eric Chavez struck out, Jay Payton singled, then he scored on Marco Scutaro's double. After two innings, the A's had a 2–0 lead.

Zito would shut out the Twins for six and two-third innings, when Rondell White hit a solo home run to make it 2–1.

The Twins had a great chance to tie the game after Bartlett's leadoff double in the bottom of the eighth. Gardenhire gave Luis Castillo the "move him over" sign but couldn't get the bunt down. Bartlett was too far off the bag, and catcher Jason Kendell threw down to second and almost picked Bartlett off. With first baseman Nick Swisher playing way in, Castillo was hesitant to have Castillo bunt again. Castillo grounded out to third base, which forced Bartlett to stay at second. Joe Mauer grounded to second, and Cuddyer flew out to right to end the innings.

Jesse Crain, who had pitched seven consecutive scoreless appearances and a 0.75 ERA in September, relieved Santana after eight innings of two-run ball and eight strikeouts. The first batter he faced was Frank Thomas, who hit his second home run of the game. After back-to-back ground outs, Swisher hit a single to right then advanced to second on a bad throw from Cuddyer. Pat Neshek came in and struck out Scutaro to end the inning.

Trailing 3–1 in the bottom of the ninth, Cuddyer led off the inning with a triple after Milton Bradley lost the ball in the Teflon roof. Cuddyer would score on a Hunter ground out, but closer Huston Street would secure the win as Oakland took Game 1 3–2.

"Little mistakes, man," said Hunter after the game. "That's what costs you the game. In the playoffs, everything is magnified. The game could totally be different if we get Bartlett to third base in the eighth."

Rookie Boof Bonser got the ball for the Twins in Game 2. Bonser had been sent to the minors twice that season, and he only made one start for the Twins in August: in place of the injured Liriano, who missed the start to rest his sore forearm. He gave up four runs and six hits in four innings against the Rangers. He was sent back to the minors right after the game. After Liriano was put on the disabled list, the Twins recalled Bonser to take his place in the rotation. He was 5–3 with a 3.26 ERA down the stretch, including 4–1 with a 2.63 ERA in September.

He was opposed by a familiar face to Twins fans: Esteban Loaiza, who had been a perennial Cy Young candidate with the Chicago White Sox in 2003–04. Loaiza had started the 2004 All-Star Game in Houston and was traded to the Yankees at the end of July. He spent 2005 with the Washington Nationals before signing with the A's. He had a rough start to the 2006 season (0–3, 8.35 ERA) and a stint on the disabled list. He finished a respectable 11–9 with a 4.89 ERA.

Bonser and Loaiza were both dealing, shutting out the other's offense through four innings. Swisher doubled off Bonser to lead off the fifth, then he scored on Scutaro's double. Kendall knocked Scutaro in with an RBI single to make it 2–0. The Twins flashed their power in the bottom of the sixth with back-to-back home runs from Cuddyer and Morneau (the first time the Twins had back-to-back home runs in the playoffs since Tony Oliva and Harmon Killebrew in Game 4 of the 1970 ALCS) to tie the game at 2–2 with nobody out. A's manager Ken Macha pulled Loaiza (5 IP, 8 J, 2 R, 2 K) for Kiko Calero after Morneau's home run, and Calero retired Twins to send the game to the seventh.

Gardenhire also went to his bullpen, relieving Bonser (7 IP, 7 H, 2 R, 3 K) in favor of Neshek.

"Here he is, pitching probably the biggest game of his life," Twins pitching coach Rick Anderson said after the game. "To give us six innings and do what he did, he did an outstanding job."

Mark Ellis singled of Neshek with one out, then Kendall hit a ground ball that forced Ellis at second base. With two outs, Gardy replaced Neshek with Dennys Reyes, who hit a line drive to Torii Hunter in right-center field. Hunter charged in and dove for the ball.

For Hunter, who would win his sixth consecutive Gold Glove in 2006, this was a routine play in what would be a career full of highlight catches stealing base hits, taking away doubles and pulling balls back across the 408 sign in center field.

But Hunter's gamble didn't pay off as he missed the ball and it rolled past him. Cuddyer had to run about sixty yards to get to the ball. By the time Mauer had the ball at home, Kotsay was already at home with an inside-the-park home run.

"I can't explain what happened," Hunter said. "It curved out at the last second. I'll take the blame for this one. It was on national TV. You've just got to go out there and take it on the chin."

"As long as he's out there, we want him diving all over the place," said Joe Nathan. Because he's going to make those plays 99 percent of the time."

Hunter knew the feeling of a missed dive in the playoffs. In the 2002 ALDS against Oakland, a Ray Durham hit got under his glove for an inside-the-park home run in Game 3 that ultimately put the A's up 2–1 in the series.

"It's the worst feeling in the world," Hunter added.

The As added one more run in the ninth to win 5–2 and take a commanding 2–0 lead in the best-of-five series. After the game, all eyes were still on the Hunter play.

"We lost as a team," Joe Mauer said. "It wasn't just Torii, and we're going to regroup and try to get back after it."

Maybe Joe was talking about the fact that the Twins were 0–5 with runners in scoring position in Game 2 and were now 0–14 in the series. After going 2–1 in his first three home postseason games, Gardenhire was now 0–7 and being outscored 39–18 in those games. The same season, the Twins were 5–1 against Oakland at the Metrodome. They were headed to the Coliseum with the backs against the walls.

The Twins turned to veteran Brad Radke, who won Game 5 against Oakland in 2002. "You can't be in any better situation than having a man with experience," Twins GM Terry Ryan said. "He's been down this path before. We're in a tough situation with a tough guy on the mound."

Radke had been pitching with a stress fracture in his throwing shoulder since the end of May. Despite the pain, he was 12–9 with a 4.32 ERA and allowed fewer than two walks per nine innings.

"It's been enjoyable, and it hasn't been enjoyable," Radke said at a presser before Game 3. "Physically, it hasn't been, but being around the guys and being around this team that's gone a long way, it's definitely been just as enjoyable as it's been my whole career."

Management and fans knew that the thirty-four-year-old Radke would retire after the season and were hoping he would extend the Twins' season with one more good start.

Despite a 2–0 lead, Oakland fans were uneasy. They had led their 2001 and 2003 series 2–0 over New York and Boston respectively, then they lost three straight games. In 2002, they had a 2–1 lead over the Twins before losing in five games. In 2001, the Yankees had lost the first two games at home before winning two straight games in Oakland, then the fifth game at home.

Radke only lasted four innings, giving up four runs on five hits, including home runs by Eric Chavez and Milton Bradley. He dropped a pop fly down the first baseline that could have been handled by Morneau that allowed D'Angelo Jiménez to reach first base.

But trailing 4–0, the Twins weren't about to give up. Hunter hit a two-out home run off A's starter Dan Haren in the fourth to make it 4–1. With Morneau and Hunter in scoring position with one out, Rondell White broke the Twins' 0–18 with runners in scoring position when he singled in Morneau from third. Hunter tried to score from second base but was thrown out at home on another controversial play.

"[Home plate umpire] Mike Everitt told me, 'He had to tag you,'" Hunter said. "'What do you mean, he had to tag me? I'm an athlete. I made a slide like an athlete. He didn't tag me.'"

Even catcher Jason Kendell wasn't sure he made the tag. Rondell White didn't advance to second on the throw to home. Jason Tyner struck out to end the inning. The Twins trailed 4–2, but their playoff woes were about to hit a new low.

Dennys Reyes got the Mark Kotsay and Milton Bradley out in the bottom of the seventh. After intentionally walking Frank Thomas, he walked Eric Chavez. Reyes was pulled for Jesse Crain. Jay Payton hit a ground ball to first base that should have ended the inning, but it was booted by Morneau. With bases loaded and two outs, Crain walked Nick Swisher. Macro Scutaro hit a three-run double that broke the game open.

"These are probably three of the worst games we played since I got called up," Bartlett said, who committed an error at short right before Milton Bradley's two-run home run in the third. "We picked a bad time to have some bad ball games."

Morneau added a solo home run in the eighth, but the Twins watched Luis Castillo fly out to left to end the game and the series.

The Twins finished the series 1–19 with runners in scoring position (.053). They had three errors in Game 3, which led to five unearned runs. The Twins, who were the second best fielding team in the majors, had five errors in the last two games of the series. Three and four hitters Mauer and Cuddyer had more strikeouts than RBI and were a combined 5-for-23 (.217). Despite having the same number of hits as the A's (26), the Twins were outscored 16–7 in the three games.

Meanwhile, on the other side of the bracket, the Detroit Tigers beat the New York Yankees in four games. The As, in their first ALCS since 1992, were swept by the Tigers.

<<BONUS ACHE>>

The 1984 Minnesota Twins

The 2006 Minnesota Twins put together the greatest second half in team history. In 1984, they were on the other side of the comeback.

Only two seasons after losing 102 games, the Twins were in contention for the American League West pennant in 1984 thanks to the emergency of rookie Kirby Puckett, an MVP-caliber season from Kent Hrbek, and the development of players like Gary Gaetti, Tom Brunansky, and Frank Viola. They had a five-and-a-half-game lead in the division on August 22, but a couple losing streaks had them tied with the Kansas City Royals at 80–75 atop the division with seven games to play. The Twins won the next game over the Chicago White Sox, then they lost the next six games—two of them walk-off losses given up by closer Ron Davis. The Twins finished 81–81 and three games behind Kansas City in what would have been their first postseason appearance since 1970.

DECEMBER 29, 2006

Gopher Football versus Texas Tech—the Insight Bowl

If we had not lost the way we lost, we probably wouldn't be here today.
—Gophers athletic director Joel Maturi announcing Glen Mason's dismissal

The 2006 Minnesota Gophers football team finished the season 6–6 (3–5 in the Big Ten) in Glen Mason's tenth season with the team, good enough for the team's seventh bowl invite in eight seasons. And a year after losing the 2005 Music City Bowl to Virginia in the closing minutes after blowing a 14–0 lead, the Gophers were itching to get back in the win column during Bowl season.

The Gophers were invited to the Insight Bowl in Tempe, Arizona, and were matched up against sophomore phenom Graham Harrell (4,555 passing yards, 38 touchdowns); Joel Filani (91 receptions, 1,300 yards, 13 touchdowns); Shannon Woods (926 yards, 10 touchdowns); and the 7–5 Texas Tech Red Raiders, coached by Mike Leach.

The Gophers jumped out to a 7–0 lead after an aggressive play-call by Mike Leach backfired. On fourth and one from their own 45, Harrell was stopped on a quarterback sneak, and the Gophers got the ball after the Red Raiders turned it over on downs. Six plays later, Gophers quarterback Bryan Cupito hit tight end Jack Simmons for a two-yard touchdown with 9:27 left in the first quarter.

Four minutes later, linebacker Mike Sherels picked off Harrell at Tech's thirty-seven-yard line. Running back Amir Pinnix, who would finish the game with 179 rushing yards, extended the Gopher lead to 14–0 with a two-yard touchdown run.

Harrell turned the ball over again on Tech's next possession. Willie VanDeSteeg strip-sacked Harrell, and Steve Davis recovered the loose ball at the Gophers' 13. Minnesota marched down the field on an eighty-seven-yard drive (their longest scoring drive of the season) to take a 21–0 lead on a Justin Valentine one-yard plunge into the end zone.

Tech had a chance to cut into the Gophers' lead after cornerback Antonio Huffman intercepted a Cuptio pass at Minnesota's twenty-yard line, but Pinnix forced a fumble. The Gophers recovered the ball in the end zone for a touchback. The Gophers took advantage and would score another touchdown (fourteen-yard pass from Cupito to Ernie Wheelwright) for their fourth consecutive scoring drive.

The Red Raiders would score in the first half with a Shannon Woods, finishing off a seven-play seventy-seven-yard drive with a one-yard touchdown run, only for the defense to give up another long Gopher drive and another passing touchdown (to Logan Payne) in the final minute of the first half for a 35–7 halftime lead.

Minnesota got the ball to start the third quarter and opened the second half with a sixteen-play seventy-eight-yard drive that ate 7:13 off the clock. Kicker Joel Monroe kicked a thirty-two-yard field goal to give the 38–14 lead with 7:47 left in the third quarter.

What transpired the rest of the game would ultimately cost Glen Mason his job. Harrell, who would set multiple NCAA records during his career and finish in the top 4 of the Heisman Voting in 2008, woke up. Harrell started the comeback with a forty-three-yard touchdown pass to Filani with 4:58 left in quarter three. The Tech defense forced a Gophers punt, then they scored another touchdown with an eight-yard pass from Harrell to Robert Johnson on the first play of the fourth quarter.

Minnesota drove the ball to the Tech thirty-yard line, but on fourth and seven, Mason decided to go for it rather than kick the field goal. Cupito was sacked and gave the ball back to Tech without putting points on the board. Tech would on a one-yard Harrell touchdown run to cut the score to 38–28.

The Gophers went three-and-out on their next possession and punted the ball to Texas Tech. Danny Amendola returned the punt forty yards to set up the Red Raiders up on their own forty-four-yard line. Nine plays later, they were in the end zone again as Woods scored his second touchdown of the game on a one-yard run to make it a three-point game, 38–35, after scoring 21 unanswered fourth-quarter points.

Texas Tech attempted the onside kick, but it was recovered by the Gophers. The Gophers offense went three-and-out for the second consecutive drive, but they forced Tech to burn two of their time-outs on the drive. The Gophers punted the ball away again and was downed by the Red Raiders at their own twelve-yard line. A false start penalty on the first play of the drive moved them back to the seven-yard line.

Harrell ran Tech's two-minute offense efficiently, completing five of seven passes, working the sidelines to stop the clock. Two of the catches stopped the clock for measurements. On the eighth play of the drive, Tech kicker Alex Trlica (who was 15-for-21 kicking field goals that season) drilled a fifty-two-yard field goal to tie the game at 38–38 as time expired to send the game to overtime.

The Gophers got the ball first in overtime, and Joel Monroe kicked a thirty-two-yard field goal to give Minnesota the lead at 41–38. College football overtime rules let each team have a chance with the ball. If Minnesota stops the Tech offense, they win the game. A field goal, and the game continues. But if the Red Raiders score a touchdown, the game would be over.

In only five plays, Tech was knocking on the door. Woods would run in his third touchdown from three yards out, completing the 44–41 comeback.

The comeback was the largest in Division I bowl history (it has since been tied by a 31-point TCU comeback over Oregon in the 2016 Alamo Bowl).

Graham Harrell finished with 445 yards and two touchdowns while rushing for another one and was named the Offensive MVP. Cuptio finished with 263 yards and three touchdowns in the loss.

Two days after losing, Gophers athletic director Joel Maturi fired Glen Mason after the game following another historic collapse under Mason, adding the Insight Bowl to the list of Gopher meltdowns in the past decade. Maturi would hire Denver Broncos tight ends coach Tim Brewster as the team's next head coach.

<<BONUS ACHE>>

Gopher Football versus Ohio State: October 28, 1989

The Gophers led the Ohio State Buckeyes 17–0 after the first quarter, and 31–0 in the second quarter. With the Buckeyes getting ready to punt back to the Gophers with three minutes left in the first half, the Gophers were penalized for twelve men on the field. OSU took advantage and scored a touchdown and a two-point conversion just before halftime to trail 31–8. The Buckeyes opened the second half with a field goal to trail 31–11, then they scored a touchdown on their next possession (31–18). The Gophers kicked a field goal to make the score 34–18, but the Buckeyes scored another quick touchdown (34–26). The Gophers got another field goal, opening up a 37–26 lead. Facing a fourth and goal from the Gophers one-yard line, OSU went for it and punched it in to cut the deficit to 37–34. After forcing another Gophers punt with fifty-one seconds left, OSU completed a long touchdown pass to take a 41–37 lead. The Gophers had a chance at the end, but receiver Steve Rhem could only get his fingertips on the game-winning touchdown pass from Scott Schaffner. Minnesota lost 41–37 despite forcing six OSU turnovers. The Buckeyes outscored the Gophers 41–6 in the second half.

Gopher Football versus Michigan: October 10, 2003

The 6–0 #17 Gophers led the #20 Michigan Wolverines 28–7 at the beginning of the fourth quarter at the Metrodome in what was the hundredth anniversary of the game that began the trophy series for the iconic Little Brown Jug. A week before, a loss to Iowa had dropped Michigan from #9 to #20 in the polls, and things looked like they were going to drop further in the BCS rankings. But Michigan scored 31 points in the fourth quarter, taking the lead on Garrett Rivas's thirty-three-yard field goal with forty-seven seconds left in the game. Michigan won 38–35. It was the biggest comeback in Michigan history and the program's fifteenth straight win over the Gophers.

Gopher Football versus Wisconsin: October 15, 2005

#22 Gophers faced #23 Wisconsin at the Metrodome on October 15, 2005. They took a 34–24 lead with 3:27 left in the game. Wisconsin scored a touchdown with 2:10 remaining, but the Gophers couldn't run out the clock and were forced to punt inside their own end zone. Justin Kucek blocked the punt, and Ben Strickland recovered it in the end zone for a 38–34 Badgers win.

2005 Music City Bowl—Gophers versus Virginia

The Gophers were 7.5-point favorites against the 6–5 Virginia Cavaliers at the 2005 Music City Bowl. The Gophers led at halftime 21–10 and 24–17 late in the third quarter. Virginia tied the game at 31–31 with 8:48 left, then they kicked the game-winning thirty-nine-yard field goal with 1:08 remaining to win 34–31. The Gophers started the season 4–0 but lost four of their last six games of the season.

Gopher Football versus South Dakota: September 11, 2010

The Gophers played the South Dakota Coyotes at their home opener at TCF Bank Stadium after a 24–17 win at Middle Tennessee. South Dakota opened up a 21–10 halftime lead over the Gophers. While Adam Weber did tie a school record with his fifty-fifth career touchdown pass and throw for 258 yards and 3 touchdowns, South Dakota Dante Warren made a lasting impression on Gophers fans. Of the 444 yards the Gophers defense allowed that Saturday, Warren accounted for 433 of them (352 through the air, 81 on the ground, 5 total touchdowns). Warren also iced the game late with a thirty-six-yard touchdown run on a fourth and one boot leg that put South Dakota up 41–31 midway through the fourth quarter. USD won 41–38, and head coach Tim Brewster was fired after a 1–6 start.

Gopher Football versus NDSU: September 24, 2011

The Gophers played the North Dakota State Bison in Jerry Kill's first season as head coach of the program, and it didn't go well. The Gophers led 7–0 after the first quarter before NDSU put up twenty-eight-second quarter points en route to a 37–24 win. The Bison returned two interceptions for touchdowns in the game, including a fifty-two yarder as time expired in the first half. Quarterbacks Marquies Gray and Max Shortell combined for only 124 passing yards in the game. NDSU would win the first of seven FCS Championships in the 2010s that season. The Gophers also lost to the Bison 27–21 in 2007 in the middle of a ten-game losing streak. They haven't played North Dakota State since.

Minnesota Football at Michigan—October 1, 2011

Michigan welcomed first-year head coach Jerry Kill and the Gophers to the Big House on October 1, 2011, and in front of a crowd of 111,000 strong for his first Big Ten game; and they proceeded to absolutely dismantle the Gophers. Michigan outgained Minnesota in yardage 580–177 on their way to a 58–0 win. Junior running back Vincent Smith had touchdowns rushing, passing, and receiving on Michigan's first four drives. Denard Robinson was 15–19 for 169 yards and 2 TDs along with 53 rushing yards and a TD before being pulled after jumping out to a 38–0 halftime lead. The Gophers were in a great position to score and break the shut out before a David Cobb fumble was returned eighty-three yards for a touchdown by Courtney Avery. While the numbers were ugly, the outcome was much worse. Backup running back Fitzgerald Toussaint had 108 yards and a touchdown. It was Michigan's first Big Ten shutout since 2001, and their first shutout of any opponent since 2007.

Gopher Football versus Wisconsin: November 26, 2016

Minnesota led 17–7 at halftime before Mitch Leidner threw four second-half interceptions as the Badgers scored 24 unanswered points to beat the Gophers for the thirteenth straight time, 31–17.

July 31, 2007

The Wolves Trade Kevin Garnett

"ANYTHING IS POSSIBLE!"
—Kevin Garnett after winning the 2008 NBA Title with Boston

There is only one player that leads an NBA franchise in scoring, rebounds, blocks, assists, and steals: Kevin Garnett. The Wolves drafted Garnett fifth overall straight out of high school in the 1995 NBA Draft, becoming the first player since Darryl Dawkins in 1975 to bypass college. He played in eighty games (forty-three starts) his rookie year, averaging 10 points, 6 rebounds, a block, an assist, and a steal in just over twenty-eight minutes.

The next season, he became the face of the franchise, earning the first of 10 All-Star Game appearances with the Wolves and—teamed with Stephon Marbury, Tom Gugliotta, and Sam Mitchell—led the Wolves to the playoffs for the first time with a 40–42 record.

The Wolves would be fixtures in the playoffs for eight consecutive seasons, but were bounced in the first-round seven consecutive years. During those seven years, Garnett established himself as one of the best players in the NBA, averaging 20 points, 11 rebounds, and 5 assists per game.

While players came and went, Garnett remained a constant for the Wolves, basically willing them to the playoffs by himself. While every other successful team of that era had a duo of players (Jordan and Pippen, Malone and Stockton, Kobe and Shaq, Robinson and Duncan, Webber and Stojakovic, Nash and Stoudemire), Garnett was basically a one-man show.

Things changed for KG in 2003 with the addition of two-time NBA champion Sam Cassell and All-Star Latrell Sprewell. The "Three Wolves" won a franchise-record fifty-eight games and were the top seed in the Western Conference playoffs. With Cassell and Sprewell, Garnett got past the first round for the first time in franchise history, beating Carmelo Anthony and the Denver Nuggets. In the second round, the Wolves got 32 points and 21 rebounds from Garnett in a Game 7 against the Sacramento Kings; but they would lose in six games to the LA Lakers in the Western Conference Finals.

Garnett posted career highs in points, rebounds, assists, and blocks and was named the NBA MVP.

Things began to crumble with the Wolves after that. A year after their fifty-eight-win season, the team missed the playoffs for the first time since Garnett's rookie year. Flip Saunders was fired midseason, Wolves GM Kevin McHale traded Cassell to the LA Clippers, and Sprewell opted not to sign a $21 million extension. Garnett was back to relying on average NBA players again like Ricky Davis, Trenton Hassell, and Marko Jaric. The next season, the Wolves fell below .500 at 33–49. Wolves owner Glen Taylor wanted Garnett to be a Timberwolf for life but realized that trading KG would be the best thing for the franchise to rebuild. When he announced that he would listen to trade offers for Garnett, he immediately began fielding phone calls.

There were reportedly seven teams involved in the Kevin Garnett sweepstakes: Chicago, Golden State, Indiana, Boston, Phoenix, Dallas, and the LA Lakers. Trade rumors swirled. There was reportedly a handshake deal that would have sent Garnett to the Lakers for Lamar Odom, Andrew Bynum, and Kwame Brown. There was a rumor of a three-way trade that would have sent Garnett to Phoenix, Amare Stoudemire to Atlanta, and the third and eleventh picks in the upcoming draft to Minnesota. Boston was also offering a haul of young players for Garnett too.

The issue? Garnett had a no-trade clause in his $126 million contract. His preferred destination was Phoenix to play with Steve Nash. McHale wanted draft picks and young players to retool the Wolves. The Suns had three valuable pieces: Amare Stoudemire, Shawn Marion, and Atlanta's unprotected first-round pick in the 2008 draft. The Suns thought Stoudemire and the draft pick were too much, and the Wolves thought Marion and the draft pick weren't enough. There was a possible three-way trade involving Minnesota, Phoenix, and Boston on the table; but Marion was set to become a free agent after the season and let everyone know he had no intention of re-signing with either the Wolves or Celtics. Ultimately, talks fell through.

Garnett was also rumored to be headed to Golden State to play with Baron Davis, Stephen Jackson, Monta Ellis, and Al Harrington in a deal that would have sent Jason Richardson to Charlotte and draft picks to Minnesota; but Warriors owner Chris Cohan decided not to make the trade (he did trade Richardson to Charlotte for rookie Brandan Wright).

Before the 2006 season, the Chicago Bulls had offered the Wolves a package that included Luol Deng, Tyson Chandler, and the second overall pick in the draft (LaMarcus Aldridge). The Wolves declined. The following year, they offered the ninth overall pick (Joakim Noah), a future first rounder (which would have ended up being the top pick in the 2008 Draft and Derrick Rose), Tyrus Thomas, and P. J. Brown.

What people tend to forget is that Garnett didn't want to be traded. He was extremely loyal to the franchise he had spent the first twelve years of his career with, the franchise that took a chance on a high school prospect.

McHale, Garnett's agent Andy Miller, and Celtics GM Danny Ainge eventually convinced Garnett to waive his no-trade clause and be traded to the Boston Celtics in a move that sent seven players to the Wolves: Al Jefferson, Ryan Gomes, Gerald Green, Sebastian Telfair, Theo Ratliff, and two first-round picks—the most players traded for an individual player in the history of the league.

The 2006–07 Boston Celtics were terrible: 24–58 (they were 66–16 with Garnett, Ray Allen, and Paul Pierce) and most of those young pieces from that team came to Minnesota.

The centerpiece of the deal was twenty-two-year-old Al Jefferson. He had a strong first year with the Wolves, averaging 21 points and 11 rebounds. In year 2, he only played in fifty games before tearing his ACL. His numbers decreased to 17 points and 9 rebounds. He didn't fit in with the Wolves coach Kurt Rambis's offense, and his interior defense didn't mesh with eventual-teammate Kevin Love. So he was traded to Utah after three seasons in Minnesota.

Ryan Gomes may have been the one player that lived up to expectations in the trade. He started 214 games over three seasons and averaged 14 points and 5 rebounds per game before he was traded to the LA Clippers.

Gerald Green was a first-round pick by the Celtics in 2005. His most memorable moment as a member of the Timberwolves came in the 2008 Slam Dunk Contest where he blew out the candle on a cupcake sitting on the back of the rim while executing a dunk (he finished second to Dwight Howard). He only appeared in twenty-nine games before being traded to Houston for Kirk Snyder and a second-round pick.

Sebastian Telfair's first stint with the team lasted two seasons before he was traded with Mark Madsen and Craig Smith for Quentin Richardson. He was traded back to the Wolves a year later. The journeyman averaged 9 points and 5 assists in parts of three seasons.

Theo Ratliff, once a dominant center in the NBA, was a Celtics contract dump in the Garnett trade. Ratliff played in ten games for the Wolves before being cut.

The two first-round picks ended up being sixth overall pick Jonny Flynn and twenty-ninth overall pick Wayne Ellington.

Kevin Garnett, meanwhile, led the Celtics to a sixty-six-win season and the 2008 NBA Championship.

October 1, 2007

The Twins Hire Bill Smith as General Manager

"We're going to continue to build a winner."

- Bill Smith

Bill Smith had huge shoes to fill when he was hired to succeed Terry Ryan as the general manager of the Twins. Ryan, who also had big shoes to fill when he was hired in 1994, succeeded Andy MacPhail—the architect of the 1987 and 1991 World Series teams. Ryan had taken one of the worst teams from the 1990s and transformed them into a perennial division winner. He drafted players like Joe Mauer, Justin Morneau, Torii Hunter, and Michael Cuddyer. He turned a disgruntled Chuck Knoblauch into Christian Guzman and Eric Milton. He swapped rule 5 players with the Florida Marlins in 1999 to acquire Johan Santana. He turned A. J. Pierzynski into Joe Nathan and Francisco Liriano in 2003; he solidified second base for two seasons by getting Luis Castillo from Florida in 2005.

While Ryan did have his list of blunders (Brett Boone, Butch Huskey, Rondell White, Tony Batista, Reuben Sierra, Sidney Ponson, and flat out releasing David Ortiz), he made enough good ones to get the Twins out of the basement in the American League and return the team to respectability.

Then, Terry Ryan retired after thirteen seasons at the helm, saying the stress of the job had a negative effect on his health and general outlook on life. The Twins promoted Ryan's top assistant Bill Smith the GM job for the 2008 season.

Smith had two tall tasks in his first few months on the job: try and resign free agent Torii Hunter and see what he could get for Johan Santana, whose contract expired after the 2008 season. Hunter left the Twins for the Los Angeles Angels, and Smith replaced him by dealing Johan Santana to the New York Mets in a deal that brought Carlos Gomez to replace Hunter in center field as well as three other pitching prospects.

Smith also traded away starting pitcher Matt Garza and shortstop Jason Bartlett (who would become key members of Tampa Bay's American League pennant team that year) for outfielder Delmon Young and utility infielder Brendan Harris. Even with the losses of Hunter, Santana, Bartlett, and Garza, the Twins had a surprise season and were one win away from making the playoffs.

2009 was one of the most exciting finishes to a non-World Series winning season in Twins history. Away from the field, Smith drafted future All-Star Brian Dozier in the eighth round of the MLB Draft and signed international prospects Miguel Sano, Jorge Polanco, and Max Kepler. On the field, Smith added relievers Ron Mahay and Jon Rauch, starter Carl Pavano, and shortstop Orlando Cabrera. The Twins won the AL Central, this time winning Game 163 in walk-off fashion against the Detroit Tigers. After the Twins were swept out of the playoffs by the New York Yankees, Smith began leaving his fingerprint on the franchise. He replaced Cabrera (who signed as a free agent with the Cincinnati Reds) by trading Carlos Gomez for shortstop J. J. Hardy, which both filled his vacant shortstop position and opened a full-time position in the outfield for Delmon Young. He also locked up reigning AL MVP Joe Mauer with an eight-year $186 million contract.

The Twins won the Central again in 2010, despite losing Justin Morneau for the second half of the season with a concussion and Joe Nathan the entire year after undergoing Tommy John surgery. Forty-year-old Jim Thome, who was added in the off-season, hit 25 home runs, and Smith added closer Matt Capps at the trade deadline to solidify his bullpen. But the Twins were swept out of the playoffs again.

In 2011, the Twins went from a ninety-four-win team to a ninety-nine-loss team. Smith traded J. J. Hardy to Baltimore for two minor league relievers that never panned out. He signed Japanese infielder Tsuyoshi Nishioka and promoted Alexi Casilla to the starting shortstop. He let two of the best bullpen arms in the game in Jesse Crain and Matt Guerrier walk away in free agency (likely strapped for cash with the Mauer signing) and had to rely on a who's who of Alex Burnett, Phil Dumatrait, Lester Oliveros, Chuck James, Dusty Hughes, Jim Hoey, Scott Diamond, and Kevin Slowey. Matt Capps imploded, Joe Mauer and Justin Morneau both suffered concussions, and the starting rotation crumbled. Following the 2011 season, the Pohlads had seen enough. He wasn't fired, but reassigned within the organization. Six weeks after Terry Ryan pulled a Bud Grant and accepted his old job, Smith was given the job assistant to the GM and club president. He held that position until 2017, when he accepted a job in the president of Minor League Baseball's office.

Meanwhile Terry Ryan spent the next four years trying to rebuild what Smith had destroyed. He was fired midway through the 2016 season as Minnesota lost a franchise-record 103 games.

<<BONUS ACHE>>

The Twins Trade for Delmon Young

Nearly two months after taking over as general manager of the Twins, Bill Smith made his first big trade by acquiring one of the best young players in baseball in Delmon Young. Young was the first pick by the Tampa Bay Rays in the 2003 MLB Draft and had already played a 162-game season as a twenty-one-year-old in which he hit .288 with 13 home runs and 93 RBI. Smith sent pitcher Matt Garza and shortstop Jason Bartlett to Tampa Bay for Young and utility infielder Brendan Harris. With Torii Hunter signing with the LA Angels six days before the trade, Smith had a huge outfield piece to replace Hunter's bat in the lineup.

Young had decent offensive numbers in four seasons with the Twins, his best coming in 2010 with a .298 average, 21 home runs, and 112 RBI. His bat easily replaced that of Torii Hunter. Unfortunately, his glove didn't. Despite hitting .287 with 47 home runs and 276 RBI, his WAR with Minnesota was 1.1 because his defense was terrible. Brendan Harris wasn't much better. He hit .251 in 296 games with 14 home runs and 90 RBI in a utility role. He's best known for being attacked by a squirrel while playing third base for the Twins in May 2010.

Meanwhile, Jason Bartlett became an All-Star for Tampa Bay, and Matt Garza was the ALCS MVP as Tampa Bay won the American League pennant. Delmon Young won an ALCS MVP too . . . playing for the Detroit Tigers in 2012.

February 2, 2008

The Twins Trade Johan Santana

We're getting arguably the best pitcher in the game.
—Mets third baseman David Wright

Johan Santana is on the short list of best pitchers the organization has had since moving from Washington in 1961. His .679 winning percentage (93–44 in eight seasons) is tied for the best mark in Twins franchise history and his 1,381 strikeouts rank is fifth all-time. The left-hander was a two-time Cy Young Winner, led the league in strikeouts for three consecutive years, was a four-time All-Star and a Gold Glove winner, and won pitching's Triple Crown in 2006 (19–6, 2.77 ERA, 245 strikeouts).

In 2004, he had one of the best second halves in modern baseball: allowing four or fewer hits in ten consecutive starts, averaged 11 strikeouts per nine innings, had a 13–0 record and set the Twins' single-season strikeout record.

Santana is one of fourteen players to win multiple Cy Young Awards, and from 2004 to 2006, he was 55–19 with a 2.75 ERA and 748 strikeouts.

But following the 2007 season, it was decision time for GM Bill Smith and the Twins. Santana was in-store for a massive contract, and the Twins weren't going to be able to afford him. So they began looking for trade partners before Santana entered the final year of his contract. Santana, who had a full no-trade clause in his current contract, was due $13.25 million in 2008 and was seeking a record-setting six-year $150 million deal.

There were two main suitors for Santana during the 2008 winter meetings: the Boston Red Sox and the New York Yankees, battling for supremacy in the AL East. Each team had the money to sign Santana to a long-term deal and had the prospects the Twins wanted in exchange for him.

The thing both teams were wary of was giving up a ton of young prospects then shelling out a record-setting contract.

The Yankees had the first crack at him. The key players they offered the Twins were outfielder Melky Cabrera and pitcher Phil Hughes. They were also willing to include pitcher Jeffery Marquez in the deal. But the Twins wanted the Yankees to include pitchers Ian Kennedy, Alan Horne or outfielder Austin Jackson, but the Yankees didn't want to part with them.

The Red Sox looked to add Santana to a rotation that already included Josh Beckett, Curt Schilling, Daisuke Matsuzaka, and Clay Buchholz. There were multiple reports of what Boston was offering: some package involving outfielder Jacoby Ellsbury or pitcher John Lester as well as pitcher Justin Masterson, infielder Jed Lowrie, and outfielder Coco Crisp. The Twins wanted all five. Boston said no.

The New York Mets were a dark horse in the Johan Santana sweepstakes. Because of Santana's no-trade clause, he could pick and choose where he wanted to go, and the Mets were near the top of his list. General Manager Omar Minaya was looking for a top pitcher to add to his rotation to help future Hall of Famer Pedro Martinez and some of the younger guys like John Maine and Oliver Perez. The Mets had two players that should have headlined a trade: All-Star shortstop José Reyes and outfielder Fernando Martinez. But Minaya was able to get Santana and keep his best player and top prospect.

Bill Smith agreed to send Santana to the Mets for four prospects: outfielder Carlos Gomez and pitchers Kevin Mulvey, Philip Humber, and Deolis Guerra.

Gomez joined the Twins in an already-crowded outfield with Denard Span, Delmon Young, Michael Cuddyer, and Jason Kubel. The speedster was the opening day center fielder in 2008 after Torii Hunter signed with the LA Angels. His best year was his first year with the Twins, batting .253 with 33 stolen bases. He became the third youngest player to hit for the cycle in May 2008. He led the league with 30 bunt hits but was also picked off a league-leading ten times and led all center fielders with eight errors. In 2009, his averaged dropped to .229, as did his hits (149 to 72), RBI (59 to 28) and stolen bases (33 to 14). After only two years in Minnesota, he was traded to the Milwaukee Brewers for shortstop J.J. Hardy. Gomez turned into an All-Star in Milwaukee. He hit a career high 24 home runs and stole 40 bases, finished in the top 10 in the NL MVP voting and won an NL Gold Glove in in 2013. In 2018, while playing for the Tampa Bay Rays, he hit his first career walk-off home run . . . against the Twins.

Mulvey would pitch exactly 1.1 innings with the Twins, ending his Twins career with a 27.00 ERA. When the Twins claimed closer Jon Rauch off waivers from the Arizona Diamondbacks in September 2009, they sent Mulvey as the "player to be named later." Mulvey wasn't much better for the D-backs, finishing his time in the desert with a 0–3 record and a 6.92 ERA in eight games.

Humber was a little bit better than Mulvey, but not much. He pitched 20.2 innings for the Twins from 2008 to 2009, putting up an ERA of 6.10. The Twins would cut him following the 2009 season. His claim to fame is the perfect game he threw against the Mariners while pitching for the Chicago White Sox in April

2012 (he finished the year 5–5 with a 6.44 ERA). He was claimed off waivers by the Astros before the 2013 season, where he was 0–8 with a 7.90 ERA.

Guerra would never pitch for the Twins. He has a career record of 7–2, a 4.17 ERA, and 75 strikeouts in three seasons between the Pittsburgh Pirates and LA Angels.

Santana, on the other hand, signed a six-year $137.5 million deal with the Mets. He had a good first year in New York, although it was cut short due to a torn meniscus. He had a career-best 2.53 ERA and 206 strikeouts with a 16–7 record and would finish third in the NL Cy Young voting. His most memorable moment as a Met came in 2012. After missing the entire 2011 season recovering from shoulder surgery, Santana threw the only no-hitter in Mets history.

None of the pieces acquired from the Mets lasted more than three seasons with the Twins.

September 30, 2008

Twins at Chicago White Sox—the Blackout Game 163

When you mention "Game 163" up here in Twins Territory, most Twins fans will smile. They remember Alexi Casilla knocking in Carlos Gomez in the bottom of the tenth inning for the 2009 AL Central title.

What fans have erased from their memory is the Game 163 when the ball didn't bounce their way. The Blackout Game 163 against the Chicago White Sox on September 30, 2008.

A little background on the 2008 season first: nobody expected the Twins to even be relevant enough for a Game 163. Torii Hunter had signed with the Angels after the 2007 season. Johan Santana was traded to the Mets for a handful of prospects. The Twins also lost Carlos Silva in free agency to the Mariners and traded pitcher Matt Garza to the Devil Rays for Delmon Young and utility infielder Brendan Harris. Francisco Liriano's dominant rookie season had been cut short by Tommy John surgery, which forced him to miss the entire 2007 season.

The Twins proved the experts wrong.

The young outfield featuring Young (the 2007 Rookie of the Year runner-up), Carlos Gomez (who was centerpiece of the Johan Santana trade), and Denard Span (the Twins first-round pick in 2002) held their own. The combination of Nick Punto, Brian Buscher, and Brendan Harris at third base didn't solve the long-term need but got the job done.

Livan Hernandez won ten games for the Twins before being placed on waivers in August, while Glen Perkins and Kevin Slowey led the team with twelve wins apiece in a new-look rotation that also featured Nick Blackburn, Scott Baker, and occasionally Boof Bonser.

Joe Mauer, Justin Morneau, and Joe Nathan were all All-Stars. Morneau won the Home Run Derby. Carlos Gomez hit for the cycle. Mauer won his second Batting Title and his first Gold Glove.

And most importantly, the Twins were in position to win their fifth AL Central title in seven years at the end of September.

After falling to six games under .500 in June, they rattled off ten wins in a row to get back in the race. After August 1, the division leader changed eighteen times. The Twins were 2.5 games back in entering a crucial three-game series at the Metrodome with the first-place White Sox on September 23 with six games left. The Twins swept the series, including a series finale in which the Twins erased a 6–2 deficit before winning the game in extra innings to take a half-game lead into the final regular season series against the lowly Royals (75–87), while the White Sox had a four-game series against the Indians (81–81).

The Royals won the series against the Twins 2–1. The White Sox split the four-game series with Cleveland to force a tie atop the division.

The Twins and White Sox finished with an identical 88–74 record, meaning the two teams would play one game to determine the 2008 AL Central champion. A major factor in Game 163 in 2008 would be home field advantage. In 2008, home field advantage during a one-game playoff was determined by a coin flip. The Twins and White Sox were both 53–28 at home and 35–46 on the road, so whomever was given home field would have a considerable advantage. Chicago won the coin flip, so the Twins would have to travel to US Cellular for the game. However, the Twins had won the season series over Chicago 11–8, and fans argued that the Twins should have had home field advantage. The rule was changed during the off season.

White Sox fans were encouraged to wear black, which is why the game is referred to by many as the Blackout Game. The Twins started Nick Blackburn (11–11, 4.05 ERA) against John Danks (12–9, 3.32 ERA), who was pitching on three days' rest after allowed 7 ER against Cleveland in first game of Chicago's final regular season series.

Danks allowed 2 hits over 8 scoreless innings. The middle of the Twins lineup (Mauer, Morneau, and Cuddyer) went a combined 1-for-9. The one hit was a Michael Cuddyer double in the fifth inning. A Delmon Young sac fly moved Cuddyer to third base with one out. Brendan Harris hit a shallow fly ball to Ken Griffey Jr. in center field. Cuddyer tried to tag up and score, but Griffey threw a bullet to catcher A. J. Pierzynski to gun down Cuddyer at the plate. Nick Blackburn also pitched a great game, except for one pitch to Jim Thome in the bottom of the seventh inning.

Thome's solo blast was the difference maker as the White Sox won the game 1–0 and won the AL Central Division title. The White Sox would lose to eventual American League champion Tampa Bay in four games in the American League Division Series.

November 22, 2008

Gopher Football versus Iowa—the Final Game in the Metrodome

We didn't do anything to stop them, so they kept making plays.
—Adam Weber

It's never good when the first thing out of your head coach's mouth after a loss is an apology. That's exactly what Tim Brewster did after Minnesota's annual game with the Iowa Hawkeyes in 2008.

Gophers fans were pumped for the game, which was the final game in the Metrodome before the team moved back to campus and beautiful TCF Bank Stadium.

A year after finishing 1–11 and ranked number 116 (out of 120), the Gophers won seven of their first eight games in Tim Brewster's second season. After winning at Purdue for the first time since 1990, the Gophers were ranked #17 in the country. Their 2–1 Conference record was the first time the program had been above .500 in the Big Ten in three years. But losses against Northwestern, Michigan, and at Wisconsin (in a game that they led 21–7) dropped them to 7–4 and 2–4 in the Big Ten. On November 22, 2008, over 64,000 Minnesota Golden Gophers fans filled the Metrodome for the final Gopher football game at the Dome.

The opponent was the 7–4 Iowa Hawkeyes. Iowa had won six of the last seven meetings between the two teams, and the Gophers were looking for a poetic end to the Metrodome—by keeping Floyd of Rosedale with them. Minnesota was close to reclaiming Floyd in 2007, playing a competitive game in Iowa City and only losing 21–16.

But Iowa quarterback Ricky Stanzi and running back Shonn Green had no plans to leave their trophy in Minneapolis.

Greene break Iowa's single-season rushing record (22 carries, 144 yards, 2 touchdowns); and Stanzi took advantage of a terrible Gophers pass defense, carving up the secondary for 255 yards and 3 touchdowns as the Hawkeyes shut out Minnesota 55–0. Adam Webber completed 14 of 28 passes for 127 yards and two interceptions as Iowa's big defensive line manhandled Minnesota (Iowa's defensive line outweighed Minnesota's line by at least twenty-five pounds per player). Mike Maciejowski was the team's leading rusher with thirteen yards. The Iowa defense held the Gophers to six first downs, 134 total yards, and forced three turnovers.

After losing four consecutive games to end the season, the Gophers accepted an invitation to the Insight Bowl against Kansas. They lost 42–21.

January 24, 2009

The NFC Championship Game versus New Orleans

You usually don't expect somebody to throw across the middle that late, but Brett's a Hall of Fame quarterback who's been making that throw his whole career.
—Saints defensive back Tracy Porter

August 18, 2009, was one of the most celebrated days in Vikings history. Six months after retiring from the NFL and after speculation and rumors of a comeback, Brett Favre arrived in Minneapolis on a private plane to sign a two-year contract with the Minnesota Vikings. Favre was named to the AFC Pro Bowl roster despite playing the final five games with a torn biceps (3,472 yards, 22 touchdowns, league-leading 22 interceptions). When Favre got walked through the doors at Winter Park and put pen to paper, Vikings fans and media knew that the 2008 would be an unforgettable season.

With Favre under center, receiver Sidney Rice would have a career year (1,312 yards, 8 touchdowns), first-round pick Percy Harvin would win Rookie of the Year (2,081 all-purpose yards and 8 touchdowns), and All-Pro running back Adrian Peterson would score 18 rushing touchdowns. Favre had his best season since his MVP season in 1995: 4,202 yards, 33 touchdowns, and only 7 interceptions.

The Vikings finished 12–4 in a season that will be remembered as the Year of Favre: his game-winning touchdown pass to Greg Lewis against San Francisco as the clock expired, eclipsing Jim Marshall's mark of 289 consecutive starts, beating Green Bay twice, and becoming the first quarterback in NFL history to beat all thirty-two teams.

The Vikings won the NFC North and earned a first-round bye in the playoffs as the number 2 seed. They beat Tony Romo and the Dallas Cowboys at the Metrodome 34–3 to advance to the ninth NFC Championship Game in team history. After winning the first four ('70, '73, '74, '76), the Vikings had lost their last four ('78, '87, '98, '00).

Their opponent in the conference title game was the 13–3 New Orleans Saints. As good as the Vikings offensive attach was in 2009, the Saints was even better. Drew Brees was now in his fourth season in New Orleans. After a torn labrum in his throwing shoulder put his career in jeopardy while with the San Diego Chargers in 2005, he had signed with the Saints after getting little intereste from the other thirty-one teams. The Miami Dolphins had reportedly been interested in Brees, but team doctors were worried his shoulder wasn't healed and advised against signing the former Purdue Boilermaker. So the team instead traded a second-round pick to Minnesota for Daunte Culpepper to fill their void at quarterback.

Brees was a Pro Bowl selection three times in his first four seasons and threw for 4,388 yards, 34 touchdowns, and 11 interceptions in 2009. His favorite targets were Marques Colston (1,074 yards and 9 touchdowns), Devery Henderson (804 yards and 2 touchdowns), Robert Meachem (722 yards and 9 touchdowns) and Jeremy Shockey (569 yards and 3 touchdowns). The two-headed rushing attack of Pierre Thomas and Reggie Bush combined for 1,820 rushing and receiving yards plus 16 total touchdowns. The Saints won their playoff game against Arizona 45–14.

The Vikings traveled to New Orleans for the second game of Championship Sunday. Peyton Manning and the Indianapolis Colts beat the New York Jets to advance to their second Super Bowl in four seasons.

Favre picked the Saints' defense apart on the opening drive, completing six passes to five different receivers. Peterson scored a nineteen-yard touchdown to cap off an eighty-yard drive and give the Vikings a 7–0 lead. The Saints offense matched that touchdown with one of their own, a thirty-eight-yard pass from Brees to Thomas to tie the game at 7–7. The Vikings' offense kept rolling, scoring a touchdown on their second drive, this time a five-yard touchdown pass from Favre to Rice.

After Brees tied the game with a nine-yard touchdown pass to Henderson, the Vikings caught a break. Reggie Bush, who had gone from second overall pick in 2005 to second-string running back/punt returner, muffed a punt at the Vikings ten-yard line as he was hit by Eric Frampton. The fumble was recovered by backup linebacker Kenny Onatolu with about a minute left in the first half.

"I thought I had some time, but he was right in my face," Bush said. "The defense got the ball right back."

Looking to take a seven-point lead into half time, the Vikings needed a score . . . especially after punting four straight times after their first two scoring drives.

On the second play of the drive from the ten-yard line, Peterson fumbled the handoff from Favre in the backfield, and the Saints recovered the ball.

"No problem," said Scott Fujita, who wrestled the fumble away from Jim Kleinsasser. "There's no chance that guy was going to get it from me. Whatever it took."

While Favre was credited with the fumble, Peterson knew whose shoulders the blame fell upon.

"It was poor execution by me," he said. "I didn't make a big enough pocket, and it hit my elbow. Hold onto the ball. I've been saying that all year, but it's a battle you have to fight."

Both teams headed to the locker room with the game tied at 14–14.

Saints returner Courtney Roby began the second half with a sixty-seven-yard kickoff return. Four plays later, New Orleans took their first lead of the game with a nine-yard Thomas touchdown run, 21–14.

Favre returned to the field to rally the Vikings, but he started taking a beating from the Saints' defense. Favre was never officially sacked in the game, but he took the brunt of a lot of knockdowns from Saints' defensive line. He turned to tight end Visanthe Shaincoe three times on the next drive, completing all three of his targets for sixty-seven yards, capped off by a Peterson one-yard touchdown run to tie the game at 21–21.

The Saints punted back to the Vikings after a three-and-out. Again, Favre took a beating, but he drove the Vikings down to the Saints' thirty-four-yard line. The drive was aided by an Anthony Hargrove roughing-the-passer penalty after leveling Favre after he threw. Four plays later, Favre he dropped back to pass to Sidney Rice, he was high-lowed by Bobby McCray and Remi Ayodele. The pass hung in the air and was intercepted by linebacker Jonathan Vilma at the 31. Favre was basically carried off the field by his teammates and taken to the trainer's table to get looked at.

"We tried to put everything on him," McCray said after the game. "But he just kept coming back."

The Vikings' defense kept Minnesota in the game, forcing another three-and-out deep in New Orleans territory as rookie punter Thomas Morstead came out and pinned the Vikings offense at their own seventeen-yard line.

Harvin ran for a ten-yard gain on the first play of the fourth quarter to get the offense going after the Favre interception two minutes earlier. The next play, he took another handoff in the backfield and tried to run around the left end. He was hit in the backfield by Will Smith and fumbled the ball, which was recovered by Ayodele for the Vikings' second turnover in three offensive plays.

New Orleans had the ball at the Minnesota seven-yard line. After two runs by Thomas, Brees threw a pass to Bush on third and goal. Bush leapt for the goal line in the front corner of the end zone and was met by defensive back Tyrell Johnson, who pushed him out of bounds at the one-yard line before the ball crossed the plain, bringing up fourth and goal. New Orleans coach Sean Payton challenged the ruling on the field. The call was overturned, and New Orleans led 28–21.

"I'll have to see that replay again," said linebacker Ben Leber. "I didn't agree with that one. I thought TJ did a good job getting the guy out of bounds."

Favre limped back onto the field, trailing by seven with 7:57 left in the game. Starting from their own twenty-yard line, Peterson broke free for his largest run of the game, a twenty-seven-yard gain into New Orleans territory. On third and ten from midfield, Favre connected with Bernard Berrian for a thirty-yard gain to set up a first down from the Saints 20.

Berrian had been signed as a free agent by the Vikings for the 2008 season, signing a six-year $42 million contract after spending his first four season with the Chicago Bears. Berrian led the NFL in yards-per-catch in 2008 (20.1 yards) but saw his numbers drop with the emergence of Rice and Harvin. When the Vikings played the Saints in 2008, he torched them with six catches for 110 yards and a touchdown.

The Vikings were twenty yards away from tying the game. The Vikings went to Peterson on first down for a two-yard gain. Favre completed another pass to Berrian inside the ten-yard line, but defensive back Tracy Porter forced a fumble that was recovered by Vilma (his second takeaway of the game). The Vikings had now committed turnovers on three straight drives.

The Saints had the ball on their own five-yard line with 9:37 left. A four-yard Thomas run and a five-yard Henderson reception set up third and short from the 14. Brees tried a QB sneak to pick up the first down, but fumbled. He recovered his fumble and signaled first down. The officials disagreed and signaled fourth and short. Payton again challenged the play, but the play was upheld burning up another New Orleans time-out.

Morstead punted forty-three yards out of bounds. Favre, in obvious pain from the beating he was taking from the defense, hobbled back into the huddle. He hung in the pocket, allowing his receivers to get open, throwing the ball and taking his lumps from the defense. After a sixteen-yard completion to Shaincoe, an eighteen-yard run by Peterson, and an eighteen-yard pass interference call on Porter, the Vikings were first and goal from the one-yard line.

The first carry by Peterson went for negative yards. The second was Peterson's third touchdown of the game and tied it 28–28 with 5:03 left.

Jared Allen, Ray Edwards, and Kevin Williams continued to bottle up the Saints' offense. Edwards had a strip-sack on Brees at the Saints' nineteen-yard line, but it was recovered by offensive lineman Jahari Evans. On third and eighteen, Brees completed a sixteen-yard pass to Henderson, but he was eaten up by Pro Bowler Antoine Winfield short of the first down marker. After the three-and-out, Morstead once again punted the ball back to Minnesota, a booming fifty-eight-yard punt that sent Darius Reynaud back to the twenty-one-yard line.

This was why Vikings head coach Brad Childress had recruited Favre so hard during the off-season, even after Favre had continuously told him no.

"When Brad called [the last time], it was kind of like 'This is it. Now or never,'" Favre said after signing with the Vikings. "Everyone who I've talked to—former players, coaches, people in general—said if I were to come back, this is a perfect fit."

Favre the gun-slinger. Forty-three game-winning drives in his career. This was why he was here.

"The story is too good to die," *Star Tribune* columnist Jim Souhan predicted in his NFC Championship preview the day before the game. "Brett Favre leads a last-minute drive to set up a game-winning field goal by his buddy and fellow former Packer Ryan Longwell. Packer Nation weeps."

The Vikings tried to ride the hot hand in Peterson (finished the game with 25 carries, 125 yards, and 3 touchdowns). After his first two carries went a total of two yards, the Vikings faced a passing down. A ten-yard completion to Berrian on third and eight and a twenty-yard connection with Rice on first and ten had the ball in New Orleans territory. Chester Taylor ran the ball fourteen yards to the New Orleans' thirty-three-yard line, which would have been a fifty-five-yard game-winning field goal attempt by Ryan Longwell.

New Orleans called their final time-out with 1:14 left. The Vikings tried to get a little closer for Longwell, but Ayodele stuffed Taylor and Peterson at the line of scrimmage on consecutive plays.

Facing third and ten, the Vikings huddled up as the play came in from the sideline. Then the whistles blew.

"We just had a fullback in there, and we changed up and broke the huddle with 12," Childress explained.

The extra man in the huddle was fullback Naufahu Tahi. The penalty pushed the Vikings back five yards. Now third and fifteen, the Vikings needed one more big play to set up the game-winning field goal and send the Vikings to their first Super Bowl in thirty three years.

Favre took the snap from John Sullivan and rolled to his right. He had a split second to make one of two decisions: run the ball up the sideline for five yards and step out of bounds or find an open receiver.

He did neither. He didn't see Harvin wide open down the sideline that likely would have been the game-winning touchdown. Instead, Favre threw across his body to the middle of the field to Sidney Rice, who was standing at the twenty-one-yard line. Porter jumped the route and intercepted the pass with seven seconds left.

"You've gotta be kidding me," a bewildered Paul Allen said over the radio broadcast. "Why do you even ponder passing? I mean, you can take a knee and try a fifty-six-yard field goal! This is not Detroit, man! This is the Super Bowl!"

Brees kneeled the ball to send the game to overtime.

The NFC Championship Game had only gone to overtime twice before 2009. The first time was in 1998, which saw the Vikings lose to the Atlanta

Falcons 31–28. The other time was at Lambeau Field in 2007: Favre's final game as a Packer. Lawrence Tynes kicked a forty-seven-yard field goal to send the New York Giants into Super Bowl XLII.

The Saints won the toss and wanted the ball. Starting on his own thirty-nine-yard line, Brees began marching the Saints toward the end zone, trying to get New Orleans to their first ever Super Bowl. An Asher Allen defensive holding call on third and six, which resulted in an automatic first down, helped the cause. After back-to-back incompletions, followed by a nine-yard pass to Henderson, the Saints faced fourth and short at the Minnesota 43. Payton sent his offense back onto the field. The Vikings defense, which had stymied the Saints run game all night long needed one more big stop. Thomas dove over the line to pick up the first down to give Brees a fresh set of downs. As he was hit by Chad Greenway at the top of the pile, he almost fumbled the ball but was ruled down before the ball came out.

The next play, Brees targeted tight end David Thomas over the middle of the field. He was defended perfectly by Leber, but the flags came out of the ref's pocket. Defensive pass interference.

"I don't think it was catchable," Leber said afterward. "I don't agree with the call."

The PI call moved the ball from the Vikings 41 to the 29. Leber tacked Bush for a five-yard loss on the next play. Brees found Meachem for a twelve-yard gain (that once again needed a replay review to see if the ball was caught) to the 22. After another incompletion to Thomas, kicker Garrett Hartley came onto the field to attempt the game-winning field goal.

2009 was an up-and-down year for Hartley. The undrafted kicker out of Oklahoma signed with the Saints midway through the 2008 season to replace the struggling rookie Taylor Mehlhaff. Hartley hit all thirteen of his field goals that year.

He was expected to be the kicker in 2009 but was handed a four-game suspension for testing positive for Adderall. When he returned, he set the NFL record for consecutive field goals to begin his career with 16 (a record since broken by Kai Forbath).

And now, Hartley faced the biggest kick of his career.

On fourth and three, he connected on the forty yarder to send the Saints to the Super Bowl, keeping Favre and the Vikings offense on the sidelines with a 31–28 win.

"It was painful," said Peterson after watching the Saints celebrate from the tunnel. "Especially the way the game ended."

"We lost the game ourselves," said Shiancoe, who finished with four catches for eighty-three yards. "It's as simple as that. With all the fumbles and turnovers, you can't win."

A quick look at the box score would imply the Vikings had won. Their offense outgained 475 to 257: 165 to 68 on the ground. It was 310 to 197 through the air. The Vikings had 31 first downs to New Orleans' 15. Then you get to the turnovers. Six fumbles, three lost by the Vikings. Five total turnovers.

New Orleans would beat Indianapolis in Super Bowl XLIV 31–17 for the first championship in franchise history, but the story doesn't end there.

After the season, a whistleblower within the Saints organization claimed that head coach Sean Payton and defensive coordinator Gregg Williams had set up a "bounty" system during games and handed out money for knocking opposing players out of games.

The Vikings said that Favre took thirteen unnecessary hits in the championship game, including the high-low hit by McCray and Ayodele. No penalty was called, even though NFL VP of officiating Mike Pereira said there should have been. It was later revealed that linebacker Jonathan Vilma had offered $10,000 cash to whoever knocked Favre out of the game.

There were other bounty targets as well, including the previous week against Arizona's Kurt Warner.

It wasn't until the 2012 season that the NFL did something about it. After finding significant and credible information, NFL commissioner Roger Goodell came down hard on the Saints. In their investigation, the NFL found more evidence of the Saints' bounty system: targeting Aaron Rodgers and Cam Newton during the regular season and Matt Hasselbeck during the 2011 playoffs. It was discovered that Reggie Bush's agent also chipped in $10,000 to whoever knocked Favre out of the championship game and $5,000 to whoever took Rodgers out during the 2011 season opener. Several Chicago Bears players came forward and accused the Saints of a bounty system in their regular season game in 2011—a game in which Jay Cutler nearly lost his voice when a Saints player kicked him in the throat.

Saints players earned $1,000 for cart-offs and $400 when an opposing player had to leave the game.

Sean Payton not only knew about the bounty program but tried to cover it up. And the NFL crushed him for it. Payton was suspended for the entire 2012 season and became the only head coach in league history to receive a suspension. Williams was suspended indefinitely (players that played for Williams while he was with the Houston Oilers and Washington Redskins claim that he had a similar setup while he was coaching there). Saints owner Mickey Lumis was suspended for the first eight games of the 2012 season. Assistant coach Joe Vitt, the likely candidate to replace Payton while was suspended, was also suspended for six games. Vilma was suspended the entire 2012 season. Suspensions were also handed out to Anthony Hargrove, Will Smith, and Scott Fujita—all four players had huge roles in the win against the Vikings and were found to have a hand in organizing the program. The Saints were also fined the league max $500,000 and lost two second-round picks (the Saints had already traded their 2012 first-round pick to New England).

But the one thing the NFL couldn't take away was the Super Bowl trophy that now resides in New Orleans.

May 22, 2009

The Wolves Hire David Kahn as General Manager

He's a very intelligent guy and knows the ins and outs of this league as well as anyone. He has all the tools to get the job done in Minnesota.

—former Pacers coach Larry Bird

David Kahn's first job in the sports landscape was as a sports journalist for the *Oregonian* in 1983, covering the Portland Trail Blazers, as well as other local and national headlines. In 1989, he moved to New York to study law at NYU. He stayed in sports, however, working with Proskauer Rose LLC, which represents just about every major US sports organization, including the NBA, NFL, NHL, MLS, MLB, Association of Tennis Professionals, as well as college's Pac-12 and Big East conferences. While at PR, he provided legal counsel to the NBA.

In 1995, he was hired by the Indiana Pacers. He began working in business side and played a major role in helping the franchise design and develop the new Conseco Fieldhouse, now known as Bankers Life Fieldhouse in 1999. In 2000, he began assisting president of basketball operations Donnie Walsh in the day-to-day operations of the team, including overseeing signing players, hiring coaches, making trades, and managing the salary cap.

While he was with the Pacers (from 1995 to 2004), the team was 430–276, made eight playoff times, and made four appearances in the Eastern Conference Finals, advancing to the NBA Finals in 2000. During his last four seasons in Indiana, he was the acting general manager under Walsh.

In 2004, he left the Pacers and moved home to Portland where he was part of a group that tried to bring Major League Baseball to Portland. When their target franchise Montreal Expos moved to Washington, DC, he acquired several D-league franchises and began developing his players into NBA-level talent.

In 2009, Timberwolves owner Glen Taylor relieved Kevin McHale of his president of basketball operations/head coach duties. Several candidates interviewed for the position, and Taylor even offered it to three candidates before Kahn: San Antonio Spurs assistant GM Dennis Lindsey (who would become the GM of the Utah Jazz in 2012), former Miami Heat GM Randy Pfund, and Portland Trail Blazer assistant GM Tom Penn (who instead accepted a promotion to vice president of basketball operations with the Blazers). After missing out on their top 4 choices, NBA Commissioner David Stern recommended Kahn for the job, and on May 23, 2009, he was announced as the new president.

Kahn had just over a month to prepare for the upcoming NBA draft on June 25. McHale had traded Garnett to the Boston Celtics two years earlier, and the team was still in hard-core rebuilding mode. They had only won forty-six games over the last two years but had some good building blocks for the future with Al Jefferson, Kevin Love, Corey Brewer, and Randy Foye.

The Wolves had three first-round picks to build around in the draft: Their own selection at number 6, pick number 18 (which was acquired in 2007 from Miami with Antoine Walker, Wayne Simien, and Michael Doleac for Ricky Davis and Mark Blount) and pick number 28 (which was acquired from Boston in the Kevin Garnett trade). The day before the draft, Kahn made his first big move with the Wolves, trading Randy Foye and Mike Miller for the fifth overall pick, Etan Thomas, Darius Songaila, and Oleksiy Pecherov.

Now with four first-round picks (two in the top 10) as well as two second-round picks, the Wolves were ready to build. After Blake Griffin, Hasheem Thabeet, James Harden, and Tyreke Evans went off the board, the Timberwolves were on the clock with back-to-back picks. With forwards Jefferson and Love, Kahn's goal was to stock up on guards. With the fifth pick, he took Spanish superstar point guard Ricky Rubio, knowing full well that the eighteen-year-old Rubio would stay in Spain for a couple seasons to develop. Khan then selected Syracuse point guard Jonny Flynn with the sixth pick—a pick that would garner lots of criticism over the next decade with players like Steph Curry (seventh overall pick) and DeMar DeRozen (ninth overall pick) still on the board.

With the eighteenth overall pick, Kahn selected another point guard in UNC's Ty Lawson, who was immediately traded to the Denver Nuggets for a 2010 first-round pick. Lawson would develop into a good point guard for the Nuggets, averaging 14 points and 6 assists per game over six seasons in Denver. The Nuggets made the playoffs four straight years with Lawson on the team.

With the twenty-eighth overall pick, the Wolves drafted another guard: Lawson's backcourt teammate at UNC, Wayne Ellington. With the forty-fifth pick in the second round, ANOTHER guard was drafted: Nick Calathes. He was traded to Dallas for a 2010 second-round pick and cash. Two picks later, one of Rubio's DKV Joventut teammates, power forward Henk Norel was drafted

(the Calathes and Norel picks were acquired in 2008 in the trade that sent Mario Chalmers to Miami. The picks originally belonged to Philadelphia and Miami.)

But the roster overhaul wasn't done there. In July, he traded fan favorite Mark Madsen, Craig Smith, and Sebastian Telfair (the first of the Garnett trade pieces to move) to the LA Clippers for Quentin Richardson, who was traded less than a month later to Miami for Mark Blount (who was waived by the Wolves four months earlier). He also flipped Etan Thomas and two 2010 second-round picks to Oklahoma City for Chucky Atkins and Damien Wilkins.

In August, he hired Kurt Rambis to a four-year $8 million deal to become the ninth head coach in Timberwolves history (and the fifth in the previous five seasons).

In September, he traded guard Bobby Brown and Darius Songaila to New Orleans for Antonio Daniels, then he signed guard Ramon Sessions and forward Sasha Pavlovic. Three weeks after acquiring Atkins, he was waived.

The Wolves opened the 2009–10 season at home against the New Jersey Nets with a starting lineup of Corey Brewer, Jonny Flynn, Damien Wilkins, Al Jefferson, and Ryan Gomes. (Kevin Love missed the first eighteen games of the season after breaking his hand in a preseason game.) Wilkins, starting in the place of Love, had the game-winning offensive put back in a 95–93 Timberwolves win.

The Wolves would then lose the next fifteen consecutive games. And that wasn't even their longest losing streak of the season (sixteen). They finished 15–67, tying the worst record in team history (1991–92).

Other notable Kahn moves from 2009 to 2010 include trading Jason Hart to Phoenix for Alando Tucker (who was waived three months later) and a second-round pick, trading Brian Cardinal to New York for Darko Milicic (famous for being drafted ahead of Carmelo Anthony, Chris Bosh, and Dwayne Wade in the 2003 Draft) then re-signing Cardinal when New York waived him three weeks later.

2010–11

One season after watching his team lose sixty-seven games, he was ready to make some changes. Despite having the second worst record in the NBA (New Jersey was 12–70), the Wolves were awarded the fourth pick in the NBA Draft Lottery. Kahn had three first-round picks and two second rounders to use.

Washington and Philadelphia each leapfrogged New Jersey and Minnesota in the draft order and took Kentucky point guard John Wall and Ohio State shooting guard Evan Turner, respectively. New Jersey took Georgia Tech power forward Derrick Favors with the third pick, and a year after selecting four point guards in the first round, Kahn decided to go add some depth to the front court with Big East Player of the Year forward Wesley Johnson from Syracuse with DeMarcus Cousins, Gordon Hayward, and Paul George still available.

With the eighteenth overall pick, acquired from Denver in the Lawson trade at the last draft, Kahn took Nevada forward Luke Babbitt but almost immediately packaged him with Ryan Gomes to Portland for forward Martell Webster, who was in year 2 of a four-year $20 million contract. Minnesota's third first-round pick was acquired in 2008 for Rodney Carney and Calvin Booth. With the twenty-third pick in the draft, Kahn selected Clemson forward Trevor Booker. In the second round, the Wolves selected centers Paulao Prestes (forty-fifth overall) and Hamady N'Diaye (fifty-sixth overall). After the draft, he traded Booker and N'Diaye to Washington for forward Lazar Hawyard (thirtieth overall pick) and future Euro League MVP forward Nemanja Bjelica (thirty-fifth overall).

After the draft, Kahn continued to retool the roster. On July 12, he traded two second-round picks and cash to the Miami Heat for former number 2 overall pick Michael Beasley, who the Heat were anxious to get rid of to create roster space for impending free agents LeBron James and Chris Bosh. Beasley was an All-American at Kansas State and was named the National Freshman of the Year. Beasley averaged 14 points per game during his first stint in Miami.

The next day, he traded forward Al Jefferson, the centerpiece of the Kevin Garnett trade. Jefferson averaged 20 points and 10 rebounds per game in three seasons, but Rambis thought he was too slow to center his fast-paced offense around. And with an emerging Kevin Love, Jefferson was expendable. Kahn was able to get two first-round picks and Kosta Koufos from Utah for Jefferson.

He signed failed big-man Darko Milicic to a four-year $20 million contract and had him work extensively with Coach Rambis and Assistant Coach Bill Laimbeer to try to save his career.

A week later, he signed veteran point guard Luke Ridnour. Then he traded Ryan Hollins, Ramon Sessions, and a second-round pick to Cleveland for Sebastian Telfair (whom he had traded to the LA Clippers a year prior) and Delonte West. West was cut a week later. Anthony Tolliver, Maurice Ager, and Sundiata Gaines appeared to be the final pieces for the 2010–11 squad.

Things looked positive in the early going. The Wolves were 6–2 in the preseasons with Webster, Beasley, and Love stuffing the stat sheet. But it was a different story once the regular season started, winning only one of their first eight games. Despite all the roster moves and nearly 40 combined points per game from Kevin Love (20 PPG) and Beasley (19 PPG), the Wolves only improved by two wins from the previous season. Jonny Flynn bounced back and forth from the NBA to the G-League. Martell Webster only played in forty-six games while recovering from back surgery that he needed before even playing a game in Minnesota. Kahn and the Wolves were involved in the trade-deadline deal that would send Carmelo Anthony and Chauncey Billups to the New York Knicks. As a part of the trade, Kahn sent Corey Brewer to the Knicks and Kosta Koufos to the Nuggets. When the dust settled, the Wolves got a second-round pick,

Eddy Curry, Anthony Randolph, and cash in the three-team trade that involved fourteen players and six draft picks.

The Wolves would win back-to-back games four times all season and ended the year on a fifteen-game losing streak to finish 17–65.

After the season, Kahn fired Kurt Rambis. Rambis was 32–132 in two seasons.

2011–12

Kahn decided to hire an established coach after releasing Rambis, bringing in Rick Adelman. Adelman had been a head coach in the NBA since 1988 and was an assistant for six years prior to that. He had coached the Portland Trail Blazers to two NBA Finals appearances in the early 1990s and had a very successful run as the head coach of the Sacramento Kings in the early 2000s.

The Wolves' 17–65 record in 2011–12 was the worst in the NBA, and the Wolves had the best chance to get the number 1 overall pick in the NBA Draft. The 32–50 LA Clippers, with less than a 3 percent chance to get the top pick, won the draft lottery. However, they had traded their first-round pick to the Cleveland Cavaliers earlier that season. Minnesota was awarded the second pick.

There was a debate over who the top pick in the 2011 NBA Draft should be: Duke guard Kyrie Irving or Arizona forward Derrick Williams. Irving had gotten hurt that season and had only played in eleven games that season but averaged 17 points per game and had returned to lead Duke to the Sweet 16 in the NCAA tournament. Williams averaged 20 points per game at Arizona and was named Pac-10 Player of the Year. Analysts and experts went back and forth with who Cleveland should take with the first overall pick. Ultimately, they went with Irving, and Minnesota was satisfied in taking Williams with the second pick. Other players still on the board included Enes Kanter, Kemba Walker, Klay Thompson, Kawhi Leonard, Nikola Vucevic, and Jimmy Butler.

Kahn also had Utah's first-round pick from the Jefferson trade and selected Donatas Motiejūnas with the twentieth pick. He had decided to cut his losses with Jonny Flynn and traded him, Motiejūnas, and a second-round pick to his predecessor Kevin McHale (who was now a head coach) in Houston for center Brad Miller, forward Nikola Mirotic, forward Chandler Parsons, and a 2013 first-round pick.

In hindsight, getting Mirotic and Parsons for Flynn was a great move. The Wolves only had the two first-round picks, so getting a solid veteran and two young players was a solid move. But Kahn wasn't done yet. He traded Mirotic to Chicago for guard Norris Cole, who he then traded to Miami for forward Bojan Bogdanovic, a 2014 second-round pick, and cash. Bogey was immediately traded to New Jersey for another future second-round pick and cash. Parsons was traded back to Houston for cash considerations only. So instead of getting pair of All-Rookie Team players in Mirotic and Parsons for arguably the biggest draft bust in team history, Kahn got two second-round picks and cash.

The cherry on top of the 2011 trade spree came from the Portland Trail Blazers. The hidden gem of the 2011 draft was Targuy Ngombo, a twenty-one-year-old forward from the Congo who had been playing in Qatar. The Dallas Mavericks had drafted Ngombo with the fifty-seventh overall pick, then had been moved in a three-team deal to Portland. Portland immediately flipped the draft rights to Ngombo to Khan and the Timberwolves for a future second-round pick. It turned out that Ngombo had lied about his name and his age prior to entering the NBA draft. His real name was Tanguy Ngombo, and he was twenty-six . . . not twenty-one. NBA rules state that international players over the age of twenty-two aren't eligible for the draft but are unrestricted free agents. By the time the reports had surfaced about his ineligibility, he had already been drafted and traded twice. Rather than canceling each transaction, his rights were removed by Minnesota, and they gave up the second-round pick to Portland for nothing.

Khan only had one more trade before the season started: sending former first-round pick Lazar Hayward to Oklahoma City for guard Robert Vaden (who never played an NBA game) and two future second-round picks. Ricky Rubio finally came over from Barcelona to play in the NBA. Kahn also signed guard J. J. Barea to bring a scoring boost off the bench.

The year 2011–12 was a contract year for Kevin Love. He wanted a five-year deal, but Kahn only offered him four. Kahn was saving the max five-year deal for Rubio. Contract negotiations became heated, and at one point, Kahn burst into the training room and shoved an offer sheet in Love's face. The two sides eventually agreed on a three-year deal with a player option for the fourth year worth $62 million. Love has said that if he were offered the full five-year deal, he would have played his entire career in Minnesota. In the final year of his rookie contract, Love averaged a career-high 26 points and pulled down 13 rebounds per game.

The Wolves were a lot better under Adelman than Rambis. On March 7, they were two games above .500 at 21–19. They would let the season slip away though, finishing the season 5–21. The Wolves' twenty-six wins was their highest win total since 2006–07—Kevin Garnett's last year with the team (32).

Two days before the 2012 Draft, Kahn traded the Wolves' first-round pick to his buddies in Houston for guard Chase Budinger and forward Lior Eliyahu. The Wolves' lone pick in the 2012 draft was explosive but often-injured forward Robbie Hummel from Purdue.

2012–13: the End

The 2012–13 season was the final year of David Kahn's contract, and he needed to have an incredible season to keep his job. Over the first three years, his teams had a combined 58–172.

He needed to make a big move. The two best players on his team, Kevin Love and Nikola Pekovic, were scouted and drafted by McHale. Kahn's answer was

Nic Batum of the Trail Blazers, who was a restricted free agent. Batum signed a $46 million offer sheet with the Wolves. The problem was Minnesota didn't have the cap space after the offer had already been extended. So to make space, Kahn had to cut his losses on Darko Milicic (8 points, 4 rebounds in twenty-two minutes over three seasons) and Martell Webster (played in ninety-three games over two seasons due to multiple back surgeries), saving $5.5 million by waiving the two players so they could extend the offer to Batum. Portland matched the offer sheet, so it didn't matter anyways.

Kahn also gave Brad Miller and two second-round picks to New Orleans for a protected 2017 second-round pick. Wayne Ellington was traded to Memphis for Dante Cunningham. Kahn also traded Wes Johnson and two second-round picks to Phoenix in a three-team deal that ultimately landed Minnesota three second-round picks (Brad Miller also went from New Orleans to Phoenix in the same deal).

Michael Beasley, Anthony Randolph, and Anthony Tolliver all left via free agency; but Kahn bought in two former All-Star players looking to make NBA comebacks: Brandon Roy, who was dealing with knee issues, and Andrei Kirilenko, who had spent the 2011–12 season playing in Russia. With the freed-up cap space from the botched Batum deal, he offered Roy a two-year $10 million deal after Roy miraculously recovered from a degenerative knee condition that had forced him to retire a year earlier.

Injuries were the storyline for the Wolves in 2012. Roy only lasted five games with the Wolves. Kevin Love only played in eighteen games, Chase Budinger only played in twenty-three games, and Rubio tore his ACL midway through the season. Despite that, Adelman and the Wolves won thirty-one games.

The fifth year of Kahn's deal included a team option, which he thought would be exercised.

It wasn't.

Instead, Glen Taylor offered the job to former Wolves coach Flip Saunders, who took over the position for the 2013–14 season.

The Wolves were 89–223 during Kahn's tenure, the worst record in the NBA over that four-year period.

<<BONUS ACHE>>

The Wild hire Paul Fenton

Paul Fenton was hired as the third general manager in Minnesota Wild history, replacing the fired Chuck Fletcher for the 2018 season. And less than fifteen months later, he was fired. Wild owner Craig Leipold cited that "it wasn't a good fit" and "the culture wasn't the same." The issue was that Fenton knew the Wild needed to rebuild. Leipold wanted to win now.

Already facing an uphill battle with the massive contracts of Zach Parise and Ryan Suter on the books (for which Chuck Fletcher was responsible), Fenton knew that he wouldn't be able to re-sign all his impending free agents: notably Charlie Coyle, Mikael Granlund, and Nino Niederreiter. The problem was, the Wild were still in the playoff hunt at the trade deadline. On January 17, he traded Nino to Carolina for Victor Rask. After scoring 9 goals and 23 points in forty-six games for the Wild, Nino played the final thirty-six games for the Hurricanes, scoring 14 goals and 30 points. Nino helped Carolina advance to the Eastern Conference Finals. Charlie Coyle was traded to the Boston Bruins for Ryan Donato. Coyle shined on the third line for the Boston as the Bruins advanced to the Stanley Cup Finals. He traded Mikael Granlund to Nashville for Kevin Fiala. For a long time, a rumor of Jason Zucker being traded to Calgary was the talk of the town, although the deal was never made. Instead of "tweaking" the roster like Leipold wanted, Fenton began trading quality players and rebuilding. Oddly enough, Fenton's final move as GM was signing forward Mats Zuccarello to a five-year $30 million contract with a full no-trade clause on July 1. Bruce Boudreau's reaction to Fenton calling him to tell him Zucarrello was added to the team was, "You've got to do what you've got to do." Fenton was fired on July 30, 2019.

June 25, 2009

The Wolves Draft Jonny Flynn over Steph Curry

The 2009 NBA Draft was loaded with guard prospects: James Harden from Arizona State, Tyreke Evans from Memphis, Stephen Curry from Davidson, DeMar DeRozan from USC, Jrue Holiday from UCLA, Ty Lawson from North Carolina, Terrence Williams from Louisville, Jeff Teague from Wake Forest, Jonny Flynn from Syracuse, and tantalizing EuroLeague star Ricky Rubio.

Coming off a 24–58 season that saw Randy Wittman fired after only nineteen games (the Wolves were 4–15), the Timberwolves front office was looking for some backcourt help for the upcoming season.

The Wolves had reacquired their 2009 first-round pick from the Boston Celtics (sixth overall) that they had traded in 2006 with Wally Szczerbiak, Michael Olowokandi, and Dwayne Jones for Ricky Davis, Marcus Banks, Mark Blount, Justin Reed, and two second rounders. It came back in the Kevin Garnett trade in 2007.

Wolves GM David Khan wanted two of the guards in the draft. His trade target? Flip Saunders and the Washington Wizards.

Washington finished with the league's second worst record in 2008 but had fallen out of the top 3 on NBA Lottery night and had the fifth overall pick. Khan traded guards Randy Foye (61 starts, 16.3 PPG) and Mike Miller (47 starts, 9.9 PPG) to the Washington for the Wizards' first-round pick and three players (Etan Thomas, Darius Songalia, and Oleksiy Pecherov).

The Wolves also had the Miami Heat's first-round pick (eighteenth overall) from an October 2007 trade that sent Davis and Blount to South Beach for Antoine Walker, Wayne Simien, and Michael Doleac.

Oklahoma's Blake Griffin was the conscientious best player in the draft and went first overall to the LA Clippers. Connecticut center Hasheem Thabeet went second to Memphis. Two guards went of the board with the third pick (James Harden/OKC) and fourth pick (Tyreke Evans/Sacramento).

With the fifth pick, David Khan took Spanish superstar Ricky Rubio.

And with players like DeMar DeRozen and Stephen Curry still on the board, he took Jonny Flynn.

At the time, it made sense to take Flynn. While Curry was the best pure shooter in the draft, he flat out said that he only wanted to play for the Knicks. (The Knicks had the eighth pick. Golden State had the seventh and didn't give a crap where he wanted to play.)

Flynn was impressive in college for the Syracuse Orange. He showed his scoring ability (16.6 PPG over two seasons), conditioning (played sixty-seven of seventy minutes in a 5OT game against UConn), clutch free throw shooting (was 16/16 from the line in that UConn game), and was known for his lockdown defense on the perimeter. He showed flashes of brilliance during his rookie year with the Wolves. In an October game against the New Jersey Nets, he sparked a rally and led the Wolves back from a 19-point deficit, scoring 13 fourth-quarter points. In December, he hit the game winner in a 28-point effort against the Utah Jazz. In January, he scored 29 points in an overtime win against the Philadelphia 76ers.

He started all eighty-one games his rookie year while averaging 13.5 PPG, 2.4 rebounds, 4.4 assists, and shot 35 percent from beyond the arc—good enough to make the All-Rookie Second Team.

After hip surgery following the season, Flynn wasn't the same player. He played in fifty-three games (started eight), and his numbers dipped dramatically: 5.3 PPG during his sophomore season. He was traded to the Houston Rockets during the 2011 NBA Draft for Brad Miller and three draft picks.

Following the trade, Flynn would only appear in twenty-nine more NBA games between the Rockets and Portland Trail Blazers.

The fact that Flynn's success only lasted for one season is just the tip of the iceberg here. Sports fans know the success that Steph Curry has had in Oakland (3x NBA Champion, 2x NBA MVP). But in 2010, the year after Flynn's rookie season, the Indiana Pacers offered their tenth overall draft selection in exchange for Flynn: Paul George. David Khan turned it down.

<<BONUS ACHE>>

Other Wolves Draft Misses

The Flynn/Curry miss wasn't the only draft mistake that night. The Wolves took Nick Calathes forty-sixth overall that night. The San Antonio Spurs drafted Danny Green with the next pick.

In 2010, the Wolves took Wesley Johnson fourth overall, one pick ahead of All-Star DeMarcus Cousins.

In 2011, the Wolves selected Arizona Wildcat Derrick Williams second overall, one pick ahead of All-Star Enes "the Menace" Kanter.

But 2014 could have been the turning point. The traded Kevin Love (who they had drafted in 2008 with Russell Westbrook still on the board) to Cleveland for top pick Andrew Wigging out of Kansas. They selected Slam Dunk Champion Zach LaVine (who immediately put his head down and muttered "F—— me" when drafted) thirteenth overall. Dario Saric, Adreian Payne, and Shabazz Napier were all first-round picks that have played for Minnesota. In the second round, the Wolves selected Glenn Robinson III out of Michigan with the fortieth pick.

Robinson averaged 13.1 points and shot 49 percent from the field in his sophomore season, and Saunders drafted him to get more athletic. Robinson would play twenty-five games and average four minutes a game for the Wolves before he was waived and claimed by Philadelphia. One pick after Robinson, the Denver Nuggets selected Serbian center Nikola Jokic. Jokic is an All-NBA center, averaging 16 points and 10 rebounds a game through his first four seasons.

In 2013, the Wolves traded the twenty-sixth pick and Malcom Brown to the Golden State Warriors for a second-round pick. The Warriors selected All-Defensive guard Andre Roberson. Utah selected two-time Defensive Player of the Year center Rudy Gobert with the twenty-sixth pick.

Also in 2013, the Wolves passed on Giannis Antetokounmpo for Trey Burke. If you're keeping track at home, the Wolves could have potentially boasted a lineup of Russell Westbrook, Steph Curry, Giannis Antetokounmpo, DeMarcus Cousins, and Rudy Gobert with Danny Green, Enes Kanter, and Nikola Jokic coming off the bench.

August 9, 2009

The Wolves Hire Kurt Rambis and the Triangle Offense

The Triangle Offense has been, pretty much irrefutable, the single most dominant offensive attack (in any major sport) over the past 20 years.
—Chuck Klosterman

Things were going downhill for the Minnesota Timberwolves in 2009. Kevin Garnett, traded two years earlier, had gone to back-to-back NBA Finals. Meanwhile, the Wolves had gone through five head coaches in five seasons. Following a twenty-four-win season in 2009, Kevin McHale fired Randy Witman (who was 38–105 in two-plus seasons) and hired longtime LA Lakers assistant coach Kurt Rambis.

Rambis, an assistant under Phil Jackson with the LA Lakers, was a student of the Triangle Offense—an offense that produced eleven NBA titles. An offense that had produced eleven NBA Titles was worth a shot, right?

The Triangle Offense was designed by Sam Berry at USC in the 1940s. It was picked up and developed further by Tex Winter, who would coach at Kansas State as well as for the Houston Rockets. It really took off when Winter became an assistant coach for the Chicago Bulls in 1985 and began to teach the offense to Michael Jordan. Two years later, the Bulls hired the head coach of the CBA's Albany Patroons Phil Jackson (as an assistant), who immediately became obsessed with learning the style under Winter.

When Phil Jackson was promoted to head coach of the Bulls in 1989, he had mastered it and coached the Bulls to six NBA titles between 1989 and 1998, then he would win four more titles with the LA Lakers from 2000 to 2010, including a three-peat in the early 2000s.

The Triangle focuses on three players: the center at the low post, the forward at the wing, and the guard in the corner. The strategy is to create good spacing between players and allows each one to pass to four teammates. Every pass is dictated by what the defense does.

Phil Jackson had a couple once-in-a-generation players playing for him: Michael Jordan, Scottie Pippen, Kobe Bryant, and Shaquille O'Neil.

Kurt Rambis did not.

He would have to make do with the youngest roster in the NBA featuring Kevin Love, Al Jefferson, Corey Brewer, and rookie Jonny Flynn. Also, David Kahn was putting together his roster.

A key component of the Triangle is the players you have on the court. To say the Wolves didn't have the talent of the Bulls or Lakers dynasties is a dramatic understatement. In Rambis' first year with the Wolves in 2009, the team won fifteen games—their lowest win total since the 1991–92 season.

Rambis and Kahn agreed that the reason the team wasn't clicking was because they weren't "athletic enough." The Wolves ranked twentieth in PPG (98.2) and twenty-ninth in opponent PPG (107.8). They figured the odd man out on the offense was 290-pound center Al Jefferson (the Triangle suited 325-pound Shaquille O'Neil just fine . . .). Jefferson averaged 17 points and 9 rebounds that year.

Following the 2009 season, Kahn traded Jefferson (the final remaining piece of the Kevin Garnett trade three seasons earlier) to the Utah Jazz for Kosta Koufas (who played thirty-nine games for the Wolves) and two first-round picks: Donatas Motiejūnas (round 1, pick 20 in 2011) and Terrence Jones (round 1, pick 18 in 2012).

D-Mo and Jones never played for the Wolves. Motiejūnas was drafted by the Wolves then immediately traded to Houston with Jonny Flynn for Brad Miller (who played fifteen games for the Wolves). Nikola Mirotic (who never played for the Wolves but was immediately traded to the Chicago Bulls for Norris Cole and Malcom Lee), Chandler Parsons (who refused to play for the Wolves, so he was traded back to the Houston Rockets for cash), and a first-round pick in 2012, which ended up being Andre Robertson (who never played for the Wolves but was traded with Malcolm Lee to Golden State for cash. Robertson was taken one pick ahead of NBA Defensive Player of the Year Rudy Gobert).

With Jefferson gone, it opened the door for recently signed draft bust Darko Milicic to assume the center role with second-round pick Nikola Pekovic (six feet eleven, 307 pounds, seemed to fit the mold of a David Kahn athletic center) coming off the bench. The Wolves also acquired Michael Beasley, Luke Ridnour, and Sebastian Telfair and drafted Jonny Flynn's former Syracuse teammate Wesley Johnson with the fourth overall pick (over players like DeMarcus Cousins, Paul George, and Gordon Hayward).

Rambis had his retooled, athletic, and faster roster. This would be the breakout year for the Wolves, right? The pieces were in place.

Spoiler alert: they weren't.

The Wolves won seventeen games in 2010, and Rambis was fired in the second year of a four-year deal. He went 32–132 in his two seasons with the Wolves. The Wolves hired Rick Adelman to replace him.

Adelman won managed to win twenty-six games in 2011 and improved the Wolves to 40–42 in 2012—their best season since 2004.

Rambis was rehired by the Lakers as an assistant after getting canned by the Wolves. A year later, he would follow Phil Jackson to New York after Jackson was hired as the president of the New York Knicks. He worked as an assistant under Derrick Fisher for two seasons until Fisher was fired by Jackson in 2016. Rambis was named the interim coach and led the Knicks to 9–19 record over the final thirty games that year.

July 13, 2010

Royce White

The Gophers have a recent history of losing their best in-state recruits to outside schools. Prospects like Cole Aldrich (from Thomas Jefferson High School in Bloomington, attended Kansas), Tyus and Tre Jones (from Apple Valley High School, both attended Duke), and Jon Leur (from Orono High School, attended Wisconsin). After Aldrich and Jones won NCAA championships with their respective teams, Gopher fans began pleading for the coaching staff and administration to start keep Minnesota's high school stars in state. In 2009, fans got their wish.

Royce White, the Hopkins star that led the Royals to a perfect 31–0 season, was Mr. Basketball that season and committed to join the Gophers. The six-foot-eight White was ranked the nineteenth best player in the class for 2009 on the Rivals.com board and was all set to join Hopkins hero Blake Hoffarber in maroon and gold that next season.

Gopher basketball had a couple down years prior to White's arrival. After Clem Haskins' resignation following the academic fraud scandal that vacated the Gopher's Final Four run in 1997, U of M Athletic Director Joel Maturi hired Dan Munson away from Gonzaga to replace Haskins.

Monson coached the Gophers for part of eight roller-coaster seasons. He finished with a respectable 118–106 overall record, but the Gophers struggled in Big Ten play with a 44–68 record. Monson resigned seven games into the 2006–07 season, and interim coach Jim Molinari finished the season 7–17. Monson led the Gophers to one NCAA tournament. Despite Monson's inability to consistently put a winning product on the court, he was heralded for his ability to bring integrity and cleanliness back to the program that was still in the shadow of the Haskins scandal.

The next season, Maturi replaced Molinari with a big-name hire: former Kentucky coach Tubby Smith, who had a national championship on his resume. Tubby recruited Royce White, and the tide seemed to be turning.

But that tide turned into a tsunami that engulfed the U of M campus. Before ever taking the court for the Gophers, White was suspended after an incident at the Mall of America and later pleaded guilty to fifth-degree theft and disorderly conduct. Later that academic year, White was charged with trespassing in connection to an alleged theft of a laptop from a dorm room. He left the team in February, never appearing in a game for the Gophers.

Tubby won twenty or more games in five of his six seasons in Minnesota but didn't see any Big Ten or NCAA tournament success. He was fired after another first round NCAA exit following the 2012–13 season and would have undoubtedly benefited from Royce White being on the court.

White, on the other hand, transferred to Iowa State. According to the *Star Tribune*, White asked Tubby if he could stay on the team, but concerns about his behavioral challenges and social circle raised too many red flags.

So Iowa State and Coach Fred Hoiberg got a former Top 20 prospect.

Due to NCAA transfer regulations, White was ineligible to play the 2010–11 season, so after two years away from a regular season game, he suited up for the Cyclones on November 12 and posted a double-double against Lehigh with 25 points and 11 rebounds. Three weeks later against Big Ten powerhouse number 15 Michigan State, White recorded another double-double with 22 points and 13 rebounds as well as 4 steals. After leading Iowa State to the NCAA tournament, the postseason awards came rolling in, including the Big 12 Newcomer of the Year and First Team All-Big 12. White was also the only player in the country to lead his team in the five major statistical categories: points, rebounds, assists, steals, and blocks.

White declared for the 2012 NBA Draft in March and was selected sixteenth overall by the Houston Rockets in the NBA draft.

<<BONUS ACHE>>

Reggie Lynch

Reggie Lynch was a Gopher Basketball transfer from Illinois State in 2015. After sitting out the abysmal 2015–16 season (the Gophers were 8–23 overall), the Edina HS graduate took the Big Ten by storm. The junior helped turn the Gophers around from an eight-win team to 24–10 and the Gophers' first winning Big Ten record (11–7) since 2004–05 and an NCAA tournament appearance. Lynch was the 2017 Big Ten Defensive Player of the Year and recorded a school-record 114 blocks. He played sixteen games for the Gophers in 2017–18, averaging 11 points, 8.5 rebounds, 4.5 blocks, and 2 assists before being kicked off the team and expelled from the U due to allegations of sexual misconduct.

Injuries Derail Joe Mauer, Justin Morneau, Nikola Pekovic, and Percy Harvin

Work hard, be humble, and don't break up a double play with your head!
—Justin Morneau

With Justin Morneau and Joe Mauer in their primes, the Twins won three AL Central titles (and were one win away from a fourth. See Game 163 versus Chicago White Sox) in five seasons from 2006 to 2010. Morneau was the AL MVP in 2006, Home Run Derby Champion in 2008, and a four-time All-Star. Mauer won the MVP in 2009 as well as three batting titles as a catcher.

The only things that could slow the M&M Boys down were injuries. On July 7, 2010, Morneau suffered a concussion while sliding into second base. Blue Jays infielder John McDonald tried to leap over the sliding Morneau but hit him in the head with his knee. Morneau's MVP-caliber season ended with 18 home runs, 56 RBI, and a .345 batting average after eighty-one games.

In August 2011, he missed the last two months of the season after experiencing concussion-like symptoms after diving for a ground ball at first base.

From 2006 to 2009, Morneau hit .292 and averaged 30 home runs, 118 RBI, and 153 games a year. After his July 7 concussion, he hit .256, averaged 13 home runs, 61 RBI, and 118 games from 2011 to 2013. Morneau was traded to Pittsburgh in 2013. While he did win an NL Batting Title (.319 in 135 games) with Colorado in 2014, it was the only strong year after his concussion.

Joe Mauer was bitten by the injury bug early in his career. In his second career game (April 6, 2004), a knee injury sidelined him for a month. After coming back for thirty-two more games, complications from the injury shut down his season.

After that, Mauer became an All-Star catcher for the Twins, hitting .327 from 2006 to 2013. He became the first American League catcher to win a batting title with a .347 average in 2006. He won two more batting titles over the next three seasons, including career highs with a .365 average, 28 home runs, and 96 RBI in his MVP season in 2009. He signed an eight-year $184 million extension after the season.

Beginning in 2011, Mauer missed games with what was diagnosed as bilateral leg weakness, which was later found to be caused by a viral infection. He drew the ire from fans who wanted him to play through the injury, not taking into consideration the long-term health of their franchise catcher and the fact that the Twins (63–99) were terrible that season.

Joe Mauer suffered his first concussion on August 19, 2013. With the Twins trailing the New York Mets 4–0 in the seventh inning, Mauer took an Ike Davis (son of Ron Davis) foul ball off the top of his catching helmet with enough force to send the ball over the backstop. Mauer fell to his knees, dazed, but stayed finished the game in the eventual 6–1 loss. He would go on the DL with a concussion and miss the rest of the season from the symptoms. The game against the Mets would be the last time Mauer would start a game at catcher. His 921 games at catcher (885 starts) are a team record.

Mauer moved to first base for the 2014 season to prolong his health and his career. From 2014 to 2018, Mauer would average 136 games a year but would only post a .278 average. He played in a career-high 158 games in 2015 but hit over .300 (.305 in 2017) one more time.

In 2018, Mauer's concussions symptoms returned after diving for a ground ball against the Angels on May 11. He would miss a total of thirty-five games in his final season, retiring with a total of 2,123 hits, 428 doubles (a Twins record), 143 home runs, 923 RBI, and a .306 average—numbers way below where they would have been if he hadn't taken that foul ball off the top of his head.

For the Timberwolves, center Nikola Pekovic was considered a Top 10 prospect in the 2008 NBA Draft, but uncertainty with his contract with Panathinaikos of the Greek league saw him fall out of the first round. Pek had signed a three-year contract with Panathinaikos that summer, and he likely wouldn't make the jump to the NBA until that contract was fulfilled. The Wolves selected the seven-foot-eleven, 307-pound center with the first pick of the second round.

He played his first NBA game in 2010 and averaged 5.5 points and 3.0 rebounds a game his rookie year. In 2011, he stepped in the starting role for the injured Darko Milicic and finished third in the NBA's Most Improved Player award after increasing his numbers to 13.9 points and 7.4 rebounds a game. His numbers continued to climb, averaging a career-high 17.5 points and 8.7 rebounds a game in 2013. That off-season, in an attempt to show disgruntled superstar Kevin Love that the franchise was committed to winning, they signed Pekovic to a five-year $60 million extension.

Love was traded a year later.

In 2014, Pekovic only played in thirty-one games after suffering an ankle injury. In 2015, he had surgery on his Achilles to relieve pain in his ankle and only played in thirty-one games. Still dealing with the ankle injury, he only played in twelve games in 2016 and didn't appear on the court at all in 2017. He was waived by the Wolves after the season with one year left on his contract. After signing the big contract on August 14, 2013, Pekovic only played in forty-three games (thirty-two starts).

Injuries killed the career of a promising Minnesota Viking too. The 2009 Offensive Rookie of the Year Percy Harvin was one of the most explosive players in the NFL. In his first NFL season after being drafted twenty-second overall out of Florida, Harvin caught 60 passes for 790 yards and a career-high 6 touchdowns, plus returned two kickoffs for touchdowns, which was good enough to earn him a Pro Bowl nod.

But during the season, Harvin began having chronic migraine headaches that caused him to miss practice. He was inactive due to headaches for a 30–10 win against Cincinnati in Week 14 and missed practices leading up the NFC Championship Game against the Saints a month later.

"Take a hammer, and beat it on the side of your head nonstop," Harvin told *Sports Illustrated* in 2010. "If you're trying to relax, if someone's trying to talk to you, that hammer is still going off. You're trying to eat, still going off."

Harvin had been having the migraines since he was ten but didn't tell many people about them—his family, a select group of friends, and some coaches at the University of Florida. The Vikings were unaware of Harvin's condition when they drafted him.

Harvin collapsed at a Vikings practice during training camp 2010, increasing concern over his career. Despite multiple trips to the Mayo Clinic in Rochester, he was unable to find a treatment that worked.

Harvin would play in fourteen games in 2010 and saw an increase in his targets and receptions, while Sydney Rice recovered from off-season hip surgery.

After two more years in Minnesota that featured day-to-day migraine issues, an IR stint with an ankle injury, rigid contract negotiations, and a sideline meltdown aimed at Coach Les Frazier, the Vikings traded Harvin to Seattle prior to the 2013 NFL Draft for three draft picks (that turned into Xavier Rhodes, Jerick McKinnon, and Travis Bond).

Seattle signed Harvin to a six-year $67 million contract. He had one regular season catch for seventeen yards (in a game against the Vikings) after dealing with a torn labrum but did return a kickoff to help Seattle win their first Super Bowl title in franchise history.

Harvin's migraine and attitude issues continued in Seattle to the point where he would fight with teammates and take himself out of games. He was traded to the New York Jets in 2014, then he signed with the Bills in 2015 after he was cut by the Jets. A knee injury forced him to retire in 2016, but he left the door open for a return. That November, he came out of retirement to play for the Bills again, but he began experiencing more migraines that forced him to the nonfootball illness list and a second retirement.

<<BONUS ACHE>>

Glen Williams Disloactes His Shoulder

While he didn't have the same impact on the Twins that Morneau or Mauer did, the story of Glenn Williams is a great one.

In 1993, Williams, a native of Australia, was the most coveted international signees of all time. The sixteen-year-old phenom got an unheard of $825,000 signing bonus from the Atlanta Braves. Braves management compared his game to another highly touted prospect in their organization: Chipper Jones. He played in the minors for Atlanta from 1994 to 1999, never making it above AA, dealing with injuries, and batting in the low .200s. In 2000, he signed a minor league contract with the Toronto and spent the next five seasons in the minors of the Blue Jays' organization. Despite having his best minor-league season with Syracuse (.264, 23 home runs, 79 RBI) the Jays released the twenty-seven-year-old Williams. He signed with the Twins in 2005 and, after eleven years in the minor leagues, got his first big league call up as an emergency infielder after hitting .302 in 47 games. Michael Cuddyer had lost his job as the third baseman, and his replacement Nick Punto got hurt. Williams got a hit in his first plate appearance as a pinch hitter on June 7, 2005. Ron Gardenhire even gave Williams two starts at third base while he was with the Twins. He had a walk-off, pinch-hit single against the Padres on June 17. After thirteen games with the Twins, had a hit in every game he appeared in. On June 28, after an RBI single off Mike Wood of the Kansas City Royals, Williams slid into third base after Lew Ford doubled to left field. While sliding, Williams dislocated his shoulder, which effectively ended his season. It was the last time he would play in the majors. He battled Tony Batista for the starting third base job in 2006 but didn't make the team out of camp. He currently has a thirteen-game hitting streak and a career .425 batting average.

July 29, 2010

The Twins Trade Wilson Ramos for Matt Capps

In 2010, the Minnesota Twins were in the thick of the AL Central race. After leading the division for most of the first half, the Twins had dropped thirteen of their last nineteen heading into the All-Star Break and trailed the Chicago White Sox by 3.5 games.

The Twins' offense was solid, led by reigning AL MVP Joe Mauer (.327, 75 RBI), Michael Cuddyer (.271, 81 RBI), Delmon Young (.298, 21 HR), and Jim Thome (.283, 25 HR). The starting rotation featured Carl Pavano (17–11, 3.75), Kevin Slowey (13–6, 4.45), and a comeback year from Francisco Liriano (14–10, 3.62).

But the Twins knew they could improve. And they needed to if they wanted to win the division.

There were several prospects the Twins could use as trade bait to make an upgrade somewhere, none as valued as highly as catcher Wilson Ramos.

In 2010, Ramos was an expendable piece. He had batted .296 in twenty-eight plate appearances for the Twins in 2010 after batting .332 at AA the year before. He was the fifty-ninth best prospect in baseball and the fifth best catching prospect in baseball.

But the Twins had an MVP catcher behind the plate that had just signed a ten-year contract extension. Twins GM Bill Smith knew he had a valuable piece to deal and took a long, hard look at the Twins bullpen. Jon Rauch had taken over the closer role for Joe Nathan, who was out for the year while recovering from Tommy John surgery. The Twins were 22–12 after acquiring Rauch from Arizona that August (Rauch was 5–1 with a 1.72 ERA). The bullpen also leaned on guys like Jesse Crain, Matt Guerrier, José Mijares, and spot-starter Brian Duensing.

Smith decided the weak link was at closer, despite Rauch's good numbers (2.38 ERA, 20 saves at the All-Star Break). On July 29, and a game out of first place, Smith traded Ramos, along with Joe Testa, to the Washington Nationals for All-Star closer Matt Capps (2.74 ERA, 26 saves at the time of the trade). Smith also brought in guys like Brian Fuentes and Randy Flores to shore up the bullpen for the playoff push.

"Having him for 2011 was critical," Smith said. "We would not have had interest in having him for just two months."

Capps had a great second half for the Twins (2–0, 2.00 ERA, 16 saves) to solidify the bullpen. The Twins finished 36–22 and won the AL Central title for the second time in as many years. And then were swept by the New York Yankees in the ALDS.

The Ramos/Capps looked good at the time but, like many Bill Smith moves, crippled the franchise for years to come.

A lot of fans don't remember how good Capps was for the Twins in 2010. He had an ERA of 2.00 and only gave up one home run in twenty-seven innings pitched. Meanwhile, Jon Rauch struggled and posted a 4.18 ERA in the second half.

Rauch signed a contract with the Toronto Blue Jays after the 2010 season. Meanwhile, Capps struggled with a 5–11 record with a 4.07 ERA with 15 HR allowed in 99 appearances in 2011 and 2012. The Twins went from a ninety-four-win team in 2010 to a hundred-loss team in 2011. Not only was Capps in a funk, so was Mauer. After batting .365 with 28 HR and 96 RBI in his MVP season in 2009, Mauer only hit 12 home runs total in 2010–11 as he battled various injuries from complications from off-season knee surgery to bilateral leg weakness to pneumonia and had the worst season of his career. It wouldn't have been a bad time to have a certain twenty-three-year-old prospect at catcher instead of trotting Drew Butera and his .197 average out there every night.

With Mauer's struggles and eventual move to first base, would the decline have happened with Ramos with the Twins? Throughout Twins history, the good runs in the 1960s and 2000s had catchers who could play defense and hit (Earl Battey, A.J. Pierzynski, and Joe Mauer). Instead, the Twins have started guys like Steve Holm, Josmil Pinto, Bobby Wilson, John Ryan Murphy, and Drew Butera at catcher. The Twins learned the hard way that if you have a young catcher who can catch, hit, and is major-league ready, do not trade him . . . no matter how good your number 1 catcher is.

Although he's battled injuries throughout his career, when Ramos is healthy, he is very good. In his first full season in Washington, he hit .267 with 15 HR and 52 RBI and finished fourth in the NL Rookie of the Year voting. The two-time All-Star (he was the starting catcher for the American League in 2018 before he was replaced due to an injury) also won a Silver Slugger award in 2016.

<<BONUS ACHE>>

The Twins Don't Trade for Cliff Lee

Cliff Lee, two years removed from winning the AL Cy Young Award, was being shopped by the Seattle Mariners. At the time, Lee was 8–3 with a 2.34 ERA for an eventual hundred-loss Mariners club. It was reported at one point that the Mariners wanted Ramos and either a prospect (outfielder Aaron Hicks) or an MLB-ready pitcher (Brian Duensing) for the ace. The Twins decided not to pull the trigger. Hicks was being groomed to take over an outfield spot, and Duensing was a key member of the bullpen (the rookie Duensing was 4–1 with a 2.92 ERA down the stretch for the Twins in 2009).

The Twins balked, even though the move would have given the Twins an elite playoff rotation. Lee was eventually traded to the Texas Rangers and led the team to their first ever AL Pennant. He was 3–0 in the first two rounds of the playoffs, including a two-hit, thirteen-strikeout performance at Yankee Stadium in the ALCS. He also beat the Yankees twice in the World Series with the Phillies in 2009.

Meanwhile, Aaron Hicks was eventually traded to the Yankees for catcher (ironically) John Ryan Murphy (.146, 3 RBI in one season with Minnesota). Brian Duensing, who was 0–2 with an 11.25 career playoff ERA against the Yankees, had a 4.68 ERA over the next five seasons and left via free agency after the 2015 season. Meanwhile, Hicks posted career highs in average, home runs, and RBIs while playing in New York before signing a seven-year contract extension before the 2019 season.

NOVEMBER 3, 2010

Randy Moss's Final Minnesota Meltdown

He won't be on our board on draft day . . . I don't need any more problems.
—St. Louis Rams head coach Dick Vermeil

There is no doubt that Moss is one of the all-time greats. He was a first ballot NFL Hall of Famer. He is the most athletic wideout to ever put on a jersey. He is the best deep threat the game has ever seen. Moss was so good that the Cover 2 was created to try and stop him. In 1999, the year following Moss' rookie campaign that included a rookie record 17 touchdowns, the division rival Green Bay Packers first three draft choices were defensive backs (Antuan Edwards, Fred Vinson, and Mike McKenzie) to stop Moss.

But as great as Moss and his 151 touchdowns were, one thing that will always overshadow his career numbers were his issues off the field.

Moss's flaws go back to when he was in high school. A highly touted prospect, Moss was courted by Notre Dame and Florida State. But stints in jail for drug use and a battery charge forced them to withdraw their scholarship offers. Moss ended up going to NCAA Division I-AA school Marshall, where he flourished. He led them to the Division I-AA title the season before the school moved to Division I-A.

Moss' reputation upheld during the 1998 NFL Draft. The Fred Biletnikoff Award winner and Heisman finalist was expected to be the most watched contestant of the NFL Combine, but he was a no-show. Rumors began to swirl that Moss was absent to avoid the drug test. He opted to work out at the Marshall pro day, where scouts from nearly every NFL team came to watch him work out. Moss turned in a legendary performance, running the forty-yard dash in just 4.25 seconds, despite running into the wind. He also posted a forty-seven-inch vertical while catching nearly every pass thrown.

Despite that, Moss slipped to the Minnesota Vikings with the twenty-first overall pick.

While Moss established himself as one of the best wide receivers in NFL history, he was also upholding his reputation for off-the-field issues:

2000—Moss was fined $25,000 for squirting an official with a water bottle and another $25,000 for touching an official.

2001—Moss was fined $15,000 by the Vikings and required to receive anger management counseling for verbally abusing corporate sponsors. In a separate incident, he told a newspaper columnist that he "plays when he wants to play."

2002—Moss was arrested after an incident in Minneapolis in which he bumped traffic control officer Amy Zaccardi with his car, knocking her to the ground. He was ordered to pay a $1,200 fine and perform forty hours of community service. Marijuana was allegedly found in his vehicle as well, but charges were later dropped.

2003—Moss was fined $5,000 for his role in a fight with the Chicago Bears during a September game. In November, he was fined another $5,000 for spiking a ball at the foot of Detroit Lions cornerback Dre' Bly.

2004—With the Vikings trailing 21–18 to the Washington Redskins with two seconds left, Moss walked off the field to the locker room and drew criticism for quitting on his team.

2005—In a playoff game against the Green Bay Packers, he was fined $10,000 by the NFL after an end-zone celebration in which he pretended to pull down his pants and "moon" Green Bay Packers fans.

And that's just from his time with the Vikings. Two months after the playoff game against the Packers, Moss was traded to the Oakland Raiders for a first-round pick (7th overall, Troy Williamson), a seventh-round pick (219th overall, Adrian Ward), and linebacker Napoleon Harris.

Moss wasn't spectacular in his two seasons in Oakland, catching 102 passes for 1,558 yards and 11 touchdowns. In 2006, he put up career lows in receptions, yards, and touchdowns despite playing in thirteen games. The Raiders were 6–26 with Moss on the team.

During the second day of the 2007 NFL Draft, the Raiders traded him to the New England Patriots for a fourth-round pick. He responded with an All-Pro season, setting the NFL's single-season receiving touchdown record (23) and helped lead New England to a 16–0 record and an NFL-record 589 points (a record that has since been broken by the 2013 Denver Broncos).

In three full seasons with the Patriots, Moss regained freak status, catching 250 passes for 3,765 yards and 47 touchdowns and starting every game each year he was there.

Moss wanted a contract extension in 2010, but the Patriots didn't give him one. He told the media he felt unwanted. After he caught five passes for fifty-nine yards in the 2010 season opener against Miami, he announced in his postgame press conference that it would be his final season with the Patriots. It was reported later in the week that Moss had requested a trade.

Moss's targets decreased exponentially over the next three games. In games against the Jets and Bills, he only had four catches although three of those catches were touchdowns. The following week against Miami, he had zero catches in a game for the first time with the Patriots.

2010 was a desperate season for Brad Childress and the Vikings. A year after a 12-4 record and an NFC Championship berth, the bottom had fallen out. Age had caught up to Brett Favre, and Pro Bowl wide receiver Sidney Rice missed the first half of the season from a hip surgery.

The league's number 2 scoring offense from the previous year only scored 19 total points in the first two games and lost both despite the defense only giving up 14 points each game. They beat the Lions 24-10 in Week 3 thanks to 160 yards and 2 touchdowns from Adrian Peterson. Without Rice, the Vikings weren't getting the production they needed from Percy Harvin (12 catches, 106 yards, and 1 touchdown), Greg Lewis (5 catches, 56 yards), Greg Camarillo (4 catches, 48 yards), Bernard Berrian (5 catches, 38 yards), or Hank Baskett (1 catch, 18 yards).

The Vikings traded a third-round pick to the Patriots for Randy Moss. While the Vikings lost Moss's first game back to the Jets following their Bye Week, the NFL world was treated to a regular-season Favre-to-Moss touchdowns, the five hundredth of Favre's career.

After four weeks back in Minnesota, Moss found himself at the center of two controversies. The Vikings went 1-3 with Moss, including an 18-28 loss to the Patriots in Foxboro. After the game, Moss gushed about the genius of Patriots coach Bill Belichick and the Patriots organization and criticized Childress for not taking his advice in game planning against him (Moss had one catch for eight yards in the game). Moss also alienated some of his teammates when, during a catered postpractice meal, he verbally accosted the spread by saying he wouldn't feed it to his dog.

Childress, who had control of the fifty-three-man roster, decided to place Moss on waivers. Childress made the announcement to the team that Moss would be leaving at a team meeting, saying he "didn't fit with how we treat people, how we talk to people and how we act." Moss's subpar play and praise of the Patriots would have been enough reason, but the food incident was the final straw.

Childress didn't tell initially tell Vikings owner Zygi Wilf that he had waived Moss. Wilf was instrumental in organizing Randy's return to Minnesota and was furious that Moss had been cut after only a month. After Moss was cut, there were various reports that he had been talking to Wilf about Childress, saying he didn't have what it takes to become a head coach in the NFL. Childress, fighting for his job, got rid of Moss before Moss could get rid of him. Childress was eventually fired ten games into the season with a 3-7 record.

Randy was claimed off waivers by the Tennessee Titans—the only team in the league to place a claim.

<<BONUS ACHE>>

Adrian Peterson's Child Abuse Charges

Adrian Peterson is arguably one of the greatest running backs in NFL history. Through his first seven seasons in the NFL, he had averaged 1,145 yards and scored 86 touchdowns despite tearing his ACL in 2011. He won the NFL MVP the following season with a 2,097-yard season . . . just nine yards shy of breaking Eric Dickerson's all-time single season record of 2,105.

In 2014, Peterson only played in one game (21 carries, 75 yards) after he was suspended without pay after he was indicted on child abuse charges. Court documents stated that Peterson had beaten his child with a switch, which cut and bruised his back, buttocks, ankles, and legs and left defensive wounds on his hands. Peterson hoped to be reinstated by the NFL by November, but the NFL announced that he would be suspended for the remainder of the season.

Without Peterson, the Vikings finished 7–9. Matt Asiata (570 yards, nine touchdowns) split carries with rookie Jerick McKinnon (538 yards, no touchdowns).

DECEMBER 12, 2010
The Final Metrodome Roof Collapse

The Teflon roof on the old Metrodome Stadium deflated on five separate occasions:

The first time was in November 1981, before the stadium was even open, after the Twin Cities received ten inches of heavy snowfall.

The second time was thirteen months later, in December 1982, only a few days before the final regular season game between Vikings and Dallas Cowboys in the strike-shortened season.

The third collapse in April 1983, which postponed a Twins-Angels game after a late-season snow caused a tear in the roof.

The fourth happened during a game against the California Angels in April 1986. Eighty mph winds tore through the metro area, tearing a hole in the eighth inning of a Twins-Angels game, delaying the game for nine minutes (The Twins led 6–1 in the ninth inning before the Angels rallied off Ron Davis to win 7–6).

Then, the Metrodome went twenty-four years without any roof issues. But on December 12, 2010, the night before a Vikings-Giants Sunday Night primetime game, a severe winter storm dumped about two feet of snow on the roof. Usually, crews can clear the snow from the roof to prevent any issues, but the storm was so bad that workers were unable to get up there. Around 5:00 a.m., three panels tore open and dumped snow and ice all over the field.

With sixty-four thousand tickets sold to the game, the NFL had a quick decision to make. The game was postponed to Monday night and moved to Ford Field in Detroit. Vikings fans that had tickets to the original game were given priority seating on the fifty-yard line, while all other tickets were refunded. In Detroit, the NFL handed out free tickets to the game to fill the stadium. The Vikings lost millions in tickets sales, merchandise, and concessions.

The Dome roof collapsing was the icing on the cake of a disappointing season. One season removed from their NFC Championship Game loss to the

New Orleans Saints, the Vikings were 5–7 and needed a miracle to return to the playoffs. Brad Childress was fired ten games into the season with a 3–7 record, and Les Frazier was named the interim head coach. Brett Favre was starting to show his age; Percy Harvin began missing games with migraines, and Randy Moss's triumphant return to Minnesota lasted four games before he was traded to Tennessee. And now their home stadium was possibly lost for the season. Following their game against the Giants, the Vikings had a Monday Night home game scheduled against the Chicago Bears.

The Vikings played their primetime game against the New York Giants on Monday, December 13, in Detroit in the first ever Monday Night game in Detroit. Ironically, it didn't involve the Lions. It was also the game in which Brett Favre's 297 consecutive starts streak would end. The previous week, he sprained a joint in his throwing shoulder on the third play of the game against the Buffalo Bills. For the first time since September 27, 1992, Brett Favre was not going to start a game.

Tarvaris Jackson got the start, and the Vikings lost at "home" to the Eli Manning and the Giants 21–3.

After the Giants loss, it was time to look ahead to the following week and find a venue for the Bears game for Monday Night Football on December 20. The first choice was the home of the Gophers, TCF Bank Stadium. But the Gophers' home schedule had wrapped up on November 27, and the stadium was shut down for the winter. It would be expensive to reopen the stadium and to take it out of hibernation. There were no heating coils beneath the field, so field conditions would be rough.

They decided to move forward with TCF Bank Stadium, and the Vikings would play their first outdoor game in Minnesota in exactly twenty-nine years (December 20, 1981, versus Kansas City). Fifteen thousand man hours went into getting the stadium ready: restoring plumbing, shoveling the two feet of snow out of the seats, and thawing the field with four giant heaters.

The Bears needed one win to clinch the NFC North division title. The Vikings were trying to avoid their first last-place finish since 1990. It was the perfect situation to honor the fifty greatest Vikings, which the team did at halftime of the game. The game time temperature was twenty-four degrees, but that didn't stop Bud Grant from wearing a short-sleeve golf shirt while being honored. But that was about the only good thing to happen that night.

After missing the Giants game, Favre started against the Bears. He threw a touchdown to Percy Harvin on the first drive of the game. But Favre was knocked out of the game after being sacked by Corey Wooten in the second quarter and hitting his head on the frozen turf. It would be the last time Favre would see the field during an NFL game. The Bears won 40–14.

The Metrodome wasn't only the home for the Vikings. The Gopher baseball team was scheduled to play a game there on February 5. When it was decided that the entire roof would need to be replaced, and wouldn't be repaired until the spring, the Gophers had to cancel all their March home games as well as their annual Metrodome Tournament. They played their outdoor Big Ten games at Target Field and nonconference games at Siebert Field.

The cost to repair the roof cost an estimated $18 million, and most of it was covered by the Metrodome's insurance. Repairs were completed in July 2011, and the roof was inflated.

Less than two years after the brand-new roof went up, the Dome was deflated for the final time. On January 18, 2014, the ten acres of Teflon went down in step 1 of the demolition of the Metrodome to begin the $1 billion US Bank Stadium project.

December 9, 2010

The Twins Trade J. J. Hardy to Baltimore

Bill Smith isn't afraid to make deals. Even terrible deals.
—Jim Souhan, *Star Tribune*

The Twins acquired shortstop J. J. Hardy from the Milwaukee Brewers on November 6, 2009, straight up for outfielder Carlos Gomez in what Jim Souhan of the *Star Tribune* called an "amazing deal for the Twins."

Hardy, an All-Star for the Brewers in 2007, was coming off his worst statistical year as a pro: a .229 average with 11 home runs and 38 RBI in 115 games. Gomez, the key player in the 2007 Johan Santana trade, had two disappointing seasons as a Twins. In 2009, he hit .229 with a .287 OBP, 3 home runs, and 28 RBI. The swap made sense for both teams: to take on two players who had down seasons. Not only did this open a full-time spot in the outfield for former number 1 overall pick Delmon Young, whom they had traded for in 2008, to play along Denard Span and Michael Cuddyer in the outfield but it also gave the Twins a solid bat at shortstop—something the team hadn't had since Cristian Guzman in the mid-2000s or Greg Gagne in the early 1990s.

Hardy was the opening day shortstop at the brand-new Target Field in 2010 with newly acquired second baseman Orlando Hudson, Nick Punto at third, Justin Morneau at first, reigning AL MVP Joe Mauer behind the plate, and Young, Span, and Cuddyer in the outfield. Hardy hit .268 with 6 home runs and 38 RBI in 101 games that season as he dealt with a wrist injury a good chunk of the season.

After a division title in 2010 with a 94–68 record (and a second consecutive first-round sweep at the hand of the New York Yankees), GM Bill Smith wanted to put together a faster lineup. Hardy, despite a big bat and solid glove, was slow. A twenty-six-year-old infielder from Japan named Tsuyoshi Nishioka had declared a desire to move from the NPB league in Japan to the MLB after leading the league with 206 hits, a .346 average, and 121 runs scored. Nishioka was also a three-time Nippon Gold Glove winner, a five-time All-Star, and two-time stolen base leader. He was exactly what Smith was looking for in a shortstop. The Twins put in a $5 million bid, which was accepted by the Chiba Lotte Marines to negotiate a contract with Nishioka. The Twins signed him to a three-year $9 million deal.

This made Hardy expendable. Smith traded him along with utility infielder Brendan Harris to the Baltimore Orioles for minor league pitchers Jim Hoey and Brett Jacobson.

Hoey, who had a 3–5 record and an 8.13 ERA in thirty-five relief appearances with the Orioles in 2006 and 2007, appeared in twenty-six games for the Twins in 2011 with a 5.47 ERA in twenty-four innings. The Twins placed him on waivers after the season, where he was claimed by the Toronto Blue Jays. Jacobson never made it to the major league club.

Meanwhile, Hardy had a career resurgence for the Orioles. He hit a career-high 30 home runs and knocked in 80 runs in 2011. He played in all but seven games from 2012 to 2013 and was named the starter for the AL All-Star squad in 2013. In seven seasons in Baltimore, Hardy hit .252 with 188 home runs, 688 RBI, won three-straight Gold Gloves and a Silver Slugger award while helping the Os make the playoffs three times, including the 2014 AL East crown.

Also, don't forget that Carlos Gomez flourished in Milwaukee. In five and a half seasons, he hit .267 (including a career-high .284 in 2013 and 2014), appeared in two All-Star Games (including starting in center field at the 2014 All-Star Game at Target Field), and led the Brew Crew to their first ever NL Central Division title in 2011.

<<BONUS ACHE>>

The Twins trade Eduardo Escobar

The Twins had received Eduardo Escobar from the Chicago White Sox in July 2012 for Francisco Liriano. The utility infielder became an everyday player in 2014, and by 2018, he was a fan favorite. Despite a big year from Escobar in 2019, the Twins took a step backward from their wild card season in 2018. Big off-season signings like Logan Morrison, Lance Lynn, Zach Duke, and Addison Reed were all flops; and the Twins became sellers. Brian Dozier was dealt to the Los Angeles Dodgers, Ryan Pressley was traded to the Houston Astros and became an All-Star reliever, Phil Hughes was sent to the San Diego Padres, and Lynn went to the New York Yankees.

Escobar was among the league leaders in doubles and having a career year with 15 home runs and 63 RBI, and he was in the final year of his contract. He was moved at the trade deadline to the Arizona Diamondbacks for minor leaguers

Ernie De La Trinidad, Jhoan Duran, and Gabriel Maciel. Escobar would finish the 2018 season with career highs in home runs (23), RBI (84), doubles (48), and average (.272). Twins fans were hoping the Twins would re-sign him, but he decided to re-sign with Arizona on a three-year contract.

In 2019, Escobar was even better than he was in 2018, hitting 35 home runs and driving in 118 runs. The Twins signed Jonathan Schoop on a one-year "prove it" contract to play second base. Schoop wasn't terrible offensively (20 home runs, 59 RBI), but he missed time due to injury and his numbers were nowhere near Escobar's.

December 16, 2010

The Twins Win the Bid for Tsuyoshi Nishioka

I take full responsibility for my performance which was below my own expectations.
—Tsuyoshi Nishioka

Despite winning the AL Central in 2010, Twins GM Bill Smith thought the lineup needed a speedy makeover, specifically in the middle infield. J. J. Hardy had been hampered by a wrist injury for a good chunk of the 2010 season, and Orlando Hudson's contract had expired after hitting .268/.338 with 10 stolen bases and 80 runs scored in 126 games.

He decided Alexi Casilla, who came over from the Angels as a twenty-year-old prospect in the 2005 J. C. Romero trade, was ready to start after hitting .276 in a utility role in 2010. Hudson signed a two-year deal with the San Diego Padres after one season in Minnesota.

Even though Hardy was still under contract, Smith started looking for other options at shortstop: Willie Bloomquist, Orlando Cabrera, Cristian Guzman, Cesar Izturis, Julio Lugo, and Edgar Renteria were all a part of the 2010 shortstop free agent class.

While the Twins were able to re-sign two of their key free agents in Carl Pavano and Jim Thome, they didn't sign an MLB shortstop and also let players like Jesse Crain, Randy Flores, Brian Fuentes, Matt Guerrier, Ron Mahay, Nick Punto, and Jon Rauch leave via free agency.

Smith had his sights set on one player: a twenty-six-year-old phenom from Japan named Tsuyoshi Nishioka. He was a two-time Japan Series champion, was a five-time Nippon Professional Baseball League All-Star, was a two-time stolen bases leader, and was the reigning NPB batting champion (.346) and hits leader (206) and had scored 121 runs for the Chiba Lotte Marines in 2010. He was exactly what the Twins were looking for.

The Twins posted a $5 million bid for the rights to negotiate a contract with Chiba Lotte, which they accepted. On December 17, 2010, the Twins officially signed their new shortstop to a three-year $9 million contract. To make room for Nishioka, Smith traded J.J. Hardy to Baltimore for a pair of minor league pitchers.

During training camp, manager Ron Gardenhire announced that Casilla would be the starting shortstop for the Twins, with Nishioka moving to second base for his rookie MLB season.

Nishioka's season got off to a rough start. After hitting .208 (5-for-24) in his first week in the major league, he broke his leg as New York Yankees outfielder Nick Swisher slid into second base trying to break up a double play. Nishioka missed the next fifty-nine games, returning against the White Sox on June 16. He hit .226 with 14 runs scored, 19 RBI, a .278 OBP, and a .249 slugging percentage in 221 at bats. He also had twelve errors in sixty-eight games.

Nishioka broke camp with the AAA Rochester Red Wings to start the 2012 season. He was called up in early August after Trevor Plouffe got hurt, and Danny Valencia was traded to the Boston Red Sox. He was 0-12 and committed two errors in three games before being sent back to Rochester.

After hitting .258 with two home runs, 34 RBI, and 42 runs scored in 101 games at Rochester, Nishioka asked the Twins for his release so he could return to Japan and not honor the third year of his contract. The Twins agreed, saving the $4 million in salary for 2013, plus the $250,000 buyout in his contract. Nishioka felt so bad about his play that he gave the Twins back $3.2 million. He signed with the Hanshin Tigers in the NBP and helped the Tigers reach the Japan Series against the Fukuoka Hawks. Facing elimination with one out and bases loaded in the top of the ninth, Nishioka was hit by the ball thrown by the catcher after a play at home plate. Nishioka was called out for interference because he was running inside the baseline. The play ended the series and gave Fukuoka the title.

He played for Hanshin until he retired in 2018.

<<BONUS ACHE>>

The Twins sign Byung-Ho Park

Twins GM Terry Ryan signed Korean masher Byung Ho Park to a four-year $12 million contract during the 2015 Winter Meetings after winning exclusive negotiation rights for $12.8 million. Park had averaged 43 home runs over the previous four seasons and hit .343 in 2015 in the KBO. "Park Bang" only played sixty-two games for the Twins, all in 2016. He hit .191 with 12 home runs and 24 RBI. He didn't make the big-league club in 2017 and batted .253 with 14 home runs and 60 RBI in 111 games with AAA Rochester before asking for his release to return to the KBO. He hit .345 with 43 home runs and 112 RBI with the Nexen Heroes in 2018.

April 11, 2011

The Wild Hire Todd Richards as Head Coach

I think your skill set and your overall talent takes precedence over experience.
—Chuck Fletcher

The Wild hired Todd Richards to succeed Jacques Lemaire as head coach of the team in 2011. Lemaire had been the head coach since the team began playing in 2000. In eight seasons with the Wild, Lemaire won 293 games and led the team to four playoff appearances.

Wild GM Chuck Fletcher had worked with Todd Richards when the two of them were both with the Pittsburgh Penguins organization. Prior to becoming the head coach of the Wild, Richards had just one season of coaching in the NHL as a bench coach with the San Jose Sharks. Prior to that, he spent four seasons as an assistant coach with the Nashville Predators AHL affiliate Milwaukee Admirals, winning the Calder Cup with the team in 2004. Two years later, he joined the Pittsburgh Penguins affiliate Wilkes-Barre/Scranton Penguins, which is where he met Fletcher.

With Richards, Fletcher hoped to get away from Lemaire's defensive-minded hockey philosophy. A lot Wild fans felt like Lemaire's style of coaching wasn't fun to watch. Richards promised a fresh, up-tempo style of play. A "youth" movement of head coaches was trending: the Pittsburgh Penguins had promoted thirty-eight-year-old Dan Bylsma to head coach midway through the season, and he led the Pens to the Stanley Cup title. The previous season, forty-one-year-old Todd McLellan coached the San Jose Sharks to the President's Trophy with an NHL-leading 117 points.

With the Wild, Richards acquired superstar-caliber players Mikko Koivu, Martin Havlat, Niklas Backstrom, and Brent Burns, plus other key players like Nick Schultz and Andrew Brunette. Richards and the Wild lost their first game of the season to the Columbus Blue Jackets 2–1. Andrew Brunette delivered a power play goal in overtime against the Anaheim Ducks in the second game of the season to get Richards his first NHL win. The Wild would lose their next six games to drop to 1–6. They'd spend most of the season climbing out of the early hole and would finish 11 points out of the playoffs with 84 points (38–36–8).

The following year, the Wild were in the playoff hunt and sat in fifth place in the standings at the All-Star Break and were 30–20–5 after a home-and-home sweep of the St. Louis Blues in mid-February. But the Wild would falter down the stretch again, only winning eight of the next twenty-seven games to finish the season, finishing with 86 and once again missing the playoffs.

Fletcher fired Richards after two seasons. Richards was 77–71–16 in his two seasons with the Wild.

The following off-season, he became a bench coach for the Columbus Blue Jackets before ultimately becoming the head coach forty-one games into the season (he would lead Columbus to the postseason one time in four full seasons. He was fired after starting the 2015–16 season 0–7).

Fletcher, meanwhile, hired another unproven young head coach from the Pittsburgh Penguins coaching tree in thirty-four-year-old Mike Yeo.

April 28, 2011
The Vikings Draft Christian Ponder

The Vikings fired Brad Childress after a 3–7 start and named Leslie Frazier the interim coach. The Vikings finished 6–10, missed the playoffs, and had the twelfth overall selection in the 2011 NFL Draft. With the retirement of Brett Favre and no confidence in the other quarterbacks on the roster (Rhett Bomar, Patrick Ramsey, and Joe Webb), the Vikings signed free agent Donovan McNabb and looked to the draft for the next franchise quarterback. The 2011 Draft was flush with Pro Bowl talent, with the first seven picks all being named to a Pro Bowl in their careers. Two quarterbacks were off the board in the first eight picks (Auburn's Cam Newton went number 1 to Carolina, and Washington's Jake Locker was taken by Tennessee with the eighth pick). With the twelfth pick, the Vikings selected Florida State standout Christian Ponder. Ponder would take over six games into his rookie season after McNabb struggled. Overall, he would play thirty-eight games for the Vikings over four seasons, was 14–21–1 as a starter, and threw for 6,658 yards, 38 touchdowns, and 36 interceptions. He did lead the Vikings to the playoffs at 10–6 in 2012 but missed the playoff game with a deep triceps bruise (the Vikings lost to Green Bay 24–10 with Joe Webb starting at quarterback). After a 0–3 start in 2013, Ponder was benched. Inconsistent play from Matt Cassell and Josh Freeman put Ponder back in the starting role, but his season ended in week 13 after a concussion.

In 2014, Matt Cassell was named the starter with rookie Teddy Bridgewater as his backup. He did play in two games that season (one start) with a QB rating of 45.8. The Vikings released him following the season. He spent time with the Oakland Raiders, Denver Broncos, and San Francisco 49ers the following two seasons; but he never played a down in the NFL after his final game in Minnesota.

Taken two picks after Ponder in the 2011 Draft was future Defensive Player of the Year Robert Quinn. Pro Bowlers Mike Pouncey, Ryan Kerrigan, Cameron Jordan, Mark Ingram, Muhammad Wilkerson, and Cameron Heyward were all taken in the first round after Ponder; and Pro Bowl Quarterback Andy Dalton was the first quarterback selected in the second round.

<<BONUS ACHE>>

Vikings Quarterbacks

Here is a list of quarterbacks to start a regular season game for the Green Bay Packers from 1992 to 2018: Brett Favre (243), Aaron Rodgers (160), Matt Flynn (6), Scott Tolzien (2), Seneca Wallace (1), and Brett Hundley (9).

Here is a list of quarterbacks to start a regular season game for the Minnesota Vikings from 1992 to 2018: Rich Gannon (12), Sean Salisbury (9), Jim McMahon (12), Warren Moon (39), Brad Johnson (46), Randall Cunningham (23), Jeff George (10), Daunte Culpepper (80), Todd Bouman (3), Spergeon Wynn (2), Gus Frerotte (13), Tarvaris Jackson (20), Kelly Holcomb (3), Brooks Bollinger (1), Brett Favre (29), Joe Webb (2), Christian Ponder (36), Donovan McNabb (6), Matt Cassel (9), Josh Freeman (1), Teddy Bridgewater (28), Sam Bradford (17), Shawn Hill (1), Case Keenum (14), and Kirk Cousins (16).

2013 was probably the worst year for Vikings quarterbacks. Ponder was benched, and Cassel wasn't much better. After the Tampa Bay Buccaneers released former first-round pick Josh Freeman, Les Fraiser and the Vikings took a flyer on him. He was signed on October 6, and ten days later, he was the starting quarterback in a Monday Night game against the New York Giants. He turned in one of the most disastrous performances in Vikings history. He was 20 of 53 passing for 190 yards and one interception. The Vikings lost 23–7, with the lone touchdown coming on a Marcus Sherels punt return. Fraiser went back to Ponder the following week, and Freeman was the third-string quarterback for the rest of the season.

June 23, 2011
The Wolves Draft Derrick Williams

The Timberwolves finished an NBA-worst 17–65 in 2010. They were going through the growing pains of a young roster. Only four members of the squad (Martell Webster, Sebastian Telfair, Luke Ridnour, and Darko Milicic) had more than four years in the league.

There were two elite prospects in the upcoming draft to add their young core: Duke G Kyrie Irving, despite only playing 11 games his freshman season, and Arizona F Derrick Williams, who many analysts thought should be the top pick in the draft.

The Wolves, with the worst record in the league, had a 25 percent chance of getting the top pick; but their bad lottery luck struck again. The top pick was awarded to the LA Clippers, who had a 2.80 percent of being awarded the top pick. But LA had traded their first rounder pick to the Cleveland Cavaliers along with Baron Davis in exchange for Jamario Moon and Mo Williams.

The Wolves were awarded the second overall pick. The Cavs, still reeling from LeBron James's move to Miami, took Irving as the next star of the Cavaliers.

The Wolves had a variety of options for the second pick. They didn't necessarily need to draft a forward at number two. They had a blossoming Kevin Love on the roster, as well as other young assets like Michael Beasley, Corey Brewer, Wesley Johnson and Anthony Tolliver. In addition, they were still invested in the often-injured Martell Webster, whom they had acquired in a trade from Portland.

Other than Irving, there weren't any really any standout guards in the draft worthy of the second overall pick. Plus, in hindsight, somebody like Kemba Walker or Klay Thompson would have been a great pick at two (Walker went ninth to Charlotte, Thompson went eleventh to Golden State).

The Wolves had used six consecutive first-round picks on guards: O.J. Mayo (who was traded for Kevin Love) in 2008, Ricky Rubio, Jonny Flynn, Ty Lawson,

Wayne Ellington in 2009, and Wesley Johnson (who was converted to small forward) in 2010. Or they could do what Wolves GM David Khan did best: they could trade back in the draft and amass picks.

Khan went with his "asset accumulation" strategy and selected who he thought was the best player available: Derrick Williams.

Not many people thought Williams would be in Minnesota for very long. The sophomore had a very high ceiling. He was a critical part in knocking defending champion Duke from the NCAA tournament that year, plus he had a great blend of size, athleticism, and scoring ability. He was named PAC-10 Player of the Year, averaged nearly 20 points per game, and shot 60 percent from the floor including 57 percent from beyond the arc.

But Khan kept him on the roster, and the twenty-year-old Williams broke camp with the Wolves.

Williams had a disappointing rookie campaign, averaging 8 points per game off the bench while shooting 41 percent from the floor and only 26 percent from three-point range. While he was able to assert his six-foot-eight, 240-pound frame in college, it wasn't working in the NBA. He showed glimmers of potential, but nothing consistent. His speed was an issue on defense because he wasn't fast enough to guard small forwards and not big enough to handle power forwards in the paint.

His sophomore season was better, averaging career highs in points (12.0), minutes (24.6), and three-point percentage (33 percent) and starting fifty-six games; but his consistency was still an issue.

After appearing in only eleven games for the Wolves in 2013, he was traded to the Sacramento Kings for Luc Mbah a Moute. New Wolves GM Flip Saunders said the while he liked Derrick, he didn't think he could fit in as a small forward in Rick Adelman's system. He started to find his niche as a rotation guy off the bench for the Kings. In his sixth game as a King, he scored a career-high 31 points against the Mavericks and then dropped 26 against the Wolves a couple months later. It looked like the Wolves had given up on him too early.

But he would have one big game then disappear for the next six or seven. He began to see fewer and fewer minutes once the Kings traded for Rudy Gay.

He averaged 8 points and 22 minutes per game during his year and a half in Sacramento. His rookie contract expired after the 2013 season, and he bounced around the league with the New York Knicks, Miami Heath, Cleveland Cavaliers, and LA Lakers before disappearing completely.

Once heralded as the top prospect in the draft, Williams was out of the league by the time he was twenty-seven years old.

<<BONUS ACHE>>

The Wonder Bread Wolves

Even with the addition of Williams in 2011, the Wolves faced a lot of criticism in 2012. The team was a mess. They had four head coaches in foureasons and were coming off the Kurt Rambis era in which they won thirty-two games over two seasons. Now coached by Rick Adelman, the team had taken a positive step forward and won the most games (twenty-six) in five seasons. But the media didn't see the nine-game improvement. They saw one thing: the Timberwolves were very "white": Kevin Love, J. J. Barea, Chase Budinger, Lou Amundson, Andrei Kirilenko, Nikola Pekovic, Luke Ridnour, Ricky Rubio, Alexey Shved, and Greg Stiemsma. Even though the Wolves were represented by nineteen men from six different countries, they were labeled "too white to win in the NBA."

June 24, 2011

The Wild Trade Brent Burns to San Jose

I think today, we added the equivalent of four first-round picks.
—Wild GM Chuck Fletcher

The Wild missed the playoffs for the fourth straight season after a 39–35–8 record in 2010–11. Fans from the State of Hockey were getting anxious, with the Wild's only two playoff appearances over a seven-year period ended in the first round. Second-year owner Craig Leopold wanted to get away from defensive-minded schemes of Jacques Lemaire and Todd Richards.

Richards was fired after the season, and GM Chuck Fletcher began building his team. All he needed were offensive pieces to fit the puzzle. But changing a roster to fit a specific scheme takes a lot of time. But fans didn't want to wait.

Fletcher hired Mike Yeo to usher in a new era of high-flying hockey. Then he looked at the roster to see who had the highest trade value.

He didn't want to get burned like his predecessor Doug Risebrough did in 2008 when Marian Gaborik left. Gaborik only played in seventeen games during his final season in St. Paul due to a hip injury and had no value on the trade market with an expiring contract. He signed a seven-year deal with the New York Rangers, and the Wild got nothing in return, wherein in a normal year, they could have potentially dealt him for a haul of prospects knowing that he was going to walk in free agency anyways.

The Wild had a couple intriguing trade pieces on their roster: Mikko Koivu, Martin Havlat, Pierre-Marc Brouchard, Kyle Brodziak, and Brent Burns. Burns, the Wild's first-round pick in 2003, was coming off a career year with 17 goals and 46 points. And he was about to be in a similar situation as Gaborik was a few years earlier—an expiring contract and a big contract on the way. And after losing Gabby for nothing, Fletcher had three options: trade him, sign him, or lose him for nothing. The team needed scoring, and they needed it fast.

The 2011 NHL Draft was in St. Paul, and about a half hour after the Wild selected Jonas Brodin with the tenth overall pick, Commissioner Gary Bettman stepped to the podium to announce a trade: Burns had been traded to San Jose.

In return, Minnesota got goal-scorer Devin Setoguchi, rookie center Charlie Coyle, and San Jose's first-round pick (number 28 overall). Wild fans were shocked.

"We gave up a very good piece in Brent Burns," said Fletcher after the announcement was made. "We felt that we needed to add talent. I think we did that."

"I love this place," Burns said. "I live here all year. I'm the only guy that does that. This is the team that brought me in when I was eighteen and gave me livelihood."

The jewel of the trade was twenty-four-year-old Setoguchi, a pure scorer who scored 84 goals and 159 points in 267 games with the Sharks, including three consecutive twenty-goal season. He had signed a three-year $9 million extension the day before the trade was made.

"He's a streaky guy," Sharks coach Todd McLellan said. "But he's still a young player. When he gets scoring, he's extremely dangerous."

Along with Seto came Charlie Coyle, who was San Jose's first-round pick the year before. As a freshman at Boston College, Coyle had scored 7 goals and notched 19 assists and was one of the US's best players at the world junior championships.

"I watched him last year at Boston College," longtime NHL scout Grand Sonier said of the nineteen-year-old Coyle. "I think he's ready to come out and play pro hockey right now."

With their extra first-round pick, Minnesota selected Zach Phillips, a high-scoring two-way center from St. John's.

Fletcher made a second deal with San Jose the following week, trading Martin Havlat for former 50-goal-scorer Dany Heatley. Neither trade worked out for the Wild.

Setoguchi was underwhelming for the Wild. He scored 32 goals and 63 points in 117 games. After trading Cal Clutterbuck for Nino Niederreiter, adding Zach Parise and Jason Pominville and young players like Coyle, Jason Zucker, and Mikael Granlund battling for top-six spots, Fletcher traded Seto to Winnipeg for a second-round pick in 2013.

Phillips would spend three seasons in the AHL and, with Coyle, led the Sault Ste Marie Greyhounds to the 2012 Memorial Cup. Phillips had 80 points in 60 games that season and along with Coyle's 38 points in 23 games, the expectation was that the two of them would build on that success in the pros. The Wild would trade Phillips to Boston for Jared Knight in March 2015 without suiting up for the Wild. Still on the board when Phillips was selected were Brandon Saad and Nikita Kucherov, who were both taken in the second round.

Coyle spend the first seven years of his career with the Wild, playing 242 points (91 goals, 151 assists) in 479 games. With the Wild floundering at the 2019 trade deadline, Fletcher traded Coyle to the Boston Bruins for Ryan Donato and a conditional pick. Coyle would have been an unrestricted free agent after the next season, and with cap space issues, the Wild likely wouldn't have been able to retain him. Coyle helped the Bruins reach the Stanley Cup Finals, where they lost to St. Louis in seven games.

Meanwhile, Brent Burns exploded in San Jose. After being acquired by the Sharks, he signed a five-year $5.76 million contract. Over the past eight seasons, Burns has been a consistent All-Star, a Norris Trophy Winner and has been a finalist for the Hart Trophy as League MVP twice. In 2016–17, he scored 29 goals and 76 points and helped lead San Jose to the Stanley Cup Finals in 2016.

Instead of paying Burns, Fletcher used that money to hand out megacontracts (thirteen years, $98 million each) to Zach Parise and Ryan Suter the following season when Burns's contract expired.

<<BONUS ACHE>>

More Bad Wild Trades

The Wild Trade Dwayne Roloson to Edmonton

Dwayne Roloson was an All-Star for the Minnesota Wild in 2003–04, led the league with a .933 save percentage, only allowed 1.88 goals per game, and was the number 1 goalie in the tandem with Manny Fernandez. But after the 2004 season was lost due to the lockout, Roloson (now thirty-six years old) struggled in 2005, allowing 3.00 goals per game (the highest of his career) and only winning six of his first twenty-four starts. He was dealt to the Edmonton Oilers at the trade deadline for a first-round pick and a future conditional pick.

The Wild traded the pick to Los Angeles (which became Trevor Lewis) along with Patrick O'Sullivan for Pavol Demitra during the 2006 NHL Draft. The conditional pick became a third rounder in 2007, which was traded to Atlanta (Spencer Machacek) for Petteri Nummelin.

Roloson reestablished his career as an Oiler and would play three seasons in Edmonton. He was still a starting-caliber goaltender at age forty-one, leading the Tampa Bay Lightning to within one game of the 2012 Stanley Cup Finals.

The Wild Trade Nick Leddy to Chicago

The Wild drafted hometown star defenseman Nick Leddy with the sixteenth overall pick in the 2009 NHL Draft. Leddy, a University of Minnesota commit, was named Minnesota's "Mr. Hockey" after leading Eden Prairie to their ever first state championship.

While he was playing for the Gophers, the Wild were struggling to make the playoffs. With two solid defensemen prospects in Marco Scandella and Tyler Cuma waiting in the wings and a rough start to Leddy's collegiate career (which included missed time due to a broken jaw), Wild GM Doug Risebrough decided to mortgage the future. Eight months after being drafted by the Wild, Leddy was traded, along with Kim Johnsson, to Chicago for Cam Barker.

Barker had scored 40 points in his second NHL season, but he had only scored 14 through his first fifty-one games in 2009–10. He only lasted one injury-plagued season in Minnesota, scoring 5 points in fifty-two games.

Meanwhile, Leddy took off with Chicago and was a key member of the 2012–13 Stanley Cup champion team. In four years in Chicago, he played in 258 consecutive games before signing as a free agent with the New York Islanders. The two-time All-Star has never missed more than three games in a season and scored 40+ points in his first three seasons with the Islanders.

As terrible as Barker was, Cuma (who was valued more than Leddy) was worse, only playing in one game for Minnesota.

November 2012

Josh Harding Diagnosed with Multiple Sclerosis

There's things in life that happen. Sometimes you can't explain it. You deal with it.
—Josh Harding

The Wild selected goaltender Josh Harding thirty-eighth overall (eighth pick in the second round) in the 2002 NHL Entry Draft. He played three seasons of junior hockey in the WHL for the Brandon Wheat Kings and Regina Pats. In 2003, he was the WHL's top goalie prospect, winning the Del Wilson trophy (best goaltender) and four Broncos Memorial trophy (Most Outstanding WHL Player). In 2004, he won a silver medal with Team Canada at the World Junior Ice Hockey Championships. When he turned pro, the Wild assigned him to their AHL affiliate, the Houston Aeros. As an Aero in 2004–05, Harding was 21–16–3 and surrendered two goals per game.

He was called up to the Wild in March 2006 after the team traded Dwayne Roloson to Edmonton. In limited action, he was 3–2 with a 2.59 GAA. He would bounce back and forth between Houston and Minnesota in 2006 and 2007 before getting the backup job behind Nicklas Backstrom. Despite only appearing in nineteen games in 2008–09 and posting a 3–9 record, his 2.21 GAA turned some heads.

On September 24, 2010, Harding tore his ACL and MCL in a preseason game against the St. Louis Blues and missed the entire 2010–11 season. But coming back from that injury was nothing compared to what was next for Harding.

In November 2012, a few months after signing a three-year contract with the Wild, Harding was diagnosed with multiple sclerosis, an incurable autoimmune disease that results in problems with balance, fatigue, and blurred vision. At the time of the diagnosis, Harding had appeared in 117 NHL games, winning 41 of them with a .916 save percentage and a 2.65 GAA.

Harding had no plans to retire. "Josh's competitive fire has led him to a successful career in the NHL," said Wild GM Chuck Fletcher. "We know he will approach this new battle in the same manner."

And he did. In his first game back after the diagnosis, he stopped 24 shots in a 1–0 shutout of the Dallas Stars on January 20, 2013. In the first round of the playoffs, Backstrom got hurt during warm-ups before Game 1 against the President's Cup winner Chicago Blackhawks. Harding stepped into the game and stopped 35 of 37 shots in a 2–1 overtime loss. Harding would start all five games in the eventual 4–1 series loss. He was awarded the Bill Masterton Memorial Trophy at the end of the season. As it turns out, Game 5 of that playoff series would by Harding's final game in a Wild sweater.

Despite the MS diagnosis, Harding was expected to compete for the starting goaltender job with Backstrom and Darcy Kuemper, but a broken foot kept him sidelined. When he was activated from injured reserve, he was waived by the Wild and assigned to their AHL affiliate, the Iowa Wild. In his second game for Iowa, in a game against the Charlotte Checkers, he began suffering from severe dehydration as a result of his MS. His body was in such bad shape that he had to be taken by ambulance from the visitor's locker room. While lying in the hospital bed in Charlotte with his family, he decided that it was time to retire.

Only two years prior to his diagnosis, he was viewed by many as the Wild's goaltender of the future. He finished his NHL career with a 60–59–11 record with a .918 save percentage and a 2.45 GAA. In his final NHL season in 2013–14, he was 18–7–3 with a league-leading .933 save percentage and a 1.66 GAA at only twenty-nine years old.

March 1, 2012

Wild at Montreal Canadiens— Devin Setoguchi's Shoot-Out

That is the most bizarre ending to a hockey game I've seen in a long, long time.
—Pierre Houde on the Montreal Canadiens TV broadcast

The Wild started the season 2011–12 NHL season 20–7–3, but a pair of long losing streaks in December (5–6–3 with an eight-game winless streak) and February (3–7–2 with a seven-game winless streak) had them two games over .500 at 28–26–10 and fighting for their playoff lives.

In a Thursday night game at the Bell Center on March 1, 2012, the Wild trailed the Montreal Canadiens 4–1 after two and a half periods of play. The Habs, who were in last place in the Eastern Conference, had scored three power play goals (PK Subban, Lars Eller, Max Pacioretty) then added a David Desharnais goal at the 8:50 mark in the third. Wild starting goalie Niklas Backstrom had left the game with an injury after facing six shots in the first period and was replaced by Josh Harding.

But, with four minutes left in the game, the Wild came to life. Matt Kassian scored his second goal of the night (he had his first career goal at 15:27 in the first period) with four minutes left in the game to make it 4–2. Head coach Mike Yeo pulled Harding for the extra attacker with about 2:15 left. Dany Heatley scored his twentieth goal of the season at 18:17 to cut the deficit to one.

With the Wild still empty, Heatley intercepted a Carey Price-to-Tomas Plekanec, then Devin Setoguchi tied the game at 4–4 with ten seconds left.

After erasing a three-goal deficit with less than four minutes left, the Wild were headed to overtime. With twenty-six seconds left in extra time, Harding made a huge pad save on Subban to send the game to a shoot-out.

This was great news for the Wild, because the Canadiens were terrible in the shoot-out. With the Wild in desperate need of two points, head coach Mike Yeo elected to have Heatley, Setoguchi, and Matt Cullen take the shots for the Wild. For Montreal, it was Pacioretty, Desharnais, and Rene Bourque.

Josh Harding was in net for the Wild and stopped Pacioretty's attempt. Future Hart Memorial and Venzia Trophy winner Carey Price denied Cullen's first shot. Desharnais beat Harding with a nice deke move to give Montreal the goal advantage in the shoot-out. Price had no problem stopping Heatley's attempt. Harding stopped Bourque to give Setoguchi a chance.

Unfortunately, Seto's game-tying goal wouldn't be remembered after this game. As he came at Price to tie the shoot-out, the puck hit a rut. As he tried to regain the puck, he tripped and slid on the ice. Price came out of the crease to tap the puck as Setoguchi lay facedown on the ice in embarrassment.

The Wild followed up the 5–4 shoot-out loss with a 6–0 loss against the Detroit Red Wings to drop to .500. They wouldn't have a winning record for the rest of the season, finished 35–36–11, and would miss the playoffs for the fourth straight year.

June 27, 2013

The Wolves Pass on Giannis Antetokounmpo . . . Twice

Giannis Antetokounmpo is a beast. In his first six NBA seasons with the Milwaukee Bucks, the All-Star forward averaged 19 points, 8 rebounds, and 4 assists per game.

In 2012, he was a nineteen-year-old kid playing in the Greek A2 League. He played in twenty-six games, averaged nearly 10 points and 8 boards per game. That year, he was a special participant in the league's All-Star game—not because he was selected to the team but because the coaches let him play as a special treat to the fans because Greece had never seen anything like him before.

The next year, Antetokounmpo declared for the NBA draft. His 2013 draft profile wasn't that impressive. He was listed at six feet nine and only 196 pounds (he is six feet eleven, 222 pounds today). He was knocked for his inexperience, ineptitude on defense, consistency, lack of a jump shot, and the adjustment needed in moving from overseas competition to the NBA.

One anonymous Western Conference executive told *Sports Illustrated*, "I wouldn't touch him. I don't even know how good he is going to be once he reaches his potential."

There's a decent chance that the exec was Timberwolves general manager Flip Saunders, who had just rejoined the team after an eight-year absence. But considering he took a risk on a certain six-foot-eleven high school kid out of Farragut Academy High School with the fifth overall pick in 1995, I doubt that it was him.

The 2013 NBA Draft was Flip's first as an NBA general manager, and he and head coach Rick Adelman had the ninth overall pick in the draft.

After seeing Anthony Bennett, Victor Oladipo, Otto Porter, Cody Zeller, Alex Len, Nerlens Noel, Ben McLemore, and Kentavious Caldwell-Pope taken off the draft board, Flip had options with the pick. He could select the National

College Player of the Year in Trey Burke from Michigan or another guard like Michael Carter-Williams from Syracuse or C. J. McCollum from Lehigh. The unproven Antetokounmpo was on the board yet, too, but probably not worthy (at the time) of the ninth pick. Or he could trade the pick.

Utah and their two first-round picks (fourteenth and twenty-first) called and offered both picks if the Wolves would select Trey Burke for them. Flip agreed.

When it was the Wolves pick again at fourteen, McCollum and Carter-Williams had both been taken. As had a pair of big men in Steven Adams and Kelly Olynyk.

An enticing player sat on the board at fourteen. Shabazz Muhammad, the Pac-12 Freshman of the Year, averaged 18 points and 5 boards at UCLA that season. Although he was a forward in college, he planned on transitioning to shooting guard in the NBA. Character issues had taken him from a top three pick to a mid-first-round grade (after he was drafted, he was sent home from Summer League due to rules violations) but there was no question the talent and drive were there.

Saunders passed on the unknown Antetokounmpo again and selected Muhammad with the fourteenth pick. The Wolves used the other pick acquired in the Burke deal to select center Gorgui Dieng out of Louisville.

Antetokounmpo was taken off the board by the Milwaukee Bucks at fifteen.

In five short seasons, Antetokounmpo has gone from green prospect to All-NBA. The player who was once questioned for experience and defensive abilities won the NBA's Most Improved Player of the Year, was named to the NBA All-Defensive Team in 2017, and was the league's Most Valuable Player in 2019.

November 27, 2013
The Twins Sign Ricky Nolasco

The Twins, after back-to-back ninety-loss seasons, went all in on acquisitions in 2013 especially to a starting rotation of being twenty-ninth in the majors with a 4.81 rotation ERA and dead last in the majors with a 5.26 team ERA in 2012. They traded for Vance Worley and signed Mike Pelfrey and Kevin Correia to the starting rotation. But the crown jewel of the off-season was starter Ricky Nolasco.

Nolasco was 81–72 with a 4.44 ERA in eight seasons with the Marlins before being traded to the LA Dodgers midway through the 2012 season. He was 8–3 with a 3.85 down the stretch for Los Angeles before hitting free agency. The Twins signed him to the largest free agent contract in team history: four years and $49 million.

To say Nolasco struggled with the Twins would be an understatement. He posted a 5.38 ERA in 2013, then a 6.75 ERA in eight starts in an injury-riddled season in 2015. In two and a half seasons, he was 15–22 with a 5.44 ERA in fifty-six starts. It looked like the Twins would have to ride out his contract or eat the millions left on his deal. They managed to deal him to the LA Angels with prospect Alex Meyer in exchange for Hector Santiago and Alan Busenitz.

December 8, 2013

Vikings at Baltimore Ravens—Five Touchdowns in 125 Seconds

It broke my heart. That's a game we should've won.
—Vikings special team coordinator Mike Priefer

Not many things went right for the Vikings in 2013. After beating the Chicago Bears in overtime on December 1, the Vikings had a whopping three wins. On December 8, they played a rare game at M&T Bank Stadium in Baltimore. The Ravens were the defending Super Bowl champions but were having a down year too and entered the game with a 6–6 record and were in danger of missing the 2013 postseason.

December 8 was a cold, snowy day in Baltimore and was the first time a couple Vikings players, including Brian Robison and Andrew Sendejo, had played in the snow. Baltimore led 7–6 late at the start of the fourth quarter, and with bad weather, deteriorating field conditions, and Adrian Peterson leaving the game with a foot injury, it looked like there was a good chance that the scoring was about done.

But Matt Cassell connected with Jerome Simpson for an eight-yard touchdown (the two-point conversion was no good) to take a 12–7 lead. The Vikings held that lead until 2:05 left in the game.

In those final 125 seconds, the two teams combined for five touchdowns, beginning with a one-yard touchdown from Joe Flacco to tight end Dennis Pitta (the two-point conversion was successful) to give Baltimore a 15–12 lead.

One the second play of the ensuing drive, Toby Gerhard broke free up the middle for a forty-one-yard touchdown run as the Vikings retook the lead, 19–15. The lead didn't last long, though, as Jacoby Jones returned Blair Walsh's kickoff seventy-seven yards for a touchdown and a 22–19 lead.

Cassell and the Vikings responded quickly again, this time with a seventy-nine-yard touchdown screen pass and run by rookie Cordarrelle Patterson, giving Minnesota a 26–22 lead with forty-five seconds left in the game.

Starting at their own twenty-yard line, Flacco hit undrafted rookie Marlon Brown for a thirty-five-yard gain, pushing the Ravens into Minnesota territory. After throwing an incompletion, Flacco was picked off by Andrew Sendejo at the Minnesota 23 on a pass intended for Dennis Pitta that looked to seal the game. But Chad Greenway was called for pass interference.

"There were a lot of things that I thought could have been called pass interference more so than that throughout that ball game," head coach Leslie Frazier said after the game. "It bewildered me. It's disappointing."

Frazier argued that Pitta tripped over Greenway's foot, and it should be considered incidental contact. But instead of a Minnesota kneel ending the game, Baltimore still had life at the Vikings' twenty-seven-yard line.

After an eighteen-yard completion to Pitta, Baltimore had the ball on the nine-yard line with nine seconds left. With no time-outs left, Flacco found Marlon Brown in the back of the end zone for the game-winning touchdown, 29–26.

"You think you've seen everything," said Ravens kicker Justin Tucker. "And then a game like this happens. To sum it up in one word, it was pandemonium."

It was the fourth time that season that the Vikings had given up a winning touchdown after being ahead and the first time in NFL history that there had been six lead changes in the fourth quarter.

August 23, 2014

Twins Cancel Chuck Knoblauch's Twins Hall of Fame Induction

There is no greater love/hate relationship for Twins fans than that of Chuck Knoblauch.

Chuck Knoblauch was drafted by the Twins with the twenty-fifth overall pick in the 1989 amateur draft, and he saw his first playing time in 1991, where he started 151 games and hit .281 with 25 stolen bases, good enough to earn him the title of AL Rookie of the Year, receiving twenty-six of twenty-nine first-place votes, beating out Juan Guzman, Milt Cuyler, and Ivan Rodriguez for the award. The moment that solidified him as a fan favorite occurred in Game 7 of the 1991 World Series versus the Atlanta Braves. In the top of the eighth in a 0–0 ball game, with Lonnie Smith on first base, Terry Pendleton hit a double to the gap. Braves manager Bobby Cox had a hit-and-run on, and Smith took off from first on the pitch. But Knoblauch faked a scoop of the ball and flipped the imaginary ball to Greg Gagne, who threw the imaginary ball to Hrbek. The play confused Smith long enough to where he made it only to third base and did not score on the play.

Knoblauch went on to become the face of the franchise in the '90s, due to the retirements of players like Kent Hrbek and Kirby Puckett. Along with his ROY campaign in 1991, Knoblauch was a four-time All-Star for the Twins ('92, '94, '96, '97), he won two Silver Slugger awards ('94, '96), he was in the top 20 in MVP voting three times, he won a Gold Glove in '97, he led the league in doubles (45) in '94, led the league in triples (14) in '96, as well as hit a career-high .341, tying him for third in the league with teammate Paul Molitor. But the Twins couldn't field a winning team in five seasons despite Knoblauch's play, and following the 1997 season, he committed the ultimate burning-the-bridge act that a player can do to the fans: he demanded a trade out of Minnesota.

Knoblauch's wish was granted, and he was dealt to the New York Yankees for four players (All-Stars Christian Guzman and Eric Milton plus Brian Buchannan and Danny Mota). Knoblauch finished his Minnesota career with a .304 average with 210 doubles, 713 runs, 391 RBI, and 276 stolen bases. He was the 1994 doubles champion and stole over 40 bases three consecutive seasons, including 62 in 1997.

Upon his arrival in New York, Knoblauch declared that he and rising star Derek Jeter would become the best double-play combo in the history of the league. Knoblauch's dreams were cut short, however, when he came down with Steve Blass disease, a serious condition in which a talented player suddenly loses his talent and is not able to regain it. In the 1998 playoffs against Cleveland, Knoblauch began to argue with an umpire during a play, enabling Indians infielder Enrique Wilson to score from first, giving Cleveland a 2–1 edge in an eventual Yankee loss. Knoblauch began to make horrendous overthrows, one of which hit sports broadcaster Keith Olbermann's mother in the face. As bad as he played, the Yankees won the four American League Pennants and three World Series titles with Knoblauch on the roster.

In 2001, Knoblauch was released by the Yankees and signed with the Royals, where he hit a meager .210 in eighty-eight games. He left the Royals at the end of the season and retired in 2003 after being out of baseball for two seasons.

After his playing career was over, Knoblauch began getting in trouble with the law. In 2007, he was named in the Mitchell Report, a list of alleged steroids users. Brian McNamee said he injected Knoblauch seven to nine times with HGH while he was a Yankee.

Knoblauch was subpoenaed by the congressional committee investigating steroids in baseball after he failed to respond to an invitation to give a deposition by the January 18, 2008, deadline. On January 23, the Associated Press reported that federal marshals were unable to find Knoblauch to serve him with the subpoena. Five days later, it was reported that the congressional subpoena had been withdrawn after Knoblauch agreed to give a deposition on February 1, 2008.

In 2010, he pleaded to a misdemeanor assault charge filed by his wife.

He stayed out of the public eye after that, and in 2014, he was voted into the Minnesota Twins Hall of Fame. Twins management and media that voted him in showed that they were willing to put the past behind them. His induction ceremony was scheduled for August 23, 2014.

But a month before his big day, he was arrested for assaulting his (now) ex-wife. After the news broke, the Twins decided that they would not hold the Hall of Fame ceremony. As details unfolded in the case, they ultimately decided that he had no place in the Twins Hall of Fame and—despite being voted in by a sixty-two-member committee of media, club officials, fans and other Hall members—decided not to put him in the Twins Hall of Fame.

OCTOBER 25, 2015

Flip Saunders Passes Away

He was a shining example of what a true leader should be, defined by his integrity and kindness to all he encountered.
—Timberwolves owner Glen Taylor

Things were finally looking up for the Timberwolves in 2015. After missing the playoffs for eleven consecutive seasons, the Timberwolves had the pieces in place to rebuild. And it was all coordinated by Flip Saunders. Saunders had been the Timberwolves' head coach from midway through the 1995–96 season until midway through the 2004–05 season. During that time, the Wolves made the playoffs eight times.

After Saunders was fired fifty-one games into the 2004–05 season, the Wolves averaged twenty-six wins per season until he returned as the president of basketball operations in 2014. Meanwhile, Flip had led the Detroit Pistons to three consecutive Eastern Conference Finals and had also coached the Washington Wizards.

Flip took over on the Wolves on June 6, 2014. The team finished 40–42 in his first season as executive, the highest win total since 2004–05. After the season, Rick Adelman retired as head coach and Flip took over as head coach. Still serving as team president, he began retooling the team. He traded All-Star Kevin Love to the Cleveland Cavaliers for Anthony Bennett and the draft's top pick Andrew Wiggins. He drafted the high-flying Zach LaVine out of UCLA with the thirteenth pick in the 2014 draft. He also added Thad Young from the 76ers, who he later traded to the Brooklyn Nets to bring Kevin Garnett back to the Twin Cities to help mentor his young players.

That season was full of growing pains. The young roster, paired with veterans like Garnett, Kevin Martin, and Andre Miller, only won sixteen games that season; but the young-look Wolves were learning.

The Wolves won the draft lottery for the 2015 NBA Draft. With the first pick, Flip took Karl-Anthony Towns out of Kentucky. He traded a pair of second-round picks to the Cleveland Cavaliers for Duke star and Minnesota native Tyus Jones. He added one of his former Pistons stars Tayshaun Prince to help mold and coach his Timberpups of Towns, Wiggins, and LaVine.

In addition to his building projects on the court, he also facilitated the construction of a new downtown practice facility in the former Block E (now the Mayo Clinic Sports Medicine Center) and a Target Center remodel.

But on August 11, 2015, Saunders made an announcement that would shake the franchise and its fan base: he had cancer. He was undergoing treatment for Hodgkin's lymphoma. While he was undergoing treatment, he continued his work as team president, but he relinquished his duties as head coach. He appointed one of his former players and 2006–07 NBA Coach of the Year Sam Mitchell as the team's coach for the 2015–16 season.

Less than three months later, on October 25, Flip Saunders passed away at the age of sixty. Saunders's death not only left a gaping hole in the Wolves franchise but also in the NBA. Having coached for three franchises (Timberwolves, Pistons, Wizards), he also worked as an advisor for the Boston Celtics and had coached a multitude of players at the collegiate and minor-league level.

With Saunders and his vision for Timberwolves basketball gone, the franchise started heading in a new direction. Kevin Garnett, not only one of Saunders best players but also one of his best friends, had public disagreements with owner Glen Taylor and hasn't had much to do with the franchise since retiring the year after Saunders passed away. Taylor replaced Saunders's choice for head coach with Tom Thibideau, who also took over as team president. Thibideau began building the team in his own image, trading two pieces of Saunders team in LaVine and the fifth pick in the 2015 NBA Draft Kris Dunn to Chicago for one of his former players in Jimmy Butler.

The Wolves hung a "FLIP" banner from the rafters of Target Center in February 2018—more than two years after the death of pioneer of two eras of Timberwolves basketball.

The Twins Trade Aaron Hicks for John Ryan Murphy

The Twins were looking for catching depth following the 2015 season. With All-Star Kurt Suzuki (.240, 5 home runs, 50 RBI) behind the plate and little faith in backups Eric Fryer and Chris Hermann, the Twins traded for Yankees backup catcher John Ryan Murphy in exchange for outfielder Aaron Hicks, who had become expendable with the arrival of super-prospect Byron Buxton.

Murphy, a second-round pick by the Yankees in 2009, hit .277 with 3 home runs and a .327 on-base percentage in sixty-seven games while backing up Brian McCann. He had a game-winning three-run home run off Twins closer Glen Perkins the previous May. And with Suzuki only under contract one more season, Twins management hoped that Murphy would be the catcher of the future for the Twins.

Murphy started the season 3-for-40 (.075) before being optioned to AAA Rochester. He did get his average up to .146 but spent most of the season with Rochester. He lost the backup catcher job to Chris Gimenez in 2017 and never saw time with the big-league club. He was traded to Arizona for reliever Gabriel Moya in late July 2017.

Meanwhile, Hicks had become an everyday player for the Yankees. After declining to trade Hicks to the Seattle Mariners for Cliff Lee in 2010, Hicks, the Twins first-round pick in 2008, had hit .225 with 20 home runs and 78 RBI in parts of three seasons in Minnesota. After playing in a career-high 123 games in 2016, Hicks found his groove. He hit a career-high .266 in 2017, then hit 27 home runs for the Yankees in 2018 (and finished twenty-second in MVP voting) before signing a seven-year contract extension with the Yankees before the 2019 season.

To make matters worse, trading Hicks to the Yankees opened a spot in the outfield for Miguel Sano.

<<BONUS ACHE>>

Miguel Sano in Right Field

Terry Ryan thought he had a good problem in 2016. Miguel Sano, who had finished third in AL Rookie of the Year voting the year before, had primarily played DH in 2015. Sano was a natural third baseman, but that position was filled by Trevor Plouffe (.248, 74 HR, 273 RBI over the last three seasons). Ryan had just signed Korean star Byung Ho Park as the designated hitter, and he had Joe Mauer at first base. The question was, Where did Miguel Sano and his bat fit into the lineup?

Manager Paul Molitor's solution was right field. Sano worked exclusively with Torii Hunter to work on his outfield defense. But it never clicked. Sano had some awful moments in the outfield. He didn't have speed, and he never learned to play the ball off the wall. By the middle of the season, Park had been demoted to AAA, so the DH spot opened back up for Sano. The Sano experiment lasted only thirty-eight games.

January 10, 2016

Vikings versus Seattle: Blair Walsh Misses

It's my fault. I'm the only one who didn't do my job. That's on me.
—Blair Walsh

A year after the Vikings hired Mike Zimmer as the ninth head coach in franchise history, they made the playoffs with an 11–5 season. Zimmer's defense, led by Pro Bowlers Everson Griffen, Harrison Smith, and Anthony Barr, were a top five scoring defense. The offence was paced by Adrian Peterson's 1,485 rushing yards and 11 touchdowns. Teddy Bridgewater's first year as a starter ended in a Pro Bowl selection as a late addition after he threw for 3,231 yards and 14 touchdowns in sixteen starts.

The Vikings had beaten the Green Bay Packers at Lambeau Field in the final week of the season 20–13 for their first NFC North Division title since 2009, highlighted by Captain Munnerlyn's fifty-five-yard fumble recovery after a Griffen strip-sack of Aaron Rodgers to put the Vikings up 20–3 late in the third quarter.

With the division championship, the Vikings had home field advantage in the Wild Card Round (the 15–1 Carolina Panthers and 13–3 Arizona Cardinals had first-round byes). The Packers at 9–7 traveled to Washington to take on the NFC East champion Redskins as the second wild card team. The Vikings welcome the 10–6 Seattle Seahawks to Minnesota. Seattle had beaten the Vikings 38–7 at TCF Bank Stadium on December 10.

The Vikings were playing their final season at TCF Bank Stadium on the University of Minnesota campus while construction crews were finishing up the new US Bank Stadium on the site of the old Metrodome. The game against Seattle would be the first outdoor playoff game for the Vikings since beating the LA Rams in the 1976 NFC Championship Game 24–17 on December 26, 1976—a game that saw a high temperature of −7 degrees.

The NFC Wild Card game was played at TCF Bank Stadium on January 10, 2016, and saw temperatures far more frigid than the game in 1976 . . . with a wind chill of −25 degrees.

"Remember the old Met?" former Vikings head coach Bud Grant reminisced. "The teams were on the same side of the field. Next to us, the teams had heaters and any kind of thing to keep hands warm. We did not have them. Our players were looking at the field. When I looked down at the other team, they were huddled around their heaters. They weren't watching the game."

Grant set the tone as the Vikings honored him by bringing him out for the coin toss by walking to midfield in a golf shirt like it was a warm day at Hazeltine. Seahawks head coach Pete Carroll, who was a part of Grant's 1985 coaching staff as the defensive backs coach, could only smile as the eighty-eight-year-old coach took part in the ceremony while he "showed people how much we love this weather."

Charlie Newland, who calls high school sports for KDLM Radio in Detroit Lakes, attended the game and didn't love the weather.

"I wore four pairs of wool socks, two pairs of long johns, two pairs of snow pants, and two winter jackets." Charlie said. "During the game, people would go to the bathrooms and put their feet under the hand dryers to get feeling back in their toes. But as cold as that game was, Packers fans can still say they've had the coldest game." The 1967 Ice Bowl was −36 below.

While Grant loved the subzero temps, the teams playing in the game did not. At kickoff, the temperature at TCF Bank Stadium was only −25. Despite the grim forecast before the game, Seahawks cornerback Richard Sherman didn't think the weather would be a big deal. Then his eyelashes froze during pregame warm-ups.

"Then you kind of realize, *It's really kind of cold*," he said.

Offense was hard to come by in the first quarter. The longest play from scrimmage was an eleven-yard run by Seattle running back Christine Michael with a minute left in the quarter. Despite short runs and even shorter passes, the Bridgewater and the Vikings offense ate up most of the first quarter. After starting on their own twelve-yard line, Teddy converted a fourth down conversion at midfield to keep the drive alive. The next three plays netted −2 yards for the Vikings, and punter Jeff Locke booted the frozen football twenty-three yards after a seven-minute drive ended without any points.

Russell Wilson and the Seattle offense didn't move the ball as well as the Vikings did, being forced to punt after three plays. From their own twenty-five-yard line on a fourth and seven, punter Jon Ryan fielded a bad snap and tried to run for a first down, but he was tackled by Jason Trusnik at the twenty-nine-yard line.

After back-to-back receptions by Jerick McKinnon and rookie Stefon Diggs, the Vikings had the ball first and goal from Seattle's seven-yard line. Adrian Peterson got two chances to punch it in but gained three yards on two plays. After an incomplete pass to McKinnon, the Vikings settled for a twenty-two-yard Blair Walsh field goal and a 3–0 lead.

The Vikings defense continued to smother Seattle's offense, forcing four more Jon Ryan punts and a huge fourth down conversion stop in the second quarter. The fourth punt came from the Vikings thirty-eight-yard line, which in normal weather conditions would have been an easy field goal for Seattle kicker Steven Hauschka. Instead, Pete Carroll elected to pin the Vikings deep in their own territory with a minute left in the half. After a couple Bridgewater kneels from inside their ten-yard line, the Vikings went to their warm locker room with a 3–0 halftime lead.

Seattle got the ball to open the third quarter, and their offense started clicking, moving the ball from their own 20 to the Vikings 40 after a seventeen-yard reception by Doug Baldwin and a twelve-yard run by Fred Jackson. After an eight-yard carry on first and ten from the Minnesota 47, Christine Michael was studded at the line of scrimmage to bring up another fourth down conversion. This time, Carroll elected to keep his offense on the field and keep the drive alive. Vikings cornerback Trae Waynes intercepted Wilson's pass to end the drive.

Bridgewater completed an eleven-yard pass to Zach Line on the first play of the drive and got an extra fifteen yards on a roughing-the-passer call on Cliff Avril that brought the ball to the Seattle 26. But the offense stalled just outside the red zone and settled for another Walsh field goal and a 6–0 lead.

Wilson was sacked on back-to-back plays by Everson Griffen and Sharrif Floyd on the next drive as the offense went three-and-out. Jon Ryan punted back to the Vikings from their own twenty-yard line. The Vikings started their next drive at Seattle's forty-eight-yard line. A heavy dose of Peterson (four carries, eight yards) and Diggs (two catches, 10 yards) got the Vikings to the Seattle 23. On a third and six, Bridgewater was sacked by Cliff Avril. Again, Zimmer called on his All-Pro kicker, this time from forty-seven yards. And again, Walsh delivered to put the Vikings up 9–0 entering the fourth quarter.

The Vikings defense kept after Wilson to start the fourth quarter, but Seattle put together their best offensive drive of the game. After picking up a quick first down on a Vikings penalty, the Seahawks picked up their first first down since 12:36 in the third quarter. With a first and ten from the Vikings thirty-nine-yard line, things appeared to take a sharp turn when the shotgun snap flew past Wilson's shoulder. He ran backward and slid to pick up the ball at the Seattle 45, scrambled to his right, evaded the pursuing Captain Munnerlyn and hit a wide-open Tyler Lockett, who had gotten behind the defense. He was tracked down by Josh Robinson and tackled at the four-yard line for a thirty-five-yard gain.

"It was a good snap if I was expecting it," Wilson said. "I just wasn't expecting it quite yet."

Two plays later, Seattle was in the end zone for the game's only touchdown on a three-yard touchdown reception by Doug Baldwin.

Two plays later, the Vikings had the ball second and five on their own twenty-seven-yard line. Peterson took the handoff and ran eight yards for a first down. But Kam Chancellor punched the ball free. Defensive Tackle Ahtyba Rubin recovered the fumble at Minnesota's forty-yard line.

"That will haunt me throughout this off-season," Peterson said at his locker after the game. "I got careless with it, scratching for yards. They made a good play, and it cost us. It put us in a bad position."

The Seahawks turned the turnover into three points with a forty-six-yard Hauschka field goal and a 10–9 lead with 8:09 left, erasing a 9–0 deficit in 3:32.

After trading punts, the Vikings got the ball back with 1:42 left and with good field position. Starting at their own thirty-nine-yard line, Bridgewater threw deep to Kyle Rudolph. Chancellor was called for a nineteen-yard defensive pass interference that brought the ball to the Seattle 42. On the next play, Teddy looked Rudolph's way again, this time connecting for a twenty-four-yard strike that got the Vikings offense down to the Seattle 18. After running Peterson up the middle and forcing Seattle to burn their remaining time-outs, Blair Walsh set up for the game-winning field goal at the twelve-yard line with twenty-six seconds left in the game.

Before the kick, confident fans were throwing both hands up in the air as Walsh lined up for the twenty-seven-yard field goal attempt. According to NFL Stats and Into, NFL kickers were 189–191 (99 percent) from twenty-seven yards and closer that season. Walsh lined up to send the Vikings to the divisional round and a matchup with the Arizona Cardinals.

The snap was good, but Jeff Locke had the laces in. Walsh's kick missed wide left.

"It was so quick," he said. "I don't know what happened."

"He hit three field goals in −25 windchill," long snapper Kevin McDermott said. "That's really hard to do."

"It's a chip shot," Zimmer said. "He's gotta make that."

The Vikings stood stunned as the Seahawks celebrated around them.

And although you can pin the loss on Walsh's miss, the players recognized it wasn't the only thing to go wrong that day.

"You can name a hundred things that could have changed the outcome," said defensive end Brian Robison.

The Vikings converted three of thirteen third downs in the game. The Vikings' three scoring drives covered 25, 28, and 19 yards. A total of 73 yards, which included 21 penalty yards. Peterson averaged a season-low two yards per carry, and the Vikings totaled 183 yards of offense in the game.

"I never felt like there was any 'Here we go again' today," Zimmer said in his postgame press conference. "We missed the field goal. We lost the game. Other than that, they hit a kind of fluky play. We played great on defense all day . . . We missed a chip shot field goal, so that's life. The finish was disappointing, but

I thought we did a lot of good things this year. We had the best record of any team that's played in a temporary stadium, first playoff game ever in a temporary stadium, we won the NFC North for the first time in I don't know however many years."

But despite those feel-good successes, the Vikings' season ended without a championship again.

<<BONUS ACHE>>

Blair Walsh

The Vikings selected Georgia kicker Blair Walsh in the sixth round of the 2012 NFL Draft, and early in his career, it seemed like the steal of the draft. He was an All-Pro in his rookie season and was money from beyond fifty yards. He set the NFL record for most makes of fifty yards or more in a season (10), tied the Vikings franchise record for longest field goal (fifty-six yards), tied the NFL record for most field goals made by a rookie (35), and passed Randy Moss for most points scored by a rookie. The next season, he broke the NFL record for most consecutive field goals made from fifty yards or more (12). In 2015, he signed a four-year $14 million contract extension with the Vikings, making him one of the highest-paid kickers in the league. That preseason, he was 5-for-11 on field goal attempts. He saw his field goal percentage drop from 92.1 percent in 2012 to 74.3 percent in 2014. In a 20–23 loss to Denver in week 4, he missed a thirty-six-yard field goal. He picked himself up, making his next seventeen attempts and finished the season with an NFL high 34 made field goals. But the one that fans remember from that year was the twenty-seven-yard miss with twenty-six seconds left in a 10–9 loss to Seattle in the wild card round of the playoffs. After struggling early in the 2016 season, which included four missed extra points, he was cut by the Vikings. He was signed by Seattle and, in the team's second preseason game against the Vikings, was 2-of-3 from fifty yards and made both of his field goal attempts, which led to him taunting his former teammates. But Walsh spiraled in Seattle too, missing big kicks for Seattle as they fought for a playoff spot. Vikings fans had the last laugh when Walsh missed a field goal with less than a minute left in a game against Arizona that would have clinched a playoff spot for Seattle. The Seahawks lost 27–26 and were eliminated from postseason contention. Walsh was released after the season.

April 28, 2016

The Vikings Draft Laquon Treadwell

He's a natural hands catcher and will win 50–50 balls. I think the Vikings got a winner.
—NFL Network analyst Mike Mayock

The Vikings have drafted seven receivers in the first round: one is a Hall of Famer (Randy Moss), one was a Pro Bowler (Gene Washington), two were Pro Bowl kick returners (Percy Harvin and Cordarrelle Patterson), one was traded on draft day and became a Pro Bowler (Jack Snow), and one was a huge bust (Troy Williamson).

Then there is the curious case of Laquon Treadwell.

Most Vikings fans were thrilled when Treadwell was taken by Minnesota with the twenty-third pick in the 2016 NFL Draft. During his time at Ole Miss, Treadwell had set most of the school's single game receiving records and, had he returned to school for his senior year, likely would have owned most of the career-receiving records. Instead, he decided to forgo his senior year and enter the NFL Draft. Analyst Mike Mayock had Treadwell as the second-best receiver in the draft, behind Notre Dame's Will Fuller.

Despite his great college stats, it was Treadwell's pro day numbers that started to turn heads. But not in a good way. He decided not to run the forty-yard dash at the NFL Combine in Indianapolis to work on his time, but the six-foot-two, 217-pound receiver still had a relatively slow forty-yard dash time (4.63 seconds, which would have ranked twenty-eighth out of forty-three receivers at the combine). His vertical jump measurement was also disappointing (33.5 inches).

Treadwell was the fourth receiver taken in the draft behind Corey Coleman (pick 15 by Cleveland), Will Fuller (pick 21 by Houston), and Josh Doctson (pick 22 by Washington) and ahead of Pro Bowlers Michael Thomas (round 2, pick 41) and Tyreek Hill (round 5, pick 165).

Treadwell caught one pass his entire rookie season: a fifteen-yard pass from Sam Bradford against Detroit. In his second season, he caught 20 passes for two hundred yards. It wasn't until his third season that he caught his first touchdowns in a 29–29 tie against Green Bay.

Through his first three seasons, Treadwell had 56 catches (35 in 2018) for 517 yards and a touchdown while losing snaps to guys like Brandon Zylstra, Chad Beebe, and Aldrick Robinson and being a healthy scratch from multiple games. Treadwell was cut by the Vikings after training camp in 2019 after the Vikings declined to pick up his option.

Michael Thomas, who was taken by the New Orleans Saints' twenty-four picks after Treadwell, has 321 catches for 3,787 yards, 23 touchdowns, two Pro Bowl selections, and an All-NFL nod; and he signed a five-year $100 million contract.

August 30, 2016

Teddy Bridgewater Blows Out His Knee in Practice

I saw it all. I am not going to go into it. I don't have any words to describe it.
—Running back Jerick McKinnon

The 2015 NFC North Champion Minnesota Vikings had high expectations heading into 2016. Still recovering their heartbreaking loss to Seattle in the Wild Card round of the playoffs, the team had high hopes for Teddy Bridgewater, who was coming of his first career Pro Bowl season.

August 30, 2016, seemed like a normal day at Winter Park. Bridgewater was coming of an impressive showing in a 23–10 preseason win over San Diego in the first ever game in the brand-new US Bank Stadium and was going through the motions at practice as he prepared to take the final game of the preseason off.

But then, his career derailed.

As Bridgewater dropped back in a noncontact drill, his left knee buckled and snapped. Bridgewater went down, yelling in pain. Players within earshot of the snap were visibly upset. While Mike Zimmer updated the media and the state of Minnesota on Bridgewater's condition, an ambulance pulled onto the field to rush Bridgewater to the hospital.

All-Pro Safety Harrison Smith was covering a receiver downfield when the injury happened. He had his back to the play. He didn't see the injury happen, but he could gather from the reactions of his teammates that something was wrong.

"I thought he pulled a hammy," Smith said. "And then I heard the screaming."

An MRI revealed that he had a complete tear of his ACL and had suffered other structural damage, including a dislocation of the knee joint. Bridgewater was lucky that he didn't sever any arteries during the injury because he could have lost his leg, or even his life.

With Bridgewater's career in jeopardy, the Vikings had three options at quarterback: veteran Shawn Hill, rookie Joel Stave, or make personnel move to bring in somebody else.

The Vikings elected to trade a first-round pick and a conditional fourth to the Philadelphia Eagles for former first overall pick Sam Bradford.

After a week 1 start and win by Shawn Hill, Bradford took over in week 2—only fifteen days after being acquired by Minnesota. The Vikings were 5–1 at their Bye Week but would only win three of their next seven games to drop to 8–8 and miss the playoffs.

Bridgewater would not appear in an NFL game until week 15 in 2017. After months of rehab, Bridgewater attempted two passes in the Vikings 34–7 win against Cincinnati, a game at US Bank Stadium and a game where the Vikings would clinch the 2017 NFC North title.

He was released by the Vikings after the season and signed with the New York Jets, then he was traded to New Orleans before the 2018 season.

October 20, 2016

WNBA Finals versus LA Sparks—Game 5

It's not enough to just apologize and send out a memo that they got something wrong.
—Lynx head coach Cheryl Reeve

The Minnesota Lynx were the defending WNBA champions coming into the 2016 season. Led by Maya Moore, Lindsay Whalen, Seimone Augustus, Sylvia Fowles, and Rebekkah Brunson, the Lynx finished as the top seed in the playoffs with a 28–6 record and were looking for the franchise's fourth title, which would tie them with the Houston Comets for most in WNBA history.

The playoff format in the WNBA had changed in the off-season. Instead of taking the top four teams from each conference, the WNBA took the top 8 teams overall and seeded them for the tournament. With the new format, the LA Sparks (who were in the Western Conference with the Lynx) were the number 2 overall seed in the playoffs.

The first round of the playoffs is a single-elimination game with seeds 5 through 8 (number 8 Phoenix upset number 5 Indiana, and number 6 Atlanta beat number 7 Seattle in a pair of interconference playoff matchups). The second round is single elimination as well. Number 3 Chicago Sky dispatched Atlanta, and the Cinderella Mercury beat the best team from the Eastern Conference in number 3 New York.

That set up a best-of-five matchup in the semifinals between Phoenix and Minnesota and Los Angeles and Chicago. The Lynx made quick work of the Mercury, sweeping Diana Taurasi and Brittney Griner out of the postseason. LA beat Chicago in four games.

Two-time WNBA MVP Candace Parker, reigning MVP Nneka Ogwumike, and Kristi Toliver stunned the Target Center crowd in Game 1 with a 78–76 victory over the Lynx. Maya Moore responded in Game 2, scoring 21 points as Minnesota blew out the Sparks 79–60 to even the best-of-five series. A critical

Game 3 shifted to Los Angeles. Candace Parker led all scorers with 24 points in a 92–75 win, putting LA one win away from their first WNBA title in fourteen seasons.

Maya Moore stole the show in Game 4, staving off elimination with a 31-point performance and forcing a decisive Game 5 for the championship at the Target Center.

What happened the night of October 20, 2016, is a game many describe as one of the greatest games in WNBA history . . . unless you're a Lynx fan.

Minnesota led by six points at halftime, 34–28 with Ogwumike in foul trouble. Despite one of Moore's best game as a pro (23 points, 11 assists, 6 rebounds, 3 steals), the Lynx defense fell apart in the second half. With 2:16 left in the third quarter, Minnesota had a 53–47 lead. Parker and Chelsea Gray (11 straight points off the bench) fueled a ferocious Sparks comeback as they took a 71–63 lead with 3:06 left in the game. Minnesota responded with an 8–0 run, tying the game at 71–71.

The play that everybody was talking about the next morning happened with 1:12 left. With the game tied, Ogwumike hit a turnaround jumper to give the Sparks a lead. The issue was that the shot clock had expired before she got the shot off. The officials counted the basket.

The rule in the WNBA rulebook states, "The review will take place at the next clock stoppage, including immediately upon a successful basket when the clock stops in the last two minutes. If a 24-second shot clock violation is not reviewed in accordance with the foregoing timing rules, it may not be reviewed thereafter." The officials waved to indicate that they would look at the monitor to see if the basket was good, but ultimately decided not too even though the ball was still obviously in Ogwumike's hands a good second or two after the clock had expired.

"I don't get paid to enough to have to do somebody else's job too," Lynx coach Cheryl Reeves fumed after the game. "Just get the simple things right."

The shot by Ogwumike gave LA a two-point lead. The lead would change four times in the final 23.4 seconds.

The Lynx had taken a 76–75 lead with sixteen second left on a Maya Moore spin move that sent Alana Beard to the floor. With no time-outs left, the Sparks ran the ball down the court with the clock ticking down. Chelsea Gray's jumper was no good with six seconds. All the Lynx had to do was pull down one rebound, and a fourth WNBA championship in six years would be theirs.

Ogwumike got the offense rebound and put up a shot that was blocked by Fowles. Collecting her own rebound, she hit an off-balance shot falling out of the circle over the outstretched arms of Fowls to take a 77–76 lead with 3.1 seconds. Whalen got the inbound and heaved a half-court shot that clanked off the top of the backboard.

"I didn't breathe until the ball hit the backboard," said Finals MVP Candace Parker, who finished Game 5 with 28 points and 12 rebounds.

"It's a heartbreaking way to lose," said Maya Moore. "To be able to come back those last couple minutes to regain the lead, and we just weren't able to secure the rebound and get a stop. It's hard to have it come that close."

After the game, the league admitted their mistake in not reviewing Ogwumike's shot clock violation.

"It was reviewable at the time when she shot it," Reeves said. They didn't understand it was the end of the clock. They didn't hear the shot clock. When they put the ball in play, the play is no longer reviewable. It's unfortunate that we're even having this discussion."

The shot clock violation wasn't the only reason the Lynx lost the game. The Lynx outrebounded the Sparks in three of the first four games but gave up 14 offensive boards and 15 second-chance points in Game 5. They were also outscored in the paint 44–30.

But having those two LA points taken off the board with 1:12 left likely would have changed the outcome of the game.

The Lynx would matchup against the Sparks in the 2017 WNBA Finals, but this time they would win Game 5 for their fourth WNBA championship.

February 26, 2017
The Wild Trade for Martin Hanzel

Of all the guys with expiring contracts at forward, we felt he would have the biggest impact on any roster.
—Wild GM Chuck Fletcher

Minnesota Wild GM Chuck Fletcher made some good moves during his nine years as the head of the Wild: he found Mikael Granlund and Jason Zucker in the first two rounds of the 2010 NHL Draft, he dealt Cal Clutterbuck to the Islanders for Nino Niederreiter, he landed both free agents Zach Parise and Ryan Suter in one off-season, he traded a third-round pick to Arizona for All-Star goalie Devan Dubnyk, and he brought in a revitalized Eric Staal, who scored 70 goals in two seasons.

But Fletcher will always be remembered for the bad: sending a first and second to Buffalo for Jason Pominville then signing him to a five-year deal, losing Alex Tuch and Erik Haula to Las Vegas in the expansion draft (because they had to protect Pominville and his no-trade clause), signing Thomas Vanek, and he'll be blamed for the latter years of the thirteen-year contracts that Parise and Suter signed. But the thing he'll always be remembered for his bringing in duds as the team geared up for postseason runs.

In 2014, he sent two second-round picks to Buffalo for Cody McCormick (2 points in fourteen games) and Matt Moulson (13 points in twenty games). Both players re-signed with Buffalo after the season. He traded another second-round pick to Buffalo in 2015 for Chris Stewart (45 points in three seasons) and a third-round pick to Florida for seventeen games of Sean Bergenheim (1 goal, zero assists, −4).

But the midseason trade that stands out from the rest happened in the middle of what arguably could have been the best season in Wild history: 2017. On February 26, the Wild were in first place in the Western Conference as the trade deadline approached. The two big names rumored to be on the move were Tampa Bay goalie Ben Bishop and Colorado winger Jarome Iginla. The Wild were riding a red-hot Devan Dubnyk into the playoffs, and Fletcher wanted to add some scoring depth. When Fletcher couldn't make a deal with the Avs for the thirty-nine-year-old Iginla (who was later traded to the LA Kings), he turned his attention to Arizona Coyotes assistant captain Martin Hanzel. Hanzel was leading the Coyotes with 16 goals and had 26 points in fifty-one games and had 117 goals and 196 assists in his ten-year career.

Fletcher traded their 2017 first-round pick, their 2018 second-round pick, a conditional 2019 pick, and prospect Grayson Downing to Arizona for Martin Hanzal (who was in the final year of his contract), Ryan White, and a 2017 fourth-round pick.

The Wild would only earn 22 points over the final twenty-three games as they sputtered from the top overall seed in the Western Conference to second place in the division. Hanzal would only score four goals in twenty games and threw off the chemistry of the team in what has been deemed an unnecessary move by Fletcher.

The Wild would be eliminated in the first round by the St. Louis Blues. Hanzal walked away via free agency after the season, signing with the Dallas Stars. Ryan White was also released when his contract expired.

April 12, 2017

Mike Yeo's St. Louis Blues Eliminate the Wild

Usually you remember what you last saw so, unfortunately, we're going to remember getting knocked out in five games.
—Wild forward Zach Parise

General Manager Chuck Fletcher hired Mike Yeo as the head coach of the Minnesota Wild in 2011. Fletcher had just relieved former coach Todd Richards of his duties after failing to make the playoffs in his two seasons as coach.

The Wild started the season 15–7–3 but finished 35–36–11 during Yeo's first season and missed the playoffs for a fourth consecutive season, the longest stretch in franchise history. That off-season, the Wild made the highest-profile free agent signings in team history, inking Zach Parise and Ryan Suter to ten-year contracts.

In 2013–14, the Wild tallied 55 points a lockout-shortened season and made the playoffs as wild card team. They beat the Colorado Avalanche in seven games before losing to the Chicago Blackhawks in the quarterfinals.

They returned to the playoffs the following season with 98 points, their highest point total in six years, but they once again lost to the Blackhawks in the playoffs.

In 2014–15, the Wild recorded 100 points for just the second time in franchise history despite another slow start. The Wild were 18–19–5 before making a trade for journeyman goalie Devin Dubnyk and finished 46–28–8. They beat the St. Louis Blues in the first round before being bounced from the postseason by the Blackhawks for the third time in as many seasons.

With huge expectations in 2015–16, the Wild struggled. After dropping their eighth game in a row (thirteen of the last fourteen) and sitting in second to last place in the division, Fletcher fired Mike Yeo. Former Blackhawks coach John Torchetti was brought in to finish the season as head coach and try to spark some life into the team. The Wild responded by winning the next four games and finishing 15–11–1 under Torchetti to sneak into the playoffs. They lost to Dallas in the first round in six games.

Yeo wasn't out of work for long, however. After interviewing for positions with the Anaheim Ducks and Calgary Flames, he accepted a job as associate coach for on Ken Hitchcock's staff in St. Louis. Hitchcock was entering his final season as head coach and had endorsed Yeo to take his place as head coach when he was done. Yeo would spend a season working under Hitchcock before taking over in 2017–18.

He took over the Blues sooner than expected, however. Hitchcock was fired on February 1, 2017, after going 24–21–5 and losing five of the last six games. Yeo coach the Blues to a 5–1 win over Toronto in his first game on the bench and led the team to a scorching 22–8–2 record to secure a playoff spot with a total of 99 points.

His opponent in the playoffs? The Minnesota Wild.

Under new head coach Bruce Boudreau, the Wild had score a franchise-record 106 points and finished second in the Central Division (behind Chicago's 109).

The Wild led the Western Conference with 266 goals that season with a steady attack from Eric Staal (28), Mikael Granlund (26), Nino Niederreiter (25), and Jason Zucker (22).

Game 1 was played at the Xcel Energy Center. Vladimir Sobotka scored the first goal of the series at 6:21 in the first period to give St. Louis a 1–0 lead. The Wild would tie the game with twenty-two seconds left in regulation on a goal from Parise from Granlund and Koivu to knot it up at one goal apiece and send it to overtime. Yet despite firing fifty-two shots on Blues goalie Jake Allen, the Wild lost the game in overtime 2–1 when Joel Edmundson scored the game winner on Dubnyk at the 17:33 mark.

In Game 2, Edmundson picked up where he left off in Game 1, giving St. Louis a 1–0 lead early in the second period (Edmundson had three goals in sixty-nine regular season games that year). Parise tied the game for the second consecutive night with the Wild on a 5-on-3 advantage at the 17:44 mark in the second. But Blues winger Jaden Schwartz scored the game winner with 2:27 left in the third to give St. Louis another 2–1 win and a 2–0 series lead.

Game 3 shifted to the Scottrade Center in St. Louis, with Coach Bruce Boudreau looking for a spark on offense. The Wild peppered Allen with forty-one shots, but he saved forty of them as he held the conference's top offense to only one goal (Charlie Coyle) for the third consecutive game. Colton Parayko and Jaden Schwartz each scored for the Blues, with Alex Steen adding an empty netter at the end for a 3–1 final and a 3–0 series lead.

Facing elimination in Game 4, Devin Dubnyk kept the Wild alive by stopping all twenty-eight shots he faced. Coyle scored his second goal of the series at 16:50 in the first period to give the Wild their first lead of the series. Martin Hanzal would score in the second period to make it 2–0. Minnesota traveled back to St. Paul facing a 3–1 deficit in the series.

Blues All-Star Vladimir Tarasenko started the scoring in Game 5 with his first goal of the series at 7:16 of the first for a 1–0 Blues lead. Steen scored his second goal of the series at 10:31 to extend the lead to 2–0. Ryan Suter scored the Wild's first 5-on-4 power play goal of the series at 18:31 to make it 2–1 after two periods. Paul Stastny, who returned the Blues lineup after missing fourteen games with an injury, scored at 7:23 to create a two-goal deficit for the Wild.

Then, finally, the Wild's offense came alive. Wild captain Mikko Koivu scored with 9:22 left in the game, followed by a Jason Zucker goal four minutes later to tie the game at 3–3. In the closing minutes, Dubnyk made two huge saves: one on a wraparound attempt by Patrik Berglund, then the rebound attempt by David Perron to keep the game knotted at 3–3 and send it to overtime.

Game 5 went to overtime with the Wild needing a goal to stay alive in the series and needing to do it without their leading goal-scorer Eric Staal, who had left the game with a concussion after sliding into the boards in the second period. With just under ten minutes left, Devin Dubnyk turned the puck over behind the Wild net. Vladimir Sobotka centered the puck for Magnus Paajarvi (scored eight regular-season goals). He put the puck in the back of the net for the series-winning goal.

"Our goal is to advance in the playoffs, and obviously it's a little bit of irony in it, that I'm facing my former team," Mike Yeo told NHL.com after the game. "But our goal was to advance in the playoffs and for our group to continue to grow and have a chance to keep competing for a Stanley Cup, and that's what we have right now."

The Wild, who averaged just over three goals a game during the regular season, scored eight in the five-game series.

On the other side of the bracket, the Wild playoff-nemesis Chicago Blackhawks had been swept by the Nashville Predators. A Wild series win would have meant they wouldn't have had to face Chicago in the next round.

Mike Yeo and the Blues would miss the playoffs by one point (94 to Colorado's 95) the following season. After a 7–9–3 start in 2018, he was fired. Yeo was 73–49–11 with the Blues.

June 19, 2017

Chuck Fletcher and the 2017 NHL Expansion Draft

We knew were would be forced to lose quality talent. That doesn't make this any easier.
—Chuck Fletcher

In 2017, the NHL was expanding from thirty to thirty-one teams with the addition of the Las Vegas Golden Knights. It was the NHL's first expansion since 2000 when the Columbus Blue Jackets and Minnesota Wild entered the league.

With an expansion franchise comes an expansion draft and one player being plucked from every roster in the league. Minnesota lost two.

In the 2000 expansion draft, the twenty-eight NHL teams could protect nine forwards, five defensemen, and one goalie or two goalies, three defensemen, and seven forwards. But in this expansion draft, teams were only allowed to protect seven forwards, three defensemen, one goaltender or one goaltender, and eight skaters regardless of position.

Teams had to expose at least two forwards and one defenseman that had played at least forty games in 2016–17 or more than seventy games in 2015–16 and 2016–17 combined. Teams were also required to protect players with no-move clauses in their contracts.

The Wild were in a tough spot. It had to protect Jason Pominville (who had an NMC). One of the players that was left unprotected was Eric Stall (who scored 42 goals for the Wild in 2017–18). The Wild also had an outstanding core of young talent (Matt Dumba, Charlie Coyle, Jonas Brodin, Mikael Granlund, and Las Vegas native Jason Zucker).

After months of speculation, the Wild protected Pominville, Brodin, Coyle, Zucker, Granlund, Mikko Koivu, Zach Parise, Ryan Suter, Devan Dubnyk, and Nino Niederreiter.

This left players like Dumba, Eric Staal, Marco Scandella, Darcy Kuemper, and Erik Haula exposed. Wild fans were nervous that Dumba would be the one selected. He was a first-round pick by the Wild in 2012 and was regarded as one of the best young defensemen in the game. George McPhee was willing to pass over Dumba for a forward if they got a prospect in return.

The player McPhee liked was Haula, who had spent most of the previous season on Minnesota's fourth line. Haula, a seventh-round pick in the 2009 draft out of the University of Minnesota, was coming off a season in which he scored a career-high 15 goals for the Wild, while averaging just under fourteen minutes a game.

While McPhee was concentrating on building a franchise, Wild GM Chuck Fletcher was trying to protect his. He knew that logically, one of his young defensemen would likely be taken. But he wanted to try and trade one of them for some forward help while trying to clear some salary cap space.

Fletcher accomplished each of those things. After Las Vegas eventually passed on a Wild defenseman, Fletcher traded Marco Scandella and Jason Pominville (and his salary) to Buffalo for forwards Marcus Foligno and Tyler Ennis (both of whom were protected by the Sabres).

For Vegas, the one piece left in the puzzle was the prospect the Wild would send them to not take Dumba or Scandella. Three names were at the top of their list: Jordan Greenway, Kirill Kaprizov, and Alex Tuch.

Minnesota send 2014 first-round pick Tuch to complete the deal.

Tuch played in his first full NHL season for the Golden Knights and scored 15 goals. Haula went on to score 29 in seventy-nine games, nearly doubling his 2016-–7 total. It's worth noting Foligno and Ennis combined for 16.

Chuck Fletcher got inside his own head on this one. Not only did he give up two players to protect one but he also didn't realize what he had in Erik Haula. Why wasn't Haula putting up near-30 goal seasons with the Wild? The previous season, Fletcher decided he had to trade three draft picks (including a first) for Martin Hanzel and Ryan White. Then Bruce Boudreau gave Hanzel more ice time than Haula.

The Wild had Haula and wasted him, then they willingly gave him away plus another pretty good forward to boot. To put more salt in the wound, Haula, Tuch, and the Las Vegas Knights became the first expansion team to win their division and reach the Stanley Cup Finals.

The Wild's postseason struggles continued as they lost in the first round of the playoffs for the third consecutive year.

June 22, 2017

The Timberwolves Trade for Jimmy Butler

You [bleeping] need me! You can't win without me!

—Jimmy Butler

Tom Thibodeau loves "his" guys. While Thibs was the president of basketball operations and head coach of the Wolves from 2016 to 2019, he signed several former players from his days with the Chicago Bulls: Derrek Rose, Luol Deng, Taj Gibson, John Lucas III, and Aaron Brooks. But the biggest addition from his former team came on Draft Night 2017.

The Wolves won thirty-one games in 2015–16, and despite finishing in last place in the Northwest Division, they were trending up. Karl-Anthony Towns, Andrew Wiggins, Zach LaVine, and Ricky Rubio had formed a strong nucleus for the "TimberPups" that had fans excited for the future.

Their excitement escalated when Thibs made arguably the biggest trade acquisition in team history, sending LaVine, Kris Dunn, and the seventh overall pick to the Bulls for All-Star Jimmy Butler and the sixteenth pick. Wolves fans and media thought they had robbed Chicago blind. LaVine was coming off a torn ACL, and Dunn had a pretty disappointing rookie season. After the Butler trade, Thibodeau traded Ricky Rubio to Utah for guard Jeff Teague.

Butler has two more years on his contract, so he is guaranteed to play at least two seasons in Minnesota.

Butler had played for Coach Thibs for four seasons, transforming from a relatively unknown player from Marquette to a gritty defender and tough scorer that the Wolves needed meshed in with their young core. Butler averaged career highs in points (23.9), rebounds (6.2), and assists (5.5) in 2016 and his All-NBA Defensive Team picks were needed on a team that finished twenty-sixth in the NBA in defensive efficiency.

But along with Butler came some baggage. After Thibodeau was fired by the Bulls in 2015, Butler openly criticized new coach (and former Timberwolves guard) Fred Hoiberg's laid-back coaching style.

"I know Fred is a laid-back guy, and I really respect him for that," Butler said in 2015. "But when guys aren't doing what they're supposed to do, you have to get on guys."

Two years later, Butler was criticizing his Bulls teammates, wanting to "play with guys who care." Six months later, he was traded to Minnesota to reunite with Thibodeau.

The Wolves started 36–25 and were battling for home court advantage in the playoffs at the end of February. But things weren't as great behind the scenes with Butler and the Wolves as it seemed. On a flight to New Orleans to face the Pelicans on February 3, Butler called out his teammates on the plane and challenged them to raise their effort, work ethic, and defensive approach.

On February 23, he suffered a noncontact knee injury against the Houston Rockets that was initially thought to be a torn ACL. After further tests, it was determined it was only a tear in his meniscus. He underwent surgery and was ruled out indefinitely. In fifty-six games, he was averaging 22.2 points, 5.4 rebounds, and 5.0 assists.

Without Butler, the Wolves finished the season 8–9 and went from battling for home court advantage to fighting for a playoff spot. Butler was able to return for the final three games of the season against the LA Lakers, Memphis Grizzlies, and Denver Nuggets. Needing to win all three games to get into the playoffs for the first time since 2003–04, Butler averaged 29.1 minutes per game and 21.3 points per game, including the go-ahead basket in an overtime win against Denver to clinch the eighth seed in the Western Conference on the final day of the season.

But making the playoffs didn't cure all ills within the Wolves locker room. The Wolves drew the number 1 seeded Houston Rockets in the first round of the playoffs and were eliminated in five games. Before the Wolves were eliminated in Game 5, Butler again called out his teammates in a story in the *Chicago Sun-Times*.

"I put so much into this game, and I only play to win," he said. "I don't play for individual stats or accolades. And at times I get lost in how everybody is not built the way that I'm built. Sometimes I just look around, and I don't understand how or why you all don't love to get better the way I do."

After the 122–104 loss, Minnesota flew back from Houston for exit interview and medical exams... without Butler. Instead, he flew to Los Angeles and refused to take the exam. He didn't participate in team activities during the off-season, instead electing to work out in Los Angeles and Europe. More reports, through the *Chicago Sun-Times*, say that Butler was "fed up with the nonchalant attitude of his younger teammates, specifically Towns" and that he planned to become a free agent after the 2018–19 season. Thibs tried to talk him off the ledge and offered him a four-year $110 maximum contract extension. But Butler declined.

If Butler waited until the following summer, he could sign a five-year $188 million contract with the Wolves or a four-year $139 million contract with another team.

Butler stayed away from Minnesota the entire summer, but not out of the headlines. On September 19, less than a month before the start of the regular season, Butler officially requested a trade from the Timberwolves and said his preferred destinations were the New York Knicks, Brooklyn Nets, and Los Angeles Clippers. It wasn't the first time Butler had told management that he wanted to be traded. After the Houston series, Butler had talked with Thibodeau about his desire to play somewhere else and didn't want to commit to the Wolves long-term because he was frustrated with the nonchalant attitudes of Towns and Wiggins.

While Thibs reiterated his stance that Butler wouldn't be traded, Wolves owner Glen Taylor told owners that he was open to trading Butler and to deal with him directly if they got pushback from Thibodeau or Wolves GM Scott Layden.

Butler stayed in LA for the entire preseason with his status with the Wolves up in the air. With seven days left before the start of the 2018–19 season, there was still no deal for Butler. He returned to Minneapolis and Wolves practice on October 10.

What ensued was a media firestorm. Butler suited up with the third-string team and let them to a scrimmage win over the starters. He was yelling at teammates, coaches, and Layden. He turned to Layden during practice and yelled, "You [bleeping] need me! You can't win without me!"

"Jimmy's back," tweeted Adrian Wojnarowski after the practice. Butler agreed to a sit-down interview with ESPN's Rachel Nichols after the practice and stressed that just because he was back in Minnesota didn't mean his issues with the team and management had been resolved.

The next day, the Wolves canceled practice and media access to the team. Butler called a players-only meeting to clear the air. He reportedly told them that as long as he was on the team, he would show up and compete with his teammates, and he aired some of his grievances about management.

Against all odds, Butler was in the starting lineup for the Wolves on October 17 against the San Antonio Spurs. He scored 23 points and had 4 steals in a 112–108 loss. Then he scored 33 points in a win over Cleveland.

But the rifts continued. Butler sat out the third game of the season with what was called precautionary rest. Butler didn't travel with the team to Dallas. The Wolves lost to Dallas 140–136 as fans got a glimpse of what the team would look like without Butler. Derrek Rose scored 28 points and rookie Josh Okogie started in Butler's spot, scoring 6 points and grabbing 5 rebounds in twenty-eight minutes of action.

Butler met with Taylor to reach a mutual agreement while Butler was still with the team. "He will be a regular team player," Taylor told reporters. "What I said to him in the meantime is, Scott Layden will be talking to other teams to see if there is a trade that works."

"They want me to go out here and hoop to the best of my abilities," Butler said. "Make sure I'm healthy, compete, because that's what I love to do, and do it for the guys in the same jerseys as me."

Butler would miss four more games over the next month due to precautionary rest as the Wolves continued to search for a suitable trade offer. It was reported that they were nearing a deal with the Miami Heat, but trade talks fell through. Near the middle of November, the Wolves were 4–9 and had lost five straight games. Butler played in ten of those games, averaged 21.3 points and 5 rebounds per game in thirty-six minutes.

During the five-game losing streak, Thibodeau decided it was time to cut his losses. "This team can no longer function while Butler is a part of it," he told NBA.com. On November 10, Butler was traded to the Philadelphia 76ers for Robert Covington, Dario Saric, Jerryd Bayless, and a second-round pick. The Jimmy Butler era was over.

It seemed like a no-brainer risk to take for Philadelphia. Butler was added to a young core of Joel Embiid and Ben Simmons in a weak Eastern Conference as the Sixers (on paper) became instant NBA Championship contenders. While Butler didn't sign a contract extension right away with Philly, the desire by both teams was there to get something figured out after the season.

But Butler found new conflicts with his 76ers teammates and coaches. He publicly questioned Sixers coach Brett Brown's offensive system and his role in it. Embiid saw his touches and offensive production go down once Butler joined the team, and he didn't like it.

"He's a young player killer," said an anonymous Eastern Conference executive of Butler. "This too shall pass. He'll follow the money."

"You don't just click your heels and throw Jimmy Butler in and everybody's going to be playing the same way and style," Brown said. "It doesn't work like that. My job is to grow a team."

Butler averaged 18.2 points per game in fifty-five games with Philadelphia, including two games against Towns and the Timberwolves. The Sixers beat the Wolves both times. Butler led his new team to a 51–31 record, which was good for the third seed in the East behind the Milwaukee Bucks (60–22) and Toronto Raptors (58–24).

After beating the Brooklyn Nets in the opening round of the playoffs, the Sixers lost to the eventual champion Toronto Raptors on a Kawai Leonard game-winning three at the buzzer on Game 7.

The Wolves finished in last place in the division again with a 36–46 record.

After the season, Butler declined his player option and became a free agent. He signed with the Miami Heat.

Meanwhile, the trade with Chicago became tilting more and more in the Bulls' favor. Zach LaVine came back in a big way from his knee injury and scored 23 points per game in his first full season back. After scoring 3.8 points per game in his rookie season, Dunn averaged 13.4 in his first season in Chicago. The seventh overall pick became Finnish sharpshooter Lauri Markkanen (AKA the Finnisher), who was named to the All-Rookie Team and has averaged 16.7 points per game in his first two NBA seasons.

<<BONUS ACHE>>

The NBA Playoffs versus Houston

The Timberwolves made the playoffs for the first time in fourteen seasons with a 47–35 record. The addition of Jimmy Butler on draft night plus singing Taj Gibson, Jamal Crawford, Jeff Teague, and the late-addition of Derrek Rose made the Wolves an instant playoff contender alongside Karl-Anthony Towns and Andrew Wiggins. The Wolves were 36–25 and well on their way to a top 4 seed and home court advantage in the NBA Playoffs before Butler hurt his knee against the Houston Rockets in the first game after the All-Star Break. He underwent meniscus surgery and was thought to be done for the season. The Wolves went 8–9 without Butler and were in a fight with Denver for the final playoff spot in the West. Butler returned on April 6 as the Wolves won the final three games of the season, including what was basically a one-game playoff with Denver on the final day of the regular season.

The Wolves were pitted against James Harden, Chris Paul, and the Houston Rockets in the first round of the playoffs. The Wolves had a chance to steal Game 1 from Houston with Jimmy Butler missing the game-tying shot in a 104–101 loss. KAT only had eight points in his playoff debut. Houston blew out the Wolves 102–82 in Game 2, scoring 37 points in the second quarter alone. Again, Towns was nowhere to be found, scoring only five points. The Wolves played their first home playoff game since 2004 in Game 3. Butler scored 28 points, and Rose added 17 off the bench in a 121–105 win. Towns had 18 points in the win.

In Game 4, Harden poured in 36 points in a 119–110 Houston win. Towns had his best playoff game with 22 points and 15 rebounds in the loss. Game 5 shifted back to Houston with the Wolves on the brink of elimination, with the Rockets winning 122–104.

The Houston series was the beginning of the end for Jimmy Butler in Minnesota, and he requested a trade from the organization in the days after the Game 5 loss.

October 3, 2017

Twins at New York Yankees: the Wild Card Game

It's heartbreaking.
—Twins center fielder Byron Buxton

In 2016, the Twins lost a franchise-record 103 games in Paul Molitor's second year as manager. In 2017, they had completed one of the greatest turnarounds in MLB history, improving to 85–77, winning Molitor the AL Manager of the Year award, and advancing to the postseason as the American League's second wild card team.

With the Twins' turnaround came breakout years from a lot of their young players like pitcher José Berríos (14–18, 3.89 ERA), closer Brandon Kintzler (2.78 ERA, 28 saves), Miguel Sano (28 HR, 77 RBI), outfielders Eddie Rosario (.290, 27 HR, 78 RBI) and Max Kepler (19 HR, 69 RBI), and shortstop Jorge Polanco (74 RBI). Second baseman Brian Dozier followed up his record-setting 42 home run season with 34 more and scored 106 runs. First baseman Joe Mauer put up his best numbers since 2013, and free-agent acquisition Ervin Santana won sixteen games. Byron Buxton, who was batting .214 at the All-Star Break, had one of the best second halves in baseball, batting .300 with 11 HR and 40 runs scored in the last fifty-seven games. He also finished eighteenth in AL MVP voting and won a Gold Glove.

Their opponent in the winner-take-all wild card game was the New York Yankees. At this point in Twins history, their struggles against the Yankees were well-documented: a 30–76 record since 2002 and a 2–12 record in the playoffs.

The 2017 Yankees were 91–71 and featured young core of stars with catcher Gary Sanchez (33 HR, 90 RBI), Rookie of the Year outfielder Aaron Judge (52 HR, 114 RBI), and pitcher Luis Severino (14–6, 2.98 ERA).

The Twins were 2–4 against the Yankees that season, getting swept at Yankee Stadium and winning a home series against the Bombers for the first time since 2005 (they split a four-game series in 2008).

As the low seed, the Twins traveled to Yankee Stadium. The Twins sent All-Star Ervin Santana to the mound in the winner-take-all game, while the Yankees countered with Luis Severino, who finished third in the AL Cy Young voting.

The Twins got off to a hot start in the top of the first. Brian Dozier hit a leadoff home run to open the game. After Joe Mauer hit a foul pop fly, Jorge Polanco drew a full-count walk, then Eddie Rosario hit a two-run shot to make it 3–0. Severino gave up a single to Eduardo Escobar and a double to Max Kepler before being pulled, having recorded only one out in the ball game.

Reliever Chad Green (5–0, 1.83 ERA) relieved Severino with two runners in scoring position and only one out. He struck out Byron Buxton and Jason Castro to end the inning.

Santana took the mound in the bottom of the first with a 3–0 lead, but it didn't last long. After issuing a leadoff walk to Brett Gardner, Aaron Judge singled to move Gardner to third. Gary Sanchez hit a foul fly ball, then Didi Gregorius tied the game with a three-run home run.

Green came back out to pitch the second inning for the Yankees, who would need to rely heavily on their bullpen now that Severino was out of the game. Green, David Robertson, Tommy Kahnle, and Aroldis Chapman would combine for 8.2 innings, 13 strikeouts, and only one run the rest of the game. The only Twins run came on a threat in the third with a Byron Buxton RBI ground out with the bases loaded.

After giving up a solo home run to Brett Gardner in the second inning (4–3 Yankees), Molitor pulled Santana in favor of Berríos. Santana's final stat line, after being spotted a 3–0 lead, two innings pitched, four earned runs (all on home runs), and zero strikeouts.

Berríos wouldn't fare much better, giving up an RBI single to Greg Bird in the third and a two-run home run to Judge in the fourth to make it 7–3 Yankees. They added one more run on an Aaron Hicks bases-loaded walk in the bottom of the seventh to extend the lead to 8–4.

Leading by four runs in the top of the ninth, fireballer Aroldis Chapman struck out the side to end the game and send the Yankees to the American League Division Series.

The Twins lost their ninth straight postseason game to the Yankees to fall to 2–13 all-time. The Yankees upset the defending American League champion Cleveland Indians in the five-game ALDS (3–2) before losing Game 7 to the eventual World Series champion Houston Astros in the Championship Series.

January 21, 2018

The NFC Championship Game versus Philadelphia

It's not going to be very much fun watching them come to Minnesota and play in our stadium for a Super Bowl we feel like we should be in.

—Kyle Rudolph

The 2017 Minnesota Vikings season was full of ups and downs. They had missed the playoffs the year before after starting 5–0 and had traded their first-round pick to Philadelphia (the Eagles drafted Derek Barnett) for Sam Bradford after Teddy Bridgewater went down with a knee injury during a noncontact drill in practice in August 2016. With Bridgewater still rehabbing, the Vikings offense was once again Bradford's. With the offensive line being a major concern in the off-season, the Vikings added Riley Reiff (five years, $58 million), Mike Remmers (five years, $30 million), and drafted center Pat Elflein in the third round to help protect Bradford.

But after a shredding the New Orleans Saints defense for 346 yards and 3 touchdowns, he was inactive for all but one game the rest of the season after reinjuring his left knee—a knee that he had two previous ACL surgeries.

Case Keenum, who was signed in the off-season, stepped in at quarterback. In week 4 against Detroit, rookie phenom Dalvin Cook (who had 288 rushing yards on 61 carries and 10 catches for eighty-two yards coming into the game) tore his ACL on a noncontact play and was lost for the season.

But the Vikings' defense (ranked first, only allowing 15.1 points per game) carried the team. Despite losing their starting quarterback and running back for the season, the Vikings finished the regular season 13–3. The Vikings had five Pro Bowlers on defense (Anthony Barr, Everson Griffen, Linval Joseph, Xavier Rhodes, and Harrison Smith), while undrafted free agent Adam Thielen emerged to make his first Pro Bowl (91 catches for 1,276 and 4 touchdowns); and Kyle Rudolph was named to his second Pro Bowl.

The Vikings earned the number 2 seed in the playoffs, behind the 13–3 Philadelphia Eagles, which gave them a first-round bye. The Super Bowl was to be held at US Bank Stadium that season, and Vikings fans felt it would be destiny to win the first Super Bowl in franchise history in their own stadium—a feat no NFL team had ever accomplished.

The Vikings' road to Super Bowl XLII began with a week 1 rematch against the New Orleans Saints at US Bank Stadium. Sam Bradford was now healthy enough to start, but Zimmer went with the hot hand in Case Keenum. Led by the rushing attack of Jerick McKinnon and Latavius Murray, the Vikings led 17–0 at halftime. But the Saints outscored the Vikings 21–3 in the second half and took a 24–23 lead with twenty-five seconds left the game after Saints kicker Wil Lutz hit a forty-three-yard field goal.

The Vikings began their final drive on the twenty-yard line, which began with a five-yard false start penalty on Remmers. Keenum completed a pass to Stephon Diggs for nineteen yards and a first down. After two incomplete passes, the Vikings faced third down on their own thirty-nine-yard line with ten seconds left. They needed a miracle. Kicker Kai Forbath had connected from fifty-three yards earlier in the game, and the Vikings needed a play to get them to the New Orleans thirty-five-yard line to give them a chance. They needed a twenty-six-yard play.

They got the full sixty-one. Keenum threw a sideline pass to Diggs, who was freed up when Saints defensive back Marcus Williams whiffed on the tackle. Diggs took off down the sidelines for the improbable touchdown as time expired. The Vikings won 29–24 and headed to Philadelphia for their first NFC Championship Game since the 2009 season.

"I saw the play one time," Diggs said after the historic touchdown. "This is all great, but we have to move on to Philadelphia. We're done talking about that one particular play."

The Eagles were a well-balanced team, finishing in the top 10 in total offense and total defense. Philadelphia had dealt with their injuries too, namely their Pro Bowl quarterback Carson Wentz, who tore his ACL in week 14 against the Los Angeles Rams. Now led by journeyman Nick Foles, the Eagles were 8–1 at Lincoln Financial Field, including their 15–10 playoff win against the Atlanta Falcons the week before.

But the Vikings were one of the NFL's best road teams, boasting a 6–2 record. Before the game, Mike Zimmer said he knew they could expect one thing from the Eagles fans.

"I think it will be very, very loud," Zimmer said. "They're a very loud crowd. They love their Eagles. But we've played in some loud environments, and I expect us to go in there and play good. Obviously, we'd like to play in front of our fans, but if you told us at the beginning of the year that we could play in the NFC Championship Game, we would say, 'Let's go. Wherever you want us to go, we'll go.'"

The Vikings were three-point favorites in the game and were looking to break their five-game NFC Championship losing streak (with losses in 1977, 1987, 1998, 2000, and 2009). Their defense was facing a backup quarterback who hadn't thrown for three hundred yards in a game since 2014 (the Vikings only allowed three hundred passing yards once that season) and were one game away from bringing it home, which had become the team's mantra.

The Vikings scored on their opening drive—a twenty-five-yard touchdown pass from Keenum to tight end Kyle Rudolph. Kai Forbath's extra point gave the Viking a 7–0 lead with 10:14 left in the first quarter. There weren't many things that went right for the Vikings after that.

After forcing a Philadelphia punt, the Vikings got the ball back. The Vikings were driving at midfield, when Keenum threw a pick-six to Patrick Robinson, intended for Adam Thielen.

Thielen was one of eight Vikings who had played 1,000+ snaps that season and was playing with a fractured back that he suffered in the New Orleans game. From the get-go, the Eagles were physical with Thielen. Michael Jenkins gave him a late push to the ground after the game's first play, which was a run by Latavius Murray. Thielen was hit after the whistle multiple times, prompting retaliation from Diggs and Laquon Treadwell, who needed to be separated from Eagles players.

"That's playoff football," Thielen shrugged after the game. He caught three of nine targets for twenty-nine yards.

The Vikings went three-and-out on their next drive, and Philly drove seventy-five yards for another touchdown; there was an eleven-yard LaGarrette Blount run that carried Andrew Sendejo into the end zone.

It was 14–7, Philadelphia.

Two drives later, the Vikings' offense was knocking on the door to tie the game. With the ball on the sixteen-yard line, Derek Barnett (whom the Eagles selected in the draft with the Sam Bradford pick) beat David Morgan on the outside and sacked Case Keenum. Keenum fumbled, and it was recovered by Philadelphia on their own twenty-four-yard line.

A fifty-three-yard Nick Foles touchdown pass to Alshon Jeffery extend the Eagles lead to 21–7. Jake Elliot would kick a thirty-eight-yard field goal as the first half expired, and the Eagles took a 24–7 lead into the locker room.

The second half didn't start much better. Andrew Sendejo went down with a calf injury and was replaced by Anthony Harris at halftime. Foles took advantage with a forty-one-yard touchdown to Torrey Smith on the Eagles' first drive of the second half extended the lead to 31–7. Pat Elflein went down with an ankle injury (which required off-season surgery) and was mocked by Eagles fans as he was carted off the field in the third quarter, doing the SKOL chant and clap, but replacing the word *skol* with *Foles*.

Foles beat Harris again with a forty-two-yard completion to Nelson Agholor in the final minutes of the third quarter, which set up another Eagles touchdown: a five-yard touchdown pass to Alshon Jeffery.

The Vikings had one more good drive midway through the fourth quarter, driving seventy-five yards down to the Philadelphia. But Keenum threw another interception that was intended for Thielen, this time to Corey Graham.

When it was mercifully over, the scoreboard read Eagles 37, Vikings 7; and it sent the Eagles to their first Super Bowl since 2004. After leading 17–0 at halftime of the Saints playoff game, the Vikings' number 1 defense had been outscored 62–19 over the next six quarters. Nick Foles threw for 353 yards, three touchdowns, and was only sacked once (by Danielle Hunter). His 141.4 QB rating was a career high.

Tight end Zach Ertz was targeted by Foles eight times, and he finished the game with eight receptions for ninety-three yards, including a thirty-six-yard completion that set up Jake Elliot's lone field goal attempt of the game.

"We played like trash," a disappointed Xavier Rhodes said after the game.

The Vikings became the first team in NFL history to lose two conference titles by 30 points of more.

Eagles fans took to the streets and partied hard; so hard that the NFL investigated conduct of Eagles fans toward Vikings fans: full beer cans thrown at fans and vehicles, verbal assault, rape threats. As a way of apologizing, some Eagles fans donated to Mike Zimmer's foundation—$11,000 in donations sent with "heartfelt apologies."

While it was a nice gesture, it didn't negate the fact the Vikings had lost their sixth consecutive NFC Championship Game in heartbreaking fashion. To make matters worse, two weeks later, the Eagles celebrated their first ever Super Bowl victory in the streets of Minneapolis after upsetting Tom Brady and the New England Patriots 41–33. Super Bowl MVP Nick Foles threw for 373 yards, three touchdowns, and even caught a touchdown in the game.

March 17, 2018

Gopher Men's Hockey Misses the 2018 Postseason

We have a hockey program that should be competing for championships each year.
—Minnesota AD Mark Coyle

Minnesota is the state of hockey. The state high school hockey championship attendance dwarfs that of NHL teams. There are five DI hockey programs in the state with easily the most talent. But sometimes, things don't line up the way they should.

The 2017–18 Minnesota Gophers men's hockey team was a shoo-in to make the NCAA tournament. In the middle of February, the team was ranked number 8 in the country after beating and tying Ohio State and were on a 6–1–1 stretch. The Gophers lost their last two regular season games to Penn State and then drew the Nittany Lions again to open the Big Ten Tournament.

The Nittany Lions won the three-game series 2–0, ending the Gophers' chances at an automatic NCAA tournament bid. The Gophers were outscored 21–11 in the four games.

The Gophers were now scoreboard watchers. After North Dakota beat Minnesota Duluth (the 2018 NCAA Men's Hockey champion), the Gophers were up to number 12 in the rankings—the final spot for at-large bid.

There were six conference tournament games left to determine the majority of the twelve at-large teams for the tournament. Minnesota needed one of these teams to win to make the field: Providence (Hockey East), Clarkson (ECAC), Robert Morris (Atlantic Hockey), Northern Michigan (WCHA), St. Cloud State (NCHC), and Ohio State (Big Ten).

Just one of those team winning any of their respective championships would have put the Gophers in the top 12.

Here are the scores from those conference championship games:

Hockey East
>Providence—0
>Boston College—2

ECAC
>Clarkson—1
>Princeton—2 F/OT (Clarkson tied the game with seven seconds left in regulation.)

Atlantic Hockey
>Robert Morris—1
>Air Force—5

WCHA
>Michigan Tech—2
>Northern Michigan—0

NCHC
>St. Cloud State—1
>Denver—4

Big Ten
>Ohio State—2
>Notre Dame—3 F/OT

All six teams lost. The last result to come in, an OT winner by Notre Dame's Cam Mortenson 9:23 into the extra period, gave Notre Dame an automatic berth into the tournament and ended the dreams of the Gophers. The final PairWise rankings for the 2018 NCAA Men's Hockey Tournament are the following:

1. St. Cloud State
2. Notre Dame
3. Denver
4. Cornell
5. Ohio State
6. MSU–Mankato
7. Providence
8. Northeaster
9. Clarkson
10. Michigan
11. Minnesota Duluth
12. Penn State
13. Boston University

14. North Dakota (did not make tournament)
15. Minnesota (did not make tournament)

The teams that did not crack the top 20 were the following:
Air Force (automatic bid)
Michigan Tech (automatic bid)
Gopher Head Coach Don Lucia stepped following the season after nineteen years as head coach. Lucia had coached the Gophers to NCAA championships in 2002 and 2003 but hadn't won an NCAA tournament game the previous four seasons.

June 22, 2018

Tony Sparano Passes Away

He was a grumpy little Italian guy who was very, very good at his job.
—Vikings head coach Mike Zimmer

Expectations were high for the 2018 Minnesota Vikings. The season after a thirteen-win campaign and an NFC Championship Game appearance, the Vikings were ready to take the next step.

Coach Tony Sparano had a huge hand in the success of 2017. He first broke into the NFL in 1999 as their offensive quality control coach after coaching at University of New Haven and Boston College from 1984 to 1998. He was promoted to offensive line coach in 2000 before being let go in the Chris Palmer/Butch Davis coaching change following the 2000 season.

After short stints as tight ends coach for the Washington Redskins (2001) and Jacksonville Jaguars (2002), he was hired by the Dallas Cowboys to coach their tight ends. He worked his way up the coaching ladder in Dallas, eventually being promoted to offensive line and assistant head coach under Wade Phillips.

In 2008, he accepted the head coach position from the 1–15 Miami Dolphins. During his first year, he won the AFC East with an 11–5 record—the only year between 2003 and 2018 that the New England Patriots didn't win the division.

Sparano was 29–32 as head coach of the Dolphins before he was fired in 2011. He was the offensive coordinator for the New York Jets in 2012, then the assistant head coach and offensive line coach for the Oakland Raiders from 2013 to 2014. Four games into the 2014 season, he was promoted to interim head coach of the Raiders after the team moved on from Dennis Allen. After finishing 3–9, he was not retained as head coach. After a year as the tight ends coach for the San Francisco 49ers, he joined Mike Zimmer's staff as the Vikings' offensive line coach.

Sparano coached o-line for the Vikings from 2016 to 2017 and helped the Vikings survive the loss of running back Dalvin Cook to a torn ACL in week 4 in 2017. Despite losing the electric rookie from Florida State, the Vikings rode Jerick McKinnon and Latavius Murray to a rushing attack that ranked seventh in the NFL. Vikings quarterbacks were only sacked on 4.9 percent of passing attempts, which was eighth best in the NFL.

But Vikings players, coaches, and fans were stunned on the morning of Sunday July 22, 2018. Only two days before the team reported to their new training facility in Eagan for training camp, news broke that Tony Sparano had passed away from a heart attack at his home in Eden Prairie. He was fifty-six years old.

In a season-ending press conference on January 3 after finishing the season 8–8, Zimmer says the team never really recovered from the loss of Sparano. "Quite honestly, the death of Tony Sparano really kind of threw things into a little bit of a downward spiral," Zimmer said, "only because of the fact this guy was a type-A personality, he was very innovative in the running game and had a strong voice in that room and a strong voice with me. Yeah, I do feel like we lost a bit of our identity. We're going to get that back."

Without Sparano, the offensive line struggled. Zimmer promoted Andrew Janocko and Clancy Barone to co-offensive line coaches. The Vikings seventh-ranked rushing attack from 2017 plummeted to thirtieth in 2018. New quarterback Kirk Cousins was sacked on 6.1 percent of his drop backs, which tied for eleventh.

September 16, 2018

Vikings at Green Bay Packers— Daniel Carlson Misses

He missed again, and he missed it right. Daniel Carlson missed three field goals today.
—Paul Allen on the Vikings Radio Network

September 16, 2018 was the 116th meeting between the Minnesota Vikings and the Green Bay Packers. Both teams entered the Week 2 match up 1–0. The Vikings had beaten the San Francisco 49ers 24–16 at US Bank Stadium the week before. Meanwhile, Aaron Rodgers and the Packers stunned the Chicago Bears, overcoming a 20–0 deficit to win 24–23.

The good news for Vikings fans coming into the game was that Rodgers sprained his MCL in the Bears game and was questionable the entire week leading up to the game. Rodgers did start the game, and a lot of analysts assumed the injury would affect his mobility, leaving him a sitting duck for Everson Griffin, Linval Joseph, and company.

Rodgers was good, but not Aaron Rodgers good. He did finish with 281 yards passing and a touchdown. But the Packers built their lead around their special teams: a blocked punt touchdown and two Mason Crosby field goals gave Green Bay a 20–7 lead at the beginning of the fourth quarter.

That's when Captain Kirk took over.

Kirk Cousins, the Vikings key off-season acquisition, began doing what the Vikings brought him to Minnesota to do: put up points against the Packers. He started the fourth quarter with a three-yard touchdown pass to Stephan Diggs to cut the Green Bay lead to 20–14.

The Vikings held Green Bay to a Crosby field goal to make it 23–14.

Cousins then found Diggs again, this time for a seventy-five-yard touchdown strike to cut the Green Bay lead to 23–21.

The Vikings held Green Bay to a Crosby field goal to make it 26–21.

On the first play of the Vikings' next drive, a Cousins pass intended for Laquan Treadwell (who scored his first NFL touchdown in this game—the second game of his third NFL season) ricocheted off Treadwell's hands into the hands of Green Bay safety Ha Ha Clinton-Dix with just over two minutes left in the game and Green Bay leading 26–21.

The Vikings held Green Bay to a Crosby field goal to make it 29–21.

Now down by eight points, Cousins led the Vikings into Green Bay territory again and hit a double-covered Adam Thielen with a twenty-two-yard touchdown with ninety seconds left in the game. The two-point conversion attempt was a complete on a beautiful fade route to Diggs.

The game was tied at 29–29.

Rodgers drove Green Bay to Minnesota's 35 with thirty-one seconds left. Mason Crosby's first attempt at the game-winning field goal was good, but a Vikings time-out before the snap negated the try. Crosby's second attempt at the fifty-two-yard kick was no good.

The Vikings got the ball first in overtime, driving down to the Green Bay thirty-five-yard line.

Enter rookie kicker Daniel Carlson.

Carlson was the top kicking prospect in the 2018 NFL Draft. The former Auburn kicker was a three-time All-American, three-time All-SEC, and the all-time leading scorer in SEC history. The Vikings traded two picks to the New York Jets to move up and draft him in the fifth round. Carlson won the Vikings kicker job over Kai Forbath in training camp. He hit four of six field goals in the preseason and was 1/1 in 2018 with a forty-eight yarder against San Francisco the week before.

Carlson had already missed one against Green Bay: a forty-eight-yard field goal in the second quarter. And here was his chance to redeem himself and give Minnesota the lead with a forty-nine-yard field goal. He missed wide right, giving Aaron Rodgers the ball at the Green Bay 35.

Rodgers and the Packers played conservative, setting up for another potential Crosby field goal . . . and why not? The guy was 5/6 already.

On third and four from the Minnesota 32, Rodgers was sacked by Mackenzie Alexander, pushing the Packers out of Crosby's field goal range. Green Bay punted the ball back to the Vikings.

Again, Cousins and the Vikings drove deep into Packers territory, this time setting up Carlson with a thirty-five-yard field goal to send the Vikings home with a win.

He missed right. Again. The game finished tied at 29–29. The Vikings cut Carlson the next day. He was signed by the Oakland Raiders and finished his rookie season by hitting fifteen of sixteen field goals (including a game winner against San Francisco) and was 11/11 on extra points.

The Vikings signed Dan Bailey and his 88.2 percent career field goal percentage. He only hit 74 percent of his field goals with the Vikings that year.

The miss would come back to bite them in the final week of the season. In week 17 against the NFC North champion Chicago Bears, the Vikings found themselves in a win-and-in situation. Beat the Bears and they secure the sixth seed. Lose, and they miss the playoffs.

The Vikings lost 24–10 and finished the season 8–7–1. Their .531 winning percentage put them just out of the playoffs, allowing the defending Super Bowl champion Philadelphia Eagles (9–6, .563) to sneak into the playoffs.

February 2, 2019

Maya Moore sits out 2019 WNBA season

Am I living out my purpose?

—Maya Moore

The Lynx won four WNBA championship with the core of Lyndsey Whalen, Seimone Augustus, Rebekkah Brunson, and Maya Moore. Whalen retired to coach the Gophers women's basketball team in 2018, Augustus missed the first half of the 2019 season after arthroscopic knee surgery in May, and Brunson signed a one-year deal to return to the Lynx but hadn't appeared in a game in the first half of the season as she recovered from a concussion suffered late in 2018. Fans figured Maya Moore, arguably one of the greatest players of all time, would return, along with All-WNBA center Sylvia Fowles, to bring some familiarity to the court. But mid-January 2019, WCCO-TV reported that Moore was weighing her options for 2019; and in an article for *the Players' Tribune*, she announced that she had decided to spend 2019 away from professional basketball off to focus on her family and pursue ministry. Despite All-Star seasons from Fowles, Rookie of the Year Napheesa Collier, and the newly acquired Oddysey Sims, the Lynx were an even .500 at the All-Star Break and snuck into the WNBA playoffs as the seven seed where they lost to Seattle in the first round—a far cry from where fans were used to and far under where they'd be if Moore had played in 2019.

November 29, 2019

#9 Minnesota versus #13 Wisconsin with the Rose Bowl on the Line

We got the older people thinking, 'we got a chance to go back to the Rose Bowl.'
—PJ Fleck

In PJ Fleck's third season as head coach in Minnesota, the Gophers put together just the second 10-win season in school history (2003) and had their first legitimate shot at their first Rose Bowl appearance since 1961.

Despite their gaudy win total, the Gophers had struggled in early non-conference games. They needed to put together a game-winning drive to avoid being upset by South Dakota State, needed a game-sealing interception in overtime from Big Ten Defensive Back of the Year Antoine Winfield Jr against Fresno State and a game-winning touchdown pass from Tanner Morgan to All-Big Ten wide receiver Tyler Johnson to escape Georgia Southern. At a shaky 3-0, Minnesota then rolled through the first five games of Big Ten play, averaging nearly 42 points per game in their wins against Purdue, Illinois, Nebraska, Rutgers and Maryland.

The Gopher skeptics were out as Minnesota, now 8-0 and ranked #13 in the country, welcomed undefeated #5 Penn State to TCF Bank Stadium in one of the most-anticipated matchups in school history. The Gophers upset the Nittany Lions 31-26 to improve to 9-0. The win ended their 13-game losing streak to ranked opponents and was their first win against a Top-5 opponent since beating #5 Penn State in 1999. Minnesota was 9-0 for the first time since 1904 and had a two game lead over the Wisconsin Badgers in the Big Ten West division with three games to play.

Two more wins and the Gophers would earn a spot in the Big Ten Championship game with a trip to the Rose Bowl, or even the College Football Playoffs, on the line.

The Gophers, now ranked ninth in the country, were upset by #23 Iowa 23-19 in Iowa City the next week, but then smashed Northwestern in Evanston 38-22. Wisconsin won their games against Nebraska and Purdue to set up a winner-take-all matchup for the Big Ten West title and Paul Bunyan's Axe at TCF Bank Stadium.

The previous season, the Gophers had ended a 14-game losing streak against the Badgers, reclaiming the Axe at Camp Randall 37-15. With the Axe for the first time since 2003, PJ Fleck and the Gophers were determined to keep it.

With the all-time series record at tied at 60-60-8, expectations were high at a sold-out TCF Bank Stadium. ESPN's College Game Day made its first ever trip to Minneapolis for the game. Lee Corso picked the Gophers to win. Gopher great Eric Decker (one day after watching his alma mater Rocori win the Class 4A State Championship against SMB) joined the Game Day Crew as the celebrity picker.

And when Morgan connected with Big Ten Wide Receiver of the Year Rashod Bateman for a 51-yard touchdown on their first drive, expectations got even higher.

The Gophers defense forced two Badgers punts on their first two possessions of the game. Minnesota's second drive of the game stalled at the Badgers 35 yard line. Morgan and the offense failed to convert on what started as a 2nd down and 2 to go. Running back Mohamed Ibrahim was stuffed on second down, and 390 pound offensive tackle Daniel Faalele was injured on the play. The Gophers ran a Wild Cat formation on third down, and wildcat quarterback Seth Green was unable to pick up the first down as well.

Instead of try to convert the fourth down or try a field goal in the wintery conditions, PJ Fleck elected to punt the ball from the Badger 35.

""It was a fourth and long two, and the biggest thing is the field-position battle," Fleck explained after the game. "You that offense really good field position, now all of a sudden if we don't get that, now they march down the field and its 7-7. Everyone then says, 'Well, why didn't you just punt and pin them down?' I thought our defense was playing lights out at that particular time."

The Badgers put together an 11-play, 59 yard drive that included a successful fourth-and-3 conversion from Minnesota's 37 yard line. Minnesota defensive end Winston DeLattiboudere forced a fumble, which was recovered by Carter Coughlin, ending the Badgers drive.

The Gophers led 7-3 with three minutes left as the Badgers were driving before halftime. The Gophers defense sent Winfield Jr on the blitz, which forced Coughlin to take Badgers running back Jonathan Taylor and his FBS-leading 22 touchdowns in coverage. Badgers quarterback Jack Coan hit Taylor on a 28-yard wheel route for a 10-7 lead.

The Gophers punted on their first drive of the second quarter, and the Badgers quickly added to its lead with Coan hitting wide receiver Quintez Cephus for a 47-yard touchdown and a 17-7 lead. Michael Lantz kicked the Gophers back within a touchdown at 17-10 with 6:51 left in the third quarter.

On the ensuing kickoff, the Badgers special teams ran a reverse that confused the Gophers and went for 49 yards to the Minnesota 39. The Badgers called in another misdirection play as wide receiver Kendrick Pryor took the end-around run 26-yards, untouched, into the end zone for a 24-10 lead.

Needing a touchdown to stay in the game, Morgan drove the Gophers to the Wisconsin six yard line. Sitting first and goal, two Gophers runs went for a total of two yards. On third down, Morgan threw a fade to Johnson in the corner. Badger defensive back Caesar Williams was all over Johnson, grabbing his jersey but the officials kept the flags in their back pocket. On fourth down, Williams broke up another pass intended for Johnson, which turned the ball over on downs.

Badgers head coach Paul Chryst called a fullback screen to Garret Groshek on a third-and-6 that went 70 yards. The drive ended with Taylor's second touchdown of the game on an 11-yard run. On the Gophers first play of their next drive, Morgan was strip sacked and Wisconsin recovered. Four minutes later, Taylor scored his 25th touchdown of the season on a one-yard touchdown run to make it 38-10 Badgers.

A garbage time touchdown from Morgan to Johnson made it 38-17 with 5:51 left, but it was too little too late. The Badgers beat the Gophers, reclaimed Paul Bunyan's Axe (and pretended a row a boat with it a midfield…), moved to 6-0 at TCF Bank Stadium, 7-0 in games in which both teams are ranked (1942, 1954, 1962, 1999, 2005, 2014), punched their ticket to their sixth Big Ten Championship game and, in doing so, killed the Gophers dreams of their first Rose Bowl appearance in 58 years.

"We've had firsts. We've had nevers. We've restored people's beliefs of what we can do." Fleck said after the game. Let's not go back. Let's not start thinking 'well, that's typical.' That has to be out of our system. There's gonna be cynics. There's gonna be doubters. There's gonna be critics. But, the true fans, what we want them to do is get that completely out of their mind because we are not going back to that. So let it go."

BIBLIOGRAPHY

Newspapers have captured our state's history since the first issue of the *Star Tribune* hit newsstands on May 25, 1867. They were an essential resource used to write this book. That includes the first-hand accounts and award-winning reporting from the legendary Minnesota sports media that has covered the state over the past seventy years: Paul Allen, Dan Barreiro, Jon Bream, Tom Briere, Mark Brunswick, Joe Christensen, Dan "the Common Man" Cole, Dick Cullum, Norman Draper, Glen Gaff, Halsey Hall, Sid Hartman, Randy Johnson, Mike Kaszuba, Jeff Lenihan, Paul Levy, Bill McGrane, Phil Miller, Dwayne Netland, Sam Mele, Dave Mona, La Velle E. Neal III, Joe Nelson, Tom Powers, Joel Rippel, Mark Rosen, Patrick Ruesse, Jim Souhan, and Judd Zulgad.

This book includes information from articles published by the following newspapers:

Minneapolis Tribune/Star Tribune
Minneapolis Journal
St. Paul Pioneer Press
Long Beach Press-Telegram
New York Times
Los Angeles Times
St. Louis Dispatch
Kansas City Star
Chicago Sun-Times
Baltimore Sun
The Forum of Fargo-Moorhead

Books and Magazines

Aschburner, Steve. *Harmon Killebrew: Ultimate Slugger.* Triumph Books, 2012.

Aschburner, Steve. *The Good, the Bad, and the Ugly: Minnesota Twins: Heart-Pounding, Jaw-Dropping, and Gut-Wrenching Moments from Minnesota Twins History.* Triumph Books, 2008.

Craig, Mark. *100 Things Vikings Fans Should Know & Do before They Die.* Triumph Books LLC, 2016.

Dohrmann, George. "The Rise and Fall of Kirby Puckett." *Sports Illustrated*, 17 Mar. 2003.

Dohrmann, George. "U Basketball Program Accused of Academic Fraud." *St. Paul Pioneer Press*, 10 Mar. 1999.

Halsted, Alex. *100 Things Twins Fans Should Know & Do before They Die.* Triumph, 2016.

Hrbek, Kent, and Dennis Brackin. *Kent Hrbek's Tales from the Minnesota Twins Dugout.* Sports Pub., 2007.

Puckett, Kirby. *I Love This Game!: My Life and Baseball.* Harper Paperbacks, 1994.

Rippel, Joel A. *75 Memorable Moments in Minnesota Sports.* Minnesota Historical Society Press, 2003.

Rippel, Joel A. *Minnesota Sports Almanac.* Minnesota Historical Society, 2006.

Rosen, Mark, and James H. Bruton. *Mark Rosen's Book of Minnesota Sports Lists: a Compilation of Bests, Worsts, and Head-Scratchers from the Worlds of Baseball, Football, Basketball, Hockey, and More.* MVP Books, 2014.

Schumacher, Michael. *Mr. Basketball: George Mikan, the Minneapolis Lakers, and the Birth of the NBA.* University of Minnesota Press, 2008.

Wells, David, and Chris Kreski. *Perfect I'm Not: Boomer on Beer, Brawls, Backaches, and Baseball.* Perenial Currents, 2004.

The following websites were an invaluable tool for writing this book. You can get lost down the rabbit hole of Sports Reference LLC websites looking up records, stats, and players. Newspapers.com by Ancestry was the resource used to dig into the *Star Tribune* and *Minneapolis Journal* archives.

    www.baseball-reference.com
    www.pro-football-reference.com
    www.hockey-reference.com
    www.basketball-reference.com
    www.sports-reference.com/cfb
    www.bringmethenews.com
    www.newspapers.com

INDEX

A

Abdul-Jabbar, Kareem, 7, 10
Adelman, Rick, 324, 333, 360–61, 370, 377
Alexander, Derrick, 182–83, 229
Allen, Marcus, 123–24
Allen, Ray, 189–91, 301
Allison, Bob, 13, 15, 21, 39–40, 51
Antetokounmpo, Giannis, 330, 370
Arbor, Al, 64, 68, 108, 110, 112
Atlanta Falcons, 25–26, 155, 182, 205, 208, 316, 408

B

Baltimore Orioles, 13, 24, 29, 38–42, 49–51, 55, 102, 132, 231, 241, 351
Bane, Eddie, 78
Barkley, Charles, 171, 192
Bartlett, Jason, 287, 303–4
Battey, Earl, 13, 17–19, 341
Baylor, Elgin, 9
Beardsley, Dick, 116
Beasley, Michael, 323, 326, 332, 359
Belcher, Tim, 125, 181
Blackburn, Nick, 308–9
Blyleven, Bert, 49, 52, 71, 89, 132, 151
Bonser, Boof, 289–90, 308
Boogaard, Derek, 263–64
Bossy, Mike, 110, 112–13
Bostock, Lyman, 97, 99–100
Boston Bruins, 1–2, 34, 65, 68, 70, 107, 164, 262, 327, 364
Boston Celtics, 9–10, 170–72, 191, 273, 300–301, 321, 328, 378
Boudreau, Bruce, 327, 396, 399
bounty system, 318
Bradford, Sam, 358, 387, 389, 407–9
Bradshaw, Terry, 81–83, 223
Brandon, Terrell, 190, 200–201, 216, 245
Brewster, Tim, 296–97, 310
Bridgewater, Teddy, 357–58, 381, 388, 407
Brooks, Herb, 242–43
Broten, Neal, 104–5, 130, 160, 162, 164–68, 173, 177–78
Brown, Bill, 28, 82
Brunansky, Tom, 132, 151–52, 293
Bryant, Kobe, 7, 10, 36, 189, 197, 245–46, 248, 266, 268–69, 332
Burns, Brent, 355, 362–64
Butler, Jimmy, 324, 378, 400, 403–4
Buxton, Byron, 379, 405–6

C

California Angels, 9, 14, 30, 38, 55, 79, 98, 100, 144, 151, 304, 306–7, 347, 372

Campbell, Clarence, 33–34, 120, 130, 161, 174
Capps, Matt, 303, 340–41
Carew, Rod, 29, 36–40, 42, 49–50, 52–53, 72, 97–98, 100, 132, 134, 151–52, 243
Carlson, Daniel, 416–17
Carter, Cris, 205, 209, 220, 223, 225, 229–30
Casey, Jon, 160–62, 164, 166, 168, 177–78
Casilla, Alexi, 303, 308, 353–54
Cassell, Sam, 190–91, 215, 265–66, 268–69, 271–73, 299
Castillo, Luis, 287, 289, 292, 302
Chalfen, Morris, 7
Chicago Bears, 25, 73, 146–47, 182, 315, 318, 344, 348, 373, 416, 418
Chicago Black Hawks, 63, 108, 113, 120–21, 131
Chicago White Sox, 30, 38, 79, 89, 97–98, 101, 250, 254, 287–88, 290, 293, 308–9, 336, 340, 351
Childress, Brad, 315–16, 345, 348, 357
Colgate Red Raiders, 104, 294–96
Colon, Bartolo, 281
Cousins, Kirk, 358, 415–16
Cowles, Ozzie, 2
Coyle, Charlie, 327, 363, 396, 398
Crump, Harry, 232
Csonka, Larry, 75–76, 83
Cuddyer, Michael, 181, 234, 252–53, 255, 288, 302, 306, 309, 339–40, 350
Cuellar, Mike, 39, 49–51, 53
Culpepper, Daunte, 212, 220–25, 258–59, 280, 313, 358
Cuozzo, Gary, 48, 56
Curry, Stephen, 321, 328–30

D

Davis, Ricky, 300, 321, 328
Davis, Ron, 114–15, 132–33, 293, 337, 347
Davis, Tommy, 14, 288
Davis, Willie, 18–21
Dawson, Len, 45–46, 48
Denver Broncos, 26, 28, 150, 155, 209–10, 260, 275, 296, 344, 357, 366
Denver Nuggets, 265, 299, 321, 323, 330, 401
Detroit Tigers, 14, 30, 133, 151–53, 243, 252, 287, 292, 303–4
Devean George, 247, 249, 267–68
Dohrmann, George, 187, 194, 196
Doug Mohns, 64–65, 67–69
Doug Williams, 147
Dozier, D. J., 124, 148, 155
draft lottery, 170, 172, 322
Drysdale, Don, 14, 22, 37, 288
Dubnyk, Devan, 393–98
Duensing, Brian, 253, 255–56, 340, 342
Dutcher, Jim, 139, 158

E

Eller, Carl, 12, 25–26, 43, 45–47, 80, 84, 90–91, 95
Ellington, Wayne, 301, 321, 326, 360
Escobar, Eduardo, 351, 406

F

Fairly, Ron, 14, 19–20, 22–24
Favre, Brett, 220–23, 312–18, 345, 348, 357–58
Felton, Terry, 115
Finks, Jim, 25–26, 45
Fisher, Derek, 246–47, 249, 266, 269, 271–72

Fletcher, Chuck, 326–27, 355, 362, 367, 393, 395, 398–99
Flynn, Jonny, vii, 301, 321–24, 328–29, 332, 359
Foles, Nick, viii, 408–10
Foreman, Chuck, 75, 80, 82, 84, 90–91, 95
Foye, Randy, 285–86, 321, 328
Freeman, Antonio, 221–22
Freeman, Josh, 357–58

G

Gaetti, Gary, 132, 135, 144–45, 151, 293
Gainey, Bob, 160, 164, 166–68, 176, 178
Gangelhoff, Jan, 194
Gardenhire, Ron, 231, 239–40, 252–53, 255, 339, 354
Garnett, Kevin, vii, 10, 189, 191–92, 197, 200, 214–16, 245, 265, 273, 285, 299–301, 321, 331–32, 377–78
Garza, Matt, 303–4, 308
Goldsworthy, Bill, 63–65, 68–69, 176
Gomes, Ryan, 301, 322–23
Gomez, Carlos, 254, 303, 306, 308, 350–51
Gophers, 1–3, 5–7, 60–61, 87–88, 104–6, 128–29, 137–39, 141–43, 158–59, 194–96, 283–84, 294–98, 310–11, 334–35, 411–13
Goring, Butch, 109–13
Granlund, Mikael, 327, 363, 393, 396, 398
Grant, Bud, 12, 26–27, 43–45, 47, 73, 75, 93, 96, 123, 303, 348, 382
Grant, Mudcat, 13–14, 16, 21
Green, Darrell, 124, 147, 149
Green, Norm, 160, 167, 174–76

Green Bay Packers, 44, 47, 91, 156, 210, 220–22, 260–61, 343–44, 358, 381–82, 416–17
Gretzky, Wayne, 108, 130, 162
Griffin, Eddie, 217
Griffith, Calvin, 21, 29, 37, 41–42, 78, 98, 100, 125, 132, 243
Gugliotta, Tom, 192, 197, 299
Gund, George, 173–75
Gund, Gordon, 173–75
Guzman, Christian, 227, 233, 302, 375

H

Hall, Tom, 42, 49, 51
Hanzel, Martin, 393–94, 399
Harden, James, 321, 328–29, 404
Harding, Josh, 366, 368–69
Hardy, J.J., 255, 303, 306, 350, 353–54
Harrell, Graham, 294, 296
Harris, Ted, 63–64, 66
Hartman, Sid, 7–8, 10, 41, 64
Harvin, Percy, 312, 336, 338, 345, 348, 386
Haskins, Clem, 141, 158, 194–96, 334
Hassell, Trenton, 265, 268–72, 300
Haula, Erik, 393, 399
Hayden, Leo, 56
Heatley, Dany, 363, 368
Hernandez, Willie, 132–35
Herr, Tom, 151–52
Hicks, Aaron, 342, 379, 406
Hoiberg, Fred, 265, 268, 271, 335, 401
Holtz, Lou, 137
Holy Cross Crusaders, 283
Houston Rockets, 170–72, 192–93, 266, 285–86, 329, 331–32, 335, 401, 404
Hrbek, Kent, 132–36, 151, 226, 293, 375
Hudson, Troy, 245–49, 265

Hunter, Torii, 180, 227, 232–33, 239, 251, 287–90, 302, 304, 306, 308, 380

J

Jackson, Marc, 246–49
James, LeBron, 7, 10, 323, 359
Jefferson, Al, 301, 321–23, 332
Jeter, Derek, 227, 251–53, 255, 376
Johnson, Ervin, 265–66, 268, 270
Johnson, Lou, 17–18, 20–21, 23
Johnson, Magic, 7, 10
Johnson, Wesley, 322, 330, 332, 359–60
Jones, Clint, 26–28, 56
Jordan, Michael, 171–72, 197, 266, 268, 331–32

K

Kaat, Jim, 13, 15, 20, 22, 30, 41–42, 50, 52, 98
Kahn, David, vii, 320–26, 332, 406
Kansas City Chiefs, 45–47, 275
Kapp, Joe, 28, 43–45, 56
Kassulke, Karl, 48, 73
Keenum, Case, 358, 407–9
Kill, Jerry, 142, 297–98
Killebrew, Harmon, 13, 15–18, 20–21, 23–24, 29, 31, 36–40, 42, 49–51, 53, 71–72, 98, 132, 134, 151
Knoblauch, Chuck, 153, 187, 203, 226, 228, 302, 375
Koufax, Sandy, 14–15, 22, 40–41, 282
Krause, Paul, 12, 45, 47, 75, 80, 83–84, 86, 90
Kundla, John, 4, 7, 9

L

LaVine, Zach, 330, 377, 400, 403
Lawson, Ty, 321, 328, 359
Leddy, Nick, 364
Lee, Bob, 47, 56, 93–94

Lee, Cliff, 256, 341–42, 379
Lee, Mitch, 139
Lehman, Tom, 184
Lemieux, Mario, 163–66
Liriano, Francisco, 253, 255, 287–88, 302, 308, 340, 351
Little, Floyd, 27–28
Longwell, Ryan, 220–21, 316
Los Angeles Clippers, 170–71, 192, 197, 272, 300–301, 322–24, 328, 359, 402
Los Angeles Dodgers, 9, 14–24, 29, 79, 101, 115, 126–27, 204, 231–33, 250–51, 281, 288, 351, 372
Love, Kevin, 59, 301, 321–23, 325–26, 330, 332, 337, 359, 361, 377

M

Madsen, Mark, 265, 267–68, 301, 322
Malone, Karl, 10, 190, 266–67, 269
Maniago, Cesare, 35, 63, 65–66, 69–70
Marbury, Stephon, 189, 191–92, 197, 200, 299
Mariucci, John, 5
Marshall, Jim, 12, 25, 43, 47, 80, 90, 312
Martin, Billy, 17, 38–39, 41–42, 49–50, 52, 102, 243
Martin, Darrick, 267–68, 271
Martinez, Edgar, 239
Mason, Glen, 294–96
Masterton, Bill, 32–33, 176, 367
Mauer, Joe, 132, 181, 252–54, 288–89, 291, 302–3, 308, 336–37, 340–41, 350, 380, 405–6
Mays, Joe, 227, 233, 237
McCown, Josh, vii, 259
McHale, Kevin, 170, 189, 192, 215, 265, 272, 285, 300, 321, 324, 331
McKinnon, Jerick, 338, 346, 382, 388, 408, 415

McNally, Dave, 39–40, 49, 51, 53
Mele, Sam, 13–16, 29
Merritt, Jim, 16–17, 31
Metrodome, 128–29, 148, 151, 186, 188, 206, 227, 232, 234, 237, 251–52, 288–89, 296–97, 309–10, 347–49
Mijares, José, 253–55, 340
Mikan, George, 4, 8, 10–11
Mikkelsen, Vern, 8, 10
Milicic, Darko, 322–23, 326, 332, 337, 359
Miller, Bob, 22, 41, 50, 54
Milton, Eric, 227, 235, 302, 375
Minnesota Lynx, 390–92, 419
Minnesota Timberwolves, 10, 170, 172, 189, 191–92, 197, 200–201, 214–17, 245–46, 285, 300–301, 321–22, 331, 377–78, 400–404
Minnesota Vikings, 25–28, 43–48, 80–86, 90–96, 146–50, 154–57, 205–12, 220–25, 258–61, 274–80, 312–18, 343–48, 381–89, 407–10, 414–18
Molitor, Paul, 20, 186, 203, 239, 281, 375, 380, 405
Moore, Maya, 390–92, 419
Morneau, Justin, 251–52, 254, 288, 302–3, 308, 336, 350
Moss, Randy, 12, 205–6, 208–9, 211, 220, 223, 225, 258, 268, 274–75, 278, 280, 343, 345, 385–86
Murphy, John Ryan, 341–42, 379
Musselman, Bill, 60–61, 87, 139

N

Nanne, Lou, 63, 67–69, 107, 112, 163
Nathan, Joe, vii, 251–54, 288, 291, 302–3, 308, 340
National Basketball Association (NBA), 7–11, 59–60, 170–72, 189–92, 200–201, 214–17, 245–46, 265–66, 299–301, 320–26, 328–32, 337, 370–71, 378, 403–4
National Football League (NFL), 25–28, 43–47, 80, 84, 90, 123–24, 147–48, 154–56, 210–12, 229–31, 274–76, 278–79, 317–20, 343–48, 384–87
National Hockey League (NHL), 32–33, 35, 107–9, 120, 130–31, 160–61, 163, 173–76, 178–79, 219, 242, 262–63, 355–56, 363–68, 397–99
Nelson, Darrin, 123–24, 147, 149, 155–56
Newby, Alonzo, 195–96
New Jersey Nets, 190, 217, 322, 329
New York Giants, 9, 14, 26–27, 43, 155, 223, 229–30, 317, 348, 358
New York Islanders, 107–9, 111–13, 120–21, 130–31, 163, 283, 365, 393
Niederreiter, Nino, 327, 363, 393, 396, 398
Niekro, Joe, 144
Nishioka, Tsuyoshi, 303, 350, 353
Nolasco, Ricky, 372
Norman, Greg, 184–85

O

Oakland Athletics, 38, 49, 71, 126, 231–32, 250, 252, 287, 289
Ochoa, Alex, 203, 236, 238
Ogwumike, Nneka, 390–92
Ohio State Buckeyes, 60–62, 141, 279, 296
Olajuwon, Hakeem, 170–71, 192
Oliva, Tony, 13, 18–20, 30, 36, 38–41, 49–51, 53, 58, 98, 132, 151, 239, 290

Olowokandi, Michael, 265, 268, 270–71, 328
Ortiz, David, 202, 232, 235, 239, 302
Osborn, Dave, 28, 46, 48, 56, 81–82
Osteen, Claude, 14, 17–18, 21–22

P

Page, Alan, 26, 28, 43, 45–47, 80, 84, 91
Palmer, Jim, 39, 41–42, 49, 52–53, 59, 103, 282
Parise, J. P., 35, 63, 65–66, 68–69
Parise, Zach, 327, 363–64, 393, 395, 398
Parker, Candace, 390–92
Parker, Wes, 18–20, 23–24
Pascual, Camilo, 13, 16, 29
Pavano, Carl, 254–55, 303, 340, 353
Pavin, Corey, 184–85
Payton, Gary, 197–98, 266, 268
Pearson, Drew, vii, 85–86, 94
Peeler, Anthony, 197–98, 200, 245, 247, 249
Pekovic, Nikola, 325, 332, 336–37, 361
Percival, Troy, 235, 237–38
Perranoski, Ron, 16, 23, 39, 42, 49, 51, 55
Perry, Jim, 13, 21, 23, 30, 38–39, 49–51, 98
Peterson, Adrian, 312, 345–46, 373, 381–82
Philadelphia 76ers, 170–71, 190–91, 329, 377, 403
Philadelphia Eagles, viii, 138, 212, 223, 226, 389, 407–10, 418
Pierzynski, A. J., 181, 232, 239, 302, 309, 341
Pittsburgh Steelers, 46, 80–83, 92, 157, 166, 168, 210
Plager, Bob, 66, 68–69
Pohlad, Carl, 232

Pollard, Jim, 4, 7–9
Ponder, Christian, 357–58
Poole, Nate, 260–61
Portland Trail Blazers, 88, 189, 200, 216, 271, 286, 320–21, 324–26, 329
Posada, Jorge, 227, 252–56
Potvin, Denis, 108–10, 112–13
Powell, Boog, 39–40, 50–52, 58
Puckett, Kirby, 132, 136, 151–52, 186–88, 226, 287, 293, 375
Punto, Nick, 252, 254, 287, 308, 339, 350, 353
Purple People Eaters, 83, 91, 93

Q

Quillici, Frank, 15–16, 19–24

R

Radke, Brad, 227, 232, 236, 291–92
Rally Monkey, 231, 235–38
Rambis, Kurt, 301, 322, 324, 331–32, 361
Ramos, Wilson, 340
Rauch, Jon, 254–55, 303, 306, 340–41, 353
Reed, Howie, 15, 22
Rice, Sidney, 275, 312, 314, 316, 345
Richards, Todd, 355, 362, 395
Rigney, Bill, 42, 49, 51–52
Rincon, Juan, 251–52, 288
Rivera, Mariano, 251–52, 254–55, 281
Robert Horry, 247–49
Roberto, Phil, 64–66, 68
Robinson, Brooks, 13, 36, 39–41, 49, 51–52
Robinson, Frank, 39, 49, 51–52
Rochester Royals, 4, 10
Rodgers, Aaron, 279, 318, 358, 381, 416–17
Roloson, Dwayne, 364, 366

Romero, J. C., 232, 235, 237, 251, 353
Roseboro, John, 16, 18–19, 23, 39
Roy, Brandon, vii, 285–86, 326
Rubio, Ricky, 321, 325–26, 328–29, 359, 361, 400
Rush, Kareem, 272
Russell, Bill, 9–10
Ryan, Terry, 231, 239–41, 291, 302–3, 354, 380

S

Sabathia, C. C., 181, 252–53, 255
Salem, Joe, 128–29, 137
San Antonio Spurs, 64, 200–201, 266, 321, 329, 402
San Francisco 49ers, 12, 56, 123, 146, 155, 206, 225, 357, 414, 416
San Francisco Giants, 14, 37, 115, 126, 235, 238
Sano, Miguel, 256, 303, 379–80, 405
Santana, Johan, 234, 237, 251, 281–82, 288, 302, 305–6, 308, 350
Sapp, Warren, 182–83, 211
Saunders, Flip, 87, 191, 245–46, 265–66, 269–72, 300, 326, 328, 360, 370, 377–78
Sealy, Malik, 216
Setoguchi, Devin, 363, 368
Shaquille O'Neal, 10, 159, 172, 197, 245, 248, 266–67
Shay, Jerry, 25–26
Shmyr, Paul, 107, 111–12
Smith, Bill, vii, 302, 304–6, 340–41, 350, 353
Smith, Billy, 108–9, 111–13
Smith, Joe, 214, 245, 248–49
Smith, Kevin, 139, 157
Smith, Onterrio, 276–77
Smith, Robert, 207, 220–21, 223, 225, 229
Span, Denard, 254–56, 306, 308, 350

Sparano, Tony, 414–15
Sprewell, Latrell, 265, 269, 272–73, 299
Staal, Eric, 393, 396–97, 399
Staubach, Roger, vii, 76, 84–85, 94, 175
Stern, David, 170, 172, 215, 321
St. Louis, Martin, 218
St. Louis Blues, viii, 32, 35, 63–70, 108, 122, 131, 161–62, 178, 356, 366, 394–97
St. Louis Cardinals, 29, 31, 57, 80–81, 97, 145, 151–52, 205, 230, 258–61, 381, 384
Stringer, Korey, 224, 229–30
SuperSonics, 193, 197
Suter, Ryan, 327, 364, 393, 395, 397–98
Szczerbiak, Wally, 216, 245, 247, 265, 268, 328

T

Tarkenton, Fran, 25–27, 75, 80, 82, 84, 90, 94
Teixeira, Mark, 252–56
Telfair, Sebastian, 301, 322–23, 332, 359
Thibodeau, Tom, 400–402
Thielen, Adam, 275, 407, 409, 417
Thomas, Frank, 239, 289, 292
Thome, Jim, 239, 303, 309, 340, 353
Thompson, Danny, 50, 71, 89
Thompson, Mychal, 87
Thorpe, Ed, 43
Tiant, Luis, 36, 52, 54
Tice, Mike, 258, 274–75
Tingelhoff, Mick, 43, 45, 56, 90
Tinordi, Mark, 163, 166, 178
Tovar, Cesar, 13, 39–40, 49, 52–53, 72
Towns, Karl-Anthony, 378, 400–404
Treadwell, Laquon, 386, 409
Trent, Gary, 247–48, 265
Triangle Offense, 331

Trottier, Bryan, 108–11, 113, 165
Tyner, Jason, 287, 292

U

Underwood, Dimitrius, 211–13

V

Valdespino, Sandy, 15, 19
Van Brocklin, Norm, 25–26
Varitek, Jason, 180
Versalles, Zoilo, 13–21, 23–24, 30–31, 58, 134, 243
Viola, Frank, 132–33, 151, 293

W

Walker, Herschel, vii, 124, 154, 156–57, 205
Walsh, Blair, 373, 381, 383–85
Washington, Gene, 26, 28, 48, 386
Washington Redskins, 75, 80, 84, 90, 123–24, 146–50, 155, 261, 275, 278, 318, 344, 381, 414
Washington Senators, 13–14, 17, 30, 53, 231
Weaver, Earl, 39, 41–42, 49, 51, 53
Webster, Martell, 323, 326, 359
Wells, David, 202, 251
White, Royce, 334–35
Whizzinator, 276–77
Wiggins, Andrew, 280, 377–78, 400, 402, 404
Wilkins, Damien, 322
Williams, Bernie, 203, 227, 250–52
Williams, Derrick, vii, 324, 330, 359–60
Williams, George, 139
Williams, Glenn, 339
Williamson, Troy, 275, 278, 280, 344, 386
Wills, Maury, 14–15, 18–19, 22, 24, 288
Wilson, Wade, 124, 146–47, 149, 155

Wilt Chamberlain, 7, 10
Winter, Max, 7–9
Witte, Luke, 60–61
Wooden, John, 1, 3
Worsley, Gump, 63–65, 68–69
Wren Blair, 32–33

Y

Yary, Ron, 12, 43, 45, 56, 84
Yeo, Mike, 356, 362, 368, 395, 397
Young, Delmon, 254–56, 303–4, 306, 308–9, 340, 350
Yzerman, Steve, 177, 179

Z

Zholtok, Sergei, 262–63
Zimmer, Mike, 381, 388, 408, 410, 414
Zito, Barry, 181, 232, 289
Zucker, Jason, 327, 363, 393, 396–98